GLOBAL
INVESTING

1999 EDITION

GLOBAL INVESTING

1999 EDITION

A Guide to the 50 Best Stocks in the World

ANDREW LECKEY

WARNER BOOKS

A Time Warner Company

PUBLISHER'S NOTE: This book is designed to provide competent and reliable information regarding the subject matter covered. However, it is sold with the understanding that the author and publisher are not engaged in rendering financial or other professional advice. Laws and practices often vary from state to state, and if expert assistance is required, the services of a professional should be sought. The author and publisher specifically disclaim any liability that is incurred from the use or application of the contents of this book.

The opinions expressed in this book are strictly those of the author and do not necessarily reflect the opinions of either CNBC or the Tribune Company.

Warner Books, Inc., 1271 Avenue of the Americas, New York, NY 10020

Visit our Web site at http://warnerbooks.com

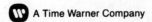 A Time Warner Company

Printed in the United States of America

First Printing: January 1999

10 9 8 7 6 5 4 3 2 1

ISBN: 0-446-67495-8

ISSN: 1520-9636

Book design and composition by L&G McRee
Cover design by George Karabotsos

Acknowledgments

You must be a bit cheeky to select the world's best global companies to invest in and then, to compound matters, actually write a book about them all. I'm grateful that a number of people were willing to help me with this rather inexact, open-to-debate pursuit. Terry Barchenko was effective both in contacting companies around the globe and making interview arrangements, while Mitchell Lavnick's exhaustive research help was invaluable. Rick Wolff of Warner Books believed in this ambitious project from the time I first proposed it, while Ed Keon and Chris Rockaway of I/B/E/S International came up with data required to understand each company better. The myriad of investment experts I have interviewed over the past two years provided great insight. Especially helpful in grading my final selections and making suggestions of their own were David Herro of Oakmark International Fund, David Lui of Strong International Fund, Marshall Acuff of Salomon Smith Barney, and Hugh Johnson of First Albany Securities. Their patience and knowledge were appreciated.

Contents

Contents

Introduction

The world's best. That's what today's stock investors demand from the volatile, complicated financial markets. In turbulent times, they aren't concerned about geographic location, so long as a company and its stock serve up terrific potential. Putting together a portfolio of quality U.S. and foreign stocks is not just a diversification or asset allocation strategy, but an acknowledgment that quality is quality wherever it is found. If market conditions make the prices of some solid long-term choices more reasonable, so much the better.

In the midst of the economic turmoil and currency fluctuations in emerging markets and Japan, the spirited move toward growth and consolidation in European Union countries, and antitrust battles and presidential intrigue in the United States, some companies have managed to stay the course. In fact, shrewd global corporations move quickly to expand their presence in troubled areas to take advantage of bargain prices, in much the same way savvy investors do with their stock purchases. Some selections in this book are at the top of their game and their stock prices reflect that, while others have been hammered by world economic and political events. Whatever their present status may be, however, flexibility, opportunism, and patience will set winners apart from losers in today's global investment race.

The companies with the best stocks in the world have one another directly in their sights. For example, London-based food and drink giant Diageo, the result of the merger of Guinness and Grand Metropolitan, intends to make a name for itself beyond its Burger King Whopper: "Our target is to equal each of the total shareholder returns of Coca-Cola, Procter & Gamble, Philip

Morris, Johnson & Johnson, and Unilever, which is a very demanding set of peers," John McGrath, Diageo group chief executive, told me firmly in an interview at his office on London's Henrietta Place, just a stone's throw from the city's bustling Oxford Street shopping district. "Everyone here is involved in this goal, and each member of our executive group participates in the review and debate about each of our businesses."

Image is everything in this new global marketplace. Even though its anti-impotence pill Viagra is the hottest drug on the planet and has bootsed company sales dramatically, pharmaceutical leader Pfizer Incorporated doesn't want to become known as a one-product company: "Our sales representatives are expected to mention our other products before they talk about Viagra," William Steere, Jr., chairman and chief executive officer of Pfizer, told me in an interview in his wood-paneled Manhattan office that overlooks New York's East River. "Not only does Viagra have a 'halo' effect that gets physicians to listen to us talk about our other drugs, but many of the patients in need of Viagra have additional ailments that require additional medications."

Having spent considerable time sitting at a television anchor desk talking with chief executive officers and overseas correspondents, as well as writing columns and books about international investing, I've learned that investor knowledge about individual world-beater companies isn't as extensive as one might think. Each day in the financial news we hear names of corporations that are making a difference in world business and economies. However, few investors know much about the comparative strengths of these companies other than the fact that one is "really big" or that it might make consumer products they're familiar with. In particular, they don't know how foreign stocks compare to those of the more familiar domestic choices in terms of their nature and growth. Even the designation of "corporation" commonly used after the names of U.S. companies varies elsewhere around the globe. For example, the designation Plc. stands for public limited company in the United Kingdom. Meanwhile, S.A. stands for Société Anonyme in Belgium, France, Luxembourg, and Switzerland, while it represents

Sociedad Anomima in Spain and Latin America. A.G. stands for the term Aktiengesellschaft in Austria, Germany, Switzerland, and Liechtenstein. Finally, N.V. stands for Naamioze Vennootschap in Belgium and the Netherlands. All of the companies described in this book are worth knowing about and tracking, whatever your home country. All but one of the companies are available to investors on U.S. exchanges, either as company stocks or American Depositary Receipts (ADRs) that represent the stocks of foreign firms.

Investors often ask whether there's a growing correlation between world stock markets that makes international investing less of a diversification move than it was in the past. Asia, for example, seems to have had an impact on every part of the globe at one time or another over the past two years, although some regions, such as Latin America, were late to experience reverberations. The answer is that there's not as much correlation as you might think. It's true that on a given day when the U.S. markets tank, that event is often immediately followed by declines in Asia and Europe. On another day, Asia may lead the way with a positive move, to be mimicked by a buoyant U.S. market. On such a day-to-day basis there is indeed close correlation that's often tied to specific events, October 1987 and October 1997 being good examples.

However, if you take the last ten years or any period over the past fifty years, you'll see very little correlation. For example, over the past eight years the U.S. market has gone up sharply, while the Tokyo stock market has gone down sharply. Despite some daily or weekly corresponding moves, they have little in common. Recent world stock market results also indicate that markets truly have minds of their own. Over the past several years, the markets of Spain, Portugal, the United States, Switzerland, Sweden, and the Netherlands have been big winners, while the biggest losers have been Malaysia and Singapore. Earnings momentum, valuations, and liquidity of individual stocks are important in the selection process, and one must also keep the macroeconomic and currency fundamentals of a country in mind because growth, earnings prospects, and interest rate factors can weigh heavily on final returns.

Even among world-class companies, the competitive advantage can vary considerably. For example, because technology changes dramatically, it might take four to six years for a rival making the right moves to overtake Intel Corporation. However, it's been estimated it would take well-financed competitors more than twenty years to catch up to Coca-Cola Company. Strong market position, solid management, good cash generation, and a focus on return are common attributes of the world's best. The companies profiled in this book and their stock have performed well over time and their managements generally take a positive attitude toward shareholders. They are steady, long-term performers dominant in their fields.

Financial strength, value, expansion, competitiveness, consistency, and performance were all considered in putting together this group of companies in a mix that is twenty-six foreign companies and twenty-four U.S. companies. Since these are very different companies and competitive advantage varies dramatically among fields, it's a gut-level rather than by-the-numbers process. Watch these companies. They're all proven winners, even though some may win more or win sooner than others. Care has been taken not to either "write off" or favor regions or stock groups because of current events. These companies for the most part have diversified their efforts globally so that one downturn won't spell disaster for them. In addition, an investor shouldn't write off anything forever. Yes, Asia will come back. After all, it turned from a leader to a laggard and the reverse will occur. Yes, technology will suffer downturns, but it is, after all, our path to the future and the future is onward and upward. Although bad news can offer opportunity to buy shares at more reasonable prices in the belief that the circumstances leading to their decline will reverse themselves, you should still buy and hold. Don't try to be an active trader in international stocks based on daily, weekly, or monthly events around the globe because you won't win at that complicated game.

The trend of looking outside one's borders is on the rise. After all, products of foreign firms are used every day by consumers in other countries. Prompted by some eye-popping returns in certain world markets, foreign stocks are gradually making their way into the portfolios of sophisticated individuals. The U.S. holdings of foreign securities in particular have taken a big jump since the mid-1990s as investors who have ridden the American bull market look to spread their assets around a bit. As this interest in global investing has accelerated, U.S. brokerage firms have been rapidly expanding their research presence to meet the demands of a global client base. It used to be difficult to find any information about foreign firms, but now there's plenty. In addition, foreign firms have improved their reporting procedures and also produce company materials or Web sites every bit the equal of the best efforts of U.S. firms.

Just being invested solely in one country doesn't give you the investment pop or diversification it once did. The makeup of world stock markets is changing, with the United States now representing less than 40 percent of total world market capitalization, versus more than 50 percent in 1980. Japan has moved up to 21 percent, while the United Kingdom has inched up to 8 percent. The rest of market capitalization is widely spread among a long list of countries, none commanding more than 3 percent of the pie. Individual investors living in those countries long ago realized the need for diversification.

The leaders of giant companies seeking to spread their power around the globe know what it takes to succeed and are making an all-out effort to emulate the best of their breed. When I arrived at Diageo's London offices, the reception area of which features a running tape of food and drink commercials from around the world, I was warned that fifty-nine-year-old Group Chief Executive John McGrath was running behind schedule. However, I was greeted by him, with a smile and handshake, exactly two-and-a-half minutes late, an obvious indication this is not a man who lets time slip by even on a busy day. With slicked-back hair and round-rimmed glasses, McGrath is a jovial fellow given to quoting global CEO superstars such as General Electric's Jack Welch, especially Welch's comment that it's important to make sure people have a lot of freedom to succeed and fail.

GE's and Coca-Cola's annual reports sit prominently on his desk and he thumbs through them for nuggets of truth as he makes points.

"We can definitely grow our market share at the expense of our competitors," McGrath said with a flourish of his right hand. "For example, you can expect to see greater non-U.S. growth for Burger King and Pillsbury." Pressing a blue felt-tipped pen to a large white easel propped up in the corner of his office, he drew a gradual upward curve indicating what was required to meet goals for return of a hypothetical division. The point, he emphasized, is that the division work earnestly toward its goal, not content with one-year measures, but thinking further ahead to more significant ultimate results. The shape of the curve means little, so long as the payoff occurs at the end, he emphasized.

Global companies aren't cowed by the competition, as indicated by the outspoken McGrath on McDonald's Corp.: "We don't want to become a toy store like them, with all those constant Beanie Babies and other things that people come to them for, but want to continue to grow by having people like our food best." McGrath on expanding marketing efforts worldwide, rather than presenting different commercials for various countries: "I've never seen so many different camera shots of Baileys Irish Cream being poured, which is bull, since there's no reason why we can't have one camera shot for around the entire world." As might be expected, in his opinion Diageo's stock price still doesn't adequately reflect the growth potential of its formidable brand names as a worldwide effort is made to significantly boost their outreach. It's his task to make sure it does.

Meanwhile, Pfizer is advancing into the position of premier U.S. drug company and expanding its already strong international roots rapidly through drugs such as Viagra. While longtime U.S. pharmaceutical industry leader Merck & Company is slipping a bit due to expiring patents on some popular drugs, Pfizer has little exposure to drugs losing patent protection and an unsurpassed drug pipeline that's growing faster than that of its rivals.

"Our company is becoming dominant because we didn't get

sidetracked by mergers, which helped us to stay focused, and because other people had bad luck because of expiring patents," related the dapper and fit sixty-one-year-old William Steere, Jr., whose wood-paneled office has a large wall sculpture depicting all the world's continents. He noted that, despite the fact his company's acquisition of Smithkline Beecham's animal business was a success, the first year it took a lot of time to draw together two very different corporate cultures. In most really big mergers, he believes, too much time is wasted with everyone worrying about their jobs, their offices, and their futures. That keeps everyone from getting the more important jobs done. If Pfizer had a failed pipeline and low growth, he'd look for a partner, but now is certainly not the time to do so.

"In the 1990s, a company must have focus, because there's never been a time when the competition has been more fierce," declared Steere, who is looking to sell the company's medical devices business because it's not a perfect fit with its pharmaceuticals, consumer products, and veterinary medicines. "You need a critical mass in this business, but after that, size isn't that important."

What's more important is Pfizer's international marketing ability to "tease out" the differences in their products, which adds up to a big difference in everyone's perception of them, Steere contends. He also sees the dark side of increased world competition, with pharmaceutical firms now suffering pervasive thefts of their patents. For example, companies in India have been sending out bulk supplies of a Viagra-type drug; Argentina has a reputation as a big pirate due to its lack of patent laws; and Egypt is also involved in unauthorized manufacture and sales. The entire world is after the properties of the world's best.

This is a time of change for investors. The Asian crisis has sparked a new global era of fierce competition characterized by currency depreciation and extensive corporate restructuring. Some companies are employing a disciplined Six Sigma approach to bring their operations as close to perfection as possible (see page 132), others are unloading unnecessary businesses while acquiring those that provide more synergy, and others are introducing their products into as many parts of the globe as possible as quickly as they can. As the competitive advantage ebbs and flows, make sure your assets stay on an upward trajectory. Do all your homework, and realize that it is the company and its management that will ultimately determine the fate of the investor. Each of the fifty companies in this book has a different story. Some are U.S.-based, while others represent Europe, Asia, Canada, or Latin America, but all do business around the globe. Their industries range from medical products to consumer products to commodities. Some of their stock prices seem to fully reflect their prospects, while others appear undervalued. Read what they're all about, track their financial data, and decide if you think the story that interests you will have a happy ending. All these large capitalization stocks of dominant companies are readily available on U.S. exchanges as either stocks or ADRs and can easily be mixed into your existing portfolio. Whether or not you agree with all of the choices included doesn't matter. Consider this a starting point for your own personal plan for world investment domination.

GLOBAL
INVESTING
1999 EDITION

1. AFLAC Incorporated

No one takes cancer lightly: Men in the United States have a one-in-two lifetime risk of getting it, while women have a one-in-three risk. Overall cancer expenses are estimated at more than $100 billion per year nationally, two-thirds of which are expenses not tied directly to treatments. That staggering health concern is why AFLAC Incorporated and its primary subsidiary, American Family Life Assurance Company of Columbus, Georgia, successfully sell supplemental medical insurance policies that cover special conditions, primarily cancer. The company's strong growth, solid profits, and healthy balance sheet have made its stock a consistently superior performer.

Cancer and other insurance needs aren't just an American preoccupation, which is why AFLAC targets both the United States and Japan as the world's best insurance markets. Japan, beset with economic problems that provide a challenge for AFLAC, is by far the largest life insurance market in the world, with more than $20 trillion of life insurance in force, while the United States ranks as the second-largest, with nearly $12 trillion in force. Together, these two markets are more than four times the combined size of the next ten largest markets.

Consumers in both markets face rising out-of-pocket health care expenses. They have access to insurance at their place of employment. They have the income to purchase additional insurance and there are millions of consumers who don't yet own supplemental insurance. AFLAC pays cash benefits for intensive care, long-term (nursing home) care, in-home care, or as a Medicare supplement. AFLAC is the largest seller of supplemental insurance in the United States, and the leading cancer-expense insurance company in Japan, which accounts for more than 80 percent of company sales.

Its Japanese sales are based on the agency system, in which a company forms a subsidiary to sell AFLAC's insurance to employees. It sells primarily through the workplace in the United States as well, with employers deducting premiums from paychecks. It is a leader in supplemental insurance sold at the work site in the United States. With 35,000 licensed agents, AFLAC sells its products through more than 120,000 U.S. payroll groups, making it the number-one company in payroll marketing.

Founded in 1955 by brothers John, Paul, and Bill Amos, AFLAC introduced one of the world's first cancer expense insurance policies in 1958. It initially operated in Georgia and Alabama, but by the mid-1960s had expanded across the Southeast. The company continued its domestic expansion throughout the 1970s and 1980s, and now operates in all fifty states. AFLAC in 1974 became the second foreign company licensed to sell insurance products in Japan. Today it is the largest foreign insurer in Japan in terms of premium income and one of the most successful foreign companies operating in any industry there. AFLAC ranks fourth in terms of individual policies in force among all of Japan's life insurers. AFLAC insures nearly one-fourth of Japan's total population, about 30 million people. More than 97 percent of the companies on the Tokyo Stock Exchange now offer AFLAC products to their employees or customers.

Recent years have obviously been tough on Japan's economy, resulting in historically low interest rates and a weakening currency. There was also a premium rate increase, an increase in the consumption tax, and the collapse of Nissan Mutual life to contend with. Yet AFLAC was gradually able to distance itself from some of those difficulties and, in fact, was recently ranked number one in financial safety among Japan's major life insurers by *Nikkei Business* magazine. Its solvency margin is among the highest in the Japanese life insurance industry, a point made clear in print advertising to that country's consumers. Rather than retrench, in 1998 the company expanded its product line to sell three new riders to its cancer life policy involving surgical benefits, accident coverage, and medical/sickness benefits. Slower sales growth in Japan has minimal effect on earnings due to the high Japanese policy renewal rate of 97 percent.

"We have not waited for the Japanese environment to brighten, but instead have refined and improved our marketing approach to combat the weak economy," AFLAC President and Chief Executive Officer Daniel Amos said at a 1998 analysts meeting in New York. "Over the long run, we know there is still a tremendous need for supplemental insurance in Japan due to demographic trends and Japan's changing health care system."

Currency fluctuations between the Japanese yen and the U.S. dollar don't generally affect AFLAC economically because all of AFLAC Japan's premiums and claims, and most of its investment income and expenses, are received or paid in yen. The majority of its invested assets are denominated in yen as well. However, for financial reporting purposes, all yen results are translated into dollars, which does affect reported earnings and balance sheets. The company doesn't hedge its earnings against yen exposure because it believes this would be hedging against a noneconomic event. Yet the company does access the foreign-currency forward markets to maximize the dollar amount of its profit repatriation to the United States. In addition, AFLAC Japan's dollar-denominated investment portfolio and AFLAC Incorporated's yen-denominated borrowings act as a hedge of AFLAC Japan's equity.

In the 1990s, AFLAC began strategically positioning to compete in a changing world insurance market. It began broadening its product line in the 1980s, after selling virtually one product for more than two decades. Besides cancer expense protection, the company now offers coverage for accident and disability, hospital indemnity, long-term care, intensive care, Medicare supplement, and more. These products now account for 64 percent of new sales in the United States, with accident/disability coverage the company's best-selling U.S. policy. New products in Japan account for nearly one-third of new sales. While AFLAC is continually assessing new markets, in recent years it has sold or closed operations in countries such as Canada, which couldn't produce near-term, sustainable profitability. Because of product broadening and enhanced distribution systems, management believes the company's greatest opportunities for growth exist in its two primary markets, Japan and the United States. In its home market, the company recently built a $15 million customer service center in Columbus, Georgia. The five-story, 133,000-square-foot building that houses the company's customer call center as well as its new business and client service functions represents AFLAC's commitment to the future.

1. AFLAC INCORPORATED

United States   Ticker symbol AFL

Stock price $32 1/4 (9/16/98)   Dividend yield .81%

(Financial data is from I/B/E/S International)*

BUSINESS DESCRIPTION

PROVIDES SUPPLEMENTAL HEALTH INSURANCE PRIMARILY IN THE UNITED STATES AND JAPAN. ALSO ENGAGES IN BROADCASTING AND COMMUNICATIONS

ADDRESS AND CONTACTS

Address	1932 Wynnton Road
	Columbus GA 31999
Telephone	1-706-323-3431

BASIC FINANCIAL INFORMATION

Capital Structure†	Long Term Debt:	483.61
	Total Debt:	523.21
	Common Sh. Equity:	2145.76

SALES BREAKDOWN

Product Segments†		NA
Geographic Segments†	United States	1160.50
	Foreign	5848.75

Displayed Currency: U.S. Dollar (1.00:1)
*I/B/E/S and I/B/E/S Express are registered trademarks of I/B/E/S International Inc.
Copyright 1993–1996 I/B/E/S International Inc. All rights reserved.
†Values are displayed in millions.

FINANCIAL STATEMENT DATA

INCOME STATEMENT	1997	1996	1995	1994	1993
Net Sales or					
Revenues	6983.48	7039.94	7190.62	6110.76	5000.62
Investment Income	1077.71	1021.96	1024.96	838.83	689.27
Total Claim and					
Loss Expense	4833.08	4895.52	5034.27	4256.54	3423.30
Operating Income	611.31	605.92	616.61	515.41	430.17
Interest Expense	13.71	16.19	15.61	13.50	10.55
Pretax Income	864.82	650.00	601.00	504.34	428.38
Net Income	585.02	394.36	349.06	292.79	243.89

BALANCE SHEET	1997	1996	1995	1994	1993
Assets					
Cash	235.68	0.00	4.14	17.64	23.41
Total Investments	22644.23	20476.53	20040.82	15976.13	12445.73
Total Assets	29454.00	25022.81	25337.99	20287.08	15442.69
Liabilities & Shareholders' Equity					
Total Insurance					
Reserves	19885.07	20234.21	19634.98	16006.61	11947.14
Total Debt	523.21	353.53	327.27	184.90	122.06
Preferred Stock	0.00	0.00	0.00	0.00	0.00
Common Equity	2145.76	1845.42	1651.35	1522.92	1350.81
Total Liabilities					
& Sh. Equity	29454.00	25022.81	25337.99	20287.08	15442.69

CASH FLOW	1997	1996	1995	1994	1993
Net Cash Flow—					
Operating	2598.45	2696.75	2944.10	2369.25	1845.25
Net Cash Flow—					
Investing	2434.32	2540.47	2863.54	2246.91	1793.65
Net Cash Flow—					
Financing	-121.64	-157.88	-93.37	-130.42	-67.68

SUPPLEMENTARY DATA	1997	1996	1995	1994	1993
Fixed Income					
Secs—Total	22437.82	20327.73	19675.01	15530.69	12137.76
Equity Securities—Total	146.33	136.33	108.06	84.37	82.07
Real Estate Assets	0.00	0.00	0.00	0.00	0.00
Mortgage Policy and					
Other Loans	16.75	17.80	22.21	25.10	57.49
Benefit and Loss					
Reserves	10090.83	18697.17	18000.30	14586.17	10932.23
Unearned Premiums	276.67	288.98	301.45	339.51	302.85

SUPPLEMENTARY DATA	1997	1996	1995	1994	1993
Policy and Contract Claims	1010.52	1039.26	1016.29	929.35	712.07
Employees	4032	4066	4070	4000	3902
Goodwill/Cost in Excess of Assets Purchased	NA	NA	NA	NA	NA
Extra Items & Gain/Loss in Sale of Assets	0.00	0.00	0.00	0.00	11.44

Displayed Currency: U.S. Dollar (1.00:1)
All values are displayed in millions (except employees).

FINANCIAL RATIOS AND GROWTH RATES

PROFITABILITY	1997	1996	1995	1994	1993	5YR AVG
Return on Assets %	2.37	1.60	1.77	1.94	2.16	1.97
Return on Equity—Total %	31.70	23.88	22.92	21.68	23.71	24.78
Tax Rate %	32.35	39.33	41.92	41.95	43.07	39.72
Net Premiums Written % Equity	318.28	357.89	398.63	383.53	392.43	370.15
Combined Ratio	106.68	106.15	105.92	105.41	105.37	105.91
Investment Income % Inv Assets	5.19	5.10	6.42	6.74	7.31	6.15

LEVERAGE	1997	1996	1995	1994	1993	5YR AVG
Total Capital % Total Assets	13.29	9.49	9.40	9.32	9.53	10.21
Common Equity % Total Assets	7.29	7.37	6.52	7.51	8.75	7.49

LIQUIDITY	1997	1996	1995	1994	1993	5YR AVG
Benefit & Loss Res % Tot Cap	470.07	787.38	755.42	771.56	742.48	705.38

ASSET UTILIZATION	1997	1996	1995	1994	1993	5YR AVG
Assets per Employee (in 000s)	7305	6154	6226	5072	3958	5743

OTHER	1997	1996	1995	1994	1993	5YR AVG
Invested Assets % Total Liab	82.92	89.51	84.61	85.14	88.32	86.10
Invested Assets % Total Assets	76.88	82.91	79.09	78.75	80.59	79.65
Eq Secs & Real Estate % Inv Assets	0.65	0.66	0.54	0.53	0.66	0.61

6

AFLAC Incorporated

GROWTH %	1997	1996	1995	1994	1993	5YR GR
Total Assets	17.71	-1.24	24.90	31.37	29.76	19.87
Total Insurance Reserves	-1.73	3.05	22.67	33.98	28.98	16.51
Net Sales or Revenues	-0.80	-2.10	17.67	22.20	25.44	11.87
Operating Income	0.89	-1.73	19.63	19.82	30.17	13.09
Earings per Share*	52.38	17.17	23.06	22.41	29.47	28.34
Dividends per Share*	15.09	14.85	13.48	14.69	12.79	14.18
Book Value per Share	19.35	14.43	14.67	15.04	24.41	17.52

Displayed Currency: U.S. Dollar (1.00:1)
*Source: Worldscope. Value may differ from I/B/E/S.
Note: 5-Year Average calculations exclude NAs.

PER SHARE AND RELATED DATA

SOURCE: WORLDSCOPE	1997	1996	1995	1994	1993
Earnings per Share	4.16	2.73	2.33	1.89	1.55
Dividends per Share	0.45	0.39	0.34	0.30	0.26
Book Value per Share	15.44	12.94	11.31	9.86	8.57
Total Investment Return	NA	NA	37.52	13.84	4.67
Market Price (Year-end)	51.13	42.75	29.00	21.33	19.00
Market Capitalization (in millions)	6861.90	5894.58	4117.27	3188.35	2948.92
Price/Earnings Ratio	12.29	15.66	12.45	11.27	12.28
Price/Book Value	3.31	3.30	2.56	2.16	2.22
Dividend Yield	0.87	0.90	1.16	1.39	1.36
Dividend Payout per Share	10.70	14.16	14.45	15.67	16.72
Common Shares Outstanding (Year-end) in Millions	134.22	137.89	141.97	149.45	155.21
Stock Split/Dividend Ratio	NA	NA	0.67	0.67	0.67
Type of Share	*Common*				

Displayed Currency: U.S. Dollar (1.00:1)
Note: Date is sourced from Worldscope and may differ from I/B/E/S historical data.

2. AlliedSignal Incorporated

The sky is not the limit at aerospace giant AlliedSignal Incorporated. This advanced technology and manufacturing company is widely diversified in automotive and engineered materials in addition to its better-known aerospace business. AlliedSignal, whose stock is a component of the Dow Jones industrial average, takes a worldview. Despite its enormous size, it displays flexibility and is comfortable with change. Tough-guy Chairman and Chief Executive Officer Larry Bossidy, who came to the company in 1991 after spending thirty-four years with General Electric Credit, fashioned a dynamic turnaround by streamlining the conglomerate's operations. He has emphasized global reach, an increasing number of new products, and plenty of acquisitions. A strong portfolio of growth businesses has also served to strengthen the company. Bossidy has also been committed since 1992 to the Six Sigma program of excellence (see page 132), as Motorola Incorporated was before it and General Electric Company more recently has become, in order to emphasize a companywide goal of improving quality.

"I think you have to position organizations to continue to take steps up. Companies don't change incrementally," Bossidy told *Harvard Business Review* as he completed the first four years of the firm's transformation. "They change in quantum jumps. If you shoot for anything less, you don't get any change. You may fall short, but still you've made a difference."

The globalization favored by AlliedSignal targets rapidly growing markets like China, instead of more developed ones that have fewer opportunities for growth. For example, AlliedSignal operates an aircraft wheel/brake repair and overhaul facility in

8

Shanghai through a joint venture with China Eastern Airlines, that nation's second-largest airline. It brought China Eastern technicians to the United States for months of training in the latest repair and overhaul techniques. As a result, the Shanghai facility was the first in China to be certified by both the Civil Aviation Administration of China and the U.S. Federal Aviation Administration. International customers now provide 28 percent of AlliedSignal's aerospace sales and it continues to form joint ventures and other alliances in Russia, Europe, and in the Asia-Pacific area to grow and establish a global presence in these markets. Diversity helped it avoid at least some of the problems stemming from economic turmoil in Asia in 1997 and 1998 that stymied so many other global companies.

AlliedSignal has been built by merger. The company was established in 1985 through the merger of Allied Corporation and the Signal Companies, Inc., a transaction in which Allied also sold a 50 percent interest in Union Texas Petroleum. Allied Chemical & Dye Corporation had begun in 1920 as a combination of five American chemical firms, and eventually expanded into automotive products and aerospace through the acquisition of the Bendix Corporation in 1983. Signal started life in 1928 as a regional gasoline company in California and also drilled for oil before it expanded through numerous acquisitions such as that of the Garrett Corporation aerospace manufacturer in 1964. Acquisitions still power AlliedSignal in the 1990s. It has completed more than twenty acquisitions since 1991, adding combined revenues of $2 billion. For example, in 1998 it acquired the hardware group and PacAero unit of Banner Aerospace, an independent distributor of aircraft hardware available for "just-in-time" delivery. Annualized sales of the operations acquired were about $250 million, primarily to commercial air transport and general aviation customers. It also completed the acquisition of British Airways' wheel and brake operations in 1998 and signed a ten-year deal with the airline to supply those services, potentially worth $150 million in annual revenue. However, in May 1998, AlliedSignal said it would repurchase up to $2.2 billion of its stock over the following two years. It also launched a hostile takeover bid for electronic connector firm AMP, Inc.

"Fix it or sell it" is Chairman Bossidy's credo. Willing to adjust his gameplan when results missed Wall Street analyst expectations in 1997, the CEO boldly eliminated the company's "sector structure" and reorganized into eleven separate business units. This major reorganization removed a layer of management to allow faster decisions and speedier serving of customers. AlliedSignal boasts a long list of innovative aerospace products. These include airplane engines, climate control systems, airborne weather-radar systems, wind-shear detection systems, and traffic collision avoidance radar systems. Management estimates that the worldwide potential market for one of its proprietary products, Enhanced Ground Proximity Warning Systems, is $1 billion. This process uses global positioning systems and a unique onboard global terrain database to provide pilots with a graphic picture of terrain in front of them. It also gives up to a full minute of advance audio warning if the aircraft is on a course to collide with terrain, versus the short ten to fifteen seconds common with traditional systems. The company also makes guidance systems for missiles and spacecraft.

How big is AlliedSignal in the automotive industry? It's one of the world's largest producers of truck brakes and friction materials, the world's leading manufacturer of turbochargers and oil-air filters, number two in spark plugs, and a major manufacturer of air bags and seat belt systems. Brand-name automotive products include FRAM filters, Autolite spark plugs, Prestone antifreeze, and Bendix and Jurid friction materials. Although analysts contend that automotive would be the division most likely to be sold off if a good deal could be made, Bossidy for now has maintained a belief in its future. New products include refrigerants that complete the transition from the manufacture of CFCs to environmentally friendly substitutes. Another product is the variable nozzle turbocharger, which improves acceleration of diesel-powered cars to give quicker pickup with smaller engines and reduced emissions.

Carpet is just one of the products produced by AlliedSignal's engineered materials division. It's the leading producer of Nylon 6 fiber for carpet manufacturing, as well as the world's largest producer of hydrofluoric acid, a primary industrial building block and raw material. It makes a variety of chemicals, fibers, and plastics used by industries such as refrigeration, construction, electronics, computers, utilities, automotive, and carpeting. The engineered materials business holds the number-two position in the North American industrial polyester and fluorocarbon markets.

Continuous growth, even in mature businesses, is urged by Bossidy, who plans to leave the giant company functioning as a lean, mean, fightin' machine when he retires in the year 2000. His model factory program, which focuses on reengineering individual plants, has made impressive productivity gains while improving speed and quality. Since 1992 AlliedSignal has been devoted to Six Sigma, achieving a ratio of 3.4 defective parts per million or near-perfection. Through its Operational Excellence program, AlliedSignal's goal is to reach that manufacturing standard achieved by only a handful of companies in the world. To underscore its seriousness, AlliedSignal hired more than 200 of the world's foremost manufacturing experts to train employees in advanced manufacturing techniques. Trainees learn how to analyze each manufacturing process in a factory, determine where the most defects are occurring, and attack the processes in order to fix or eliminate them.

"With $1.5 billion in estimated savings already achieved, Six Sigma is one of the most ambitious projects we have ever undertaken," Bossidy said in his letter in the most recent annual report. "When our Six Sigma defect reduction program began, AlliedSignal was an average-quality manufacturer. Today, we're substantially above average, and getting better." Finally, through its Materials Management program, AlliedSignal has reduced its number of suppliers from more than 10,000 to less than 3,000. Preferred suppliers receive a greater volume of business in return for better quality, lower prices, and increased productivity. Following the success of its Total Quality Leadership initiative in 1992, in which every employee received several days of extensive skills training, it launched Total Quality Leadership II. Employees now go through training with their daily work teams and select the most appropriate tools to improve their focus areas. All of which is evidence that a modern conglomerate must continue to change and reinvent itself, rather than simply relax and enjoy its supposed economies of scale.

2. ALLIEDSIGNAL INCORPORATED

United States   Ticker symbol ALD

Stock price $36 (9/16/98)   Dividend yield 1.67%

(Financial data is from I/B/E/S International)*

BUSINESS DESCRIPTION

AEROSPACE ACCOUNTED FOR 45% OF 1997 REVENUES, ENGINEERED MATERIALS 29%, AND AUTOMOTIVE 26%

ADDRESS AND CONTACTS

Address	101 Columbia Road
	Morristown NJ 07962
Telephone	1-973-455-2000

BASIC FINANCIAL INFORMATION

Capital Structure[†]		
	Long Term Debt:	1215.00
	Total Debt:	2307.00
	Common Sh. Equity:	4386.00

SALES BREAKDOWN

Product Segments[†]		
	Aerospace	6412.00
	Engineered Materials	4254.00
	Automotive	3802.00

Geographic Segments[†]		
	United States	11319.00
	Europe	2171.00
	Canada	361.00
	Other International	621.00

Displayed Currency: U.S. Dollar (1.00:1)
*I/B/E/S/ and I/B/E/S Express are registered trademarks of I/B/E/S/ International Inc. Copyright 1993–1996 I/B/E/S International Inc. All rights reserved.
[†]Values are displayed in millions.

FINANCIAL STATEMENT DATA

INCOME STATEMENT	1997	1996	1995	1994	1993
Net Sales or Revenues	14472.00	13971.00	14346.00	12817.00	11837.00
EBITDA	2367.00	2216.00	1850.00	1685.00	1492.00
Depreciation Depletion & Amort	609.00	602.00	612.00	560.00	547.00
Operating Income	1647.00	1491.00	1260.00	1152.00	938.00
Interest Expense	209.00	209.00	189.00	166.00	186.00
Pretax Income	1583.00	1428.00	1070.00	982.00	788.00
Net Income	1170.00	1020.00	875.00	759.00	656.00

BALANCE SHEET	1997	1996	1995	1994	1993
Assets					
Cash & Equivalents	1041.00	1766.00	540.00	508.00	892.00
Receivables—Net	1886.00	1661.00	1751.00	1697.00	1343.00
Inventories	2093.00	1946.00	1991.00	1743.00	1745.00
Total Current Assets	5573.00	5839.00	4890.00	4585.00	4567.00
Property Plant & Eq.— Net	4251.00	4219.00	4742.00	4260.00	4094.00
Total Assets	13590.00	12651.00	12465.00	11321.00	10829.00
Liabilities & Shareholders' Equity					
Total Curent Liabilites	4436.00	3696.00	3804.00	3391.00	3489.00
Long Term Debt	1215.00	1317.00	1366.00	1424.00	1602.00
Preferred Stock	0.00	0.00	0.00	0.00	0.00
Common Equity	4386.00	4180.00	3592.00	2982.00	2390.00
Total Liabilities & Sh. Equity	13590.00	12651.00	12465.00	11321.00	10829.00

CASH FLOW	1997	1996	1995	1994	1993
Net Cash Flow— Operating	1306.00	1196.00	1216.00	1043.00	1180.00
Net Cash Flow— Investing	1283.00	-273.00	1104.00	872.00	819.00
Net Cash Flow— Financing	-877.00	-544.00	-80.00	-555.00	-400.00
Incr/Decr in Working Capital	-1006.00	1057.00	-108.00	116.00	-336.00
Free Cash Flow	1650.00	1461.00	1104.00	1046.00	774.00

INTERNATIONAL BUSINESS	1997	1996	1995	1994	1993
Foreign Assets	3586.00	2949.00	3087.00	2344.00	2186.00
Foreign Sales	3153.00	3197.00	3612.00	3078.00	2607.00
Foreign Income	84.00	284.00	141.00	105.00	86.00

SUPPLEMENTARY DATA	1997	1996	1995	1994	1993
Employees	70500	76600	88500	87500	86400
R&D Expenses	349.00	345.00	353.00	318.00	313.00
Goodwill/Cost in Excess of Assets Purchased	2426.00	1418.00	1572.00	1349.00	1087.00
Extra Items & Gain/Loss in Sale of Assets	0.00	0.00	0.00	0.00	-245.00

Displayed Currency: U.S. Dollar (1.00:1)
All values are displayed in millions (except employees).

FINANCIAL RATIOS AND GROWTH RATES

PROFITABILITY	1997	1996	1995	1994	1993	5YR AVG
Operating Profit Margin %	11.38	10.67	8.78	8.99	7.93	9.55
Tax Rate %	34.49	37.32	36.07	35.85	32.23	35.19
Net Margin %	8.08	7.30	6.10	5.92	3.48	6.18
Return on Assets %	10.16	9.17	8.71	7.88	4.78	8.14
Return on Equity— Total %	27.99	28.40	29.34	31.76	18.26	27.15
Cash Flow % Sales	10.72	9.10	9.88	8.68	6.60	9.00
Sales per Employee (in 000s)	205	182	162	146	137	167

ASSET UTILIZATION	1997	1996	1995	1994	1993	5YR AVG
Total Asset Turnover	1.06	1.10	1.15	1.13	1.09	1.11
Capital Exp % Gross Fixed Assets	7.80	8.41	7.62	7.27	8.79	7.98
Acc Depreciation % Gross Fixed Assets	53.74	53.00	51.54	51.55	49.88	51.94
Assets per Employee (in 000s)	193	165	141	129	125	151

LIQUIDITY	1997	1996	1995	1994	1993	5YR AVG
Current Ratio	1.26	1.58	1.29	1.35	1.31	1.36
Quick Ratio	0.66	0.93	0.60	0.65	0.64	0.70

LEVERAGE	1997	1996	1995	1994	1993	5YR AVG
Total Debt % Common Equity	52.60	46.20	55.96	56.57	82.01	58.67
Long Term Debt % Common Equity	27.70	31.51	38.03	47.75	67.03	42.40

AlliedSignal Incorporated

Common Equity %						
Total Assets	32.27	33.04	28.82	26.34	22.07	28.51
Long Term Debt %						
Total Capital	21.69	23.96	27.55	32.32	40.13	29.13
Operating Cash/						
Fixed Charges	7.92	6.09	7.50	6.70	4.20	6.48

GROWTH %	1997	1996	1995	1994	1993	5YR AVG
Net Sales	3.59	-2.61	11.93	8.37	-1.79	3.74
Operating Income	10.46	18.33	9.38	22.81	19.80	16.03
Total Assets	7.42	1.49	10.11	4.54	0.68	4.79
Earnings per Share*	11.91	16.83	15.30	16.02	21.58	16.29
Dividends per Share*	15.56	15.38	20.46	11.64	16.00	15.77
Book Value per Share*	1.66	16.35	20.61	25.08	6.15	13.63

Displayed Currency: U.S. Dollar (1.00:1)
*Source: Worldscope. Value may differ from I/B/E/S.
Note: 5-Year Average calculations exclude NAs.

PER SHARE AND RELATED DATA

SOURCE: WORLDSCOPE	1997	1996	1995	1994	1993
Earnings per Share	2.02	1.81	1.55	1.34	1.16
Dividends per Share	0.52	0.45	0.39	0.32	0.29
Book Value per Share	7.51	7.39	6.35	5.27	4.21
Total Investment Return	NA	NA	42.00	-12.28	32.50
Market Price (Year-end)	38.81	33.50	23.75	17.00	19.75
Market Capitalization					
(in millions)	21670.95	18948.58	13431.55	9626.48	11211.42
Price/Earnings Ratio	19.21	18.56	15.37	12.69	17.10
Price/Book Value	5.17	4.53	3.74	3.23	4.69
Dividend Yield	1.34	1.34	1.64	1.90	1.47
Dividend Payout per					
Share	25.74	24.93	25.24	24.16	25.11
Common Shares					
Outstanding					
(Year-end) in					
Millions	558.34	565.63	565.54	566.26	567.67
Stock Split/Dividend Ratio	1.00	0.50	0.50	0.50	0.25
Type of Share	*Common*				

Displayed Currency: U.S. Dollar (1.00:1)
Note: Data is sourced from Worldscope and may differ from I/B/E/S historical data.

3. Amway Japan Limited

Just what the doctor ordered: A compact home water-treatment system designed for small Japanese kitchens that features a unique ultraviolet lamp as well as a conventional filter. Over the long haul this double treatment bacteria-killer is considerably less expensive than Japanese bottled water. As Amway Japan Limited's top-selling product, it also helps direct the consumer's eyes to a brand-new purifying product that attacks another Japanese health concern, pollution. This compact wall-mounted home air-treatment system run by remote control has a filter that removes pollutants as small as 1/10,000th the diameter of a human hair.

This is targeting the local market, something Amway Japan, the largest direct-selling business in sales in Japan, does with remarkable success even in the most difficult economic times. It's the same philosophy behind a uniquely Japanese garlic-and-licorice food supplement. While that's unlikely to be a winning combination in the United States, the Japanese consider it a clever idea that effectively counteracts taste and breath concerns about healthful but ever-so-pungent garlic.

About one-third of the products sold by Amway Japan are either made in that country or made exclusively for it by other major manufacturers. For example, the company recently introduced new co-branded products developed with Rubbermaid (food storage containers), Sara Lee's Playtex Division (intimate apparel), and Corning (ceramic dinnerware). It selects the other two-thirds of its products from the lines of U.S. consumer goods firm Amway Corp., for which it is the exclusive distributor in Japan. Only Amway Japan can use the Amway trademark there.

Amway Japan works with Amway to minimize the obvious impact of currency fluctuations on distributors by adjusting prices to reflect the dollar-to-yen relationship. To manage currency fluctuations more systematically, it has begun quarterly meetings with Amway to review the exchange rate included in the products purchased from the parent company.

In all, Amway Japan distributes more than 130 different products in housewares, personal care, nutrition, and home care through an army of more than one million distributors. These folks use "personality plus" and a self-starter sales approach that puts the touch on friends and newfound friends in order to generate sales. Many actually sign up as distributors primarily for the opportunity to buy for personal use the various products sold under the Amway, Amway Queen, Artistry, Satinique, Nutrilite, Quench8, and SA8 brand names at wholesale prices. The company's discount emphasis is something very different from the attitude of stodgy old-line Japanese retailers and consumer product manufacturers who hold to their prices, a point that's not lost on the average modern consumer there.

Its Japanese roots mean the company's stock has suffered volatility over that country's economic woes in recent months, but savvy long-term investors have used downside opportunities to buy more shares. The company has real growth potential. Even with its massive distributor strength, Amway Japan still reaches merely about 5 percent of Japan's 44 million households. That's a sure indication of future possibilities, with the only concern being whether other savvy consumer product companies will try to snatch some of that business themselves by emulating Amway Japan's style.

Founded in June 1977, Amway Japan Limited began operations in 1979 and offered its stock publicly in 1991. It's a company that got off to a rousing start and, whenever experts believe it may have peaked, seems to take off again to set even more revenue and earning records. The company remains somewhat of a family affair, since the DeVos and Van Andel families, who founded both Amway Japan and privately owned parent company Amway Corp. in Ada, Michigan, own 83 percent of Amway

Japan. Rich DeVos and Jay Van Andel met as students at Grand Rapids' Christian High School, and later pioneered person-to-person sales of Nutrilite Vitamins and Food Supplements before founding Amway in 1959 in order to sell a biodegradable all-purpose cleaner.

The company's stated goal is "to be the best business opportunity in the world." As in the United States, individuals can establish their own businesses by sponsoring new Amway Japan distributors, creating layers of "downline" distributors, and earning performance bonuses based on purchases by their own distributors. More than 400 staffers spend several days in the field each year working one-on-one with distributors in order to get a better understanding of their needs. The company recently reorganized its distributor telephone support to give more accurate assistance, and expanded automated ordering through touch-tone phones and the Internet. It began introducing a mini personal computer for distributors, to give them electronic access to information and ordering.

The home care division specializes in laundry, kitchen, and car care products, household cleaners, and air fresheners. Due to discounting by competitors, this is a division under pressure. New SA8, the most concentrated laundry detergent in Japan, is designed to save on cost-per-load, storage space, and packaging waste. It's promoted as the ideal detergent for new home fabrics by Westpoint Stevens, and a set of deep-pile, Egyptian cotton bath towels that Amway Japan sells.

The personal care division, the largest of the company's businesses, offers Artistry shaded cosmetics and skin care products, as well as hair, body, and oral care products. For example, the new Artistry Swiss Serum increases the elasticity of facial skin and moisturizes for a more youthful appearance, while the Artistry Body Gel helps improve skin texture for sleeker and firmer hips, thighs, and stomach. There are more than 350,000 members of Club Artistry, which rewards members with frequent buyer points toward gifts and other incentives. Members receive beauty tips, previews of new products, and special promotions.

The nutrition division, which has been under pressure, emphasizes food supplements. Triple X Multi-Vitamin and Multi-Mineral Supplement continues to lead all nutrition products with increasing sales. Triple X consists of two different tablets and a capsule that provide a complete daily vitamin and mineral supplement. It's also strong in herbal products, with the Nutrilite Garlic with Licorice mentioned earlier being joined by Siberian Ginseng with Ginkgo Biloba and other products. Launched to coincide with the 1998 Nagano, Japan, Winter Olympics, the Nutrilite Strive sports drink powder provides vitamin C, natural beta carotene, electrolytes, and other nutrients.

Housewares is the division selling Amway Queen cookware, induction range, and coffee maker, as well as the Amway home air- and water-treatment systems. The most recent introduction was the chinalike Amway Dinnerware by Corning.

Amway Japan has completed the first year of a three-year incentive program that encourages distributors to work toward long-term goals and greater rewards. The Dream Incentive program provides progressive bonuses at each higher level of achievement. In addition, distributors can become eligible for the Millennium Growth Awards providing annual growth bonuses as well as a special growth-sharing award in the year 2000.

---

3. AMWAY JAPAN LIMITED

Japan   Ticker symbol AJL

One American Depositary Receipt represents 1/2 ordinary share

ADR price $4 11/16 (9/16/98)   Dividend yield 7.57%

(Financial data from I/B/E/S International is in Japanese yen)*

BUSINESS DESCRIPTION

PERSONAL CARE PRODUCTS ACCOUNTED FOR 34% OF FISCAL 1997 REVENUES, HOUSEWARES 29%, NUTRITION 24%, HOME CARE PRODUCTS 9%, AND OTHER 4%

ADDRESS AND CONTACTS

Address	Arco Tower
	8-1, Shimomeguro 1-Chome
	Meguro-ku Tokyo 153-8686 Japan
Telephone	81-3-54348484
Fax	81-3-54344923

BASIC FINANCIAL INFORMATION

Capital Structure[†]

Long Term Debt:	0.00
Total Debt:	0.00
Common Sh. Equity:	63.36

SALES BREAKDOWN

Product Segments[†]	NA
Geographic Segments[†] Japan	130.03

Displayed Currency: Japanese Yen (1.00:1)
I/B/E/S and I/B/E/S Express are registered trademarks of I/B/E/S International Inc. Copyright
1993–1996 I/B/E/S International Inc. All rights reserved.
[†]Values are displayed in billions.

FINANCIAL STATEMENT DATA

INCOME STATEMENT	1997	1996	1995	1994	1993
Net Sales or Revenues	203.36	212.20	177.99	157.55	130.03
EBITDA	46.50	56.51	46.78	41.70	32.91
Depreciation Depletion					
& Amort	1.65	1.13	1.44	1.18	0.70
Operating Income	41.61	54.13	43.62	37.96	31.35
Interest Expense	0.00	0.00	0.00	0.00	0.00
Pretax Income	44.85	55.38	45.35	40.52	32.21
Net Income	23.12	28.08	23.06	20.60	15.85

BALANCE SHEET	1997	1996	1995	1994	1993
Assets					
Cash & Equivalents	46.49	64.58	73.64	91.24	77.29
Receivables—Net	3.95	0.45	0.81	2.27	3.22
Inventories	16.71	12.47	11.40	10.94	9.90
Total Current Assets	68.78	79.36	87.49	106.21	91.97
Property Plant & Eq.—Net	37.59	31.17	26.79	2.52	2.32
Total Assets	110.23	116.18	119.94	114.80	101.96
Liabilities & Shareholders' Equity					
Total Current Liabilities	46.68	52.22	43.93	37.36	29.68
Long Term Debt	0.00	0.00	0.00	0.00	0.00
Preferred Stock	0.00	0.00	0.00	0.00	0.00
Common Equity	63.36	63.86	76.01	77.43	72.29
Total Liabilities					
& Sh. Equity	110.23	116.18	119.94	114.80	101.96

Amway Japan Limited

CASH FLOW	1997	1996	1995	1994	1993
Funds from Operations	22.01	30.00	26.14	22.98	18.71
Total Sources	48.21	72.46	55.76	48.62	11.80
Cash Dividends Paid—					
Total	14.68	25.44	26.18	13.47	8.23
Total Uses	48.21	72.46	55.76	48.62	11.80
Incr/Decr in Working					
Capital	-5.04	-16.42	-25.28	6.55	5.27
Free Cash Flow	38.24	51.15	21.61	40.74	32.05

INTERNATIONAL BUSINESS	1997	1996	1995	1994	1993
Foreign Assets	NA	NA	NA	NA	0.00
Foreign Sales	NA	NA	NA	NA	0.00
Foreign Income	NA	NA	NA	NA	0.00

SUPPLEMENTARY DATA	1997	1996	1995	1994	1993
Employees	1210	1044	960	871	769
R&D Expenses	NA	NA	NA	NA	NA
Goodwill/Cost in Excess of Assets Purchased	NA	NA	NA	NA	NA
Extra Items & Gain/Loss in Sale of Assets	0.00	0.00	0.00	0.00	0.00

Displayed Currency: Japanese Yen (1.00:1)
All values are displayed in billions (except employees).

FINANCIAL RATIOS AND GROWTH RATES

PROFITABILITY	1997	1996	1995	1994	1993	5YR AVG
Operating Profit Margin %	20.46	25.51	24.50	24.09	24.11	23.74
Tax Rate %	48.45	49.29	49.15	49.15	50.79	49.37
Net Margin %	11.37	13.23	12.96	13.08	12.19	12.56
Return on Assets %	19.90	23.41	20.09	20.21	17.04	20.13
Return on Equity— Total %	36.20	36.94	29.78	28.50	24.51	31.19
Cash Flow % Sales	10.82	14.14	14.69	14.59	14.39	13.72
Sales per Employee (in 000s)	168067	203252	185407	180890	169087	181341

ASSET UTILIZATION	1997	1996	1995	1994	1993	5YR AVG
Total Asset Turnover	1.84	1.83	1.48	1.37	1.28	1.56
Capital Exp % Gross Fixed Assets	19.50	15.23	83.77	17.81	18.45	30.95
Acc Depreciation % Gross Fixed Assets	11.19	11.41	10.85	53.33	50.13	27.30
Assets per Employee (in 000s)	91098	111279	124938	131798	132593	118341

21

LIQUIDITY	1997	1996	1995	1994	1993	5YR AVG
Current Ratio	1.47	1.52	1.99	2.84	3.10	2.19
Quick Ratio	1.08	1.25	1.69	2.50	2.71	1.85

LEVERAGE	1997	1996	1995	1994	1993	5YR AVG
Total Debt % Common Equity	0.00	0.00	0.00	0.00	0.00	0.00
Long Term Debt % Common Equity	0.00	0.00	0.00	0.00	0.00	0.00
Common Equity % Total Assets	57.48	54.97	63.38	67.45	70.89	62.83
Long Term Debt % Total Capital	0.00	0.00	0.00	0.00	0.00	0.00
Operating Cash/ Fixed Charges	NA	NA	NA	NA	NA	NA

GROWTH %	1997	1996	1995	1994	1993	5YR AVG
Net Sales	-4.16	19.22	12.97	21.17	5.50	10.53
Operating Income	-23.13	24.11	14.90	21.09	5.44	6.95
Total Assets	-5.12	-3.14	4.48	12.58	9.63	3.46
Earnings per Share*	-16.05	21.87	11.93	29.98	-9.44	6.15
Dividends per Share*	-20.00	-34.21	35.71	133.33	20.00	14.87
Book Value per Share	0.97	-14.38	-1.83	7.12	11.75	0.32

Displayed Currency: Japanese Yen (1.00:1)
*Source: Worldscope. Value may differ from I/B/E/S.
Note: 5-Year Average calculations exclude NAs.

PER SHARE AND RELATED DATA

SCOURCE: WORLDSCOPE	1997	1996	1995	1994	1993
Earnings per Share	157.7	187.8	154.1	137.7	105.9
Dividends per Share	100.0	125.0	190.0	140.0	60.0
Book Value per Share	439.2	435.0	508.0	517.5	483.1
Total Investment Return	NA	29.24	13.03	26.47	20.87
Market Price (Year-end)	3180.0	4450.0	3540.0	3300.0	2720.0
Market Capitalization (in billions)	458.77	653.35	529.67	493.76	406.98
Price/Earnings Ratio	20.17	23.69	22.97	23.97	25.67
Price/Book Value	7.24	10.23	6.97	6.38	5.63
Dividend Yield	3.14	2.81	5.37	4.24	2.21
Dividend Payout per Share	63.42	66.55	123.27	101.67	56.64
Common Shares Outstanding (Year-end) in Millions	144.27	146.82	149.62	149.62	149.62
Stock Split/Dividend Ratio	NA	NA	NA	NA	NA
Type of Share	*Common*				

Displayed Currency: Japanese Yen (1.00:1)
Note: Data is sourced from Worldscope and may differ from I/B/E/S historical data.

4. Automatic Data Processing Incorporated

Everybody must get paid. That reality makes payroll processing one of the best businesses in the world. It's why Automatic Data Processing Incorporated (ADP) remains committed to its goal of "achieving world class service." Not many firms make the payroll processing part of their strategic plan, so outsourcing—a concept that ADP pioneered—is an easy step. Best of all, because most employees are paid on a regular basis, there's a predictable revenue stream. That protects payroll processing from many challenges that other high-tech businesses face and places this payroll processor's stock firmly in a "defensive growth" category that has provided decades of outstanding earnings and revenue growth.

Founded in 1949, ADP is the world's biggest payroll and tax-filing processor, with more than 400,000 accounts. These services make up about half of the company's revenues. ADP is big at tax time, since it files returns for nearly 300,000 clients. Its worldwide goals include acquisitions. Each of the company's four core businesses holds leading market share positions. For example, this aggressive company recently bought a Brazilian computing services firm to give it a foothold in the growing South American employer services market; purchased the payroll businesses of Royal Bank of Canada and Scotiabank; and completed deals in Europe that boosted its market share of the automobile and truck management services market in Germany, Italy, and Scandanavia. It has worked hard to attain its position as the number-one European market share position in both payroll processing and automobile dealer management services.

This company drives the payment vehicle. Its employer services division pays more than 23 million wage earners worldwide on payday, including 2 million in Europe. It handles paychecks and payroll information for 18 million wage-earners, or about one-eighth of the U.S. work force. It handles personnel record-keeping for more than 2 million employees and 401(k) plan record-keeping for more than 5,000 clients. It prints more than 33 million W-2 tax forms and sends more than $90 billion annually to state, federal, and local taxing authorities on behalf of employers. The regulatory background is often quite favorable to ADP, since each year there are legal and procedural changes at the federal and state levels that make payroll a major problem companies must deal with. A hefty one-third of all employees in the United States are currently paid through service bureaus, and some experts predict that eventually two-thirds of employees will outsource their payroll needs. The changing corporate scene of mergers and acquisitions has increased the demand for paychecks being supplied more efficiently. For example, Pierce Leahy Corp., an international records management provider, has been actively acquiring companies, and that has meant adjustments to payroll in order to pay new employees accurately and on time. ADP developed a plan to manage the payroll conversion process for each of Pierce Leahy's acquisitions, based on a list of items that both ADP and the client needed. By following the plan and monitoring each task, the conversion of four new acquisitions to the ADP system went smoothly. Not one worker missed a paycheck.

ADP also has an impact on the brokerage industry. Its brokerage services division is the largest U.S. provider of timely market information to 96,000 investment professionals in 1,200 firms. It processes nearly 150,000 securities transactions a day, or about 20 percent of Wall Street's trades. This includes both front-office quotation workstations and back-office record-keeping. Its ADP Investor Communications Services is the biggest independent provider of shareholder communications in North America, distributing 200 million proxy and quarterly packages to shareholders of more than 11,000 publicly held corporations and mutual funds. The company has had the technology muscle to capture impressive new accounts in recent years, such as Merrill Lynch, PaineWebber Inc., and Prudential Securities. Such changeovers have gone smoothly. For example, in 1998 ADP took over the distribution of proxy statements and other corporate information to all shareholders who have securities within a Merrill Lynch account. All these functions previously performed by Merrill Lynch in New Jersey were moved to ADP's Long Island facility. In announcing the move, Merrill Lynch top brass said it made the decision in order to provide quality service and "implement the latest technology on a more cost-effective basis." ADP said the Merrill Lynch volume would enable it to push further and faster into more technologies, such as the Internet, lowering issuers' unit costs.

A visit to your local automobile dealer quickly turns up evidence of ADP's presence. Its dealer services division provides accounting, inventory, scheduling, leasing, sales activity, and other management services to more than 18,000 automobile and truck dealers in the Americas, Asia, and Europe. As the dealer who services my car told me: "The ADP system is incredibly better than the crude way we used to keep track of everything." More than 40 percent of clients are located outside the North American market. There are more than 160,000 pieces of installed hardware for this purpose. ADP's network makes it possible to quickly calculate a vehicle's purchase price, monthly payments, or lease options, or to locate a certain vehicle or part anywhere in the country.

The insurance industry also knows ADP. Its claims services group supplies fourteen of the fifteen largest auto insurance carriers with computerized repair and parts availability services. It also provides the service to claims adjusters, repair shops, and salvage yards. ADP's PenPro pen-based touch screen handheld computer is used by mobile claims adjusters. In September 1996, Hurricane Fran did more than $3.2 billion in damage to the North Carolina coast. United Services Automobile Association (USAA), a leading insurer of homes and automobiles, had to respond to a flood of insurance claims. ADP set up automated claims estimate sites, including one in a converted garage on a military base. An ADP team operated the sites eighteen hours a day for three weeks. Using ADP claims-estimating software,

USAA's estimators evaluated damaged vehicles, processed claims, and provided settlement checks on the spot.

Powerful growth has always been a characteristic of ADP. For example, in 1997, employer services revenues grew by 19 percent, brokerage services by 13 percent, dealer services by 17 percent, and claims services by 20 percent. As Chief Executive Officer Arthur Weinbach put it in ADP's most recent annual report, the company's growth "will come from further penetration of our markets, extending our market opportunities through broader product offerings, and through additional international expansion."

That report also trumpeted the fact that ADP at that point had concluded thirty-six years (144 consecutive quarters) of uninterrupted growth in both revenue and earnings per share. With a strong and experienced management team, dominant leadership position, and consistent performance that's unparalleled, this high-quality company might be considered an automatic investment.

4. AUTOMATIC DATA PROCESSING INCORPORATED

United States   Ticker symbol AUD

Stock price $72 7/16 (9/16/98)   Dividend yield .73%

(Financial data is from I/B/E/S International)*

BUSINESS DESCRIPTION

EMPLOYER SERVICES ACCOUNTED FOR 55% OF FISCAL 1997 REVENUES, BROKERAGE SERVICES 22%, DEALER SERVICES 16%, AND OTHER 7%

ADDRESS AND CONTACTS

Address   1 ADP Boulevard
                 Roseland NJ 07068
Telephone   1-973-994-5000

BASIC FINANCIAL INFORMATION

Capital Structure†	Long Term Debt:	401.16
	Total Debt:	531.42
	Common Sh. Equity:	2660.56

SALES BREAKDOWN

Product Segments†	Employer Services	2275.00
	Brokerage Services	892.00
	Dealer Services	651.00
	Other	294.00
Geographic Segments†	United States	3417.00
	Europe	512.00
	Other Non-U.S.	131.00
	Corporate	52.00

Displayed Currency: U.S. Dollar (1.00:1)

*I/B/E/S and I/B/E/S Express are registered trademarks of I/B/E/S International Inc. Copyright 1993–1996 I/B/E/S International Inc. All rights reserved.

†Values are displayed in millions.

FINANCIAL STATEMENT DATA

INCOME STATEMENT	1997	1996	1995	1994	1993
Net Sales or Revenues	4112.19	3566.60	2893.74	2468.97	2223.37
EBITDA	975.24	866.75	731.16	615.47	546.61
Depreciation Depletion & Amort	223.44	201.63	172.54	148.30	140.23
Operating Income	781.09	665.12	558.62	467.17	406.38
Interest Expense	29.73	29.73	24.34	20.84	19.82
Pretax Income	724.01	635.39	534.28	446.33	386.56
Net Income	NA	454.70	394.83	334.12	294.20

BALANCE SHEET	1997	1996	1995	1994	1993
Assets					
Cash & Equivalents	1024.92	636.16	697.62	590.60	368.16
Receivables—Net	605.07	507.20	377.14	298.10	294.28
Inventories	0.00	0.00	0.00	0.00	0.00
Total Current Assets	1805.32	1454.28	1211.14	985.42	771.30
Property Plant & Eq.— Net	519.34	468.27	415.96	395.85	361.18
Total Assets	4382.77	3839.89	3201.10	2705.56	2439.40
Liabilities & Shareholders' Equity					
Total Current Liabilities	1019.87	835.61	543.22	478.17	416.26
Long Term Debt	401.16	403.74	390.18	372.96	347.58
Preferred Stock	0.00	0.00	0.00	0.00	0.00
Common Equity	2660.56	2315.35	2096.62	1619.25	1494.46
Total Liabilities & Sh. Equity	4382.77	3839.89	3201.10	2705.56	2439.40

CASH FLOW	1997	1996	1995	1994	1993
Net Cash Flow— Operating	719.06	644.05	478.78	509.13	391.38
Net Cash Flow— Investing	299.48	547.73	414.72	321.37	431.41
Net Cash Flow— Financing	-143.41	-95.52	10.93	-129.94	-83.19
Incr/Decr in Working Capital	166.78	-49.25	160.68	152.20	-11.70
Free Cash Flow	799.95	703.23	613.46	504.73	459.20

INTERNATIONAL BUSINESS	1997	1996	1995	1994	1993
Foreign Assets	1.40	1.81	0.00	0.00	0.00
Foreign Sales	0.64	0.50	0.00	0.00	0.00
Foreign Income	0.08	0.04	0.00	0.00	0.00

SUPPLEMENTARY DATA	1997	1996	1995	1994	1993
Employees	30000	29000	25000	22000	21000
R&D Expenses	296.54	249.64	193.17	160.80	132.39
Goodwill/Cost in Excess of Assets Purchased	106.22	931.42	482.08	NA	NA
Extra Items & Gain/ Loss in Sale of Assets	0.00	0.00	0.00	-4.80	0.00

Displayed Currency: U.S. Dollar (1.00:1)
All values are displayed in millions (except employees).

FINANCIAL RATIOS AND GROWTH RATES

PROFITABILITY	1997	1996	1995	1994	1993	5YR AVG
Operating Profit Margin %	18.99	18.65	19.30	18.92	18.28	18.83
Tax Rate %	29.08	28.44	26.10	25.14	23.89	26.53
Net Margin %	12.49	12.75	13.64	13.34	13.23	13.09
Return on Assets %	13.85	14.82	15.19	14.06	14.16	14.42
Return on Equity— Total %	22.18	21.69	23.35	22.04	22.69	22.39
Cash Flow % Sales	17.06	18.79	19.22	19.54	20.08	18.94
Sales per Employee (in 000s)	137	123	116	112	106	119

ASSET UTILIZATION	1997	1996	1995	1994	1993	5YR AVG
Total Asset Turnover	0.94	0.93	0.90	0.91	0.91	0.92
Capital Exp % Gross Fixed Assets	12.97	13.27	10.72	11.06	9.59	11.52
Acc Depreciation % Gross Fixed Assets	61.58	62.01	62.12	60.47	60.39	61.31
Assets per Employee (in 000s)	146	132	128	123	116	129

Automatic Data Processing Incorporated

LIQUIDITY	1997	1996	1995	1994	1993	5YR AVG
Current Ratio	1.77	1.74	2.23	2.06	1.85	1.93
Quick Ratio	1.60	1.37	1.98	1.86	1.59	1.68

LEVERAGE	1997	1996	1995	1994	1993	5YR AVG
Total Debt % Common Equity	19.97	21.58	19.07	22.18	23.35	21.23
Long Term Debt % Common Equity	15.08	17.44	18.61	22.05	23.26	19.29
Common Equity % Total Assets	60.71	60.30	65.50	62.51	61.26	62.05
Long Term Debt % Total Capital	13.10	14.85	15.69	18.07	18.87	16.12
Operating Cash/ Fixed Charges	25.24	22.54	22.86	23.15	22.53	23.26

GROWTH %	1997	1996	1995	1994	1993	5YR AVG
Net Sales	15.30	23.25	17.20	11.05	14.57	16.21
Operating Income	17.44	19.07	19.58	14.96	14.85	17.16
Total Assets	14.14	19.96	18.32	10.91	12.45	15.10
Earnings per Share*	10.18	13.61	15.75	15.45	13.40	13.66
Dividends per Share*	15.06	18.57	20.69	14.85	13.48	16.50
Book Value per Share	13.16	11.71	17.56	16.77	13.31	14.48

Displayed Currency: U.S. Dollar (1.00:1)
*Source: Worldscope. Value may differ from I/B/E/S.
Note: 5-Year Average calculations exclude NAs.

PER SHARE AND RELATED DATA

SOURCE: WORLDSCOPE	1997	1996	1995	1994	1993
Earnings per Share	1.84	1.67	1.47	1.27	1.10
Dividends per Share	0.48	0.42	0.35	0.29	0.25
Book Value per Share	9.79	8.65	7.74	6.59	5.64
Total Investment Return	NA	NA	28.12	6.93	4.95
Market Price (Year-end)	61.38	42.88	37.13	29.25	27.63
Market Capitalization (in millions)	17973.61	12331.75	10698.24	8230.89	7796.82
Price/Earnings Ratio	33.36	25.67	25.26	23.03	25.11
Price/Book Value	6.27	4.96	4.79	4.44	4.90
Dividend Yield	0.78	0.97	0.94	0.99	0.91
Dividend Payout per Share	25.95	24.85	23.81	22.83	22.95
Common Shares Outstanding (Year-end) in Millions	292.85	287.62	288.17	281.40	282.24
Stock Split/Dividend Ratio	NA	NA	0.50	0.50	0.50
Type of Share	*Common*				

Displayed Currency: U.S. Dollar (1.00:1)
Note: Data is sourced from Worldscope and may differ from I/B/E/S historical data.

5. Bass Plc.

Cheers. Another round for everyone. Bass Ale, Carling Black Label, Caffrey's Irish Ale, Tennent's Lager, and Worthington Draught Bitter are the well-known calling cards of Britain's second-largest brewer. This company, which began life as one brewery in 1777, also makes Britvic soft drinks and owns and operates pubs and restaurants. But an investor should carefully read the fine print on any company's label to discover whether it does indeed have global staying power. That's because Bass Plc. also happens to be the world's number-one hotel operator, with more than 2,000 Holiday Inns, Crowne Plaza hotels, and Staybridge Suites hotels. Better than a quarter of its profits are generated by the Holiday Hospitality business. More than 90 percent of these hotels are franchised, effectively placing the risk from economic cycles on franchisees while Bass receives a steady earnings stream from a franchise fee of 5 percent of room revenues. Not content to stand pat with a brand name, more than 1,000 North American Holiday Inns have been renovated in a $1 billion rolling program of modernization designed to make every hotel a quality establishment. Returns from hotels and beverages have been hurt by economic realities such as the recent downturn in Asia, but the company is broadly spread throughout the globe in order to hedge its bets.

As the company teased in its 1997 annual report: "How much do you know about Bass? 392,000 bedrooms in over 2,380 hotels in 64 countries across five continents . . . over 1,050 leisure venues, 63,000 electronic entertainment machines . . . 12 million barrels of beer, 1.2 billion liters of soft drinks sold annually in over 60 countries. Now find out more."

Bass Plc. is expanding rapidly because it has the financial wherewithal to launch major takeovers in hotels or pubs wherever in the world it finds an attractive group of properties. For example, in 1998 for $2.9 billion Bass acquired from the Saison Group, owners of Inter-Continental, the entire business of Inter-Continental, including its hotel brands Inter-Continental and Forum and its hotel assets. It's being operated as part of the Holiday Hospitality business. Inter-Continental consisted of 187 hotels with 65,000 rooms in sixty-nine countries, including the main Inter-Continental brand, a leader in the global upscale market. In another move, the acquisition of Australian hotels to be converted to Holiday Inns marked the start of what Bass termed an "aggressive" drive to gain market share throughout the Asia-Pacific area. Bass makes a habit of actively buying back its own shares, while selling off less desirable holdings, such as its Bingo clubs and bookmaking business. In late 1997, Bass announced the sale of 1,428 pubs, the majority of the Bass Lease Co.'s pubs, leaving the company with a total of fifty-three leased pubs so it can instead focus on "the roll-out of its retail brands, the development of food sales, and local market share gains."

In the brewing business, Carling is Britain's biggest-selling beer and Tennent's Lager is Scotland's favorite pint. These established market leaders are complemented by innovative brands like Caffrey's Irish Ale, Hooper's Hooch, Carling Premier, and Tennent's Velvet. The company invests hundreds of millions of dollars annually to support these brands in an increasingly competitive marketplace. Meanwhile, its international business unit, created in 1995 to focus on specific international opportunities, has developed brewing interests in the Czech Republic and China. Bass's overall export brewing business makes it Britain's biggest beer exporter, serving over sixty countries. One of Britain's leading soft drink manufacturers, Britvic, is 90 percent owned by Britannia Soft Drinks, in which Bass has a controlling interest, and 10 percent by Pepsi Cola International. It has a significant presence in both the take-home and restaurant markets, selling nearly 1.2 billion liters of soft drinks every year In addition to its own best-selling brands such as Robinsons and Tango,

Britvic holds the British franchise for Pepsi and 7UP. It also produces Red Card, Britain's first sports drink, as well as fruit juices and lemon drinks. British sales of Pepsi have tripled since Britvic took on the brand ten years ago. The company continues to seek international opportunities both in export of products and development of franchise arrangements. Profits from the more mature export markets are reinvested in destinations offering the greatest potential. Britvic exports to more than thirty different countries.

At Holiday Hospitality, Crowne Plaza Hotels and Resorts provides first-class service as Bass's premium hotel brand. Lately it has been investing in new properties at the United Nations and key locations in Israel, China, and the United Arab Emirates. Holiday Inn is the world's largest hotel brand, known for dependable amenities and services. Holiday Inn Express is the firm's fastest-growing brand and targets guests looking for a complimentary breakfast bar and comfortable room. Launched in 1997, Staybridge Suites is the world's first global extended-stay brand for travelers staying more than four nights. Staybridge's studio, one-bedroom, or two-bedroom suites have fully equipped kitchens and separate living and dining areas.

Bass Leisure operates three businesses in the recreational leisure and amusement market. Barcrest is the most successful British manufacturer of "amusement with prizes" coin-operated gaming and amusement machines, while Bass Leisure Machine Services is the largest supplier to retailers of electronic amusement machines, including video games, pool tables, and music systems, as well as pay phones. With more than 66,000 electronic entertainment machines in a diverse range of locations, it supplies more than 100 corporate customers. Meanwhile, Bass Leisure Entertainment operates a range of leisure businesses such as the Hollywood Bowl sites, which include bowling, electronic entertainment, and food. Besides its two multi-entertainment complexes, the company also has the exclusive British license to operate Dave & Buster's, a new American restaurant and entertainment complex. Dave & Buster's includes, under one enormous 40,000-square-foot roof, the latest interactive electronic amusements, such as Formula 1 racing and golf simulators, as well as classic shuffleboard and pocket billiards. Bass's first Dave & Buster's opened in Solihull in mid-1997, followed by another in Bristol, with plans for more.

"Financially, Bass is very strong," Chairman Sir Ian Prosser asserted in his letter in the latest annual report. "We continue to explore acquisition opportunities that are consistent with our strategy. We have the flexibility to grasp such opportunities when they become available at the right price." There obviously will continue to be a lot more to Bass than another round of brew. It always pays to read the fine print on any label.

5. BASS PLC.

United Kingdom   Ticker symbol BAS

One American Depositary Receipt represents one ordinary share

ADR price $12 1/2 (9/16/98)   Dividend yield 3.01%

(Financial data from I/B/E/S International is in British pence)*

BUSINESS DESCRIPTION

BREWING ACCOUNTED FOR 29% OF FISCAL 1997 GROSS REVENUES, TAVERNS 26%, LEISURE 23%, HOTELS 12%, SOFT DRINKS 10%, AND OTHER NOMINAL%

ADDRESS AND CONTACTS

Address	20 North Audley Street
	London W1Y 1WE United Kingdom
Telephone	44-171-409-1919
Fax	44-171-409-8503

BASIC FINANCIAL INFORMATION

Capital Structure[†]	Long Term Debt:	1097.00
	Total Debt:	1290.00
	Common Sh. Equity:	3768.00

SALES BREAKDOWN

| Product Segments[†] | Brewing | 1498.00 |
| | Taverns | 1390.00 |

33

SALES BREAKDOWN

Product Segments†	Leisure	1193.00
	Hotels	620.00
	Soft Drinks	539.00
Geographic Segments†	United Kingdom	4531.00
	Rest of Europe	267.00
	United States	391.00
	Rest of Americas	33.00
	Asia Pacific	32.00

Displayed Currency: British Pence (1.00:1)
*I/B/E/S and I/B/E/S Express are registered trademarks of I/B/E/S International Inc. Copyright 1993–1996 I/B/E/S International Inc. All rights reserved.
†Values are displayed in millions.

FINANCIAL STATEMENT DATA

INCOME STATEMENT	1997	1996	1995	1994	1993
Net Sales or Revenues	5254.00	4509.00	3998.00	3931.00	3747.00
EBITDA	823.00	1028.00	932.00	858.00	817.00
Depreciation Depletion & Amort	243.00	229.00	206.00	186.00	180.00
Operating Income	765.00	735.00	656.00	607.00	583.00
Interest Expense	128.00	128.00	127.00	121.00	130.00
Pretax Income	462.00	671.00	599.00	552.00	508.00
Net Income	250.00	444.00	380.00	349.00	314.00

BALANCE SHEET	1997	1996	1995	1994	1993
Assets					
Cash & Equivalents	735.00	553.00	753.00	870.00	685.00
Receivables—Net	533.00	498.00	490.00	433.00	440.00
Inventories	210.00	234.00	199.00	182.00	183.00
Total Current Assets	1567.00	1355.00	1499.00	1549.00	1364.00
Property Plant & Eq. —Net	4431.00	4838.00	4416.00	4176.00	4149.00
Total Assets	6658.00	6964.00	6573.00	6373.00	6098.00
Liabilities & Shareholders' Equity					
Total Current Liabilities	1470.00	1624.00	1531.00	1431.00	1055.00
Long Term Debt	1097.00	1181.00	1177.00	1199.00	1428.00
Preferred Stock	0.00	0.00	0.00	0.00	0.00
Common Equity	3769.00	3911.00	3697.00	3582.00	3413.00
Total Liabilities & Sh. Equity	6658.00	6964.00	6573.00	6373.00	6098.00

CASH FLOW	1997	1996	1995	1994	1993
Funds From Operations	801.00	806.00	652.00	528.00	519.00
Total Sources	2463.00	2037.00	1932.00	1579.00	1686.00
Cash Dividends Paid—Total	226.00	205.00	189.00	182.00	165.00
Total Uses	2463.00	2037.00	1932.00	1579.00	1686.00
Incr/Decr in Working Capital	366.00	-237.00	-150.00	-191.00	-237.00
Free Cash Flow	220.00	481.00	560.00	502.00	320.00

Bass Plc.

INTERNATIONAL BUSINESS	1997	1996	1995	1994	1993
Foreign Assets	NA	NA	1142.00	1151.00	1162.00
Foreign Sales	723.00	808.00	700.00	610.00	595.00
Foreign Income	178.00	188.00	163.00	154.00	135.00

SUPPLEMENTARY DATA	1997	1996	1995	1994	1993
Employees	83461	84872	76919	75845	81105
R&D Expenses	NA	NA	NA	NA	NA
Goodwill/Cost in Excess of Assets Purchased	0.00	0.00	0.00	0.00	0.00
Extra Items & Gain/ Loss in Sale of Assets	0.00	0.00	0.00	0.00	0.00

Displayed Currency: British Pence (1.00:1)
All values are displayed in millions (except employees).

FINANCIAL RATIOS AND GROWTH RATES

PROFITABILITY	1997	1996	1995	1994	1993	5YR AVG
Operating Profit Margin %	14.56	16.30	16.41	15.44	15.56	15.65
Tax Rate %	45.02	32.04	33.89	34.06	35.24	36.05
Net Margin %	4.76	9.85	9.50	8.88	8.38	8.27
Return on Assets %	4.71	8.04	7.28	7.02	6.62	6.73
Return on Equity— Total %	6.39	12.01	10.61	10.23	9.39	9.73
Cash Flow % Sales	15.25	17.88	16.31	13.43	13.85	15.34
Sales per Employee (in 000s)	63	53	52	52	46	53

ASSET UTILIZATION	1997	1996	1995	1994	1993	5YR AVG
Total Asset Turnover	0.79	0.65	0.61	0.62	0.61	0.66
Capital Exp % Gross Fixed Assets	10.72	9.39	7.11	7.25	10.19	8.93
Acc Depreciation % Gross Fixed Assets	21.25	16.94	15.60	14.95	14.91	16.73
Assets per Employee (in 000s)	80	82	85	84	75	81

LIQUIDITY	1997	1996	1995	1994	1993	5YR AVG
Current Ratio	1.07	0.83	0.98	1.08	1.29	1.05
Quick Ratio	0.86	0.65	0.81	0.91	1.07	0.86

LEVERAGE	1997	1996	1995	1994	1993	5YR AVG
Total Debt % Common Equity	34.23	40.60	43.71	46.71	43.13	41.68

LEVERAGE	1997	1996	1995	1994	1993	5YR AVG
Long Term Debt %						
Common Equity	29.11	30.20	31.84	33.47	41.84	33.29
Common Equity %						
Total Assets	56.61	56.16	56.25	56.21	55.97	56.24
Long Term Debt %						
Total Capital	22.02	22.67	23.84	24.92	29.21	24.53
Operating Cash/						
Fixed Charges	6.79	6.30	5.13	4.36	3.99	5.31

GROWTH %	1997	1996	1995	1994	1993	5YR AVG
Net Sales	16.52	12.78	1.70	4.91	3.77	7.79
Operating Income	4.08	12.04	8.07	4.12	-2.02	5.15
Total Assets	-4.39	5.95	3.14	4.51	1.14	2.00
Earnings per Share*	-44.05	16.13	8.23	10.47	-8.33	-6.56
Dividends per Share*	10.00	10.13	7.58	6.57	4.76	7.79
Book Value per Share	-4.04	5.16	2.62	4.35	1.64	1.89

Displayed Currency: British Pence (1.00:1)
*Source: Worldscope. Value may differ from I/B/E/S.
Note: 5-Year Average calculations exclude NAs.

PER SHARE AND RELATED DATA

SOURCE: WORLDSCOPE	1997	1996	1995	1994	1993
Earnings per Share	0.32	0.56	0.49	0.45	0.41
Dividends per Share	0.31	0.28	0.25	0.24	0.22
Book Value per Share	4.76	4.96	4.72	4.60	4.40
Total Investment Return	NA	NA	28.43	17.53	-11.38
Market Price (Year-end)	9.36	8.73	7.17	5.78	5.12
Market Capitalization					
(in millions)	7415.32	6885.03	5619.20	4504.68	3966.76
Price/Earnings Ratio	29.65	15.47	14.75	12.87	12.59
Price/Book Value	1.97	1.76	1.52	1.26	1.16
Dividend Yield	3.29	3.21	3.55	4.09	4.33
Dividend Payout					
per Share	97.52	49.60	52.30	52.62	54.55
Common Shares					
Outstanding					
(Year-end) in Millions	791.97	788.63	783.93	779.47	775.00
Stock Split/Dividend Ratio	1.12	1.12	1.12	1.12	1.12
Type of Share Ordinary					

Displayed Currency: British Pence (1.00:1)
Note: Data is sourced from Worldscope and may differ from I/B/E/S historical data.

6. Boeing Company

Ambition, Boeing is thy name. The world's leading maker of commercial jet aircraft became the number-one aerospace company after its $14 billion acquisition of McDonnell Douglas, the world's top military aircraft maker, in 1997. Its engineering and manufacturing resources know no equal. The Boeing 737, the best-selling jetliner in history, remains the company's top seller and the newest examples of that model could soon account for at least half the company's annual jetliner output.

Criticism of the company is not about that market dominance, but rather takes the form of concern that it is trying to accomplish too much, too soon, perhaps leaving itself vulnerable. For example, weakening demand from Asian airlines dictated cutting of production of its most profitable airplane, the 747 jumbo jet, in 1999. At the same time, Boeing had difficulty meeting demand for the new version of its popular 737 narrow-body jet. Furthermore, management has candidly warned that pricing pressures and production demands will depress profits far below Wall Street expectations through 1999.

Yet this is, after all, a company with only one major competitor in a booming market. It has also been taking steps to improve its condition. If you can see beyond the ominous clouds, its stock appears to be reasonably priced. To indicate that it is now more serious about boosting declining profit margins than in increasing market share, the aircraft maker in mid-1998 raised the price of most of its jetliners by 5 percent. It also declared its production snags to be just about untangled, with delivery of fifty planes a month in the second half of 1998, compared to an average of forty-one in the first half.

The Boeing Company wants to incorporate techniques gleaned from the automotive industry that take a more generic, rather than product-specific, approach. The goal is to greatly accelerate new aircraft development time from the current sixty months to something more like twelve months. Boeing wants to offer the airline customer the right airplane for each route—long haul or short, high capacity or low—combined with all the benefits that come from common parts and systems. With a strong balance sheet, solid cash generation, and aggressive cost reductions under way, Boeing is transforming itself into a less cyclical, more efficient company.

In a speech to the National Press Club in Washington, D.C., Boeing Chairman and Chief Executive Officer Philip Condit emphasized the global aspirations his company holds: "I would like to offer two premises and then a conclusion. First premise: Technology has and will increasingly link us together as a global community. Second premise: Market economies work better than centrally planned economies. The conclusion: If we can access these new, global market economies, we will prosper."

One might think that after an especially difficult period of nagging production delays due to a big jump in orders, indigestion from the massive McDonnell acquisition, the company's first annual loss in fifty years, and a weak start in 1998, this aerospace giant would have scaled back all of its dramatic plans. That hasn't been the case. Instead, it used the company's annual meeting in 1998 as an opportunity to unveil a production plan for its new 717 jetliner. Designed to hold around 100 passengers, the jet is derived from the popular DC-9 twinjet once manufactured by McDonnell and should serve as a replacement for those aging planes. It marks the company's first entry into the regional-jet market, represents a tough competitor for rival Airbus Industrie of Europe, and could mean $3 billion in additional revenues annually. As many as ten of the planes eventually may be built each month at the Long Beach, California, assembly plant that was formerly a McDonnell facility, thereby avoiding additional demands on Boeing's busy Seattle operations. Its initial order was for fifty jets for AirTran Holdings Inc., formerly ValuJet. The company has also said it will shift some finishing work on some 737s to Long Beach, which made the International Association of Machinists union unhappy: It doesn't represent the California workers. However, the company said it may add an entire 737 production line in Long Beach.

There's a lot going on at Boeing. Its Defense & Space group has developed the F-22 fighter with Lockheed Martin, the V-22 Osprey tiltrotor aircraft with Bell Helicopter Textron, and the RAH-66 Comanche helicopter with Sikorsky. The McDonnell acquisition added the F/A-18 Hornet and F-15 Eagle warplanes to the stable. The company is building a $9 billion network of communications satellites for communications firm Teledesic, in which Boeing has 10 percent ownership. The company's goal is to improve the balance among its aerospace products. Prior to the big merger, there was a 3-to-1 ratio of commercial jetliners to all of its other products in revenue generation. The ratio is now 3-to-2. More balance enhances stability and agility. When one market is down, another is likely to be up, and this larger company has more opportunity to deploy workers from one sector to another as needs require. The industry is currently in a strong business cycle, fueled by strong growth in airline traffic, record profits for the world's airlines, and the need to replace aging aircraft. Whenever the next downturn in the commercial airline ordering cycle occurs, Boeing plans to be better prepared than at any time in the past.

The key to future success, however, is Boeing's ability to bring its production under control, for it has suffered from parts shortages and modifications required by European and U.S. safety regulators. It had to halt production of the 747 and new generation 737 planes for a one-month period, and Boeing's top two executives, in the company's combined 1997 annual report, acknowledged that "we failed to do a good job of managing a rapid ramp-up in production in commercial aircraft, aimed at more than doubling the number of aircraft rolling off our production line over a period of eighteen months." Many analysts now believe, however, that the company has addressed those problems that had tarnished its corporate credibility.

Anyone would be impressed by the airline industry's potential in the coming century. Boeing's twenty-year forecast for the average long-term growth rate in passenger traffic is approximately 5 percent annually for the first half of the twenty-year forecast period, and 4.9 percent annually for the balance. The growth in traffic, combined with the need to replace older aircraft in service, is expected to generate demand for more than 17,000 airplanes, valued at approximately $1.2 trillion, by the year 2017.

The newly merged Boeing has had to begin streamlining its workforce, announcing in 1998 that by the year 2000 it would cut 8,200 jobs, representing more than 3 percent of its workforce, a move it hopes to accomplish through attrition and that should ultimately save about $1 billion annually. That announcement came on the heels of the announcement the prior year of 12,000 job cuts in its commercial aircraft operations. In addition, coming off its poor financial performance in 1997, Boeing acknowledged its problems by freezing the base salaries of its top four executives for 1998. Boeing, with the expected delivery of about 550 jetliners in 1998, did not project any reduction in planned production levels over the next two years resulting from the economic woes of Asia. However, the company does expect an industrywide decrease of around 150 plane orders through the year 2002.

In the company's most recent annual report, Condit expressed a fighter's spirit: "We are not here to be also-rans. We are here to lead, to be the best, nothing less." If it can get its production schedules up to speed and improve its ability to deploy workers into different areas as conditions change, little stands in the way of Boeing accomplishing just that and ultimately pleasing its shareholders in the process.

6. BOEING COMPANY

United States   Ticker symbol BA

Stock price $34 1/8 (9/16/98)   Dividend yield 1.64%

(Financial data is from I/B/E/S International)*

BUSINESS DESCRIPTION

COMMERCIAL AIRCRAFT ACCOUNTED FOR 59% OF 1997 REVENUES, DEFENSE AND SPACE SYSTEMS 40%, AND OTHER 1%

Boeing Company

ADDRESS AND CONTACTS

Address	7755 East Marginal Way South
	Seattle WA 98108
Telephone	1-206-655-2121

BASIC FINANCIAL INFORMATION

Capital Structure†	Long Term Debt:	6123.00
	Total Debt:	6854.00
	Common Sh. Equity:	12953.00

SALES BREAKDOWN

Product Segments†	Commercial aircraft	26929.00
	Defense and space	18125.00
	Other	746.00
Geographic Segments†	United States	24363.00
	Asia	11437.00
	Europe	7237.00
	China	1265.00
	Other	1498.00

Displayed Currency: U.S. Dollar (1.00:1)

*I/B/E/S and I/B/E/S Express are registered trademarks of I/B/E/S International Inc. Copyright 1993–1996 I/B/E/S International Inc. All rights reserved.

†Values are displayed in millions.

FINANCIAL STATEMENT DATA

INCOME STATEMENT	1997	1996	1995	1994	1993
Net Sales or Revenues	45800.00	22681.00	19515.00	21924.00	25438.00
EBITDA	1630.00	2499.00	1544.00	2415.00	2885.00
Depreciation Depletion & Amort	1458.00	991.00	1033.00	1142.00	1025.00
Operating Income	1045.00	1354.00	902.00	1151.00	1691.00
Interest Expense	175.00	175.00	183.00	217.00	139.00
Pretax Income	-341.00	1363.00	360.00	1143.00	1821.00
Net Income	-178.00	1095.00	393.00	856.00	1244.00

BALANCE SHEET	1997	1996	1995	1994	1993
Assets					
Cash & Equivalents	5149.00	NA	3730.00	2643.00	3108.00
Receivables—Net	3382.00	NA	1675.00	1914.00	1833.00
Inventories	8967.00	NA	6933.00	4979.00	3434.00
Total Current Assets	19263.00	NA	13178.00	10414.00	9175.00
Property Plant & Eq.—Net	8391.00	NA	6456.00	6802.00	7088.00
Total Assets	38009.00	26839.00	22040.00	21463.00	20387.00

BALANCE SHEET	1997	1996	1995	1994	1993
Liabilities & Shareholders' Equity					
Total Current Liabilities	14152.00	8642.00	7415.00	6827.00	6531.00
Long Term Debt	6123.00	3980.00	2344.00	2603.00	2613.00
Preferred Stock	0.00	0.00	0.00	0.00	0.00
Common Equity	12953.00	10941.00	9898.00	9700.00	9158.00
Total Liabilities & Sh. Equity	38009.00	26839.00	22040.00	21463.00	20387.00

CASH FLOW	1997	1996	1995	1994	1993
Net Cash Flow— Operating	2100.00	2223.00	1066.00	1077.00	1217.00
Net Cash Flow— Investing	2250.00	-300.00	-770.00	1000.00	2106.00
Net Cash Flow— Financing	-899.00	-1878.00	-190.00	-335.00	520.00
Incr/Decr in Working Capital	-1327.00	675.00	2176.00	943.00	697.00
Free Cash Flow	239.00	1737.00	915.00	1620.00	1568.00

INTERNATIONAL BUSINESS	1997	1996	1995	1994	1993
Foreign Assets	NA	NA	NA	NA	NA
Foreign Sales	NA	NA	NA	NA	NA
Foreign Income	NA	NA	NA	NA	NA

SUPPLEMENTARY DATA	1997	1996	1995	1994	1993
Employees	NA	NA	105000	115000	125500
R&D Expenses	1924.00	1200.00	1267.00	1704.00	1661.00
Goodwill/Cost in Excess of Assets Purchased	2395.00	NA	0.00	0.00	0.00
Extra Items & Gain/ Loss in Sale of Assets	0.00	0.00	0.00	0.00	0.00

Displayed Currency: U.S. Dollar (1.00:1)
All values are displayed in millions (except employees).

FINANCIAL RATIOS AND GROWTH RATES

PROFITABILITY	1997	1996	1995	1994	1993	5YR AVG
Operating Profit Margin %	2.28	5.97	4.62	5.25	6.65	4.95
Tax Rate %	NA	19.66	NA	25.11	31.69	25.49
Net Margin %	-0.39	4.83	2.01	3.90	4.89	3.05
Return on Assets %	0.60	5.40	2.30	4.62	7.08	4.00
Return on Equity Total %	-1.63	11.06	4.05	9.35	15.11	7.59
Cash Flow % Sales	5.64	9.78	10.38	9.13	6.85	8.36
Sales per Employee (in 000s)	NA	NA	186	191	203	193

Boeing Company

ASSET UTILIZATION	1997	1996	1995	1994	1993	5YR AVG
Total Asset Turnover	1.20	0.85	0.89	1.02	1.25	1.04
Capital Exp % Gross Fixed Assets	7.21	NA	4.58	5.85	9.95	6.90
Acc Depreciation % Gross Fixed Assets	56.51	NA	53.03	49.94	46.43	51.48
Assets per Employee (in 000s)	NA	NA	210	187	162	186

LIQUIDITY	1997	1996	1995	1994	1993	5YR AVG
Current Ratio	1.36	NA	1.78	1.53	1.40	1.53
Quick Ratio	0.60	0.86	0.73	0.67	0.76	0.72

LEVERAGE	1997	1996	1995	1994	1993	5YR AVG
Total Debt % Common Equity	52.91	36.50	26.42	26.90	28.72	34.29
Long Term Debt % Common Equity	47.27	36.38	23.68	26.84	28.53	32.54
Common Equity % Total Assets	34.08	40.77	44.91	45.19	44.92	41.97
Long Term Debt % Total Capital	32.10	26.67	19.15	21.16	22.20	24.26
Operating Cash/ Fixed Charges	4.73	12.68	11.07	9.22	12.53	10.05

GROWTH %	1997	1996	1995	1994	1993	5YR AVG
Net Sales	101.93	16.22	-10.99	-13.81	-15.72	8.70
Operating Income	-22.82	50.11	-21.63	-31.93	-17.11	-12.52
Total Assets	41.62	21.77	2.69	5.28	13.67	16.21
Earnings per Share*	-111.29	177.39	-54.18	-31.42	-19.91	-100.00
Dividends per Share*	0.00	12.00	0.00	0.00	0.00	2.29
Book Value per Share	-15.51	9.45	1.13	-13.80	36.14	1.88

Displayed Currency: U.S. Dollar (1.00:1)
*Source: Worldscope. Value may differ from I/B/E/S.
Note: 5-Year Average calculations exclude NAs.

PER SHARE AND RELATED DATA

SOURCE: WORLDSCOPE	1997	1996	1995	1994	1993
Earnings per Share	-0.18	1.60	0.58	1.26	1.83
Dividends per Share	0.56	0.56	0.50	0.50	0.50
Book Value per Share	13.31	15.75	14.39	14.23	16.51
Total Investment Return	NA	NA	68.88	10.98	10.28
Market Price (Year-end)	48.94	53.25	39.19	23.50	21.63

SOURCE: WORLDSCOPE	1997	1996	1995	1994	1993
Market Capitalization					
(in millions)	47640.15	36994.12	26957.29	16021.32	14710.96
Price/Earnings Ratio	NM	33.39	68.15	18.73	11.82
Price/Book Value	3.68	3.38	2.72	1.65	1.31
Dividend Yield	1.14	1.05	1.28	2.13	2.31
Dividend Payout					
per Share	-311.11	35.11	86.96	39.84	27.32
Common Shares					
Outstanding					
(Year-end) in Millions	973.48	694.73	687.91	681.76	680.28
Stock Split/Dividend Ratio	NA	0.50	0.50	0.50	0.50
Type of Share	*Common*				

Displayed Currency: U.S. Dollar (1.00:1)
Note: Data is sourced from Worldscope and may differ from I/B/E/S historical data.

7. Cisco Systems Incorporated

If you consider all the hook-ups and various gizmos from different manufacturers that are required to keep today's complex computer systems and the Internet humming along, you'll find yourself pondering a daunting high-tech Tower of Babel. Cisco Systems Incorporated seeks to bring the concept down to manageable size for all types of companies. Its flexibility is in tune with a worldwide approach.

The company saw its market capitalization exceed $100 billion in 1998 after just twelve years in business, the shortest time any company has ever taken to reach that impressive milestone. Cisco has written a dramatic success story since its initial public offering in 1990, as businesses throughout the world have set up or upgraded their computer networks. It is the biggest player in the business, with a market position comparable to Intel Corporation's in semiconductors and Microsoft Corporation's in software. The company is growing 50 percent faster in revenue than most other networking companies, primarily because it's gaining market share from weaker rivals. It accounts for approximately half the networking industry's sales and nearly three-quarters of the industry's profits. An important product in which it holds 85 percent of the market is the multiprotocol router that allows data communication between distant computer networks that would otherwise be incompatible. Cisco also makes software that supports its routers, connects to the Internet, and provides network management, diagnostic, and security capabilities. The firm sells its products worldwide to computer-equipment producers who resell them under private labels to network users. Products are sold in ninety countries and foreign sales account for about 44 percent of total sales.

The company was founded in late 1984 by a small group of computer scientists from Stanford University seeking an easier way to connect different types of computer systems. It shipped its first computer product in 1986. Since then, it has grown into a multinational corporation with more than 10,000 employees in over 200 offices in fifty-four countries. Its high-profile, high-energy leader John Chambers, named CEO of the Year for 1997 by *Electronic Business* magazine, wants to avoid the complacency that led some earlier technology giants to fall by the wayside when they strayed too far from their customers and their employees. He ambitiously wants to make Cisco hardware and software as much a part of the high-tech landscape as Intel's Pentium chip and Microsoft's Windows software. Chambers energetically spends more than 40 percent of his time on the road, meeting with customers each day and typically wrapping up his activities by taking local Cisco employees out for pizza and beer.

As a technology bellwether, Cisco Systems faces constant rumors about future shipments and earnings results that can impact not only its own stock price, but the technology group and stocks as a whole. It must also continue to move decisively and successfully into new high-growth areas, realizing that its growth rate is likely to slow as the company continues to get bigger and bigger. But such concerns simply go with being considered among the technology elite, a club in which Cisco Systems fervently wants to remain an important member.

Business in Asia, usually one of Cisco's fastest-growing sources of revenue, began to slow significantly beginning in mid-1997, while a robust American market and improving European market aided overall results. However, the economic troubles also meant favorably lower memory prices for the company. Cisco no longer faces serious competition within the data networking market, but its biggest risk is that it needs to enter new markets that can support its strong historical growth rates. The voice/data integration market is one of the options available to make that possible, and the company intends to go full-speed ahead.

Of course, the company's goal has always been to provide solutions for customers without imposing a particular technology as the only "right" answer. It does so not only through innovative engineering, but through alliances, acquisitions, and minority investments. Cisco develops its products and solutions around widely accepted industry standards and, in some instances, technologies developed by Cisco have become industry standards themselves.

Cisco serves customers in three target markets:

• Enterprises, those large organizations with complex networking needs that usually involve multiple locations and types of computer systems. Enterprise customers include corporations, government agencies, utilities, and educational institutions. For example, more than 500,000 Federal Express customers are on line with the help of a Cisco-based network. In 1997, FedEx launched its "VirtualOrder" service, providing customers with a turnkey virtual marketplace on the Internet. Businesses display a list of items for sale on a customized Web page. Orders placed from that Web page are processed and delivered by FedEx. Proof of delivery and order tracking are accessed from the network. This gives customers a global presence and increases the efficiency of their operations.

• Service providers, which are companies that provide information services, including telecommunication carriers, Internet service providers, cable companies, and wireless communication providers. An example is British Telecommunications Plc., which uses Cisco products in providing managed network services for many of Britain's largest companies. Firms with as many as 2,000 locations can contract with BT, which will design, own, and operate the network on their behalf. BT now offers packaged networking solutions, including Cisco equipment and BT services, for medium-sized businesses as well. Customers can order complete off-the-shelf networks at competitive prices.

• Small/medium business, the companies with a need for data networks of their own, as well as connection to the Internet and business partners. For instance, twenty-nine-employee Caster Technology Corporation in Garden Grove, California, uses its Cisco network to market its caster, wheel, and hand-truck products. A network links the headquarters with its three remote locations, enabling a virtual warehouse so employees can provide customers with real-time pricing and availability of products from any warehouse or supplier. There are also voice communications and videoconferencing features to display items better and conduct training sessions.

Cisco has used acquisitions to broaden its product line and is licensing products in hopes of widening the influence of its Cisco Internetwork Operating System. In 1998 it bought the WheelGroup Corp. in security scanning software products, following its 1997 purchases of LightSpeed International in voice signaling technologies; Dagaz in integrated networking; Ardent Communications in voice, video, and data; Global Internet Software Group, Skystone Systems Corp. in optical networking; and Telesend in wide area network access products.

Strong alliances are another important component in Cisco's strategy, notable examples being its relationships with Microsoft, Intel, Hewlett-Packard, GTE, Alcatel, Dell Computer, and U.S. West Communications. Cisco, Dell Computer, and U.S. West announced plans in 1998 for personal computers with high-speed digital modems that work over traditional copper telephone wires. The Networked Multimedia Connection program with Microsoft and Intel was formed to encourage the widespread adoption of networked multimedia applications in businesses using intranets and the Internet. The relationship with Hewlett-Packard covers a broad range of initiatives including technology development, product integration, professional services, and customer service. GTE will build a national network based on Cisco's products, enabling service providers to deploy services and drive next-generation Internet offerings. In fact, Cisco has created a new group that includes engineering, marketing, and sales, in order to focus primarily on the development of strategic alliances.

"Customers have come to associate the Cisco brand with a secure, reliable, high-performance network; a brand in which they can have confidence," Chambers stated in the company's most recent annual report. "We will continue to enhance and expand our brand in the future."

7. CISCO SYSTEMS

United States   Ticker symbol CSCO

Stock price $64 1/4 (9/16/98)   No dividend

(Financial data is from I/B/E/S International)*

BUSINESS DESCRIPTION

DESIGNS, DEVELOPS, MANUFACTURES, MARKETS, AND PROVIDES TECH-NICAL SUPPORT TO NETWORKING PRODUCTS AND SERVICES

ADDRESS AND CONTACTS

Address	170 West Tasman Drive
	San Jose CA 95134
Telephone	1-408-526-4000
Fax	1-408-526-4100

BASIC FINANCIAL INFORMATION

Capital Structure[†]	Long Term Debt:	0.00
	Total Debt:	0.00
	Common Sh. Equity:	4289.62

SALES BREAKDOWN

Product Segments[†]	Internetworking	6440.17
Geographic		
Segments[†]	United States	6328.73
	International	863.85
	Eliminations	-752.40

Displayed Currency: U.S. Dollar (1.00:1)
*I/B/E/S and I/B/E/S Express are registered trademarks of I/B/E/S International Inc. Copyright 1993–1996 I/B/E/S International Inc. All rights reserved.
[†]Values are displayed in millions.

FINANCIAL STATEMENT DATA

INCOME STATEMENT	1997	1996	1995	1994	1993
Net Sales or Revenues	6440.17	4096.01	1978.92	1242.97	649.04
EBITDA	2101.07	15797.42	737.56	540.31	288.71
Depreciation Depletion					
& Amort	21.20	132.59	58.51	30.81	13.58
Operating Income	2135.69	1400.81	738.70	488.12	263.57
Interest Expense	0.00	0.00	0.00	0.00	0.00
Pretax Income	1888.87	1464.82	679.05	509.49	275.13
Net Income	1048.68	913.32	421.01	314.87	171.96

BALANCE SHEET	1997	1996	1995	1994	1993
Assets					
Cash & Equivalents	1275.59	1038.18	439.53	182.79	88.99
Receivables—Net	1170.40	622.86	384.24	237.57	129.11
Inventories	254.68	301.19	71.16	27.90	23.50
Total Current Assets	3101.27	2159.64	995.97	507.68	268.30
Property Plant & Eq.—Net	466.35	331.32	136.64	77.45	48.67
Total Assets	5385.98	3614.23	1745.87	1053.69	595.21
Liabilities & Shareholders' Equity					
Total Current Liabilities	1120.11	769.35	337.76	205.51	120.03
Long Term Debt	0.00	0.00	0.00	0.00	0.00
Preferred Stock	0.00	0.00	0.00	0.00	0.00
Common Equity	4289.62	2819.62	1378.73	848.18	475.18
Total Liabilities & Sh. Equity	5385.98	3614.23	1745.87	1053.69	595.21

CASH FLOW	1997	1996	1995	1994	1993
Net Cash Flow—Operating	1442.12	1062.73	395.76	317.54	176.01
Net Cash Flow—Investing	1404.01	1057.84	268.18	315.26	206.42
Net Cash Flow—Financing	-48.20	-9.58	23.71	24.04	17.70
Incr/Decr in Working Capital	590.87	732.07	356.05	154.90	-20.49
Free Cash Flow	1770.78	1314.58	625.63	480.72	254.77

INTERNATIONAL BUSINESS	1997	1996	1995	1994	1993
Foreign Assets	505.12	184.29	141.28	61.03	4.12
Foreign Sales	863.85	446.44	176.72	144.28	86.60
Foreign Income	48.75	22.70	2.52	2.23	35.73

SUPPLEMENTARY DATA	1997	1996	1995	1994	1993
Employees	11000	8782	4086	2443	1451
R&D Expenses	698.17	399.29	164.82	88.75	44.25
Goodwill/Cost in Excess of Assets Purchased	NA	NA	NA	NA	NA
Extra Items & Gain/Loss in Sale of Assets	0.00	0.00	0.00	0.00	0.00

Displayed Currency: U.S. Dollar (1.00:1)
All values are displayed in millions (except employees).

FINANCIAL RATIOS AND GROWTH RATES

PROFITABILITY	1997	1996	1995	1994	1993	5YR AVG
Operating Profit						
Margin %	33.16	34.20	37.33	39.27	40.61	36.91
Tax Rate %	44.48	37.65	38.00	38.20	37.50	39.17
Net Margin %	16.28	22.30	21.27	25.33	26.49	22.34
Return on Assets %	29.02	52.31	39.96	52.90	53.08	45.45
Return on Equity—						
Total %	37.19	66.24	49.64	66.26	70.01	57.87
Cash Flow % Sales	27.15	30.31	23.59	26.88	29.15	27.42
Sales per Employee						
(in 000s)	585	466	484	509	447	498

ASSET UTILIZATION	1997	1996	1995	1994	1993	5YR AVG
Total Asset Turnover	1.20	1.13	1.13	1.18	1.09	1.15
Capital Exp % Gross						
Fixed Assets	37.44	49.15	46.08	45.21	47.00	44.98
Acc Depreciation %						
Gross Fixed Assets	47.14	42.43	43.74	41.24	32.60	41.43
Assets per Employee						
(in 000s)	490	412	427	431	410	434

LIQUIDITY	1997	1996	1995	1994	1993	5YR AVG
Current Ratio	2.77	2.81	2.95	2.47	2.24	2.65
Quick Ratio	2.18	2.16	2.44	2.05	1.82	2.13

LEVERAGE	1997	1996	1995	1994	1993	5YR AVG
Total Debt % Common						
Equity	0.00	0.00	0.00	0.00	0.00	0.00
Long Term Debt %						
Common Equity	0.00	0.00	0.00	0.00	0.00	0.00
Common Equity %						
Total Assets	79.64	78.01	78.97	80.50	79.83	79.39
Long Term Debt %						
Total Capital	0.00	0.00	0.00	0.00	0.00	0.00
Operating Cash/						
Fixed Charges	NA	NA	NA	NA	NA	NA

GROWTH %	1997	1996	1995	1994	1993	5YR AVG
Net Sales	57.23	106.98	59.21	91.51	91.10	80.13
Operating Income	52.46	89.63	51.34	85.19	103.71	75.20
Total Assets	49.02	107.02	65.69	77.03	83.75	75.45
Earnings per Share*	32.35	59.07	29.54	70.32	90.76	55.19

GROWTH %	1997	1996	1995	1994	1993	5YR AVG
Dividends per Share*	0.00	0.00	0.00	0.00	0.00	0.00
Book Value per Share	57.56	58.14	58.94	67.82	90.30	66.11

Displayed Currency: U.S. Dollar (1.00:1)
*Source: Worldscope. Value may differ from I/B/E/S.
Note: 5-Year Average calculations exclude NAs.

PER SHARE AND RELATED DATA

SOURCE: WORLDSCOPE	1997	1996	1995	1994	1993
Earnings per Share	1.20	0.91	0.57	0.44	0.26
Dividends per Share	0.00	0.00	0.00	0.00	0.00
Book Value per Share	4.61	2.93	1.85	1.16	0.69
Total Investment Return	NA	NA	112.46	8.70	64.40
Market Price (Year-end)	55.75	42.42	24.87	11.71	10.77
Market Capitalization (in millions)	56093.89	41310.70	20316.36	9051.61	7994.63
Price/Earnings Ratio	46.46	46.78	43.64	26.61	41.69
Price/Book Value	12.08	14.49	13.43	10.05	15.52
Dividend Yield	0.00	0.00	0.00	0.00	0.00
Dividend Payout per Share	0.00	0.00	0.00	0.00	0.00
Common Shares Outstanding (Year-end) in Millions	1006.17	973.93	816.74	773.09	742.25
Stock Split/Dividend Ratio	1.00	0.67	0.33	0.33	0.17
Type of Share	*Common*				

Displayed Currency: U.S. Dollar (1.00:1)
Note: Data is sourced from Worldscope and may differ from I/B/E/S historical data.

8. Citigroup

The Citi never sleeps—worldwide. It is the only truly global consumer bank offering its customers the very same banking, savings, and financing service everywhere. But even with that might, it holds a less than 1 percent market share in global consumer financial services. It therefore sees unlimited growth potential as it boldly asserts its consumer branding from country to country.

The Federal Reserve Board and the Justice Department approved the $48 billion merger of Citicorp and Travelers Group Incorporated in October 1998, clearing the way for the creation of Citigroup Incorporated, the world's largest financial services company. The deal combined the nation's second-largest banking company with the parent of Salomon Smith Barney and Travelers insurance. Both companies had suffered significant losses during the global markets tumult of 1998 and the new entity faces job cutbacks and a potential clash in corporate cultures. Nonetheless, Citigroup will have more than 100 million customers, 70 million of them in the United States. The hope is to expand that to 1 billion customers by the year 2010. Critics of the deal felt globally aggressive Citicorp was having some of its international emphasis taken away by joining the U.S.-based Travelers. However, the fact that Travelers had announced in May 1998 that it would pump $1.5 billion into Japan's Nikko Securities Company as part of a strategic partnership in investment banking added to its international clout. It has a 25 percent stake in Nikko. The combination also means Citicorp can sell additional financial products through its existing international organization.

But long before the Travelers Group's red umbrella was added,

53

Citicorp stood as a worldwide powerhouse that set the course for the future of financial services.

Citicorp currently serves individuals, businesses, and governments through more than 3,200 banking offices in ninety-eight countries. It has operations in fifty-six countries that include private and branch banking, as well as credit and charge cards. Additional offerings are banking by personal computer and mortgage services. When it purchased AT&T's Universal Card Services in 1998 for $3.5 billion in cash, it reasserted its dominance of the U.S. credit card business. While it has more than $46 billion in credit card loans outstanding domestically and $9 billion outside the United States, other rivals had been quickly closing in. Winning the bidding war that led to the addition of AT&T's $14 billion portfolio kept it well ahead of closest rival MBNA. Because Citicorp slowed its card solicitations in 1995 when it saw deterioration in the card portfolio, its loss ratios have been considerably lower than those of the industry. The AT&T portfolio also fits into this low-loss category. Use of the credit card business to develop cross-selling of additional products is another benefit.

Citicorp is a master of shrewd global marketing, exemplified by its role as the sole sponsor of Sir Elton John's 1998 "The Big Picture Tour" to sixty-five cities in the United States, Europe, Asia, and Australia. That deal also included consumer retail promotions in fifty-six countries where Citicorp has a consumer banking presence. John, who has sold more than 200 million records, appeared in two Citibank commercials and one tour commercial. Citicorp customers had access to a Big Picture Tour store, including a pass for special offers and ticket-buying privileges when using a Citicard.

Although Citicorp sustained heavy losses from the economic woes of Asia and Russia in 1998, it considered the turmoil an excellent opportunity to enhance its position in Asian markets. While other banks cut back their ties, Citicorp increased its exposure by opening up trade lines and also saw increases in its local deposits in those regions. Citicorp derives more than 20 percent of its operating earnings from Asia and seeks to build that percentage further. For example, it has opened an expanded trading room in Singapore, one of eighty trading sites worldwide that trade currencies, bonds, and derivatives around the clock. Some traders work for corporate and institutional investors, and others for Citicorp's asset management organization, which offers mutual funds through the consumer bank. Trading is part of its global markets unit, bringing together capital markets and corporate finance in emerging markets to serve issuers and investors. Overall, Citicorp's core business income was recently 44 percent derived from developed countries and 56 percent from emerging nations.

In its most recent annual report, Citicorp said its "growth strategy begins with our globality" and pointed to the following steps to back that up:

• We are developing and marketing consumer products and services that are consistent globally, recognizing that people's financial needs and aspirations are shaped far more by lifestyle and interests than by geography.

• We are using the insight gained as an embedded bank in emerging markets to help both multinational corporations and local companies achieve their goals.

• Systems and platforms are being unified to transform our worldwide presence into integrated global operations.

• We are applying advanced technology to ensure that we offer, today and in the future, a full range of secure, easily used access points, around the world and around the clock.

• A major initiative to reduce service defects is expected to produce the quality and consistency of performance that not only creates customer satisfaction and loyalty, but also leads to fulfilled and engaged employees.

• We are committed to balance—in our businesses, across geographies, and in our performance. This is the basis for our sustained competitive advantage.

Another goal of the bank is to introduce new technology-based products and delivery systems. It lately has targeted global integration for its operations and technology organization in an ambitious cost-reduction program that could result in savings of 10 percent of its expenses. It is altering its operating base to take advantage of the regulatory environment to standardize systems and processes, creating compatibility in everything from telecommunications to opening checking accounts. Citicorp's back-office functions account for about half of its operating expenses and employ about 65 percent of its total of 94,000 workers around the world. Meanwhile, its advanced development group is using new computer and electronic technologies that cost dramatically less than traditional banking. Delivery vehicles such as the telephone, the Internet, and satellite and cable television are being used to reach customers around the globe. A new Web browser allowing direct access to home banking services is the centerpiece of Citicorp's redesigned Web site (http://www.citibank.com). It's free and lets customers check balances, review account activity, transfer funds, pay bills, and manage investments on the Internet anytime from their personal computer.

Wherever there is innovation in financial services, Citicorp is there. It was one of the earliest proponents of home banking and a leader in credit card services, two areas that will drive the new Citigroup's global future.

8. CITICORP (to become CITIGROUP)

United States   Ticker symbol CCI

Stock price $104 1/2 (9/16/98)   Dividend yield 2.20%

(Financial data is for Citicorp from I/B/E/S International)*

BUSINESS DESCRIPTION

A MAJOR BANK HOLDING COMPANY OFFERING SUBSTANTIAL WORLDWIDE CORPORATE, RETAIL, AND INVESTMENT BANKING SERVICES

ADDRESS AND CONTACTS

Address   399 Park Avenue
                 New York NY 10043
Telephone   1-212-559-1000

BASIC FINANCIAL INFORMATION

Capital Structure†	Long Term Debt:	17622.00
	Total Debt:	41016.00
	Common Sh. Equity:	19293.00

SALES BREAKDOWN

Product Segments[†]	Interest & Fees	18967.00
	Non-Interest Income	10214.00
	Other Interest Income	5516.00
Geographic Segments[†]	United States	9802.00
	Latin America	3314.00
	Western Europe	3323.00
	Asia Pacific	3475.00
	Other	1702.00

Displayed Currency: U.S. Dollar (1.00:1)
*I/B/E/S and I/B/E/S Express are registered trademarks of I/B/E/S International Inc. Copyright 1993–1996 I/B/E/S International Inc. All rights reserved.
[†]Values are displayed in millions.

FINANCIAL STATEMENT DATA

INCOME STATEMENT	1997	1996	1995	1994	1993
Net Sales or Revenues	34697.00	32605.00	31690.00	31650.00	32169.00
Interest Income—Net	11402.00	10940.00	9951.00	8911.00	7690.00
Total Non-Interest Income	10214.00	9256.00	8727.00	7837.00	8358.00
Net Income	3451.00	3631.00	3188.00	3159.00	1607.00

BALANCE SHEET	1997	1996	1995	1994	1993
Assets					
Cash & Due from Banks	21634.00	18553.00	14751.00	13332.00	4836.00
Total Investments	87465.00	70104.00	60273.00	66573.00	48036.00
Loans—Net	178197.00	169109.00	160274.01	147265.00	134588.00
Total Assets	308678.00	279730.00	255259.00	248809.00	215246.00
Liabilities & Shareholders' Equity					
Deposits—Total	199120.00	184954.99	167131.00	155726.00	145089.00
Total Debt	41016.00	37041.00	34814.00	38784.00	34910.00
Preferred Stock	1903.00	2078.00	3079.00	4204.00	3914.00
Common Equity	19293.00	18644.00	16510.00	13582.00	10066.00
Total Liabilities & Sh. Equity	308678.00	279730.00	255259.00	248809.00	215246.00

CASH FLOW	1997	1996	1995	1994	1993
Net Cash Flow— Operating	5627.00	8844.00	11154.00	3538.00	2984.00
Net Cash Flow— Investing	19329.00	23937.00	17527.00	16838.00	5110.00
Net Cash Flow— Financing	16070.00	16445.00	5608.00	14905.00	2179.00
Free Cash Flow	5827.00	6028.00	5827.00	5370.00	3794.00

SUPPLEMENTARY DATA	1997	1996	1995	1994	1993
Provision for Loan Losses	1907.00	1926.00	1991.00	1881.00	2600.00
Non-Interest Expense	13098.00	11870.00	11102.00	10256.00	10615.00
Federal Funds	10233.00	11133.00	8113.00	6995.00	7339.00
Consumer and Installment Loans	35747.00	36285.00	32429.00	29523.00	22490.00
Real Estate Mortgage Loans	24997.00	26389.00	27285.00	26705.00	30159.00
Reserve for Loan Losses	5816.00	5503.00	5368.00	5155.00	4379.00
Foreign Assets	185000.00	161000.00	155000.00	142000.00	111165.00
Demand Deposits	16901.00	14867.00	13388.00	13648.00	13442.00
Savings/Other Time Deposits	40361.00	40254.00	36700.00	35699.00	38347.00
Consumer Liability on Acceptances	1726.00	2077.00	1542.00	1420.00	1512.00
Employees	93700	89400	85300	82600	81500
Goodwill/Cost in Excess of Assets Purchased	251.00	278.00	267.00	316.00	368.00
Extra Items & Gain/ Loss in Sale of Assets	0.00	0.00	0.00	-56.00	300.00

Displayed Currency: U.S. Dollar (1.00:1)
All values are displayed in millions (except employees).

FINANCIAL RATIOS AND GROWTH RATES

PROFITABILITY	1997	1996	1995	1994	1993	5YR AVG
Return on Assets %	1.61	1.84	1.78	2.10	1.66	1.80
Return on Equity— Total %	18.51	21.99	23.02	29.88	23.93	23.47
Tax Rate %	37.24	37.63	37.98	25.79	35.52	34.83
Efficiency of Earning Assets	11.24	11.36	11.55	13.55	14.28	12.40
Total Interest Income % Earning Assets	10.23	10.59	10.74	13.04	13.16	11.55
Total Interest Exp % Interest Bearing Liabilities	5.89	6.14	6.69	8.28	8.84	7.17
Non-Interest Income % Total Revenues	29.44	28.39	27.54	24.76	25.98	27.22
Return on Earning Assets	1.50	1.72	1.62	1.84	1.23	1.58

Citigroup

LIQUIDITY	1997	1996	1995	1994	1993	5YR AVG
Total Deposits % Total Assets	64.87	66.61	65.87	62.95	67.88	65.64
Total Loans % Total Deposits	92.41	94.41	99.11	97.88	95.78	95.92
Cash & Secs % Total Deposits	54.79	47.93	44.89	51.31	36.44	47.07

Reserve for Loan
  Losses %
  Total Assets
	3.16	3.15	3.24	3.38	3.15	3.22

LEVERAGE	1997	1996	1995	1994	1993	5YR AVG
Common Equity % Total Assets	6.29	6.71	6.51	5.49	4.71	5.94
Loan Loss Coverage Ratio	4.22	4.63	4.48	5.67	2.55	4.31

OTHER	1997	1996	1995	1994	1993	5YR AVG
Earning Assets % Total Assets	86.55	86.16	86.93	86.44	85.44	86.30

GROWTH %	1997	1996	1995	1994	1993	5YR AVG
Total Assets	10.35	9.59	2.59	15.59	0.72	7.63
Net Sales or Revenues	6.42	2.89	0.13	-1.61	3.42	2.21
Earnings per Share*	-2.27	4.02	0.84	97.51	168.15	168.15
Dividends per Share*	16.67	50.00	166.67	-+	0.00	-+
Book Value per Share	8.80	3.60	16.01	38.73	14.30	15.70

*Source: Worldscope. Value may differ from I/B/E/S.
Note: 5-Year Average calculations exclude NAs.

PER SHARE AND RELATED DATA

SOURCE: WORLDSCOPE	1997	1996	1995	1994	1993
Earnings per Share	7.33	7.50	7.21	7.15	3.62
Dividends per Share	2.10	1.80	1.20	0.45	0.00
Book Value per Share	42.50	39.06	37.71	32.50	23.43
Total Investment Return	NA	NA	65.44	13.42	65.73
Market Price (Year-end)	126.44	103.00	67.25	41.38	36.88
Market Capitalization (in millions)	57395.56	47711.35	28735.19	16346.47	14251.83
Price/Earnings Ratio	17.25	13.73	9.33	5.79	10.19
Price/Book Value	2.97	2.64	1.78	1.27	1.57
Dividend Yield	1.66	1.75	1.78	1.09	0.00
Dividend Payout per Share	28.65	24.00	16.64	6.29	0.00

Common Shares
  Outstanding
  (Year-end) in Millions
	453.94	463.22	427.29	395.08	386.49

Stock Split/Dividend Ratio	NA	NA	NA	NA	1.00
Type of Share	*Common*				

Displayed Currency: U.S. Dollar (1.00:1)
Note: Data is sourced from Worldscope and may differ from I/B/E/S historical data.

9. Coca-Cola Company

Coke is still it—worldwide. It now sells 1 billion drinks a day. The difference is that Douglas Ivester is now in charge, rather than the late Robert Goizueta, and the company Ivester heads is facing pressure on its stock price and international earnings challenges caused by a strong U.S. dollar and some weakened world economies.

Coca-Cola Company is still the world's largest soft drink maker and it's growing, boasting a 50 percent market share and two of the three top-selling soft drinks in Coca-Cola Classic and Diet Coke. With its beverages sold in approximately 200 countries, 80 percent of profits now come from overseas. Coca-Cola sells more than 160 brands of beverages that include carbonated, sports, and milk-based drinks; juices; teas and coffees. It is also the world's largest distributor of juice drinks, including Minute Maid. In the United States, its Coca-Cola Classic holds the number-one beverage spot. After gaining eight-tenths of a share point in 1997 to widen its lead over PepsiCo, the company now holds a record 43.9 percent of the U.S. market. Its other brands include the number-one-selling root beer, Barq's, as well as Fruitopia and Surge. Wendy's International in 1998 named Coke its sole soft drink supplier for the next ten years.

Coca-Cola also remains the king of world marketing, with its seventy years of Olympics sponsorship a prime example. The company signed an $80 million, eight-year deal in 1998 giving it the right to use the World Cup logo in its marketing. The U.S. roll-out of Surge citrus soda in 1998 included the brand's status as the official soft drink of the National Hockey League, a national scratch-and-win promotion with an Olympic tie-in, direct-mail distribution of compact disks, and television and radio advertising.

Tough, hard-working, single-minded Ivester worked closely with Goizueta for years before assuming the top spot upon his mentor's death from the complications of lung cancer in 1997. Numbers-cruncher Ivester is just as obsessed with the company as Goizueta was, working seven-day weeks and getting involved in all aspects of the business. He's also a New Age electronic age manager. He had the company wired globally and his two-minute voicemails are quite familiar to key Coke managers. He's been able to design quick electronic means of closely tracking all information about Coke's financial results far and wide. An aggressive Ivester has also been pushing the global consolidation of the company's bottlers much faster than most analysts expected.

"I've developed a reputation around here for always asking questions, and I'll keep asking them, always looking to make us better," Ivester, chairman and chief executive officer, wrote in his letter in the most recent annual report. "I'm obsessed with all the places Coca-Cola is not, as are our people, and it's my job to elevate their aspirations as they go out and find them all."

Unfavorable foreign exchange rates have hurt profitability, but Ivester has refused to change the company's course because he claims he is not managing for the next quarter, but for the long haul. The strength of the dollar, especially against the Japanese yen and the German mark, has been of ongoing concern to Wall Street analysts, since Coke derives 80 percent of its profits from overseas. Seventeen percent of profits come from Japan and 12 percent from Germany. Weak currencies in foreign countries can result in a decline in purchasing power and a drop in the sales of soft drinks. However, the recent problem areas—Indonesia, Malaysia, Thailand, South Korea, and the Philippines—in total account for only about 4 percent of Coke earnings and their sales held up surprisingly well.

The company seized an opportunity to expand its business amid all the uncertainty in Asia, as did many other shrewd global companies like banking giant Citicorp, and in 1998 actively invested in countries whose currencies had eroded. Remember that back in the 1994 peso crisis in Mexico, Coke similarly took advantage of the uncertainty there to continue building its business, and market share there today is substantially greater than it had been.

Of course, Coca-Cola stock is certainly no hidden jewel, but a longtime worldwide success story involving one of the world's most touted companies. Reasons why its stock sells at a high premium include the fact that its global market share has never been stronger, it has superior management, its earnings are growing twice as fast as the Standard & Poor's 500 average, and booming sales in many markets such as Latin America serve to offset the downturns in troubled countries. Analysts recommending the stock despite its high price-earnings ratio say they're comfortable going out eight or more years in evaluating it (rather than projecting just into the next year as is usually the case) because it has consistently managed its business well.

The world is the company's focus. Coca-Cola's global restructuring in 1998 boosted its presence in the fast-growing, emerging markets of Eastern Europe. Coca-Cola Amatil Ltd. of Australia, which operated in eighteen countries across three continents, spun off its European bottling operations as a separate, publicly listed company in 1998. E. Neville Isdell, former chief of Coca-Cola's European operations, was named to head Amatil's European business, evidence that Ivester was moving quickly to place some of his closest executives in important worldwide positions. William Casey, with thirty years of experience at Coca-Cola, was appointed president of its Greater Europe Group, succeeding Isdell. Ivester feels strongly that Coke products must be distributed by the strongest franchises. Coke's stake in Amatil increased to 40 percent as a result of the transaction and its stake in the European spin-off is 50 percent. As part of the reorganization, Coca-Cola Beverages, the new European company, acquired Coke's bottling operations in northern and central Italy. In addition, Amatil's remaining operations in Australia and the Asia-Pacific region acquired Coke's bottling business in South Korea.

In addition, Coke purchased an additional 2.9 percent of Chilean bottler Embotelladoras Coca-Cola Polar SA for $3.5 million, bringing its interest in the company to 19.5 percent. It also bought a 2.8 percent stake in Chilean-Bolivian bottling company Embotelladora Arica SA, the first stake it has taken in that business. Shifting to Asia, it has invested $800 million in China since entering the market, and in 1998 opened an $18 million bottling plant in the capital of China's Anhui province that employs 200 workers to bottle Coca-Cola, Sprite, Fanta, and the China-specific brand Smart. It is Coke's twenty-first plant in China.

How rough is the competition in the beverage business? Bitter rival PepsiCo sued Coca-Cola in 1998, accusing it of violating antitrust law by attempting to freeze Pepsi out of the business by selling soft drinks in restaurants and movie theaters served by independent food distributors. The suit filed in U.S. District Court in New York involved fountain-dispensed drinks, an area long dominated by Coke. Coca-Cola contended the suit was without merit because there is enormous competition in the marketplace. "We're going to war against Coke in the marketplace and now we're taking the battle to the courts to ensure fair and open competition," said Philip Marineau, Pepsi's North American beverage head, in a letter to Pepsi bottlers and executives.

Coca-Cola has a lofty reputation to uphold in a dog-eat-dog business. It ranked third on *Fortune* magazine's list of Most Admired Companies in 1998, an annual survey of senior executives, outside directors, and financial analysts. It was first in the beverages/food services category. In addition, respondents named it the number-one company in the world in product quality, attracting and developing new talent, and overall global effectiveness. Those surveyed also voted Coca-Cola the world's best long-term investment. Nonetheless, its stock price was under severe pressure during a tumultuous 1998.

9. COCA-COLA COMPANY

United States   Ticker symbol KO

Stock price $60 15/16 (9/16/98)   Dividend yield .98%

(Financial data is from I/B/E/S International)*

BUSINESS DESCRIPTION

MANUFACTURES, MARKETS, AND DISTRIBUTES SOFT DRINK CONCEN-
TRATES AND SYRUPS AND JUICE AND JUICE DRINK PRODUCTS

ADDRESS AND CONTACTS

Address   One Coca-Cola Plaza
                Atlanta GA 30313
Telephone   1-404-676-2121

BASIC FINANCIAL INFORMATION

Capital Structure†	Long Term Debt:	801.00
	Total Debt:	3875.00
	Common Sh. Equity:	7311.00

SALES BREAKDOWN

Product Segments†	Nonalcoholic Beverages	18868.00
Geographic Segments†	United States	6443.00
	Africa	582.00
	Greater Europe	5395.00
	Latin America	2124.00
	Middle & Far East	4256.00
	Other	68.00

Displayed Currency: U.S. Dollar (1.00:1)
*I/B/E/S and I/B/E/S Express are registered trademarks of I/B/E/S International Inc. Copyright
1993–1996 I/B/E/S International Inc. All rights reserved.
†Values are displayed in millions.

FINANCIAL STATEMENT DATA

INCOME STATEMENT	1997	1996	1995	1994	1993
Net Sales or Revenues	18868.00	18546.00	18018.00	16172.00	13957.00
EBITDA	6784.00	5150.00	4885.00	4204.00	3622.00
Depreciation Depletion & Amort	626.00	479.00	454.00	411.00	360.00

	5061.00	4299.50	4092.00	3708.00	3102.00
Operating Income	5061.00	4299.50	4092.00	3708.00	3102.00
Interest Expense	286.00	286.00	272.00	199.00	168.00
Pretax Income	5900.00	4385.00	4159.00	3594.00	3094.00
Net Income	4129.00	3492.00	2986.00	2554.00	2188.00

BALANCE SHEET	1997	1996	1995	1994	1993
Assets					
Cash & Equivalents	1843.00	1658.00	1315.00	1531.00	1078.00
Receivables—Net	1639.00	1641.00	1750.00	1525.00	1243.00
Inventories	959.00	952.00	1117.00	1047.00	1049.00
Total Current Assets	5969.00	5910.00	5450.00	5205.00	4434.00
Property Plant & Eq.—Net	3743.00	3550.00	4336.00	4080.00	3729.00
Total Assets	16940.00	16161.00	15041.00	13873.00	12021.00
Liabilities & Shareholders' Equity					
Total Current Liabilities	7379.00	7406.00	7348.00	6177.00	5171.00
Long Term Debt	801.00	1116.00	1141.00	1426.00	1428.00
Preferred Stock	0.00	0.00	0.00	0.00	0.00
Common Equity	7311.00	6156.00	5392.00	5235.00	4584.00
Total Liabilities & Sh. Equity	16940.00	16161.00	15041.00	13873.00	12021.00

CASH FLOW	1997	1996	1995	1994	1993
Net Cash Flow— Operating	4033.00	3463.00	3115.00	3183.00	2508.00
Net Cash Flow— Investing	500.00	1050.00	1013.00	1037.00	885.00
Net Cash Flow— Financing	-3095.00	-2102.00	-2278.00	-1792.00	-1540.00
Incr/Decr in Working Capital	86.00	402.00	-926.00	-235.00	318.00
Free Cash Flow	5691.00	4160.00	3948.00	3326.00	2822.00

INTERNATIONAL BUSINESS	1997	1996	1995	1994	1993
Foreign Assets	7617.00	6090.00	7482.00	6916.00	5809.00
Foreign Sales	12425.00	12449.00	12702.00	11048.00	9205.00
Foreign Income	3690.00	3568.00	3511.00	3276.00	2753.00

SUPPLEMENTARY DATA	1997	1996	1995	1994	1993
Employees	29500	26000	32000	33000	34000
R&D Expenses	0.00	0.00	0.00	0.00	0.00
Goodwill/Cost in Excess of Assets Purchased	727.00	NA	NA	NA	NA
Extra Items & Gain/ Loss in Sale of Assets	0.00	0.00	0.00	0.00	-12.00

Displayed Currency: U.S. Dollar (1.00:1)
All values are displayed in millions (except employees).

FINANCIAL RATIOS AND GROWTH RATES

PROFITABILITY	1997	1996	1995	1994	1993	5YR AVG
Operating Profit						
Margin %	26.82	23.18	22.71	22.93	22.23	23.57
Tax Rate %	32.64	25.18	32.27	32.67	32.22	31.00
Net Margin %	21.88	18.83	16.57	15.79	15.59	17.73
Return on Assets %	26.60	24.47	22.82	22.34	20.69	23.38
Return on Equity—						
Total %	67.07	64.76	57.04	55.72	55.96	60.11
Cash Flow % Sales	21.62	18.48	19.54	18.88	17.50	19.20
Sales per Employee						
(in 000s)	640	713	563	490	411	563

ASSET UTILIZATION	1997	1996	1995	1994	1993	5YR AVG
Total Asset Turnover	1.11	1.15	1.20	1.17	1.16	1.16
Capital Exp % Gross						
Fixed Assets	18.94	17.74	14.08	14.26	14.30	15.86
Acc Depreciation %						
Gross Fixed Assets	35.14	36.39	34.87	33.73	33.36	34.70
Assets per Employee						
(in 000s)	574	622	470	420	354	488

LIQUIDITY	1997	1996	1995	1994	1993	5YR AVG
Current Ratio	0.81	0.80	0.74	0.84	0.86	0.81
Quick Ratio	0.47	0.45	0.42	0.49	0.45	0.46

LEVERAGE	1997	1996	1995	1994	1993	5YR AVG
Total Debt %						
Common Equity	53.00	73.31	75.37	67.03	67.63	67.27
Long Term Debt %						
Common Equity	10.96	18.13	21.16	27.24	31.15	21.73
Common Equity %						
Total Assets	43.16	38.09	35.85	37.74	38.13	38.59
Long Term Debt %						
Total Capital	9.87	15.35	17.47	21.41	23.75	17.57
Operating Cash/						
Fixed Charges	15.81	11.98	12.94	15.35	14.54	14.12

GROWTH %	1997	1996	1995	1994	1993	5YR AVG
Net Sales	1.74	2.93	11.41	15.87	6.76	7.61
Operating Income	17.71	5.07	10.36	19.54	11.98	12.81
Total Assets	4.82	7.45	8.42	15.41	8.77	8.92
Earnings per Share*	17.14	18.14	19.70	17.86	17.48	18.06

Coca-Cola Company

Dividends per Share*	12.00	13.64	12.82	14.71	21.43	14.87
Book Value per Share	17.29	15.26	2.48	18.92	18.74	14.36

Displayed Currency: U.S. Dollar (1.00:1)
*Source: Worldscope. Value may differ from I/B/E/S.
Note: 5-Year Average calculations exclude NAs.

PER SHARE AND RELATED DATA

SOURCE: WORLDSCOPE	1997	1996	1995	1994	1993
Earnings per Share	1.64	1.40	1.19	0.99	0.84
Dividends per Share	0.56	0.50	0.44	0.39	0.34
Book Value per Share	2.91	2.48	2.15	2.10	1.77
Total Investment Return	NA	NA	45.88	17.15	8.19
Market Price (Year-end)	66.69	52.63	37.13	25.75	22.31
Market Capitalization (in millions)	164761.32	130562.25	92983.19	64165.56	57898.82
Price/Earnings Ratio	40.66	37.59	31.33	26.01	26.56
Price/Book Value	22.91	21.21	17.24	12.26	12.63
Dividend Yield	0.84	0.95	1.19	1.51	1.52
Dividend Payout per Share	34.15	35.71	37.13	39.39	40.48
Common Shares Outstanding (Year-end) in Millions	2470.63	2480.99	2504.60	2491.87	2594.91
Stock Split/Dividend Ratio	NA	NA	0.50	0.50	0.50
Type of Share	*Common*				

Displayed Currency: U.S. Dollar (1.00:1)
Note: Data is sourced from Worldscope and may differ from I/B/E/S historical data.

10. Diageo Plc.

The words of Arthur Brown's sixties pop song "Fire" blasted from the speakers of the giant wall-size television monitor in the reception room in London corporate headquarters, the accompanying video serving up a shot of a hamburger patty being broiled on a grill, flames licking high into the air. This popular Burger King commercial featuring loud organ music was the first of dozens of worldwide commercials being shown continuously on a tape loop. Most of the products in the commercials were readily identifiable, but their parent company isn't. Diageo, you see, is the biggest global brand-name company that nobody's ever heard of.

Created by the $22 billion mega-merger of Grand Metropolitan and Guinness, Diageo is one of the world's largest food and drinks groups. Its top thirty brands all hold the number-one or -two positions in their major growth markets and its products are sold in more than 200 countries. The company offers three of the five best-selling Scotch brands in the United States in J&B, Johnnie Walker, and Scoresby. Other important products are Guinness beer, Smirnoff vodka, Gordon's—the number-one worldwide brand in gin—and Tanqueray gin. Diageo also owns leading food brands Pillsbury, Häagen-Dazs ice cream, Green Giant vegetables, and Old El Paso food; the once moribund but now booming Burger King chain that ranks second worldwide in its field; and Guinness Publishing, which publishes the *Guinness Book of Records*. The company also owns 34 percent of Moët Hennessy, the wine and spirits unit of French luxury goods maker LVMH Moët Hennessy Louis Vuitton.

Pulling all of this marketing power together, the sum is far greater than its parts. In the works, for example, are greater growth for Burger King and Pillsbury outside of the United States and increased development of truly worldwide commercials. The merger gives Diageo pricing power with dominant positions that feature the top names that consumers will see on the shelves. The only regret among analysts is that some company brands, Dewar's and Bombay, had to be divested in the merger in order to please U.S. and European regulators. The company's only regret is that not everyone realizes the tremendous potential of this merged giant. It is setting its sights high.

Most importantly, top management is dedicated to shareholder value and it has a strong balance sheet that makes it possible for it to invest in its brands. As John McGrath, Diageo group chief executive officer, told me in an interview in his London office, his target is to equal each of the total shareholder returns of Coca-Cola, Procter & Gamble, Philip Morris, Johnson & Johnson, and Unilever—certainly a tall order. Each member of his executive group participates in review and debate about each of the company's businesses as they plot their course toward that goal. "By setting difficult targets, we can no longer get away with incremental behavior," explained McGrath, who has shown an ability to keep tight financial control without putting a damper on creativity. "You can expect a series of positive surprises that will lead to share price moves."

Burger King launched its Big King, a fully garnished double cheeseburger, in the United States in 1997 and is now selling 3 million of them daily. In December 1997, it launched new french fries that are crispier on the outside and stay hot longer on the inside. It is the world's second-largest hamburger chain, with 9,400 restaurants in fifty-three countries and international territories, with plans to step up international growth. Ninety percent of these are owned and managed by franchisees. The goal of Burger King, which serves 13.2 million customers every day, is to differentiate itself by offering the best-tasting food through its brand equities of "Have It Your Way" and the flame-broiling process depicted in that commercial playing in the Diageo headquarters reception room. The company has engineered a dramatic turnaround for the chain by emphasizing taste. There are

1,024 ways to order a Whopper, the most-preferred hamburger in the United States. Burger King opened a record 866 restaurants around the world in 1997. It is increasing its presence and market share in North America, home to 7,700 Burger King restaurants, and targeting key international markets that include the United Kingdom, Germany, Spain, Mexico, Singapore, Taiwan, Korea, Japan, Australia, and New Zealand.

Pillsbury has been gaining market share in North America in categories that themselves are growing faster than the industry averages. Cost-reduction measures have also been under way to boost profitability. More than 14 million Pillsbury biscuits and 5 million scoops of Häagen-Dazs premium ice cream are consumed every day. While Pillsbury brands are becoming more known around the world, more than 60 percent of the world's population has still to experience any prepared foods, so the potential is great.

"Our Guinness and spirits businesses are highly international and we can grow at the expense of competitors," said McGrath, who is building the most comprehensive global distribution system in the spirits industry with no visible gaps in its distribution system to various countries.

Guinness Stout is the world's leading stout brand, brewed in fifty countries and sold in 150 around the world. The Guinness portfolio includes the distinctive international brands Harp lager, Kilkenny Irish Beer, and Kaliber alcohol-free lager. It also has powerful local brands with strong international potential, among them Spain's Cruzcampo lager, Jamaica's Red Stripe lager, and Ireland's Smithwick's ale. The core strategy is to grow the volume and profitability of the Guinness Stout brand worldwide by attracting new consumers in developed and emerging markets. It is investing heavily in marketing while working to improve efficiency and productivity. United Distillers & Vintners is the world's leading and most profitable spirits and wines company, bringing together leading international brands in most categories, a strong presence across all regions of the world, and access to customers in more than 200 countries. This includes name-brand whisky, vodka, gin, cognac, tequila, rum, vermouth, and liqueurs, with 10 million drinks consumed daily. There is considerable growth opportunity, for the combined business still holds only an estimated 5 percent share of total world spirits volumes.

The power of Diageo already exists and is growing. Name recognition among investors will follow.

10. DIAGEO PLC.

United Kingdom　　　Ticker symbol DEO

Each American Depositary Receipt represents four ordinary shares

ADR price $40 3/4 (9/16/98)　　　Dividend yield 4.08%

(Financial data from I/B/E/S International is in British pence)*

BUSINESS DESCRIPTION

CREATED BY MERGER OF GUINNESS AND GRAND METROPOLITAN. SPIRITS AND WINES ACCOUNT FOR 59% OF REVENUES; FOOD AND BREWING 41%

ADDRESS AND CONTACTS

Address	8 Henrietta Place
	London W1M 9AG United Kingdom
Telephone	44-171-927-5200
Fax	44-171-927-4600

BASIC FINANCIAL INFORMATION

Capital Structure[†]	Long Term Debt:	NA
	Total Debt:	NA
	Common Sh. Equity:	NA

SALES BREAKDOWN[‡]

Product Segments[†]	Spirits	2468.00
(Guinness)	Brewing	2262.00
Geographic		
Segments[†]	United Kingdom	118.00
	Rest of Europe	1782.00
	North America	659.00
	Asia Pacific	641.00
	Rest of the World	319.00
	Other	-789.00

Displayed Currency: British Pence (1.00:1)
*I/B/E/S and I/B/E/S Express are registered trademarks of I/B/E/S International Inc. Copyright 1993–1996 I/B/E/S International Inc. All rights reserved.
[†]Values are displayed in millions.
[‡]Data is for pre-merger Guinness.

71

FINANCIAL STATEMENT DATA

INCOME STATEMENT	1997	1996	1995	1994	1993
Net Sales or Revenues	NA	3562.00	3486.00	3460.00	3439.00
EBITDA	NA	1075.00	997.00	1069.00	894.00
Depreciation Depletion & Amort	NA	159.00	148.00	141.00	138.00
Operating Income	NA	884.00	873.00	894.00	894.00
Interest Expense	131.00	131.00	154.00	164.00	223.00
Pretax Income	NA	785.00	695.00	764.00	533.00
Net Income	NA	685.00	595.00	641.00	433.00

BALANCE SHEET	1997	1996	1995	1994	1993
Assets					
Cash & Equivalents	NA	327.00	694.00	476.00	399.00
Receivables—Net	NA	1170.00	1041.00	1081.00	1114.00
Inventories	NA	1867.00	1899.00	1858.00	1822.00
Total Current Assets	NA	3439.00	3690.00	3493.00	3429.00
Property Plant & Eq.— Net	NA	1750.00	1811.00	1784.00	1725.00
Total Assets	NA	7806.00	8239.00	7834.00	8019.00
Liabilities & Shareholders' Equity					
Total Current Liabilities	NA	2572.00	2627.00	2219.00	2362.00
Long Term Debt	NA	622.00	776.00	1113.00	1366.00
Preferred Stock	NA	0.00	0.00	0.00	0.00
Common Equity	NA	4145.00	4282.00	3947.00	3729.00
Total Liabilities & Sh. Equity	NA	7806.00	8239.00	7834.00	8019.00

CASH FLOW	1997	1996	1995	1994	1993
Funds from Operations	NA	663.00	752.00	750.00	631.00
Total Sources	NA	994.00	818.00	1997.00	836.00
Cash Dividends Paid— Total	NA	294.00	307.00	263.00	244.00
Total Uses	NA	994.00	818.00	1997.00	836.00
Incr/Decr in Working Capital	NA	-196.00	-211.00	207.00	-34.00
Free Cash Flow	NA	883.00	818.00	848.00	680.00

INTERNATIONAL BUSINESS	1997	1996	1995	1994	1993
Foreign Assets	NA	NA	NA	NA	NA
Foreign Sales	NA	2612.00	3273.00	3336.00	2696.00
Foreign Income	NA	NA	NA	NA	NA

Diageo Plc.

SUPPLEMENTARY DATA	1997	1996	1995	1994	1993
Employees	NA	20555	21533	23774	23264
R&D Expenses	NA	NA	NA	NA	NA
Goodwill/Cost in Excess of Assets Purchased	NA	0.00	0.00	0.00	0.00
Extra Items & Gain/Loss in Sale of Assets	NA	0.00	0.00	0.00	0.00

Displayed Currency: British Pence (1.00:1)
All values are displayed in millions (except employees).

FINANCIAL RATIOS AND GROWTH RATES

PROFITABILITY	1997	1996	1995	1994	1993	5YR AVG
Operating Profit Margin %	NA	24.82	25.04	25.84	26.00	25.42
Tax Rate %	NA	23.57	27.63	24.61	35.83	27.91
Net Margin %	NA	19.23	17.07	18.53	12.59	16.85
Return on Assets %	NA	9.36	8.89	9.34	7.04	8.66
Return on Equity—Total %	NA	16.00	15.07	17.19	12.13	15.10
Cash Flow % Sales	NA	18.61	21.57	21.68	18.35	20.05
Sales per Employee (in 000s)	NA	173	162	146	148	157

ASSET UTILIZATION	1997	1996	1995	1994	1993	5YR AVG
Total Asset Turnover	NA	0.46	0.42	0.44	0.43	0.44
Capital Exp % Gross Fixed Assets	NA	7.77	7.12	9.29	9.58	8.44
Acc Depreciation % Gross Fixed Assets	NA	29.15	27.99	24.98	22.75	26.22
Assets per Employee (in 000s)	NA	380	383	330	345	359

LIQUIDITY	1997	1996	1995	1994	1993	5YR AVG
Current Ratio	NA	1.34	1.40	1.57	1.45	1.44
Quick Ratio	NA	0.58	0.66	0.70	0.64	0.65

LEVERAGE	1997	1996	1995	1994	1993	5YR AVG
Total Debt % Common Equity	NA	42.41	44.96	47.91	60.95	49.06
Long Term Debt % Common Equity	NA	15.01	18.12	28.20	36.63	24.49
Common Equity % Total Assets	NA	53.10	51.97	50.38	46.50	50.49

LEVERAGE	1997	1996	1995	1994	1993	5YR AVG
Long Term Debt %						
Total Capital	NA	12.79	15.01	21.52	26.25	18.89
Operating Cash/						
Fixed Charges	NA	5.06	4.88	4.57	2.83	4.34

GROWTH %	1997	1996	1995	1994	1993	5YR AVG
Net Sales	NA	2.18	0.75	0.61	8.18	NA
Operating Income	NA	1.26	-2.35	0.00	-8.50	NA
Total Assets	NA	-5.26	5.17	-2.31	-2.67	NA
Earnings per Share*	-50.03	19.39	-7.55	38.86	-18.50	-9.00
Dividends per Share*	-2.36	8.05	7.97	7.81	8.02	5.81
Book Value per Share	NA	1.68	8.11	5.43	3.90	NA

Displayed Currency: British Pence (1.00:1)
*Source: Worldscope. Value may differ from I/B/E/S.
Note: 5-Year Average calculations exclude NAs.

PER SHARE AND RELATED DATA

SOURCE: WORLDSCOPE	1997	1996	1995	1994	1993
Earnings per Share	0.20	0.41	0.34	0.37	0.27
Dividends per Share	0.18	0.19	0.17	0.16	0.15
Book Value per Share	NA	2.49	2.45	2.26	2.15
Total Investment Return	NA	NA	8.64	-2.87	-4.98
Market Price (Year-end)	6.46	5.30	5.49	5.21	5.53
Market Capitalization					
(in millions)	23017.06	8834.33	9598.50	9081.00	9597.75
Price/Earnings Ratio	31.84	13.03	16.12	14.15	20.85
Price/Book Value	NA	2.13	2.24	2.30	2.57
Dividend Yield	2.81	3.52	3.14	3.07	2.68
Dividend Payout					
per Share	89.63	45.87	50.68	43.40	55.90
Common Shares					
Outstanding					
(Year-end) in					
Millions	NA	1668.38	1749.60	1743.55	1736.64
Stock Split/Dividend					
Ratio	1.16	1.16	1.16	1.16	1.16
Type of Share *Ordinary*					

Displayed Currency: British Pence (1.00:1)
Note: Data is sourced from Worldscope and may differ from I/B/E/S historical data.

11. E. I. du Pont de Nemours

Historic company E. I. du Pont de Nemours, one of the world's major chemical firms, has lately gained a reputation for its rapidly expanding biotechnology business as well. It boasts a new chief executive officer, Charles Holliday, who has a global mindset and a dogged unwillingness to accept the status quo. This company was established in 1802 by French immigrant Eleuthère Irénéé du Pont de Nemours, and, although there are no longer any du Ponts in senior management, more than 300 of his descendants still own stock in the company, which comes out to an average holding of about $36 million.

Today's DuPont has a leading market share, either globally or regionally, in 90 percent of its chemicals and specialty business segments. The chemical business includes refrigerants, pigments, and polymer intermediaries; fibers, which include Lycra, Tyvek, textiles, and nylons; polymers, such as elastomers, nylon resins, film, finishes, and packaging materials; life sciences, made up of agricultural products, biotechnology, and pharmaceuticals; and diversified businesses, including films, photopolymer, and electronics. Through its 20 percent stake in seed company Pioneer High-Bred, DuPont is in one of the world's biggest private agricultural research and development alliances. The two companies in this Optimum Quality Grains program are working to create crops with special nutritional and pharmaceutical attributes. That's in keeping with DuPont's countless existing chemical patents for bolstering the nutritional qualities of crops and its extensive research on genetically engineering nutritional attributes into crops.

Bad weather that depressed sales of agricultural chemicals,

weak demand from an Asian market that usually accounts for 10 percent of revenues, and a General Motors strike that cut demand for textiles and plastics used in automobiles all took a toll on DuPont earnings in 1998. Still, the stated corporate goal remained that of building profitably, with a near-term target of doubling the market value of DuPont (based on 1995 market value) by the year 2002, the two hundredth birthday of the company. This would provide an average total annual shareholder return of at least 15 percent. To achieve that goal, it intends to focus on growth, building on its expertise in the chemical and biological sciences. Management has adopted a strategy of becoming number one or two in each of the core chemical fibers it's in or exiting that business, which obviously requires both acquisitions and divestitures.

To the delight of investors and stock analysts alike, shortly after Holliday took over as chief executive officer in 1998, the company moved to unload its Conoco Inc. oil business through an initial public offering and additional means to be announced later. It had bought Conoco for $7 billion in 1981 and turned it into a much more productive enterprise. The expected $20 billion to $30 billion in proceeds will be invested in the profitable field of life sciences, likely through an acquisition or a joint venture. Wall Street had long contended that DuPont's ownership of a giant oil company that provided nearly half of its corporate earnings was confusing to shareholders and diluted DuPont's market share. In 1997, the company spent more than $3 billion adding to its life sciences business, paying $1.5 billion for Ralston-Purina Co. division Protein Technologies International and $1.7 billion for its stake in Pioneer Hi-Bred. Holliday has predicted that the biotechnology business will make up more than one-third of DuPont earnings in five years, versus 18 percent now. In the meantime, the proven chemical and specialty businesses provide a strong financial safety net for the company. Life sciences, a new direction for DuPont, could hurt earnings and credibility if some key products don't succeed as expected.

This company takes a worldview. It became the first U.S. business to start a commercial venture on the site of a former

Russian chemical-weapons facility when it began making agricultural herbicide there. It invested $10 million in a joint venture with Russian company A.O. Khimprom, Novocheboksarsk, to start a herbicide business to protect Russian grain and sugar-beet crops. But being modern doesn't mean forgetting cultural differences. This global company bought time on popular local and cable television stations in China and India, two of its most important markets in Asia, rather than the regional satellite networks used by other multinational companies. That's because it wants individual consumers to know its name. For example, in one advertisement emphasizing DuPont's work in pesticides, a man is shown eating his curry and rice off a banana leaf, while in another a man is eating rice out of a Chinese bowl. DuPont wants each market to feel it is a part of its culture.

The first DuPont chief executive with extensive experience outside the United States, Holliday was previously based in Tokyo as head of DuPont's Asia-Pacific operations. When he had stepped into the line of succession to the CEO post, he was little known in the investment world even though in his twenty-nine-year DuPont career, he has been involved in virtually every one of the firm's businesses. He had, for example, negotiated the Pioneer agreement, outmaneuvering rivals who also wanted the seed company for their genetically engineered products. Holliday, upon becoming CEO in 1998, outlined actions the company would take to increase the effectiveness and efficiency of global support services for its chemicals and specialties businesses. He initiated a new round of restructuring, including layoffs, with a goal of streamlining bureaucracy and giving business units more autonomy. He gave power to a small central "core" unit with stewardship over the company as a whole. "Living outside the United States for the last eight years allowed me to see DuPont's external focus in clear contrast with other great global companies," Holliday said in a letter to chemicals and specialties employees. "Even with all of our improvements we still take too much time and expend too much energy on internal processes. We must now take the bold steps necessary to further reduce internally focused work that restricts our speed of execution and external focus."

CEO Holliday, once unknown but now a headline grabber, could serve as a poster boy for the philosophy of going with the flow of worldwide growth despite stressful periods of regional economic downturn. He announced restructuring for 1999 and 2000.

"Living in Asia enabled me to realize both the complexity of the global marketplace and the regional and national interdependencies that make our economic system work," Holiday stated recently. "I often used the maxim 'think globally, act locally,' until the president of our Japanese subsidiary told me I had it wrong. He said: 'It's think locally, resource globally.' It was one of the most incisive comments I ever heard. DuPont's strength is that we have local people who understand local needs—and they know how to resource competitively in the global economy."

11. E. I. DU PONT DE NEMOURS

United States   Ticker symbol DD

Stock price $59 1/4 (9/16/98)   Dividend yield 2.36%

(Financial data is from I/B/E/S International)*

BUSINESS DESCRIPTION

PETROLEUM ACCOUNTED FOR 47% OF 1996 REVENUES, FIBERS 17%, POLYMERS 16%, CHEMICALS 9%, AND OTHER 11%

ADDRESS AND CONTACTS

Address	1007 Market Street
	Wilmington DE 19898
Telephone	1-302-774-1000
Fax	1-302-773-3423

BASIC FINANCIAL INFORMATION

Capital Structure†	Long Term Debt:	5929.00
	Total Debt:	12083.00
	Common Sh. Equity:	11033.00

SALES BREAKDOWN

Product Segments†	Petroleum	20990.00
	Fibers	7680.00
	Polymers	6830.00
	Chemicals	4267.00
	Other	5312.00

E. I. du Pont de Nemours

Geographic
  Segments[†]

United States	24648.00
Europe	15389.00
Other Regions	5042.00

Displayed Currency: U.S. Dollar (1.00:1)
*I/B/E/S and I/B/E/S Express are registered trademarks of I/B/E/S International Inc. Copyright 1993–1996 I/B/E/S International Inc. All rights reserved.
[†]Values are displayed in millions.

FINANCIAL STATEMENT DATA

INCOME STATEMENT	1997	1996	1995	1994	1993
Net Sales or Revenues	39730.00	38349.00	36508.00	34042.00	32621.00
EBITDA	7025.00	8646.00	8326.00	7709.00	4502.00
Depreciation Depletion & Amort	2385.00	2621.00	2722.00	3128.00	3034.00
Operating Income	5733.00	5354.00	4953.00	3873.00	2644.00
Interest Expense	857.00	857.00	929.00	703.00	825.00
Pretax Income	3998.00	5312.00	4845.00	4021.00	837.00
Net Income	NA	3626.00	3283.00	2717.00	556.00

BALANCE SHEET	1997	1996	1995	1994	1993
Assets					
Cash & Equivalents	1146.00	1319.00	1455.00	1109.00	1240.00
Receivables—Net	5740.00	5193.00	4912.00	5213.00	4848.00
Inventories	4070.00	3706.00	3737.00	3969.00	3818.00
Total Current Assets	11874.00	11103.00	10955.00	11108.00	10899.00
Property Plant & Eq.—Net	23583.00	21213.00	21341.00	21120.00	21423.00
Total Assets	42715.00	37864.00	37237.00	36810.00	36855.00
Liabilities & Shareholders' Equity					
Total Current Liabilities	14070.00	10987.00	12731.00	7565.00	9439.00
Long Term Debt	5929.00	5087.00	5678.00	6376.00	6531.00
Preferred Stock	237.00	237.00	237.00	237.00	237.00
Common Equity	11033.00	10472.00	8199.00	12585.00	10993.00
Total Liabilities & Sh. Equity	42715.00	37864.00	37237.00	36810.00	36855.00

CASH FLOW	1997	1996	1995	1994	1993
Net Cash Flow— Operating	6984.00	6388.00	6761.00	5664.00	5380.00
Net Cash Flow— Investing	6496.00	2660.00	2713.00	3133.00	2981.00
Net Cash Flow— Financing	-451.00	-4018.00	-3571.00	-2878.00	-2744.00

CASH FLOW	1997	1996	1995	1994	1993
Incr/Decr in Working Capital	-2312.00	1892.00	-5319.00	2083.00	-542.00
Free Cash Flow	2257.00	5343.00	5086.00	4659.00	881.00

INTERNATIONAL BUSINESS	1997	1996	1995	1994	1993
Foreign Assets	16588.00	15435.00	14367.00	14089.00	13807.00
Foreign Sales	20431.00	20841.00	20629.00	18564.00	16756.00
Foreign Income	1432.00	1330.00	1377.00	1114.00	784.00

SUPPLEMENTARY DATA	1997	1996	1995	1994	1993
Employees	98000	97000	105000	107000	114000
R&D Expenses	1116.00	1032.00	1067.00	1047.00	1132.00
Goodwill/Cost in Excess of Assets Purchased	NA	NA	NA	NA	278.00
Extra Items & Gain/ Loss in Sale of Assets	0.00	0.00	0.00	0.00	-11.00

Displayed Currency: U.S. Dollar (1.00:1)
All values are displayed in millions (except employees).

FINANCIAL RATIOS AND GROWTH RATES

PROFITABILITY	1997	1996	1995	1994	1993	5YR AVG
Operating Profit Margin %	14.43	13.96	13.57	11.38	8.11	12.29
Tax Rate %	56.90	44.15	43.28	41.16	46.83	46.46
Net Margin %	6.05	9.48	9.02	8.01	1.70	6.85
Return on Assets %	7.47	11.03	10.31	8.40	2.50	7.94
Return on Equity— Total %	22.87	44.22	26.09	24.72	4.73	24.53
Cash Flow % Sales	17.30	16.04	16.62	16.79	13.59	16.07
Sales per Employee (in 000s)	405	395	348	318	286	351

ASSET UTILIZATION	1997	1996	1995	1994	1993	5YR AVG
Total Asset Turnover	0.93	1.01	0.98	0.92	0.89	0.95
Capital Exp % Gross Fixed Assets	8.78	6.53	6.43	6.25	7.56	7.11
Acc Depreciation % Gross Fixed Assets	56.56	58.03	57.64	56.75	55.30	56.86
Assets per Employee (in 000s)	436	390	355	344	323	370

E. I. du Pont de Nemours

LIQUIDITY	1997	1996	1995	1994	1993	5YR AVG
Current Ratio	0.84	1.01	0.86	1.47	1.15	1.07
Quick Ratio	0.49	0.59	0.50	0.84	0.64	0.61

LEVERAGE	1997	1996	1995	1994	1993	5YR AVG
Total Debt % Common Equity	109.52	85.91	144.35	60.93	84.84	97.11
Long Term Debt % Common Equity	53.74	48.58	69.25	50.66	59.41	56.33
Common Equity % Total Assets	25.83	27.66	22.02	34.19	29.83	27.90
Long Term Debt % Total Capital	33.18	30.99	39.58	32.87	36.39	34.60
Operating Cash/ Fixed Charges	8.32	7.05	6.43	7.96	5.28	7.01

GROWTH %	1997	1996	1995	1994	1993	5YR AVG
Net Sales	3.60	5.04	7.24	4.36	-12.05	1.38
Operating Income	7.08	8.10	27.89	46.48	39.08	24.70
Total Assets	12.81	1.68	1.16	-0.12	-5.18	1.90
Earnings per Share*	-35.70	15.33	40.25	381.93	-41.96	23.81
Dividends per Share*	10.31	9.85	11.54	3.41	1.15	7.17
Book Value per Share	5.84	22.53	-20.13	13.91	-5.00	2.31

Displayed Currency: U.S. Dollar (1.00:1)
*Source: Worldscope. Value may differ from I/B/E/S.
Note: 5-Year Average calculations exclude NAs.

PER SHARE AND RELATED DATA

SOURCE: WORLDSCOPE	1997	1996	1995	1994	1993
Earnings per Share	2.08	3.24	2.81	2.00	0.42
Dividends per Share	1.23	1.12	1.02	0.91	0.88
Book Value per Share	9.57	9.04	7.38	9.24	8.11
Total Investment Return	NA	NA	28.12	20.09	6.12
Market Price (Year-end)	60.06	47.06	34.94	28.06	24.13
Market Capitalization (in millions)	69238.35	54502.40	38815.32	38221.40	32693.11
Price/Earnings Ratio	28.88	14.55	12.46	14.03	58.13
Price/Book Value	6.28	5.20	4.73	3.04	2.97
Dividend Yield	2.05	2.37	2.91	3.24	3.65
Dividend Payout per Share	59.13	34.47	36.19	45.50	212.05
Common Shares Outstanding (Year-end) in Millions	1152.76	1158.09	1110.99	1362.01	1355.15
Stock Split/Dividend Ratio	1.00	0.50	0.50	0.50	0.50
Type of Share	Common				

Displayed Currency: U.S. Dollar (1.00:1)
Note: Data is sourced from Worldscope and may differ from I/B/E/S historical data.

81

12. Elf Aquitaine Group S.A.

I first noticed the word "Elf" emblazoned on European Grand Prix racing cars and their drivers' uniforms years ago, but at the time didn't realize that it symbolized a giant rather than any type of diminutive creature. France's largest industrial company, Elf Aquitaine Group S.A., explores for and produces oil and natural gas and also manufactures chemicals and pharmaceuticals. Out from under the ownership of the government since it was privatized in 1994, the company is using acquisitions to expand internationally, and, in the process, transform from restructuring to growth.

Run by a chief executive officer, Phillipe Jaffre, who is boldly transforming the nature of French business by emphasizing shareholder value, Elf operates oil and natural gas wells in twenty-nine countries, with proven reserves of 2.2 billion barrels of oil and 6.2 billion cubic feet of natural gas. It sells gasoline through more than 5,300 service stations in Europe and West Africa. Other products include petrochemicals, bulk plastics, and chlorinated chemicals. The firm's 55 percent–owned Sanofi subsidiary manufactures pharmaceuticals and diagnostic equipment, as well as perfumes and beauty products. It has filed patents for three potential blockbuster drugs to treat hypertension, thrombosis, and colorectal cancer, and also has a promising AIDS-related drug.

Most important of all, however, are Elf's million-barrel-a-day, increasingly efficient upstream oil exploration efforts. West African discoveries, including the Girassol deep offshore field off Angola, promise to raise output by one-third after the year 2000. The countries where most of its production is located—namely

Gabon, Nigeria, Congo, Cameroon, and Angola—appear to be stable for now, though inevitably this core business depends on oil agreements made with somewhat unpredictable governments. Meanwhile, there is important exploration under way in the former Soviet republic of Azerbaijan; in the U.S. Gulf of Mexico; in Venezuela, Trinidad, and Tobago; and in Libya. In 1998, Elf invested $33.8 million to develop an oil field in Ecuador's Amazon region; signed an oil exploration contract with Romania's state oil company; and bought a 5 percent stake in Russian oil giant A.O. Yuksi for $528 million in a deal meant to form the foundation of a long-term strategic alliance for the development of oil and gas activities in Russia. Elf projects that in the year 2005 this new group will account for 10 percent of its total production, which currently is balanced fifty-fifty between Africa and the North Sea.

The Elf group, whose first corporate ancestor was a small gas field found in southwestern France in 1939, now comprises nearly 850 companies in eighty countries, with the parent company directly or indirectly either the sole or majority shareholder of those companies. Its history of internationalization included the takeover of the British company RTZ Oil and Gas in 1988 and the American chemical company Pennsalt Corporation in 1989. In 1993, with the acquisition of Yves Saint Laurent, it became a leader in world prestige perfumes.

The following year, it took over the Sterling Winthrop pharmaceutical company. Despite all of its expansion moves, the company was bloated with debt, earnings were declining, and many of its exploration efforts seemed to have no payoff. It was definitely time to restructure.

Philippe Jaffre, the high-profile chairman and chief executive officer of Elf Aquitaine, led the privatization of this money-losing energy company and within two years saw it post a remarkable $1 billion annual profit. To achieve those results, he cut back exploration and development spending while improving efficiency. He sold off noncore assets and decreased the workforce by 10 percent, to 85,000 employees. Jaffre had spent ten years at the French Treasury, working on reform and privatization efforts, before holding several major banking posts. At Elf Aquitaine, he immediately demanded that thirty of his senior managers do as he did, resigning as government *inspecteurs des finances* who are guaranteed long-term, safe jobs with pensions in the civil service. He felt they should be on an equal footing with all employees who can be fired, instead of functioning as executives-for-life. Most recently, he has been active in significant share repurchases. He has worked hard to woo international and U.S. investors with professional road shows. Almost half the company's investors are outside of France and 25 percent are in the United States.

"The essential is that Elf becomes more efficient year after year; the essential is that net income before special items increases year after year," Jaffre declared in a speech that coincided with the release of 1997 results. "The essential is that Elf shows, for example, with its large discoveries in Angola, that it has a true capacity for durable growth."

One persistent problem is Elf's gasoline retailing business, which must go head-to-head with large European supermarket chains that offer cheap gasoline in order to attract grocery shoppers. Elf, searching for a partner for this difficult business, has been in talks with various major world oil companies. There's also been a move to make the Elf Atochem division more cost efficient with a greater focus on lucrative new chemicals, adhesives, and polymers. While its pharmaceutical operation Sanofi—often rumored as a potential spin-off, partner with another company, or acquirer—has done well, there is concern among analysts about whether this separately traded business has enough funding or distribution power to succeed in marketing its drugs effectively. Elf must deal with the political and social ideology of the French Socialist government before making any major moves, especially any that might conceivably take some portion of the company out of French hands.

Elf Aquitaine's international operations are much more profitable than its domestic operations. France accounts for one-third of sales, one-third of invested capital, and half of its total number of employees. However, it represents only one-fifth of the company's financial results. "The reasons are, of course, multiple and well known," Jaffre bluntly asserted. "They boil down to excessive regulation and the lack of confidence in entrepreneurs. Add to that heavy taxes and welfare contributions which lead to high employment costs while net salaries remain stagnant. The upturn in our economy comes from more freedom."

Certainly not the kind of logic that prior chairmen of the company had used when running Elf Aquitaine as a state corporation. But Jaffre is indeed ready to do battle for his army of shareholders. He has jumped the fence from the public sector and has no intention of going back.

12. ELF AQUITAINE GROUP S.A.

France   Ticker symbol ELF

One American Depositary Receipt represents 1/2 of an ordinary share

ADR price $61 5/8 (9/16/98)   Dividend yield 2.02%

(Financial data from I/B/E/S is in French francs)*

BUSINESS DESCRIPTION

OIL REFINING, MARKETING, AND TRADING ACCOUNTED FOR 50% OF 1997 REVENUES, CHEMICALS 23%, HEALTH 10%, AND OIL AND GAS EXPLORATION AND PRODUCTION 8%

ADDRESS AND CONTACTS

Address	Tour Elf
	2, Place de la Coupole
	La Defense 6-92400 Courbevoie, France
Telephone	33-1-47-45-46
Fax	33-1-47-40-24

BASIC FINANCIAL INFORMATION

Capital Structure[†]	Long Term Debt:	27248.00
	Total Debt:	42742.00
	Common Sh. Equity:	83985.00

SALES BREAKDOWN

Product Segments[†]	Refining, Marketing	149737.00
	Chemicals	57520.00
	Health	25690.00
	Exploration & Production	21359.00

SALES BREAKDOWN

Geographic
    Segments†

France	81967.00
Rest of Europe	95563.00
North America	16495.00
Africa	60281.00

Displayed Currency: French Franc (1.00:1)
*I/B/E/S and I/B/E/S Express are registered trademarks of I/B/E/S International Inc. Copyright 1993–1996 I/B/E/S International Inc. All rights reserved.

†Values are displayed in millions.

FINANCIAL STATEMENT DATA

INCOME STATEMENT	1997	1996	1995	1994	1993
Net Sales or Revenues	254305.99	232707.00	208290.00	207674.00	209674.99
EBITDA	47385.00	40782.00	34714.00	29111.00	27446.00
Depreciation Depletion & Amort	25110.00	17734.00	17912.00	19188.00	18332.00
Operating Income	14120.00	15620.00	7953.00	-907.00	-1522.00
Interest Expense	3751.00	3751.00	5008.00	6235.00	6700.00
Pretax Income	19071.00	19759.00	12271.00	4331.00	3197.00
Net Income	5602.00	6977.00	5035.00	-35.00	737.00

BALANCE SHEET	1997	1996	1995	1994	1993
Assets					
Cash & Equivalents	9270.00	11252.00	13997.00	23202.00	19552.00
Receivables—Net	52787.00	49822.00	50599.00	51396.00	48867.00
Inventories	24133.00	22282.00	21233.00	21767.00	22636.00
Total Current Assets	86190.00	83356.00	85829.00	96365.00	91055.00
Property Plant & Eq.—Net	112520.00	110400.00	96453.00	111734.00	124824.00
Total Assets	253009.00	246890.00	242199.00	261430.00	269051.00
Liabilities & Shareholders' Equity					
Total Current Liabilities	75158.00	74565.00	70320.00	77910.00	74658.00
Long Term Debt	27248.00	29579.00	33431.00	44296.00	47480.00
Preferred Stock	0.00	0.00	0.00	0.00	0.00
Common Equity	83985.00	80062.00	78672.00	76472.00	84088.00
Total Liabilities & Sh. Equity	253009.00	246890.00	242199.00	261430.00	269051.00

CASH FLOW	1997	1996	1995	1994	1993
Funds from Operations	33165.00	31139.00	28626.00	24380.00	24495.00
Total Sources	43530.00	54232.00	52271.00	49014.00	52334.00
Cash Dividends Paid—Total	3569.00	3507.00	3427.00	3337.00	3337.00

Elf Aquitaine Group S.A.

	1997	1996	1995	1994	1993
Total Uses	43530.00	54232.00	52271.00	49014.00	52334.00
Incr/Decr in Working Capital	2241.00	-6718.00	-2946.00	2058.00	-7203.00
Free Cash Flow	28639.00	23426.00	19524.00	9774.00	6677.00

INTERNATIONAL BUSINESS	1997	1996	1995	1994	1993
Foreign Assets	160166.00	152670.00	131976.00	140651.00	132646.00
Foreign Sales	172339.00	155231.00	109629.00	108308.00	87788.00
Foreign Income	14886.00	18286.00	9786.00	-2023.00	4682.00

SUPPLEMENTARY DATA	1997	1996	1995	1994	1993
Employees	83700	85400	85500	89500	94300
R&D Expenses	6341.00	5881.00	5595.00	5159.00	4803.00
Goodwill/Cost in Excess of Assets Purchased	23549.00	23412.00	19788.00	21121.00	16521.00
Extra Items & Gain/ Loss in Sale of Assets	0.00	0.00	0.00	-5404.00	333.00

Displayed Currency: French Franc (1.00:1)
All values are displayed in millions (except employees).

FINANCIAL RATIOS AND GROWTH RATES

PROFITABILITY	1997	1996	1995	1994	1993	5YR AVG
Operating Profit Margin %	5.55	6.71	3.82	-0.44	-0.73	2.98
Tax Rate %	63.11	56.39	47.20	71.97	73.66	62.47
Net Margin %	2.20	3.00	2.42	-2.62	0.51	1.10
Return on Assets %	3.13	3.78	3.07	-0.65	1.99	2.26
Return on Equity— Total %	7.00	8.87	6.58	-6.47	1.23	3.44
Cash Flow % Sales	13.04	13.38	13.74	11.74	11.68	12.72
Sales per Employee (in 000s)	3038	2725	2436	2320	2223	2549

ASSET UTILIZATION	1997	1996	1995	1994	1993	5YR AVG
Total Asset Turnover	1.01	0.94	0.86	0.79	0.78	0.88
Capital Exp % Gross Fixed Assets	6.46	6.65	6.59	7.85	8.43	7.20
Acc Depreciation % Gross Fixed Assets	61.21	57.70	58.13	54.64	49.35	56.21
Assets per Employee (in 000s)	3023	2891	2833	2921	2853	2904

LIQUIDITY	1997	1996	1995	1994	1993	5YR AVG
Current Ratio	1 15	1.12	1.22	1.24	1.22	1.19
Quick Ratio	0.83	0.82	0.92	0.96	0.92	0.89

LEVERAGE	1997	1996	1995	1994	1993	5YR AVG
Total Debt % Common Equity	50.89	60.58	65.03	89.09	85.73	70.26
Long Term Debt % Common Equity	32.44	36.95	42.49	57.92	56.46	45.25
Common Equity % Total Assets	33.19	32.43	32.48	29.25	31.25	31.72
Long Term Debt % Total Capital	20.88	22.88	25.58	31.36	30.71	26.28
Operating Cash/ Fixed Charges	9.03	8.30	5.72	3.91	3.66	6.12

GROWTH %	1997	1996	1995	1994	1993	5YR AVG
Net Sales	9.28	11.72	0.30	-0.95	4.54	4.86
Operating Income	-9.60	96.40	-+	N+	-136.39	27.55
Total Assets	2.48	1.94	-7.36	-2.83	7.87	0.29
Earnings per Share*	-15.84	37.30	-+	-104.53	-88.24	-2.19
Dividends per Share*	7.14	7.69	0.00	0.00	0.00	2.90
Book Value per Share	6.34	5.84	0.54	-11.44	-3.44	-0.66

Displayed Currency: French Franc (1.00:1)
*Source: Worldscope. Value may differ from I/B/E/S.
Note: 5-Year Average calculations exclude NAs.

PER SHARE AND RELATED DATA

SOURCE: WORLDSCOPE	1997	1996	1995	1994	1993
Earnings per Share	21.84	25.95	18.90	-0.13	2.87
Dividends per Share	15.00	14.00	13.00	13.00	13.00
Book Value per Share	328.27	308.69	291.64	290.08	327.57
Total Investment Return	NA	NA	-0.56	-6.67	18.64
Market Price (Year-end)	700.00	472.30	360.80	375.90	416.70
Market Capitalization (in millions)	179089.65	122497.50	97327.82	99094.98	106968.52
Price/Earnings Ratio	32.05	18.20	19.09	NM	145.19
Price/Book Value	2.13	1.53	1.24	1.30	1.27
Dividend Yield	2.14	2.96	3.60	3.46	3.12
Dividend Payout per Share	68.68	53.95	68.78	-10000.00	452.96
Common Shares Outstanding (Year-end) in Millions	255.84	259.36	269.76	263.62	256.70
Stock Split/Dividend Ratio	NA	NA	NA	NA	1.00
Type of Share	Actions Ordinaires				

Displayed Currency: French Franc (1.00:1)
Note: Data is sourced from Worldscope and may differ from I/B/E/S historical data.

13. L. M. Ericsson
Telephone Company

It went global because it couldn't possibly prosper if it just stayed at home. Since it lacks the large home market of its rivals, Sweden's L. M. Ericsson Telephone Company became a nimble and tenacious worldwide company with 100,000 employees and a presence in more than 130 countries. Compared with most of its major competitors—Alcatel, Lucent, Motorola, Nokia, Nortel, and Siemens—Ericsson has by far the highest percentage of international sales. In times when a region is hit by an economic slowdown, broad international distribution provides considerable strength. Ericsson is well positioned for a dynamic telecommunications market in which deregulation and liberalization play important roles.

Ericsson posted stunning 70 percent profit growth in 1997, but there has been ongoing concern about the fact that economically worrisome Asia constitutes more than 25 percent of sales. That includes a fast-growing China, weighing in with 10 percent of total sales. In fact, China is Ericsson's top market in terms of orders received, having overtaken the United States. Analysts believe such Asian concerns have sometimes needlessly hurt the stock price of this company so obviously poised for significant growth. The positives also outweigh the negatives. China, for example, has 1.2 billion citizens but only 75 million fixed telephone subscribers. Another 14 million Chinese have mobile phones, but it's difficult for Chinese operators in both fixed and mobile networks to keep up with the demand. Other regions of Asia will run their course of problems and then return to contribute significantly to overall profits, analysts believe.

The firm's ability to assimilate in any part of the world is evident in Ericsson Stadium in Charlotte, North Carolina, the home of the National Football League's Carolina Panthers. The word "Ericsson" and shots of its logo are regular parts of football coverage there. Yet the company is no Johnny-come-lately marketing effort just beginning to gain attention: In 1876 mechanic Lars Magnus Ericsson opened a workshop for repair of telegraph instruments in Stockholm. Two years later, he and a partner were making and selling telephones. The company brought out its first handset in 1885 and the rest, as they say, is history.

About 40 percent of the world's mobile phone subscribers are now connected to systems Ericsson has produced. The company manufactures the telecommunications equipment used in wired, wireless, analog, and digital communications networks, and also makes the handsets that subscribers use to communicate over the networks. AXE, the digital switching system for wired and mobile networks, is the world's most successful telecom system and is installed in 125 countries. Of the 201 million subscribers to mobile networks, 75 million make their calls in networks delivered by Ericsson. It's projected there will be almost 600 million subscribers by the end of the year 2001. As a leader in its field, Ericsson is expected to grow right in line with the impressive trends of its ultramodern industry. Intent on holding its position, it invests more than 20 percent of its revenues in research and development. Ericsson frequently forms alliances with other companies—among them Texas Instruments, Hewlett-Packard, IBM, Intel, Microsoft, and Novell—to develop new technologies. In addition, it makes military electronic gear, namely radar and communications systems.

Innovative Ericsson recently found a way to provide simultaneous telephone service and Internet access over the same regular phone line. This new technology called Home Internet Solution nearly quadruples the average speed for home Internet access. Users purchase a modem from their phone company for $100 to $200 to plug into their computer and phone line. It's possible to switch the Internet connection on and off, eliminating the need for a second phone line.

There was a recent surprise change at the top of this telecommunications giant when a dark-horse candidate was chosen to lead it. Chief executive and president Lars Ramqvist resigned his offices and assumed the duties of chairman in the spring of 1998 and was replaced by the relatively unknown Sven-Christer Nilsson, head of Ericsson's Cellular Systems–American Standards unit, a move that analysts consider positive because of his background in that important area. "My initial reaction to the appointment as Ericsson's new CEO was one of great surprise," a self-effacing Sven-Christer Nilsson who is known for being a "team player" later said. "After I gathered my composure and considered the offer, I naturally accepted the finest management position in Ericsson."

Mobile telephone sales have skyrocketed in recent years, with growth in mobile systems, the company's largest business group, also quite strong. Mobile telephone prices are dropping at a 20 percent annual clip these days. Ericsson became the leader in the digital-handset market at the expense of Finland's Nokia and the U.S.'s Motorola. The bitterly fought selection of a new cellular telephone technology as a standard throughout Europe by the European Telecommunications Standards Institute should also be a plus: The group chose third-generation cellular technology developed jointly by Ericsson and Nokia. The big advantage will be in marketing, since Ericsson already supplies a large number of existing customers and they're expected to stick with the firm. The new technology adds capacity to the existing Global System for Mobile Communications, with high-speed Internet and videophone capabilities.

In a major strategic study, "2005—Ericsson entering the 21st Century," the company outlined its goals for maintaining market dominance. It stated that customers must continue to perceive the company as the best choice in the markets in which it operates and the prime innovator in setting new standards. The company has developed an organization focused on "solutions and services for our customers," a configuration in which local staff work together in global networks to make sure customers are dealt with in a uniform manner.

Looking through recent worldwide activities of the company underscores the geographic diversity of its efforts:

91

• The firm signed a five-year framework agreement with Romanian fixed network operator Rom Telecom in which it will deliver and install a minimum of 500,000 end–user lines for switching platforms.

• It received a $27 million contract to supply Paraguay's first digital wireless communications network, supplying switching centers and radio base stations.

• A memorandum of understanding was signed with Peoples Telephone Co. Ltd., a Hong Kong cellular network operator, to expand its mobile network.

• Its first mobile handphone plant in the Asia–Pacific region was opened to point out its long-term commitment to the region.

• An order worth $50 million from Russian mobile operator TAIF was inked to install a new digital mobile system.

• A $200 million contract was awarded for the digitalization and expansion of a nationwide wireless network in Venezuela.

Ericsson really gets around, and is a global player ready to take on the locals or other global competitors in any world market. It's a company that just won't take no for an answer.

13. L. M. ERICSSON TELEPHONE COMPANY

Sweden   Ticker symbol ERICY

One American Depositary Receipt represents one series "B" share

ADR price $20 3/16 (9/16/98)   Dividend yield 13.15%

(Financial data from I/B/E/S International is in Swedish krona)*

BUSINESS DESCRIPTION

MOBILE TELECOMMUNICATION SYSTEMS ACCOUNTED FOR 43% OF 1997 REVENUES, INFOCOM SYSTEMS 29%, MOBILE TELEPHONES AND TERMINALS 25%, AND OTHER 3%

ADDRESS AND CONTACTS

Address	Telefonplan
	Stockholm S-126 25 Sweden
Telephone	46-8-7190000
Fax	46-8-7191976

L. M. Ericsson Telephone Company

BASIC FINANCIAL INFORMATION

Capital Structure[†]	Long Term Debt:	10719.00
	Total Debt:	15703.00
	Common Sh. Equity:	52624.00

SALES BREAKDOWN

Product Segments[†]	Mobile telecommunication	71700.00
	Infocom systems	49204.00
	Mobile phones & terminals	42292.00
	Other	4544.00
Geographic Segments[†]	Sweden	9320.00
	Other Europe	66386.00
	Asia	37613.00
	Latin America	21267.00
	USA & Canada	18973.00
	Other	14181.00

Displayed Currency: Swedish Krona (1.00:1)

*I/B/E/S and I/B/E/S Express are registered trademarks of I/B/E/S International Inc. Copyright 1993–1996 I/B/E/S International Inc. All rights reserved.

[†]Values are displayed in millions.

FINANCIAL STATEMENT DATA

INCOME STATEMENT	1997	1996	1995	1994	1993
Net Sales or Revenues	167740.00	124266.00	98780.00	82554.00	62954.00
EBITDA	26926.00	16948.00	13495.00	10630.00	7606.00
Depreciation Depletion & Amort	5756.00	4216.00	3614.00	3004.00	2651.00
Operating Income	17411.00	9141.00	7263.00	4781.00	2966.00
Interest Expense	1562.00	1562.00	1659.00	1459.00	1417.00
Pretax Income	18805.00	11170.00	9222.00	6167.00	3538.00
Net Income	11996.00	7169.00	5439.00	4015.00	2835.00

BALANCE SHEET	1997	1996	1995	1994	1993
Assets					
Cash & Equivalents	29127.00	19060.00	15385.00	11892.00	8800.00
Receivables—Net	63731.00	35384.00	25379.00	20666.00	18159.00
Inventories	27508.00	20074.00	19805.00	13203.00	14190.00
Total Current Assets	121588.00	84577.00	67834.00	51214.00	46722.00
Property Plant & Eq.—Net	19225.00	17754.00	15521.00	13678.00	12363.00
Total Assets	151003.00	110877.00	90048.00	72375.00	66337.00

93

BALANCE SHEET	1997	1996	1995	1994	1993

Liabilities & Shareholders' Equity

	1997	1996	1995	1994	1993
Total Current Liabilities	61660.00	54922.00	42353.00	33184.00	29661.00
Long Term Debt	10719.00	4539.00	5352.00	7763.00	7444.00
Preferred Stock	0.00	0.00	0.00	0.00	0.00
Common Equity	52624.00	40456.00	34263.00	23302.00	21305.00
Total Liabilities & Sh. Equity	151003.00	110877.00	90048.00	72375.00	66337.00

CASH FLOW	1997	1996	1995	1994	1993
Funds from Operations	18958.00	12085.00	9765.00	7454.00	5201.00
Total Sources	13296.00	10776.00	9047.00	6749.00	7167.00
Cash Dividends Paid—Total	2404.00	1676.00	1195.00	977.00	722.00
Total Uses	13296.00	10776.00	9047.00	6749.00	7167.00
Incr/Decr in Working Capital	30273.00	4174.00	7451.00	969.00	2052.00
Free Cash Flow	19689.00	10658.00	7072.00	5723.00	3801.00

INTERNATIONAL BUSINESS	1997	1996	1995	1994	1993
Foreign Assets	NA	NA	NA	NA	NA
Foreign Sales	158419.00	116810.04	89889.80	74298.60	56658.60
Foreign Income	NA	NA	NA	NA	NA

SUPPLEMENTARY DATA	1997	1996	1995	1994	1993
Employees	100774	93949	84513	76144	69597
R&D Expenses	24242.00	17467.00	15093.00	13407.00	10924.00
Goodwill/Cost in Excess of Assets Purchased	541.00	695.00	823.00	944.00	1107.00
Extra Items & Gain/ Loss in Sale of Assets	0.00	0.00	0.00	0.00	0.00

Displayed Currency: Swedish Krona (1.00:1)
All values are displayed in millions (except employees).

FINANCIAL RATIOS AND GROWTH RATES

PROFITABILITY	1997	1996	1995	1994	1993	5YR AVG
Operating Profit Margin %	10.38	7.36	7.35	5.79	4.71	7.12
Tax Rate %	30.60	30.43	28.47	29.56	9.47	25.71
Net Margin %	7.12	5.72	5.51	4.78	4.50	5.53
Return on Assets %	12.18	9.04	9.03	7.40	6.72	8.87
Return on Equity— Total %	29.52	20.75	23.34	18.54	16.26	21.68
Cash Flow % Sales	11.30	9.73	9.89	9.03	8.26	9.64
Sales per Employee (in 000s)	1665	1323	1169	1084	905	1229

L. M. Ericsson Telephone Company

ASSET UTILIZATION	1997	1996	1995	1994	1993	5YR AVG
Total Asset Turnover	1.11	1.12	1.10	1.14	0.95	1.08
Capital Exp %						
Gross Fixed Assets	17.78	17.09	20.09	16.92	14.52	17.28
Acc Depreciation %						
Gross Fixed Assets	52.77	51.76	51.46	52.82	52.83	52.33
Assets per Employee						
(in 000s)	1498	1180	1065	951	953	1130

LIQUIDITY	1997	1996	1995	1994	1993	5YR AVG
Current Ratio	1.97	1.54	1.60	1.54	1.58	1.65
Quick Ratio	1.51	0.99	0.96	0.98	0.91	1.07

LEVERAGE	1997	1996	1995	1994	1993	5YR AVG
Total Debt %						
Common Equity	29.84	27.35	27.04	45.63	52.81	36.53
Long Term Debt %						
Common Equity	20.37	11.22	15.62	33.31	34.94	23.09
Common Equity %						
Total Assets	34.85	36.49	38.05	32.20	32.12	34.74
Long Term Debt %						
Total Capital	15.29	9.47	12.93	23.31	23.97	16.99
Operating Cash/						
Fixed Charges	8.02	7.74	5.89	5.11	3.67	6.08

GROWTH %	1997	1996	1995	1994	1993	5YR AVG
Net Sales	34.98	25.80	19.66	31.13	33.89	28.96
Operating Income	90.47	25.86	51.91	61.19	167.45	73.45
Total Assets	36.19	23.13	24.42	9.10	18.21	21.89
Earnings per Share*	67.13	20.56	40.57	35.43	469.40	85.29
Dividends per Share*	40.00	42.86	32.70	22.22	28.57	33.06
Book Value per Share	28.30	17.64	39.11	9.34	15.99	21.64

Displayed Currency: Swedish Krona (1.00:1)
*Source: Worldscope. Value may differ from I/B/E/S.
Note: 5-Year Average calculations exclude NAs.

PER SHARE AND RELATED DATA

SOURCE: WORLDSCOPE	1997	1996	1995	1994	1993
Earnings per Share	12.2	7.3	6.0	4.3	3.2
Dividends per Share	3.5	2.5	1.8	1.3	1.1
Book Value per Share	54.0	42.1	35.8	25.7	23.5
Total Investment Return	NA	NA	33.69	25.08	82.43

SOURCE: WORLDSCOPE	1997	1996	1995	1994	1993
Market Price (Year-end)	298.5	211.0	130.0	98.6	79.8
Market Capitalization (in millions)	290887.07	202805.23	124489.93	89281.17	72315.22
Price/Earnings Ratio	24.57	29.02	21.56	22.97	25.21
Price/Book Value	5.53	5.01	3.63	3.83	3.39
Dividend Yield	1.17	1.18	1.35	1.34	1.35
Dividend Payout per Share	28.81	34.39	29.02	30.74	34.07
Common Shares Outstanding (Year-end) in Millions	974.50	961.16	957.61	905.94	905.66
Stock Split/Dividend Ratio	NA	NA	NA	0.24	0.24
Type of Share	B Fri Aktie				

Displayed Currency: Swedish Krona (1.00:1)
Note: Data is sourced from Worldscope and may differ from I/B/E/S historical data.

14. Estée Lauder Companies Incorporated

The sweet smell of success wafts worldwide. Each time you stroll through the cosmetics and fragrances section of your local department store, you're deep in the land of Estée Lauder Companies Incorporated. While this was obvious in a recent visit I made to the exclusive Galeries Lafayette store in Paris, where the company's sales counters, under various names, are countless, it is just as obvious in a visit to your local department store. Its products are sold in more than one hundred countries and territories, with more than one-third of annual sales volume coming from products introduced in just the previous three years. Estée Lauder controls more than 45 percent of the cosmetics market in U.S. department stores, three times the volume of its nearest competitor, and the four best-selling prestige perfumes in the United States belong to Estée Lauder. It has a rapidly growing global presence, with 57 percent of net sales currently in the Americas; 27 percent in Europe, the Middle East, and Africa; and 16 percent in the Asia–Pacific region. Obviously, Japanese economic problems have pressured results, but it should be noted that in Japan Estée Lauder's Clinique brand outsells Shiseido in the outlets where they're both sold.

As might be expected, there's also glitz and personal wealth behind the Lauder name, exemplified by the much-publicized $50 million spent by Ronald Lauder, chairman of Clinique Laboratories and Estée Lauder International, to buy the large 1904–06 Paul Cézanne painting "Still Life with Flowered Curtain and Fruit." That 1997 purchase made the Cézanne the fifth most expensive painting ever sold to that date.

Beyond its own famous Estée Lauder brand, founded in 1946

by the hard-selling but elegant Estée Lauder herself and currently featuring the likeness of actress Elizabeth Hurley in its advertisements, the company owns a host of other popular and distinctive brands. Clinique, introduced in 1968, features allergy-tested, 100 percent fragrance-free skin care and makeup products based on the research of dermatologists. Aramis, introduced in 1964, pioneered the marketing of men's grooming and skin care products and fragrances. Prescriptives, introduced in 1979, features a unique system of color-printing, custom-blending, and an extensive range of makeup shades. Origins, introduced in 1990, combines time-tested botanical ingredients with modern science to promote well-being through its skin care, makeup, and sensory therapy products. In December 1994, the company acquired a majority interest in M.A.C (Make-Up Art Cosmetics), a broad line of cosmetics and professional makeup tools targeting makeup artists and fashion-conscious consumers, and was appointed the exclusive distributor of M.A.C. products outside North America. In 1998 it bought the remaining equity interest in the business. Acquired in 1995, Bobbi Brown "essentials" is a professional beauty line created by celebrated makeup artist Bobbi Brown. Meanwhile, "tommy," the firm's licensed men's fragrance launched in 1995 with fashion designer Tommy Hilfiger, has been the number-one men's fragrance where it's sold in the United States. Already a top women's fragrance is "tommy girl," launched in September 1996.

No trends miss the company's watchful eye, as evidenced by two recent unique acquisitions designed to draw profits from hair salons and mass-market retailers respectively. Added to Lauder's stable of brands was the aromatherapy and beauty-products company Aveda Corp., which sells shampoos, cosmetics, and other natural beauty products that employ the healing powers of plants and flower aromas. The all-cash $300 million deal gave the company its first major brand in the $25 billion global hair-care market, as well as access to 30,000 hair salons. About 85 percent of Aveda's sales come from hair salons, the remaining from 130 Aveda stores. In addition, the company bought Sassaby Inc., owner of "jane" color cosmetics, a fast-growing mass-market makeup brand sold through drugstores, supermarkets, and bargain retailers. The jane brand was created three years ago and drew attention with paste colors and unusual products such as "Hip Hugger" lipstick and "War Paint" nail polish, retailing for $2.99. This gets the company into the lower-priced makeup business, which represents $2.2 billion in annual industry sales. Thanks to its high-visibility products, Lauder was able to notch its first $1 billion sales quarter during the fourth quarter of 1997.

The company uses the Internet as a powerful promotional tool. While it doesn't sell on the Internet, its Clinique Web site attracts 100,000 visits a month from consumers interested in learning more about products. Clinique's latest use of the Internet is its Cyber Cafes, in-store computers linked to the Internet, which are currently in use in four U.S. locations.

Estée Lauder Companies is expanding its international presence by increasing market penetration where its brand names are already well known; selecting new markets where demand and potential are high; and introducing new brands into additional markets. In Europe, the Estée Lauder and Clinique brands are number one or two in every store where they're sold and hold a 21 percent market share. It is also a market leader in Japan, with a 33 percent share despite that nation's recent economic woes, and is building leadership in developing countries such as Russia, China, Korea, and Thailand. It's convinced the economic clout of Russia and Eastern Europe will grow. Estée Lauder has been established in Russia since 1989 when it opened its first freestanding store there. It recently opened the Estée Lauder Beauty Center in the Moscow Country Club, a second retail boutique at Moscow's GUM department store in Tverskaya, and a dramatic Clinique counter at Actor Gallery in Moscow's Pushkin Plaza. The Estée Lauder and Clinique brands have been established in Hungary and the Czech Republic for several years, and the Estée Lauder brand has been in Poland since 1993. It recently introduced Estée Lauder, Clinique, and Aramis in Romania. Another market with growth potential is Latin America, where the company has a presence in 15 countries.

The company is a master at marketing to build brand equity. Over the past five years, it has spent more than $4 billion on advertising and promotion. The Lauder name, whatever other well-known brand name it may be behind, stands for quality, a point that current top management has no intention of forgetting.

In his latest annual report letter, Leonard Lauder, chairman and chief executive officer of the firm, noted that his mother, Estée Lauder, had said fifty years ago: "If it isn't perfect, it doesn't ship." He still stands by that philosophy, and, as he also pointed out: "Our brands are who we are and we treat them that way. We give each of them a distinct position and single global image that crosses all markets and ensures that we always stand for quality."

14. ESTÉE LAUDER COMPANIES

United States   Ticker symbol EL
Stock price $54 (9/16/98)   Dividend yield .63%
(Financial data is from I/B/E/S International)*

BUSINESS DESCRIPTION

SKIN CARE PRODUCTS ACCOUNTED FOR 39% OF FISCAL 1997 REVENUES, MAKEUP PRODUCTS 37%, AND FRAGRANCE PRODUCTS 24%

ADDRESS AND CONTACTS

Address	767 Fifth Avenue
	New York NY 10153
Telephone	1-212-572-4200

BASIC FINANCIAL INFORMATION

Capital Structure[†]	Long Term Debt:	0.00
	Total Debt:	31.10
	Common Sh. Equity:	547.70

SALES BREAKDOWN

Product Segments[†]	Skin care	1305.50
	Makeup	1253.40
	Fragrance	822.70
Geographic Segments[†]	United States	1814.70
	Other Americas	124.70
	Europe & Middle East	909.30
	Asia Pacific	532.90

Displayed Currency: U.S. Dollar (1.00:1)
*I/B/E/S and I/B/E/S Express are registered trademarks of I/B/E/S International Inc. Copyright 1993–1996 I/B/E/S International Inc. All rights reserved.
[†]Values are displayed in millions.

Estée Lauder Companies Incorporated

FINANCIAL STATEMENT DATA

INCOME STATEMENT	1997	1996	1995	1994	1993
Net Sales or Revenues	3381.60	3194.50	NA	NA	NA
EBITDA	NA	NA	NA	NA	NA
Depreciation Depletion & Amort	76.00	58.80	NA	NA	NA
Operating Income	359.10	310.30	NA	NA	NA
Interest Expense	NA	NA	NA	NA	NA
Pretax Income	362.90	313.00	NA	NA	NA
Net Income	174.20	137.00	NA	NA	NA

BALANCE SHEET	1997	1996	1995	1994	1993
Assets					
Cash & Equivalents	255.60	254.80	NA	NA	NA
Receivables—Net	471.70	476.20	NA	NA	NA
Inventories	440.60	452.80	NA	NA	NA
Total Current Assets	1311.10	1332.60	NA	NA	NA
Property Plant & Eq.—	265.00	229.30	NA	NA	NA
Net	265.00	229.30	NA	NA	NA
Total Assets	1813.20	1778.50	NA	NA	NA
Liabilities & Shareholders' Equity					
Total Current Liabilities	759.50	865.10	NA	NA	NA
Long Term Debt	0.00	21.90	NA	NA	NA
Preferred Stock	360.00	360.00	NA	NA	NA
Common Equity	547.70	394.20	NA	NA	NA
Total Liabilities & Sh. Equity	1813.20	1778.50	NA	NA	NA

CASH FLOW	1997	1996	1995	1994	1993
Net Cash Flow— Operating	253.10	172.00	NA	NA	NA
Net Cash Flow— Investing	130.70	74.50	NA	NA	NA
Net Cash Flow— Financing	-116.80	-113.40	NA	NA	NA
Incr/Decr in Working Capital	84.10	NA	NA	NA	NA
Free Cash Flow	NA	NA	NA	NA	NA

INTERNATIONAL BUSINESS	1997	1996	1995	1994	1993
Foreign Assets	702.80	831.00	NA	NA	NA
Foreign Sales	1442.20	1511.50	NA	NA	NA
Foreign Income	169.20	195.90	NA	NA	NA

SUPPLEMENTARY DATA	1997	1996	1995	1994	1993
Employees	14700	13500	NA	NA	NA
R&D Expenses	35.30	32.90	NA	NA	NA
Goodwill/Cost in Excess of Assets Purchased	NA	NA	NA	NA	NA
Extra Items & Gain/ Loss in Sale of Assets	0.00	0.00	NA	NA	NA

Displayed Currency: U.S. Dollar (1.00:1)
All values are displayed in millions (except employees).

FINANCIAL RATIOS AND GROWTH RATES

PROFITABILITY	1997	1996	1995	1994	1993	5YR AVG
Operating Profit Margin %	10.62	9.71	NA	NA	NA	10.17
Tax Rate %	42.00	44.19	NA	NA	NA	43.09
Net Margin %	5.84	5.02	NA	NA	NA	5.43
Return on Assets %	11.11	NA	NA	NA	NA	11.11
Return on Equity— Total %	44.19	NA	NA	NA	NA	44.19
Cash Flow % Sales	8.11	7.28	NA	NA	NA	7.69
Sales per Employee (in 000s)	230	237	NA	NA	NA	233

ASSET UTILIZATION	1997	1996	1995	1994	1993	5YR AVG
Total Asset Turnover	1.86	1.80	NA	NA	NA	1.83
Capital Exp % Gross Fixed Assets	13.75	11.97	NA	NA	NA	12.86
Acc Depreciation % Gross Fixed Assets	56.05	56.70	NA	NA	NA	56.38
Assets per Employee (in 000s)	123	132	NA	NA	NA	128

LIQUIDITY	1997	1996	1995	1994	1993	5YR AVG
Current Ratio	1.73	1.54	NA	NA	NA	1.63
Quick Ratio	0.96	0.84	NA	NA	NA	0.90

Estée Lauder Companies Incorporated

LEVERAGE	1997	1996	1995	1994	1993	5YR AVG
Total Debt %						
Common Equity	5.68	32.34	NA	NA	NA	19.01
Long Term Debt %						
Common Equity	0.00	5.56	NA	NA	NA	2.78
Common Equity %						
Total Assets	30.21	22.16	NA	NA	NA	26.19
Long Term Debt %						
Total Capital	0.00	2.82	NA	NA	NA	1.41
Operating Cash/						
Fixed Charges	NA	NA	NA	NA	NA	NA

GROWTH %	1997	1996	1995	1994	1993	5YR AVG
Net Sales	5.86	NA	NA	NA	NA	NA
Operating Income	15.73	NA	NA	NA	NA	NA
Total Assets	1.95	NA	NA	NA	NA	NA
Earnings per Share*	28.46	NA	NA	NA	NA	NA
Dividends per Share*	0.00	NA	NA	NA	NA	NA
Book Value per Share	32.86	NA	NA	NA	NA	NA

Displayed Currency: U.S. Dollar (1.00:1)
*Source: Worldscope. Value may differ from I/B/E/S.
Note: 5-Year Average calculations exclude NAs.

PER SHARE AND RELATED DATA

SOURCE: WORLDSCOPE	1997	1996	1995	1994	1993
Earnings per Share	1.67	1.30	NA	NA	NA
Dividends per Share	0.34	0.34	NA	NA	NA
Book Value per Share	5.44	4.09	NA	NA	NA
Total Investment Return	NA	46.85	NA	NA	NA
Market Price (Year-end)	51.44	50.88	34.88	NA	NA
Market Capitalization					
(in millions)	6083.90	5967.53	NA	NA	NA
Price/Earnings Ratio	30.80	39.13	NA	NA	NA
Price/Book Value	9.46	12.43	NA	NA	NA
Dividend Yield	0.66	0.67	NA	NA	NA
Dividend Payout per					
Share	20.36	26.15	NA	NA	NA
Common Shares					
Outstanding					
(Year-end) in					
Millions	118.28	117.30	NA	NA	NA
Stock Split/Dividend Ratio	NA	NA	NA	NA	NA
Type of Share	*Class A*				

Displayed Currency. U.S. Dollar (1.00:1)
Note: Data is sourced from Worldscope and may differ from I/B/E/S historical data.

15. FDX Corporation

When you absolutely, positively, want a solid investment, there's FDX Corporation, whose FedEx business—famous for getting important items to places in a hurry—delivers 2.9 million express packages to 212 countries each working day. In the cutthroat world of express delivery, it has introduced Sunday delivery of packages and the only overnight shipping from major Asian markets to most cities in North America. The company's impressive express army includes 141,000 employees worldwide and a fleet of 610 aircraft and 38,500 vehicles, all followed with an advanced electronic tracking system. It receives millions of tracking requests on its World Wide Web site each month and handles more than 60 million electronic transmissions daily.

FDX holds nearly a 50 percent market share in the U.S. package express industry, leading its next competitor by a wide margin. It's also a global powerhouse, deriving about 28 percent of revenues from outside the United States, a percentage that could grow by more than half within five years. Over the next ten years, it's projected that the world express transportation market in which it plays such an important role will grow from $12 billion annually to more than $150 billion. In addition, subsidiary RPS Inc. is the second-largest ground carrier of small packages under 150 pounds in the United States, while its Roberts Express Inc., the largest surface-expedited carrier in North America, provides delivery of time-critical shipments. Viking Freight Inc. is a less-than-truckload carrier in the western United States. The acquisition of nonexpress carrier Caliber Systems Inc. in 1998 led to the formation of the $15 billion holding company FDX.

Founded by Frederick Smith in 1971, the company became the first to win the Malcolm Baldridge National Quality Award in the service category. Chairman, President, and Chief Executive Officer Smith, a Yale graduate who served two combat tours in Vietnam, recalls that a marine sergeant once told him: "Lieutenant, there's only three things you gotta remember: shoot, move, and communicate." He converted that battlefield logic into a delivery company big on communicating knowledge about cargo's origin, present whereabouts, destination, estimated time of arrival, price, and cost of shipment. His information systems featuring laser scanners, bar codes, software, and electronics were revolutionary. Ten years after start-up, FedEx reached $1 billion in revenues, becoming the first U.S. business to achieve that status without the benefit of mergers or acquisitions. It was the first company dedicated to overnight package delivery, the first express company to introduce the Overnight Letter, the first to offer 10:30 A.M. next-day delivery, the first to offer Saturday and Sunday deliveries, the first to offer time-definite service for freight, and the first to offer money-back guarantees.

Technology remains a vital part of FDX's future. It has launched a newly redesigned World Wide Web site and installed its one-millionth customer electronic online shipping connection. Its original proprietary PowerShip automated hardware/software shipping system is available in a number of configurations based on customers' individual needs. This stand-alone desktop system lets customers ship and track the status of packages online and print thermal airbills and keeps them updated on billing and other relevant information. In addition, FedEx customers around the world can now access a FedEx home page that displays shipping, tracking, and customer service options available in the country where the customer is located. This new look for fedex.com includes several enhancements such as pop-up help pages for each function, an improved keyword search engine, and an easier-to-use design. Through FedEx interNetShip, customers in thirty-eight countries can ship via the Internet to more than 160 countries served by FedEx, eliminating the need to handwrite airbills. InterNetShip users can also access an online address book and FedEx ShipAlert e-mail notification.

Promotion is a vital part of FDX's business. Besides its catchy television commercials, which run around the globe, it has a major sponsorship deal with the Benetton Formula I auto racing team in which its logo is prominently positioned on both race cars and on the uniforms of its drivers as they speed throughout Europe's raceways. For its employees, the company has a good profit-sharing plan and sticks with a no-layoff policy. After the 1997 United Parcel Service strike in which FedEx employees worked around the clock to handle an extra 800,000 packages a day, FedEx distributed a $20 million Special Appreciation Bonus to 90,000 operations employees. The bonus, valued at 10 percent of eligible pay, including overtime, for the four-week period between July 27 and August 23, was distributed that September.

Expansion is carefully planned by the company. Following months of heated competition among several Southeast cities, the company announced plans in 1998 to build a $300 million air hub and package-sorting facility in Greensboro, North Carolina, helping to reduce the delivery firm's reliance on the airport in Memphis, Tennessee, where the company is based. That hub will be the sixth regional air facility built by FedEx since it began shifting operations out of Memphis. The company recently built a hub at Subic Bay in the Philippines and completed a new facility in Taiwan. Not a week goes by that FDX isn't making deals to better its system, such as a deal to buy twenty used McDonnell Douglas MD-11 aircraft from Flightlease Ltd., with delivery to begin in August 2002 and end in December 2006.

As many companies around the world seek to cut costs tied to their enormous inventories, express delivery offers a worthwhile service. The company has trained many of its salespeople as consultants who can offer sophisticated suggestions to help a firm's bottom line. Its joint venture with Temic Semiconductor of California, a $1 billion subsidiary of Daimler-Benz, uses a global center at the Philippines facility in Subic Bay to deliver confirmation of a customer order within thirty seconds. After the product requested is manufactured and sent to that global center, FDX receives it and ships it to the customer. In Asia, orders can be received within eight hours, while it takes forty-eight hours to reach U.S. and European destinations. This important hub, however, won't be able to reach full utilization until open skies negotiations with Japan are concluded. In addition, financial woes in Asia are likely to limit revenue growth in this part of FedEx's business until they improve. Its business within Asia is new and coming off low base, but growth has been promising.

"The core strengths of FedEx—brand recognition, global presence, customer base, asset base, customer service, technological expertise, regulatory rights, and the experience, skill, and motivation of our people—place us in a strong and defensible position in this high-growth industry," Smith stated in his letter in the most recent annual report. "If you believe, as I do, in the trends shaping express distribution, and the commitment and ability of our employees to extend our leadership edge, you know as stockholders you're positioned to enjoy superior financial returns."

15. FDX CORPORATION

United States   Ticker symbol FDX

Stock price $49 15/16 (9/16/98)   No dividend

(Financial data is from I/B/E/S International)*

BUSINESS DESCRIPTION

PROVIDES A WIDE RANGE OF EXPRESS SERVICE FOR THE TIME-DEFINITE TRANSPORTATION OF GOODS AND DOCUMENTS THROUGHOUT THE WORLD

ADDRESS AND CONTACTS

Address	2005 Corporate Avenue
	Memphis TN 38132
Telephone	1-901-369-3600

BASIC FINANCIAL INFORMATION

Capital Structure†		
	Long Term Debt:	1397.95
	Total Debt:	1524.62
	Common Sh. Equity·	2962.51

SALES BREAKDOWN

Product Segments†	Express services	11519.75
Geographic Segments†	United States	8322.04
	International	3197.71

Displayed Currency: U.S. Dollar (1.00:1)
*I/B/E/S and I/B/E/S Express are registered trademarks of I/B/E/S International Inc. Copyright 1993–1996 I/B/E/S International Inc. All rights reserved.

†Values are displayed in millions.

FINANCIAL STATEMENT DATA

INCOME STATEMENT	1997	1996	1995	1994	1993
Net Sales or Revenues	11519.75	10273.62	9392.07	8479.46	7808.04
EBITDA	1501.28	1365.02	1305.29	1129.99	952.23
Depreciation Depletion & Amort	777.37	719.61	652.29	599.36	579.90
Operating Income	684.04	623.82	591.14	530.63	377.17
Interest Expense	144.70	144.70	158.30	181.91	200.02
Pretax Income	628.22	539.96	522.08	378.46	203.58
Net Income	361.23	307.78	297.59	204.37	109.81

BALANCE SHEET	1997	1996	1995	1994	1993
Assets					
Cash & Equivalents	122.02	93.42	357.55	392.92	155.46
Receivables—Net	1512.94	1271.60	1130.25	1020.51	922.73
Inventories	313.34	222.11	193.25	173.99	164.09
Total Current Assets	2132.59	1728.26	1869.08	1761.70	1439.72
Property Plant & Eq.— Net	4622.08	4116.60	3715.24	3449.09	3476.27
Total Assets	7625.49	6698.97	6433.37	5992.50	5793.06
Liabilities & Shareholders' Equity					
Total Current Liabilities	1962.78	1618.40	1778.54	1536.43	1449.27
Long Term Debt	1397.95	1325.28	1324.71	1632.20	1882.28
Preferred Stock	0.00	0.00	0.00	0.00	0.00
Common Equity	2962.51	2576.14	2245.57	1924.71	1671.38
Total Liabilities & Sh. Equity	7625.49	6698.97	6433.37	5992.50	5793.06
	7625.49	6698.97	6433.37	5992.50	5793.06

CASH FLOW	1997	1996	1995	1994	1993
Net Cash Flow— Operating	1007.49	946.58	1030.72	767.28	725.08
Net Cash Flow— Investing	1191.39	988.17	775.11	393.52	799.30
Net Cash Flow— Financing	212.51	-222.54	-290.98	-136.29	151.50

FDX Corporation

Incr/Decr in Working					
Capital	59.94	19.32	-134.72	234.82	169.30
Free Cash Flow	30.69	-47.22	244.53	42.28	-71.49

INTERNATIONAL BUSINESS	1997	1996	1995	1994	1993
Foreign Assets	1502.60	1249.62	1111.56	1108.85	1360.49
Foreign Sales	3197.71	2807.31	2552.66	2279.52	2140.08
Foreign Income	141.00	81.66	126.52	-29.00	-181.97

SUPPLEMENTARY DATA	1997	1996	1995	1994	1993
Employees	126000	99999	107000	101000	95000
R&D Expenses	NA	NA	NA	NA	NA
Goodwill/Cost in Excess of Assets Purchased	365.33	380.75	397.27	415.18	432.22
Extra Items & Gain/ Loss in Sale of Assets	0.00	0.00	0.00	0.00	-55.94

Displayed Currency: U.S. Dollar (1.00:1)
All values are displayed in millions (except employees).

FINANCIAL RATIOS AND GROWTH RATES

PROFITABILITY	1997	1996	1995	1994	1993	5YR AVG
Operating Profit Margin %	5.94	6.07	6.29	6.26	4.83	5.88
Tax Rate %	42.50	43.00	43.00	46.00	46.06	44.11
Net Margin %	3.14	3.00	3.17	2.41	0.69	2.48
Return on Assets %	6.34	5.87	6.41	5.26	3.02	5.38
Return on Equity— Total %	14.02	13.71	15.46	12.23	3.41	11.77
Cash Flow % Sales	10.46	10.51	10.26	9.89	9.72	10.17
Sales per Employee (in 000s)	91	103	88	84	82	90

ASSET UTILIZATION	1997	1996	1995	1994	1993	5YR AVG
Total Asset Turnover	1.51	1.53	1.46	1.42	1.35	1.45
Capital Exp % Gross Fixed Assets	14.98	16.27	13.78	15.79	15.27	15.22
Acc Depreciation % Gross Fixed Assets	52.93	52.57	51.74	49.94	48.16	51.07
Assets per Employee (in 000s)	61	67	60	59	61	62

LIQUIDITY	1997	1996	1995	1994	1993	5YR AVG
Current Ratio	1.09	1.07	1.05	1.15	0.99	1.07
Quick Ratio	0.83	0.84	0.84	0.92	0.74	0.84

109

LEVERAGE	1997	1996	1995	1994	1993	5YR AVG
Total Debt % Common Equity	51.46	51.76	70.37	95.10	120.62	77.86
Long Term Debt % Common Equity	47.19	51.44	58.99	84.80	112.62	71.01
Common Equity % Total Assets	38.85	38.46	34.91	32.12	28.85	34.64
Long Term Debt % Total Capital	32.06	33.97	37.10	45.89	52.97	40.40
Operating Cash/ Fixed Charges	8.92	7.46	6.09	4.61	3.79	6.17

GROWTH %	1997	1996	1995	1994	1993	5YR AVG
Net Sales	12.13	9.39	10.76	8.60	3.42	8.82
Operating Income	9.65	5.53	11.40	40.69	36.18	19.82
Total Assets	13.83	4.13	7.36	3.44	6.04	6.90
Earnings per Share*	-3.05	-7.09	84.31	61.62	-+	-+
Dividends per Share*	0.00	0.00	0.00	0.00	0.00	0.00
Book Value per Share	19.79	7.81	14.18	15.09	5.50	12.35

Displayed Currency: U.S. Dollar (1.00:1)
*Source: Worldscope. Value may differ from I/B/E/S.
Note: 5-Year Average calculations exclude NAs.

PER SHARE AND RELATED DATA

SOURCE: WORLDSCOPE	1997	1996	1995	1994	1993
Earnings per Share	3.81	3.93	4.23	2.30	1.42
Dividends per Share	0.00	0.00	0.00	0.00	0.00
Book Value per Share	27.07	22.60	20.96	18.36	15.95
Total Investment Return	37.22	20.47	22.61	-14.99	30.05
Market Price (Year-end)	61.06	44.50	36.94	30.13	35.44
Market Capitalization (in millions)	7016.57	5062.77	4149.85	3367.07	3879.91
Price/Earnings Ratio	16.03	11.32	8.73	13.13	24.96
Price/Book Value	2.26	1.97	1.76	1.64	2.22
Dividend Yield	0.00	0.00	0.00	0.00	0.00
Dividend Payout per Share	0.00	0.00	0.00	0.00	0.00
Common Shares Outstanding (Year-end) in Millions	114.91	113.77	112.35	111.77	109.49
Stock Split/Dividend Ratio	NA	NA	0.50	0.50	0.50
Type of Share	Common				

Displayed Currency: U.S. Dollar (1.00:1)
Note: Data is sourced from Worldscope and may differ from I/B/E/S historical data.

16. Four Seasons Hotels and Resorts

And the winner is: Four Seasons Hotels and Resorts.

Each year this prestigious hotel management company reaps more worldwide hospitality awards than any other luxury hotel company in surveys conducted by the American Automobile Association (AAA), *Conde Nast Traveler*, *Institutional Investor*, *Gourmet*, *Andrew Harper's Hideaway Report*, and *Travel & Leisure*. Its properties snared fourteen of the fifty-seven AAA Five Diamond lodging awards for 1998, as well as seventeen slots among *Travel & Leisure* magazine's Top 100 Hotels.

Four Seasons operates an international chain of hotels famous for luxury accommodations and the ultimate in customer service. Investors also note that it's a debt-free cash machine with unlimited potential for global expansion. Responsible for the world's largest network of five-star hotels and resorts under the Four Seasons and Regent names, it produces revenue for each available room that far exceeds other luxury operators', yet its strong brand name is still not fully tapped.

The company is in charge of forty-one hotels and resorts with 11,900 rooms in seventeen countries, and has another fourteen properties under construction or development in six additional countries. Four Seasons also leases three hotels and owns a minority equity interest in eight properties that are under its management. Systemwide sales total more than $1.5 billion. About 62 percent of consolidated revenues are derived from hotels and resorts in North America.

Worry about the impact of Asian turmoil on Four Seasons has had some negative effect on the company's perceived prospects.

111

Yet while about one-third of Four Seasons' rooms are located in the Asian market, that region produces about 25 percent of revenue, and Four Seasons' ownership interests are largely limited to a 25 percent interest in the Regent Hong Kong. In addition, the overall percentage of involvement in Asia will continue to decrease because the firm's new development is centering on Europe, the Middle East, India, North America, and South America. Four Seasons is also less effected by market fluctuations than other hotel companies because it's primarily a management firm whose fees are based on a percentage of its managed hotels' gross revenues.

This has been a time of strong fundamentals in the cyclical luxury lodging business, with demand exceeding supply. An aggressive expansion strategy at Four Seasons is expected to add at least fifteen hotels and increase the number of rooms managed by more than 30 percent over the next four years. The company took over management of the Ritz Hotel in Lisbon, Portugal, in 1998 and rebranded it a Four Seasons. In 1998 it also opened Four Seasons Resort Bali at Sayan, Indonesia, and Four Seasons Resort—The Leela Beach, Goa, India. In 1999 it begins managing the George V Hotel in Paris and will also start operating properties in Las Vegas, Nevada; Caracas, Venezuela; Bombay, India; Bangalore, India; First Residence Egypt, Sharm El Sheikh, Egypt; Dublin, Ireland; Amman, Jordan; Riyadh, Saudi Arabia; and Nile Plaza, Egypt. Some analysts expect the company to ultimately exceed two hundred city hotels and at least fifty resorts, as it continues its pace of adding four to five new hotels and resorts annually for the foreseeable future.

Founded in Toronto in 1960 by Isadore Sharp, its chairman and chief executive officer, it was based on what he modestly calls "an idea that grew." Four Seasons' innovations have included European-style concierge service with twenty-four-hour room service, brand-name shampoos, complimentary overnight shoeshine, and twice-daily housekeeping services. His focus has always relentlessly been on pleasing guests so they will come back and come back often. "The customer, not the producer, now holds the levers of power, which makes conventional management priorities and practices obsolete," Sharp said in a recent speech about the global market. "Until this basic turnaround in economic control, management decided what it would offer customers. Now we have to tailor our product to what the customer wants, a new priority that redirects focus and energy."

Four Seasons acquired ownership of Regent International Hotels in 1992. Saudi Prince Alwaleed's $10 billion Kingdom Investments Inc. bought approximately 25 percent of the company in 1994 and provided it with financial fuel for worldwide growth. Kingdom's initial investment in Four Seasons of $124 million is now worth an estimated $317 million. Carlson Hospitality Worldwide acquired the rights to the Regent brand name from Four Seasons in 1997 in order to expand and develop it, with Four Seasons continuing to manage the existing nine Regent hotels with the option to manage new Regent hotels. The financial power of Kingdom Investments' resources was behind Four Seasons developments in Paris, Cairo, Riyadh, Amman, and Damascus. In addition, Four Seasons and Kingdom acquired the remaining 50 percent of the Four Seasons Hotel London that Kingdom didn't previously own. Four Seasons holds a 12.5 percent ownership interest in that hotel, the company's second most profitable establishment, behind the Pierre in New York. In addition, Kingdom has ambitiously stated that it would like to see eighty or more Four Seasons hotels by the year 2005.

Employees get first-class treatment at Four Seasons as well. The company ranked among the top thirty of *Fortune* magazine's 100 Best Companies to Work For, with the special perks for workers including free meals in the company cafeteria, tailored uniforms cleaned and pressed daily, and free nights at any Four Seasons in the world. "The only way a brand can now command a premium price, whether in taste, style, function, or status, is to typify a fairly priced distinctive product," Sharp has pointed out. "And when we have a workforce which can deliver that consistently, our brands stand out like beacons, making choice safer and easier for overloaded consumers, and commanding instant attention in a new country."

The Four Seasons blue-chip brand is undeniably a powerful selling point as it enters into each new agreement around the globe. Its name helps it garner new properties and new capital on its way to becoming a much larger force in the future. Awards are just the icing on the cake.

16. FOUR SEASONS HOTELS AND RESORTS

Canada   Ticker symbol FS

Stock price $19 7/16 (9/16/98)   Dividend yield .38%

(Financial data from I/B/E/S International is in Canadian dollar)*

BUSINESS DESCRIPTION

ENGAGED IN THE MANAGEMENT OF AND INVESTMENT IN HOTELS, RESORTS, AND VACATION OWNERSHIP PROPERTIES THROUGHOUT THE WORLD

ADDRESS AND CONTACTS

Address	1165 Leslie Street
	Toronto Ontario M3C 2K8 Canada
Telephone	1-416-449-1750
Fax	1-416-441-4374

BASIC FINANCIAL INFORMATION

Capital Structure†	Long Term Debt:	138.95
	Total Debt:	140.24
	Common Sh. Equity:	254.51

SALES BREAKDOWN

Product Segments†	Hotels & Motels	241.30
Geographic Segments†	Canada	39.37
	United States	168.87
	United Kingdom & Europe	5.70
	Asia Pacific	33.35
	Intersegment	-7.26

Displayed Currency: Canadian Dollar (1.00:1)

*I/B/E/S and I/B/E/S Express are registered trademarks of I/B/E/S International Inc. Copyright 1993–1996 I/B/E/S International Inc. All rights reserved.

†Values are displayed in millions.

FINANCIAL STATEMENT DATA

INCOME STATEMENT	1997	1996	1995	1994	1993
Net Sales or Revenues	241.30	112.37	130.89	122.98	99.61
EBITDA	73.48	68.25	-26.90	55.91	-82.01
Depreciation Depletion					
& Amort	15.75	13.99	16.88	15.70	13.22
Operating Income	56.97	41.18	43.77	37.54	1.03
Interest Expense	22.43	22.43	26.90	29.43	22.99
Pretax Income	42.37	31.83	-70.69	10.78	-118.22
Net Income	40.77	29.87	-74.57	8.02	-119.23

BALANCE SHEET	1997	1996	1995	1994	1993
Assets					
Cash & Equivalents	25.34	15.39	36.77	9.44	11.93
Receivables—Net	44.75	51.21	21.57	38.18	26.58
Inventories	1.59	1.63	0.51	0.81	0.75
Total Current Assets	73.46	69.86	59.76	50.87	41.06
Property Plant & Eq.—					
Net	43.42	33.15	32.12	68.05	72.61
Total Assets	453.21	385.29	388.45	497.54	522.90
Liabilities & Shareholders' Equity					
Total Current Liabilities	58.54	68.07	146.80	45.78	40.90
Long Term Debt	138.95	226.59	181.74	307.72	352.90
Preferred Stock	0.00	0.00	0.91	0.92	1.23
Common Equity	254.51	88.06	56.32	139.59	125.56
Total Liabilities					
& Sh. Equity	453.21	385.29	388.45	497.54	522.90

CASH FLOW	1997	1996	1995	1994	1993
Funds from Operations	70.47	41.99	39.29	39.51	15.75
Total Sources	297.80	136.88	91.49	113.79	211.33
Cash Dividends Paid—					
Total	3.18	3.04	3.13	3.09	3.05
Total Uses	297.80	136.88	91.49	113.79	211.33
Incr/Decr in Working					
Capital	13.13	88.83	-92.13	4.94	15.85
Free Cash Flow	62.97	66.91	-29.33	54.33	83.53

INTERNATIONAL BUSINESS	1997	1996	1995	1994	1993
Foreign Assets	386.67	318.74	309.89	402.59	432.68
Foreign Sales	207.93	116.92	131.67	121.73	NA
Foreign Income	60.21	73.78	-8.35	-14.07	-40.30

SUPPLEMENTARY DATA	1997	1996	1995	1994	1993
Employees	22000	21000	21500	21500	20050
R&D Expenses	NA	NA	NA	NA	NA
Goodwill/Cost in Excess of Assets Purchased	NA	NA	NA	NA	NA
Extra Items & Gain/ Loss in Sale of Assets	0.00	0.00	0.00	0.00	0.00

Displayed Currency: Canadian Dollar (1.00:1)
All values are displayed in millions (except employees).

FINANCIAL RATIOS AND GROWTH RATES

PROFITABILITY	1997	1996	1995	1994	1993	5YR AVG
Operating Profit Margin %	23.61	36.65	33.44	30.53	1.03	25.05
Tax Rate %	3.79	6.16	NA	25.57	NA	11.84
Net Margin %	16.90	26.58	-56.97	6.52	-119.70	-25.34
Return on Assets %	13.21	11.50	-11.42	5.25	-17.04	0.30
Return on Equity— Total %	46.30	53.03	-53.42	6.39	-48.37	0.78
Cash Flow % Sales	29.21	37.37	30.01	32.12	15.81	28.91
Sales per Employee (in 000s)	11	5	6	6	5	7

ASSET UTILIZATION	1997	1996	1995	1994	1993	5YR AVG
Total Asset Turnover	0.53	0.29	0.34	0.25	0.19	0.32
Capital Exp % Gross Fixed Assets	16.12	2.62	4.91	1.47	1.45	5.32
Acc Depreciation % Gross Fixed Assets	33.41	35.34	34.93	36.37	30.59	34.13
Assets per Employee (in 000s)	21	18	18	23	26	21

LIQUIDITY	1997	1996	1995	1994	1993	5YR AVG
Current Ratio	1.25	1.03	0.41	1.11	1.00	0.96
Quick Ratio	1.20	0.98	0.40	1.06	0.94	0.92

Four Seasons Hotels and Resorts

LEVERAGE	1997	1996	1995	1994	1993	5YR AVG
Total Debt %						
Common Equity	55.10	272.53	475.17	221.08	284.76	261.73
Long Term Debt %						
Common Equity	54.59	257.31	322.68	220.45	281.06	227.22
Common Equity %						
Total Assets	56.16	22.86	14.50	28.06	24.01	29.12
Long Term Debt %						
Total Capital	35.31	72.01	76.05	68.65	73.57	65.12
Operating Cash/						
Fixed Charges	4.59	1.87	1.46	1.34	0.69	1.99

GROWTH %	1997	1996	1995	1994	1993	5YR AVG
Net Sales	114.74	-14.15	6.43	23.46	-26.52	12.23
Operating Income	38.35	-5.92	16.60	3555.31	-+	-+
Total Assets	17.63	-0.81	-21.93	-4.85	-14.37	-5.79
Earnings per Share*	19.23	-+	-1003.45	-+	-1443.75	31.12
Dividends per Share*	0.00	0.00	0.00	0.00	0.00	0.00
Book Value per Share	146.23	55.06	-59.75	8.64	-49.13	-3.21

Displayed Currency: Canadian Dollar (1.00:1)
*Source: Worldscope. Value may differ from I/B/E/S.
Note: 5-Year Average calculations exclude NAs.

PER SHARE AND RELATED DATA

SOURCE: WORLDSCOPE	1997	1996	1995	1994	1993
Earnings per Share	1.24	1.04	-2.62	0.29	-4.30
Dividends per Share	0.11	0.11	0.11	0.11	0.11
Book Value per Share	7.55	3.07	1.98	4.91	4.52
Total Investment Return	NA	NA	17.60	25.85	-32.34
Market Price (Year-end)	45.00	27.75	19.00	16.25	13.00
Market Capitalization					
(in millions)	1517.37	797.17	541.30	461.87	361.08
Price/Earnings Ratio	36.29	26.68	NM	56.03	NM
Price/Book Value	5.96	9.05	9.61	3.31	2.88
Dividend Yield	0.24	0.40	0.58	0.68	0.85
Dividend Payout per					
Share	8.87	10.58	-4.20	37.93	-2.56
Common Shares					
Outstanding					
(Year-end) in					
Millions	33.72	28.73	28.49	28.42	27.78
Stock Split/Dividend					
Ratio	NA	NA	NA	NA	NA
Type of Share	*Subordinate Voting*				

Displayed Currency: Canadian Dollar (1.00:1)
Note: Data is sourced from Worldscope and may differ from I/B/E/S historical data.

17. Fuji Photo Film Company Limited

Investors like this picture: Fuji Photo Film Company is Japan's number-one photographic film producer and ranks second worldwide to rival Eastman Kodak. Due in part to lower film prices than Kodak, Fuji has the potential to surpass its competitor globally in the near future. A new plant in Greenwood, South Carolina, opened in 1998 and helped it increase its monthly production capacity from 3 million rolls of film to 20 million. The plant eliminated the need for shipping costs, which are about 3 percent of the total cost of film, and a 3.7 percent duty on base film that was being imported from the Netherlands to be cut, rolled, and wrapped in the United States. The Greenwood plant also produces one-time use cameras, VHS videotapes, color print paper, and plates for offset printing, which it sells in forty countries nationwide.

Fuji's stock is a bet on the long-term potential of the company as a truly global player. It has suffered from sluggish consumer spending at home, as well as the effects of currency and financial problems in Southeast Asia. A major risk for Fuji is always yen appreciation, since it harms the company's export profitability and triggers price declines in its largest market, Japan. Yet its strong photographic film and paper revenues from the United States and Europe have helped to offset slumping demand in Japan and Southeast Asia. Sales outside Japan account for about 46 percent of company revenues.

Fuji holds a commanding 70 percent market share at home in Japan, a country that has faced its share of economic pressures, and 37 percent internationally. Information systems equipment such as floppy disks for computers, electronic filing systems, and microfilming products fill out a product line famous for film and cameras. It is broadening its lineup of data storage products and is the exclusive supplier of ZIP high-density disks and DLT Tape IV computer backup tape, using exclusive technology that provides significant profits. Fuji has expanded its U.S. photo-developing services through the purchase of six wholesale photo labs from Wal-Mart.

Fuji's Imaging and Information corporate philosophy stresses "extending possibilities for the capture of an image and its enhancement through use of recording systems and information, and use of image-related electronics and computer technologies to create high-quality image information systems in a variety of fields." That's the philosophy, but the reality is hard-nosed competition among world competitors who frankly don't like each other much.

"Today we operate in a market characterized by intense price competition and a fierce struggle for market domination," Chairman and Chief Executive Officer Minoru Ohnishi acknowledged in his letter in the most recent Fuji Photo annual report. "In response, we are taking decisive steps to sharpen our competitive edge by further reinforcing our international manufacturing, sales, and service networks and maximizing group capabilities."

Trade wars are intense affairs. The World Trade Organization (WTO) in 1998 formally adopted a dispute panel ruling which favored the Japanese in a disagreement over access to Japan's photo film market. The United States didn't appeal the decision, but U.S. officials emphasized that they would continue a monitoring operation to make sure foreign companies were able to enter the market. The U.S. action followed a final ruling by the WTO that rejected claims by Kodak that the Japanese government had conspired with Fuji to keep Kodak products out of Japan. Meanwhile, Fuji itself filed a complaint with the U.S. International Trade Commission charging that a group of twenty-eight companies violated a total of fifteen Fuji patents related to disposable cameras. It asked for a cease-and-desist order against the alleged violators, to prevent them from selling the cameras in the United States.

Fuji's global expansion has been dramatic, and it now operates forty-five consolidated subsidiaries in North America, Europe, Brazil, and the Pacific Basin for the manufacture and distribution of its products. In China, Fujifilm Imaging Systems Co. Ltd. has been established in Suzhou, Jiangsu Province, to produce digital and Advanced Photo System cameras. Advanced Photo System is a new global photographic standard developed by Fuji, Kodak, Canon Inc., Minolta Co. Ltd., and Nikon Corp. that "expands the frontiers of photography." Such products currently include color print films, a color slide film, one-time use cameras, print paper, and cameras. By applying digital technology, Fuji developed a photo player and an image scanner that enable users to display images from a processed film cartridge on television or personal computer screens. Such products offer new ways of enjoying photography, while also creating new demand. Fuji has also introduced a variety of APS-compatible photo-finishing systems and the Digital Image Workstation AL-1000. Meanwhile, nearly all disposable cameras that Fuji will market and distribute domestically in 1999 will contain the APS. Currently, less than 40 percent of the company's 60 million disposable cameras shipped in Japan each year use these special APS film cartridges. Fuji expects the disposable camera with 25-exposure APS will be its main seller in the year 2000.

Since its founding in 1934 as a manufacturer of silver-halide photographic products, Fuji Photo has pioneered numerous revolutionary technologies while bringing a wide range of products to market. There's an impressive pipeline of new products and enhancements under way. For example, in 1998 Fuji started selling new lines of CD-recordable and magneto-optical disks designed to offer superior recording accuracy and better compatibility with CD-R recorders.

Fuji reinforces its global image through high-profile marketing and advertising. It was an official sponsor of the 1998 World Cup in France, as well as European and World Figure Skating championships and the U.S. Open and French Open tennis championships each year. It supplies the official photographic film, videotape, film processing services, and other forms of support for each of these events. The company also has its eye on worker efficiency in this price-conscious business. To better adapt to the competitive future, Fuji expanded its goal management evaluation system for bonuses in 1998 to include qualified sales and administrative staff, in addition to the researchers already included. Under this bonus system, a supervisor evaluates how much of an employee's agreed-upon goal has actually been achieved, then adds to his or her bonus accordingly.

Fuji Photo doesn't miss a trick. It's a fiercely competitive company in a field that thrives on technological advances, mass production, and pricing. With prospects for increased pricing competition with Kodak on the horizon and continued uncertainties over Asian currencies and economies, its task will be challenging. But it has positioned itself well to offer great potential for investors who believe this film giant is more than up to the task. That's a pretty picture.

17. FUJI PHOTO FILM COMPANY LIMITED

Japan   Ticker symbol FUJIY

One American Depositary Receipt represents one common share

ADR price $35 1/4 (9/16/98)   Dividend yield .90%

(Financial data from I/B/E/S International is in Japanese yen)*

BUSINESS DESCRIPTION

INFORMATION SYSTEMS ACCOUNTED FOR 41% OF FISCAL 1997 REVENUES, IMAGING SYSTEMS 35%, AND PHOTOFINISHING SYSTEMS 24%

ADDRESS AND CONTACTS

Address	26-30, Nishiazabu 2-Chome
	Minato-ku Tokyo 106 Japan
Telephone	81-3-34062111
Fax	81-3-34062193

BASIC FINANCIAL INFORMATION

Capital Structure†		
	Long Term Debt:	NA
	Total Debt:	NA
	Common Sh. Equity:	NA

SALES BREAKDOWN

Product Segments†	Information Systems	517.09
	Imaging Systems	433.67
	Photofinishing Systems	301.35
Geographic Segments†		
	Japan	979.10
	Outside Japan	441.41
	Eliminations/Corporate	-168.39

Displayed Currency: Japanese Yen (1.00:1)

*I/B/E/S and I/B/E/S Express are registered trademarks of I/B/E/S International Inc. Copyright 1993–1996 I/B/E/S International Inc. All rights reserved.

†Values are displayed in billions.

FINANCIAL STATEMENT DATA

INCOME STATEMENT	1998	1997	1996	1995	1994
Net Sales or Revenues	1378.10	1252.12	1084.96	1089.93	1066.75
EBITDA	NA	255.78	221.84	234.55	235.82
Depreciation Depletion & Amort	NA	83.75	79.13	93.58	90.31
Operating Income	NA	164.70	133.44	127.99	134.85
Interest Expense	11.70	11.70	11.57	12.38	10.68
Pretax Income	NA	160.32	131.14	128.59	134.83
Net Income	88.83	85.35	72.87	64.48	63.77

BALANCE SHEET	1998	1997	1996	1995	1994
Assets					
Cash & Equivalents	NA	707.21	726.87	655.05	629.60
Receivables—Net	NA	240.83	218.57	209.69	219.08
Inventories	NA	218.84	200.54	187.88	174.55
Total Current Assets	NA	1215.35	1187.71	1090.05	1064.05
Property Plant & Eq.— Net	NA	438.19	408.40	393.82	397.19
Total Assets	NA	1965.58	1828.54	1722.89	1699.92
Liabilities & Shareholders' Equity					
Total Current Liabilities	NA	450.14	397.52	368.62	376.69
Long Term Debt	NA	47.04	63.92	65.27	61.50
Preferred Stock	NA	0.00	0.00	0.00	0.00
Common Equity	NA	1344.93	1252.52	1180.48	1155.58
Total Liabilities & Sh. Equity	NA	1965.58	1828.54	1722.89	1699.92

CASH FLOW	1998	1997	1996	1995	1994
Funds from Operations	NA	162.82	136.90	57.69	149.72
Total Sources	NA	237.76	227.99	48.41	81.93
Cash Dividends Paid— Total	NA	11.06	9.91	4.63	9.78

Fuji Photo Film Company

Total Uses	NA	237.36	227.99	48.41	81.93
Incr/Decr in Working Capital	NA	-24.97	68.76	34.08	106.21
Free Cash Flow	NA	167.05	144.31	211.61	183.44

INTERNATIONAL BUSINESS	1998	1997	1996	1995	1994
Foreign Assets	NA	484.22	330.94	NA	NA
Foreign Sales	NA	441.41	330.68	307.37	293.70
Foreign Income	NA	19.04	11.21	NA	NA

SUPPLEMENTARY DATA	1998	1997	1996	1995	1994
Employees	NA	33154	29903	27565	11692
R&D Expenses	NA	75.92	73.19	76.77	73.90
Goodwill/Cost in Excess of Assets Purchased	NA	NA	NA	NA	NA
Extra Items & Gain/ Loss in Sale of Assets	NA	0.00	0.00	0.00	0.00

Displayed Currency: Japanese Yen (1.00:1)
All values are displayed in billions (except employees).

FINANCIAL RATIOS AND GROWTH RATES

PROFITABILITY	1998	1997	1996	1995	1994	5YR AVG
Operating Profit Margin %	NA	13.15	12.30	11.74	12.64	12.46
Tax Rate %	NA	53.32	51.08	54.55	55.27	53.56
Net Margin %	NA	6.82	6.72	5.92	5.98	6.36
Return on Assets %	NA	5.09	4.67	4.27	4.31	4.59
Return on Equity— Total %	NA	6.81	6.17	5.58	5.78	6.09
Cash Flow % Sales	NA	13.00	12.62	5.29	14.04	11.24
Sales per Employee (in 000s)	NA	37767	36283	39540	91237	51207

ASSET UTILIZATION	1998	1997	1996	1995	1994	5YR AVG
Total Asset Turnover	NA	0.64	0.59	0.63	0.63	0.62
Capital Exp % Gross Fixed Assets	NA	6.98	6.55	2.05	4.83	5.10
Acc Depreciation % Gross Fixed Assets	NA	65.52	65.50	64.77	63.37	64.79
Assets per Employee (in 000s)	NA	59286	61149	62503	145392	82083

LIQUIDITY	1998	1997	1996	1995	1994	5YR AVG
Current Ratio	NA	2.70	2.99	2.96	2.82	2.87
Quick Ratio	NA	2.11	2.38	2.35	2.25	2.27

LEVERAGE	1998	1997	1996	1995	1994	5YR AVG
Total Debt % Common Equity	NA	14.47	15.66	16.47	17.40	16.00
Long Term Debt % Common Equity	NA	3.50	5.10	5.53	5.32	4.86
Common Equity % Total Assets	NA	68.42	68.50	68.52	67.98	68.35
Long Term Debt % Total Capital	NA	3.33	4.79	5.18	4.99	4.57
Operating Cash/ Fixed Charges	NA	13.91	11.83	4.66	14.02	11.10

GROWTH %	1998	1997	1996	1995	1994	5YR AVG
Net Sales	10.06	15.41	-0.46	2.17	-1.84	4.86
Operating Income	NA	23.42	4.26	-5.09	-3.92	NA
Total Assets	NA	7.49	6.13	1.35	3.39	NA
Earnings per Share*	4.07	17.13	13.02	1.11	4.65	7.83
Dividends per Share*	2.27	4.76	7.69	8.33	0.00	4.56
Book Value per Share	NA	7.38	6.10	2.15	4.69	NA

Displayed Currency: Japanese Yen (1.00:1)
*Source: Worldscope. Value may differ from I/B/E/S.
Note: 5-Year Average calculations exclude NAs.

PER SHARE AND RELATED DATA

SOURCE: WORLDSCOPE	1998	1997	1996	1995	1994
Earnings per Share	172.6	165.9	141.6	125.3	123.9
Dividends per Share	22.5	22.0	21.0	19.5	18.0
Book Value per Share	NA	2613.5	2433.8	2293.9	2245.5
Total Investment Return	NA	NA	49.56	-9.59	-8.34
Market Price (Year-end)	4960.0	4070.0	3060.0	2060.0	2300.0
Market Capitalization (in billions)	NA	2094.43	1574.75	1060.12	1183.62
Price/Earnings Ratio	28.74	24.54	21.61	16.44	18.56
Price/Book Value	NA	1.56	1.26	0.90	1.02
Dividend Yield	0.45	0.54	0.69	0.95	0.78
Dividend Payout per Share	13.04	13.26	14.83	15.56	14.53
Common Shares Outstanding (Year-end) in Millions	NA	514.60	514.63	514.63	514.63
Stock Split/Dividend Ratio	NA	NA	NA	NA	NA
Type of Share	Common				

Displayed Currency: Japanese Yen (1.00:1)
Note: Data is sourced from Worldscope and may differ from I/B/E/S historical data.

18. Fujitsu Limited

Japan's most aggressive computer company has adopted the motto of providing "global solution links." It's the best equipped and most motivated of companies seeking profits in Internet and multimedia-related products and service. It's plowing billions of dollars into the research performed by the many bright young minds it hires.

Fujitsu Limited runs a close second with Hitachi for the number-two position behind IBM in the world mainframe computer market. It also makes telecommunications systems, information processing systems, semiconductors and electronic devices, and software. Slow demand and falling prices in personal computers and mobile telephones in Japan, declining semiconductor prices, Asian currency turmoil, and restructuring have taken their toll on its bottom line recently. That makes it crucial that the company make all of its worldwide efforts count more than ever. A giant global and vertically integrated firm such as Fujitsu—with leadership in networks, computers, electronic devices, software, and services—has the necessary staying power to weather a storm in any of its many regions.

Specifically, the company's products include hard disk drives, computer chips, image scanners, cellular phones, optical transmission systems, and telecommunications switches used to build networks. Its goal is to make notebook shipments about 50 percent of total personal computer sales. Fujitsu operates Japan's leading commercial online service, Nifty-Serve, with more than 1.5 million subscribers. It runs the WorldsAway graphics-supported chat room on the CompuServe online service. In addition, it holds U.S. patent rights for plasma display tech-

125

nology. Internet software products include Jasmine, a database for text and images built from chunks of software code called objects; Team Office, a "groupware" product similar to Lotus Notes; and Atlas translation software, used to translate Japanese into English. Its hardware includes personal computers and ultra–high-speed telecom automated teller machine switches. Fujitsu, Toshiba Corp., and Toyota Motor Corp. established a joint-venture company in 1998 to bring digital satellite broadcasts and information services to mobile users throughout Japan. The new company, called Nihon Mobile Broadcasting Corporation, is expected to start nationwide broadcasts of multichannel programming and multimedia services by the year 2001. It will target mobile users for the first time, including drivers and passengers, providing them with quality digital music, video, and information services, including car navigation and Internet services.

Founded in 1935, Fujitsu includes more than four hundred companies worldwide with offices, factories, and laboratories in over a hundred localities around the globe. From Australia to Zimbabwe, from Asia to Africa, Fujitsu is in a country nearby. This network keeps its customers at the cutting edge of information technology. Actively promoting the globalization of the entire group, Fujitsu consistently structures all of its development, manufacturing, and sales activities with a view to international markets.

"The global market environment has been favorable, with the world's markets uniting as globalization continues to speed ahead, and competition is intensifying," Tadashi Sekizawa, president and representative director, wrote in his letter in the most recent annual report.

Subsidiary Fujitsu Computer Products of America, which shipped 11 million computer disk drives in 1997, increased production significantly in 1998, with a goal of becoming one of the top three manufacturers. The company, which moved up from sixth place to fifth place in 1997, has ample backing from its parent firm to help it make its way in this volatile business. Price drops and oversupply were behind losses, layoffs, and dropping sales at the top three drive makers, who hold 20 percent of market share, and demand for under-$1,000 PCs squeezed margins tighter.

The company puts its money where its ambitions are. Subsidiary Fujitsu Microelectronics Incorporated (FMI) opened its expanded semiconductor manufacturing facility on a 200-acre site in Gresham, Oregon, in fall 1997. Representing a total investment of more than $41 billion, the enlarged 545,000-square-foot plant doubled FMI's production capacity in the United States. It mass produces 64-megabit SDRAM (Synchronous Dynamic Random Access Memory devices), processing eight-inch wafers in its personal computers, as well as in scientific computers, parallel processors, and other medical and instrument equipment.

Amdahl Corporation, a manufacturer of large computer systems and software, became a wholly-owned subsidiary of Fujitsu in fall 1997 when Fujitsu purchased all outstanding shares of Amdahl beyond the 42 percent it already owned. The Amdahl name and management team was retained and there were no employment-level reductions. That new relationship is the result of ties going back 25 years, when Fujitsu made its first investment in the start-up American firm. The two companies had jointly developed "mission-critical" servers, storage, and peripheral technologies for the U.S. and world markets. With the acquisition, the company has established an organizational structure in four major markets—the United States, Europe, Japan, and Asia—offering services globally. Uniform information systems and support are crucial throughout the world, and more and more products are being jointly developed and marketed worldwide.

Fujitsu Limited can be a good partner. It received GTE Corporation's 1997 Supplier of the Year award, providing GTE with equipment through two business units, Fujitsu Network Communications Inc. of Richardson, Texas, and Fujitsu Business Communication Systems in Anaheim, California. "Fujitsu's large size does not by itself guarantee stability," Sekizawa warned in a speech to new employees, who must take a test in English pro-

127

ficiency prior to their hiring because 90 percent of global Internet content is written in English. "The business environment in which we operate has changed greatly. It would be a mistake to assume that it will be easy for Fujitsu to continue to grow as fast as we have in the past."

18. FUJIITSU LIMITED

Japan   Ticker symbol FJTSY

One American Depositary Receipt represents five ordinary shares

ADR price $44 1/2 (9/16/98)   Dividend yield .80%

(Financial data from I/B/E/S International is in Japanese yen)*

BUSINESS DESCRIPTION

COMPUTERS/DATA PROCESSING SYSTEMS ACCOUNTED FOR 68% OF FISCAL 1997 REVENUES, COMMUNICATIONS SYSTEMS 23%, ELECTRONIC DEVICES, AND OTHER 9%

ADDRESS AND CONTACTS

Address	Marunouchi Center Building
	6-1, Marunouchi 1-Chome
	Chiyoda-ku Tokyo 100 Japan
Telephone	81-3-32167953
Fax	81-3-32169365

BASIC FINANCIAL INFORMATION

Capital Structure†	Long Term Debt:	NA
	Total Debt:	NA
	Common Sh. Equity:	NA

SALES BREAKDOWN

Product Segments†	Computers & Data	2974.95
	Communications Systems	855.05
	Electronic Devices	511.84
	Other Operations	161.64
Geographic Segments†	Japan	3762.23
	Outside Japan	1405.39
	Eliminations/Corporate	-664.14

Displayed Currency: Japanese Yen (1.00:1)
*I/B/E/S and I/B/E/S Express are registered trademarks of I/B/E/S International Inc. Copyright 1993–1996 I/B/E/S International Inc. All rights reserved.
†Values are displayed in billions.

Fujitsu Limited

FINANCIAL STATEMENT DATA

INCOME STATEMENT	1998	1997	1996	1995	1994
Net Sales or Revenues	NA	4503.47	3761.97	3257.71	3139.33
EBITDA	NA	481.48	413.88	355.69	305.14
Depreciation Depletion & Amort	NA	299.89	241.54	211.80	208.17
Operating Income	NA	179.02	190.93	156.00	97.27
Interest Expense	49.28	49.28	48.59	55.45	64.58
Pretax Income	NA	132.31	123.75	88.43	32.39
Net Income	NA	46.15	63.11	45.02	-37.67

BALANCE SHEET	1998	1997	1996	1995	1994
Assets					
Cash & Equivalents	NA	452.14	460.93	430.35	416.71
Receivables—Net	NA	1153.64	949.33	769.17	777.31
Inventories	NA	880.58	822.74	623.88	569.32
Total Current Assets	NA	2659.60	2423.90	2017.42	1914.94
Property Plant & Eq.— Net	NA	1261.28	1124.92	940.80	922.27
Total Assets	NA	4727.69	4324.49	3713.82	3594.74
Liabilities & Shareholders' Equity					
Total Current Liabilities	NA	2244.28	1955.93	1488.43	1479.95
Long Term Debt	NA	843.83	774.85	713.67	656.62
Preferred Stock	NA	0.00	0.00	0.00	0.00
Common Equity	NA	1181.49	1149.40	1100.31	1057.91
Total Liabilities & Sh. Equity	NA	4727.69	4324.82	3713.82	3594.74

CASH FLOW	1998	1997	1996	1995	1994
Funds from Operations	NA	392.06	313.44	255.35	278.27
Total Sources	NA	625.35	553.47	441.72	536.04
Cash Dividends Paid— Total	NA	18.41	18.29	18.17	10.88
Total Uses	NA	625.35	553.47	441.72	536.04
Incr/Decr in Working Capital	NA	-52.65	-61.02	94.00	15.78
Free Cash Flow	NA	42.51	25.02	127.40	103.95

INTERNATIONAL BUSINESS	1998	1997	1996	1995	1994
Foreign Assets	NA	1099.05	886.16	NA	NA
Foreign Sales	NA	1405.39	1102.69	881.74	812.10
Foreign Income	NA	-20.41	15.03	23.23	NA

SUPPLEMENTARY DATA	1998	1997	1996	1995	1994
Employees	NA	46795	165056	164364	163990
R&D Expenses	NA	352.82	346.39	323.90	329.92
Goodwill/Cost in Excess of Assets Purchased	NA	137.67	133.96	158.22	170.01
Extra Items & Gain/ Loss in Sale of Assets	NA	0.00	0.00	0.00	0.00

Displayed Currency: Japanese Yen (1.00:1)
All values are displayed in billions (except employees).

FINANCIAL RATIOS AND GROWTH RATES

PROFITABILITY	1998	1997	1996	1995	1994	5YR AVG
Operating Profit Margin %	NA	3.98	5.08	4.79	3.10	4.23
Tax Rate %	NA	56.56	45.83	45.81	88.96	59.29
Net Margin %	NA	1.02	1.68	1.38	-1.20	0.72
Return on Assets %	NA	1.82	2.56	2.27	0.13	1.70
Return on Equity— Total %	NA	4.01	5.74	4.26	-3.42	2.65
Cash Flow % Sales	NA	8.71	8.33	7.84	8.86	8.44
Sales per Employee (in 000s)	NA	96238	22792	19820	19143	39498

ASSET UTILIZATION	1998	1997	1996	1995	1994	5YR AVG
Total Asset Turnover	NA	0.95	0.87	0.88	0.87	0.89
Capital Exp % Gross Fixed Assets	NA	13.73	13.51	8.85	8.11	11.05
Acc Depreciation % Gross Fixed Assets	NA	60.55	60.91	63.52	62.83	61.95
Assets per Employee (in 000s)	NA	101030	26200	22595	21921	42936

LIQUIDITY	1998	1997	1996	1995	1994	5YR AVG
Current Ratio	NA	1.19	1.24	1.36	1.29	1.27
Quick Ratio	NA	0.72	0.72	0.81	0.81	0.76

LEVERAGE	1998	1997	1996	1995	1994	5YR AVG
Total Debt % Common Equity	NA	144.89	133.33	116.79	122.27	129.32
Long Term Debt % Common Equity	NA	71.42	67.41	64.86	62.07	66.44
Common Equity % Total Assets	NA	24.99	26.58	29.63	29.43	27.66

Fujitsu Limited

Long Term Debt %						
Total Capital	NA	38.48	37.22	36.36	35.43	36.87
Operating Cash/						
Fixed Charges	NA	7.96	6.45	4.60	4.31	5.83

GROWTH %	1998	1997	1996	1995	1994	5YR AVG
Net Sales	NA	19.71	15.48	3.77	-9.32	NA
Operating Income	NA	-6.24	22.39	60.38	61.88	NA
Total Assets	NA	9.32	16.44	3.31	-4.80	NA
Earnings per Share*	NA	-27.30	39.10	-+	N-	NA
Dividends per Share*	NA	0.00	0.00	25.00	0.00	NA
Book Value per Share	NA	2.79	3.08	3.99	-4.10	NA

Displayed Currency: Japanese Yen (1.00:1)
*Source: Worldscope. Value may differ from I/B/E/S.
Note: 5-Year Average calculations exclude NAs.

PER SHARE AND RELATED DATA

SOURCE: WORLDSCOPE	1998	1997	1996	1995	1994
Earnings per Share	NA	25.1	34.5	24.8	-20.8
Dividends per Share	NA	10.0	10.0	10.0	8.0
Book Value per Share	NA	641.6	624.2	605.6	582.4
Total Investment Return	NA	NA	15.26	-14.22	63.17
Market Price (Year-end)	NA	1260.0	987.0	865.0	1020.0
Market Capitalization					
(in billions)	NA	2320.13	1817.33	1571.57	1852.85
Price/Earnings Ratio	NA	50.28	28.63	34.91	NM
Price/Book Value	NA	1.96	1.58	1.43	1.75
Dividend Yield	NA	0.79	1.01	1.16	0.78
Dividend Payout per					
Share	NA	39.90	29.01	40.36	-38.54
Common Shares					
Outstanding					
(Year-end) in					
Millions	NA	1841.37	1841.27	1816.84	1816.52
Stock Split/Dividend					
Ratio	NA	NA	NA	NA	NA
Type of Share Common					

Displayed Currency: Japanese Yen (1.00:1)
Note: Data is sourced from Worldscope and may differ from I/B/E/S historical data.

131

19. General Electric Company

The Six Sigma approach to running a company is not new. This highly disciplined methodology of working companywide toward the engineer's concept of near-perfect quality was pioneered by Motorola Inc. and successfully carried out by Allied-Signal as well.

However, when it is taken seriously by someone with the stature of Jack Welch, General Electric Company's dynamic chairman and chief executive officer, it's elevated to a new prominence. The man who boldly restructured GE in the early 1980s is emphasizing Six Sigma as a centerpiece of his celebrated career as he aims toward his scheduled retirement in the year 2000. Six Sigma–trained GE employees are called "master black belts" or "black belts" and focus on every product and service that touches GE customers.

The five basic activities of Six Sigma are defining, measuring, analyzing, improving, and controlling. The focus is on improving employee productivity and reducing the company's capital expenditures, while increasing the quality, speed, and efficiency of the operation. As Six Sigma has expanded throughout GE over the past three years, projections of progress have repeatedly been scrapped because they underestimated what could be accomplished. For example, Six Sigma efforts have led to a tenfold increase in the life of CT scanner X-ray tubes, quadrupled the return on investment in its superabrasives business, and cut the repair time in its railcar leasing operations by 62 percent. It's no wonder GE's 1997 annual report was in large part dedicated to integrating the Six Sigma approach into all aspects of the company. The prediction now is that Six Sigma will contribute an extra $10 to $15 billion annually in revenue and cost savings by the end of the century.

Of course, General Electric already had a lot going for it before Six Sigma. Wall Street analysts have recommended its stock not just as a defensive safe haven with a stellar name, but because it's a good investment idea on its own. An enthusiastic attitude toward its own future, aggressive preparation to position itself to benefit from difficult environments, and a commitment to achieving worldwide leadership in each of its businesses are all parts of the total GE package. Among a myriad of other honors, it has been ranked America's Most Admired Company in the 1998 *Fortune* magazine survey of the country's business men and women. It was rated first in wealth creation by that same publication. Welch has been depicted on the cover of virtually every business magazine as a heavyweight among the world's CEOs.

Globalization is considered one of the engines of GE growth now and into the next century. Asia represents about 9 percent of revenues, about half of those in Japan, and the company is confident it can minimize any impact on existing operations from the Asian downturn. Welch is concerned about global over-capacity for GE businesses and for the world at large. However, as other top global companies have, GE sees the Asian situation as a unique opportunity to make strategic moves that will increase its presence and participation in one of the world's great markets of the twenty-first century. In fact, a number of Wall Street analysts expect to see modest ($100 to $200 million) opportunistic Asian acquisitions in areas such as financial services and manufacturing. GE views opportunities for such growth in the context of the European revival and the Mexican comeback, two markets that were written off by many pundits during their downturns. GE successfully used these downturns to expand its operations for future profitability. The company is convinced that bad business management or bad government policies can be remedied by tough restructuring and policy change.

As the company's top executives confidently pointed out in their letter to shareholders in the most recent annual report: "The same conditions that made restructuring and reform nec-

133

essary frequently create a currency weakness that, when coupled with the increased competitiveness brought about by restructuring, leads the country out of recession, via internal growth and increased exports. The path to greatness in Asia is irreversible, and GE will be there."

GE traces its beginnings to Thomas Edison, who established the Edison Electric Light Company in 1878. In 1892, a merger of the Edison General Electric company and the Thomson-Houston Electric Company created General Electric Company. GE is the only company listed on the Dow Jones industrial average today that was included in the original index in 1896. The fifth-largest U.S. corporation and world's third most profitable company has a vast empire with strong cash flow. If ranked independently, eight of GE's business units would be on the *Fortune* 500. GE provides financial services and produces industrial products, power-generation systems, aerospace systems, home appliances, locomotives, and engineered materials. It offers consumer- and commercial-financial and equipment-management services through its GE Capital Corp. subsidiary, which is one of the largest financial services companies in the United States. In addition, it owns the National Broadcasting Company, which includes the broadcast network, its owned-and-operated stations, and cable television interests. It has nearly 150 manufacturing plants throughout the United States and Puerto Rico, as well as more than a hundred plants in other countries. It employs 276,000 people worldwide, including 165,000 in the United States, and sells its products and services worldwide. It acquired the Greenwich/UNC jet engine service for $1.5 billion and the $600 million gas-turbine–related businesses of Stewart & Stevenson Services.

More than two-thirds of GE revenues now come from financial, information, and product services—an indication of its strength in global services. Analysts consider GE Capital the growth powerhouse in this mature company. If it were an independent company, GE Capital annual revenues would rank it number twenty on the *Fortune* 500, ahead of Citicorp. That's a long way from its beginnings in the 1930s as a captive finance subsidiary tied to the household appliance business. It has grown through acquisitions and expanded services to become the world's biggest equipment lessor, with, for example, 900 airplanes and 188,000 railcars, and has also been quickly expanding into computer services and life insurance as well. Rapid worldwide growth is undeniably its long-term future course.

19. GENERAL ELECTRIC COMPANY

United States   Ticker symbol GE

Stock price $80 7/8 (9/16/98)   Dividend yield 1.48%

(Financial data is from I/B/E/S International)*

BUSINESS DESCRIPTION

FINANCING ACTIVITIES ACCOUNTED FOR 33% OF 1997 REVENUES, INDUSTRIAL PRODUCTS 12%, POWER GENERATION 8%, MATERIALS 7%, AND OTHER PRODUCTS 40%

ADDRESS AND CONTACTS

Address	3135 Easton Turnpike
	Fairfield CT 06431-0001
Telephone	1-203-373-2211

BASIC FINANCIAL INFORMATION

Capital Structure†	Long Term Debt:	46603.00
	Total Debt:	144677.99
	Common Sh. Equity:	34438.00

SALES BREAKDOWN

Product Segments†	GE Capital Services	39931.00
	Aircraft Engines	7698.00
	Appliances	6733.00
	Broadcasting	5153.00
	Industrial	10464.00
Geographic Segments†	United States	63859.00
	Europe	17379.00
	Pacific Basin	3862.00
	Other	5740.00

Displayed Currency: U.S. Dollar (1.00:1)
*I/B/E/S and I/B/E/S Express are registered trademarks of I/B/E/S International Inc. Copyright 1993–1996 I/B/E/S International Inc. All rights reserved.
†Values are displayed in millions.

FINANCIAL STATEMENT DATA

INCOME STATEMENT	1997	1996	1995	1994	1993
Net Sales or Revenues	90777.00	79082.00	69948.00	60026.00	59827.00
EBITDA	22347.00	22764.00	20821.00	16987.00	17018.00
Depreciation Depletion & Amort	4082.00	3785.00	3594.00	3207.00	3261.00
Operating Income	42604.00	38500.00	32576.00	26684.00	30913.00
Interest Expense	7904.00	7904.00	7286.00	4970.00	7057.00
Pretax Income	9881.00	11075.00	9941.00	8831.00	6726.00
Net Income	NA	7280.00	6573.00	4726.00	4424.00

BALANCE SHEET	1997	1996	1995	1994	1993
Assets					
Cash & Equivalents	76482.00	64080.00	43890.00	33556.00	60194.00
Receivables—Net	8924.00	8704.00	8735.00	7527.00	8195.00
Inventories	5895.00	4473.00	4395.00	3880.00	3824.00
Total Current Assets	91301.00	77257.00	57020.00	44962.00	115676.00
Property Plant & Eq.— Net	32316.00	28795.00	25679.00	23465.00	21228.00
Total Assets	304012.00	272402.01	228035.00	194483.99	251506.00
Liabilities & Shareholders' Equity					
Total Current Liabilities	120668.00	100507.00	82001.00	72854.00	155729.00
Long Term Debt	46603.00	49246.00	51027.00	36979.00	28270.00
Preferred Stock	0.00	0.00	0.00	0.00	0.00
Common Equity	34438.00	31125.00	29690.00	26387.00	25824.00
Total Liabilities & Sh. Equity	304012.00	272402.01	228035.00	194483.99	251506.00

CASH FLOW	1997	1996	1995	1994	1993
Net Cash Flow— Operating	14240.00	17851.00	14946.00	13392.00	10187.00
Net Cash Flow— Investing	18275.00	20212.00	25217.00	16411.00	15591.00
Net Cash Flow— Financing	5705.00	3729.00	10503.00	2554.00	5493.00
Incr/Decr in Working Capital	-6117.00	1731.00	2910.00	12162.00	3371.00
Free Cash Flow	13959.00	15004.00	14374.00	9495.00	12279.00

INTERNATIONAL BUSINESS	1997	1996	1995	1994	1993
Foreign Assets	97357.00	82809.00	59331.00	33903.00	31798.00
Foreign Sales	24510.00	21069.00	17832.00	11872.00	10036.00
Foreign Income	3009.00	2576.00	1788.00	1268.00	793.00

General Electric Company

SUPPLEMENTARY

DATA	1997	1996	1995	1994	1993
Employees	276000	239000	222000	221000	222000
R&D Expenses	1891.00	1886.00	1299.00	1176.00	1297.00
Goodwill/Cost in Excess of Assets Purchased	16136.00	12523.00	9885.00	8118.00	7846.00
Extra Items & Gain/ Loss in Sale of Assets	0.00	0.00	0.00	0.00	-109.00

Displayed Currency: U.S. Dollar (1.00:1)
All values are displayed in millions (except employees).

FINANCIAL RATIOS AND GROWTH RATES

PROFITABILITY	1997	1996	1995	1994	1993	5YR AVG
Operating Profit Margin %	46.93	48.68	46.57	44.45	51.67	47.66
Tax Rate %	30.12	31.84	31.83	31.10	31.98	31.37
Net Margin %	9.04	9.21	9.40	7.87	7.21	8.54
Return on Assets %	5.04	5.48	5.85	3.18	4.64	4.84
Return on Equity— Total %	26.36	24.59	24.91	18.30	18.39	22.51
Cash Flow % Sales	15.62	21.71	21.84	15.97	6.38	16.30
Sales per Employee (in 000s)	329	331	315	272	269	303

ASSET UTILIZATION	1997	1996	1995	1994	1993	5YR AVG
Total Asset Turnover	0.30	0.29	0.31	0.31	0.24	0.29
Capital Exp % Gross Fixed Assets	15.07	15.28	14.03	17.98	12.41	14.95
Acc Depreciation % GrossFixed Assets	41.94	43.30	44.11	43.69	44.40	43.49
Assets per Employee (in 000s)	1101	1140	1027	880	1133	1056

LIQUIDITY	1997	1996	1995	1994	1993	5YR AVG
Current Ratio	0.76	0.77	0.70	0.62	0.74	0.72
Quick Ratio	0.71	0.72	0.64	0.56	0.44	0.62

LEVERAGE	1997	1996	1995	1994	1993	5YR AVG
Total Debt % Common Equity	420.11	415.89	390.05	359.12	350.08	387.05
Long Term Debt % Common Equity	135.32	158.22	172.34	140.14	109.47	143.10

LEVERAGE	1997	1996	1995	1994	1993	5YR AVG
Common Equity % Total Assets	11.33	11.43	12.98	13.57	10.27	11.91
Long Term Debt % Total Capital	55.01	59.06	61.04	56.70	50.71	56.51
Operating Cash/ Fixed Charges	1.69	2.17	2.10	1.93	0.54	1.69

GROWTH %	1997	1996	1995	1994	1993	5YR AVG
Net Sales	14.79	13.06	16.53	0.33	6.31	10.04
Operating Income	10.66	18.19	22.08	-13.68	10.82	8.84
Total Assets	11.60	19.46	17.25	-22.67	30.40	9.53
Earnings per Share*	11.82	12.53	41.16	6.74	-5.81	12.30
Dividends per Share*	13.68	12.43	13.42	14.18	12.50	13.24
Book Value per Share	11.68	6.52	14.87	2.26	10.31	9.04

Displayed Currency: U.S. Dollar (1.00:1)
*Source: Worldscope. Value may differ from I/B/E/S.
Note: 5-Year Average calculations exclude NAs.

PER SHARE AND RELATED DATA

SOURCE: WORLDSCOPE	1997	1996	1995	1994	1993
Earnings per Share	2.46	2.20	1.96	1.39	1.30
Dividends per Share	1.08	0.95	0.85	0.75	0.65
Book Value per Share	10.57	9.46	8.88	7.73	7.56
Total Investment Return	NA	NA	44.49	0.10	25.71
Market Price (Year-end)	73.38	49.44	36.00	25.50	26.22
Market Capitalization (in millions)	239539.44	162604.09	119988.86	87004.32	89526.65
Price/Earnings Ratio	29.83	22.47	18.41	18.41	20.21
Price/Book Value	6.94	5.22	4.05	3.30	3.47
Dividend Yield	1.47	1.92	2.35	2.92	2.49
Dividend Payout per Share	43.90	43.18	43.22	53.79	50.29
Common Shares Outstanding (Year-end) in Millions	3264.59	3289.08	3333.02	3411.93	3414.60
Stock Split/Dividend Ratio	1.00	0.50	0.50	0.50	0.25
Type of Share	*Common*				

Displayed Currency: U.S. Dollar (1.00:1)
Note: Data is sourced from Worldscope and may differ from I/B/E/S historical data.

20. Gucci Group N.V.

Quality, attention to detail, and a prestige brand name sell the world over.

Gucci Group, a turnaround success story, designs, produces, and distributes personal accessories with the famous interlocking G logo. Its products include leather handbags and luggage, which comprise 60 percent of sales, as well as shoes, ties, scarves, watches, jewelry, eyewear, and perfume. It also makes fashionable women's and men's ready-to-wear, a growth vehicle whose sales have been up significantly and have helped build local customer traffic. While Gucci manufactures some of its leather goods, other firms manufacture most of its leather goods and the rest of its products. The company directly operates eighty stores worldwide which exclusively carry Gucci items and has seventy-six franchise stores. Items are also sold in department stores and duty-free boutiques.

Nearly half of Gucci sales are from Asia and one-third from the United States. Japan has reeled from economic concerns and neither Hong Kong nor Hawaii have been particularly encouraging. Gucci's results and stock price have reflected those conditions, yet both should do well even if Japan's situation just manages to stay at an even keel. In fact, during an impressive 1997 fiscal year that ended January 31, 1998, Gucci's Japanese retail business grew at a double-digit rate, in part because consumers accelerated their spending in anticipation of a pending consumption tax. The yen-dollar rate, consumer confidence in Japan, and consumption in that country will continue to have an impact. The United States has also been under pressure, but sales have been strong in Europe, especially in key markets such as Italy, France, and Germany. Second quarter earnings rose 5.9 percent.

Gucci's investment profile has lately become more prominent, due in part to the attention of others. Privately-owned Italian fashion house Prada spent $240 million to buy 9.5 percent of Gucci in June 1998, thereby becoming its largest shareholder. That led to speculation that Prada would join with another company in a takeover of Gucci. In a U.S. Securities and Exchange Commission filing, Prada said it might consider a merger, an asset sale, a joint venture, or a change in Gucci's corporate structure. Still, Prada sent rather mixed signals after the purchase, stating that it was merely making an investment and then saying it hadn't actually ruled out a takeover. For its part, Gucci said it didn't think a merger would be a good idea. In addition, both companies have significant exposure to Asia. In the eyes of a number of stock analysts, underlying company fundamentals and takeover speculation combine to make Gucci shares a stylish choice.

Gucci was founded as a leather goods boutique in Florence, Italy, in 1923 by Guccio Gucci and remained in the founder's family until 1987 when Bahrain-based Investcorp began acquiring a stake in the company, completing the acquisition in 1993 before taking it public in 1994 and selling most of its stake. Family infighting and overproduction had left Gucci in deep, deep trouble and close to bankruptcy. There was no clear positioning of the company as either fashion-conscious or classic and its products were a jumble of items with no unified point of view. There had even been franchise negotiations with a tobacco company to market a Gucci cigarette.

However, in 1993 when President and Chief Executive Officer Domenico De Sole took over, he effectively cut production, improved quality, and refurbished stores in order to revitalize the company. This Harvard-educated attorney, who began his association with Gucci since the early seventies as its legal adviser and later ran Gucci U.S.A., emphasized fashion and quality, while repricing items lower to provide more value to the customer. He did away with unsuccessful product lines and closed the lavish Milan headquarters, relocating the company back to Florence. He's also been reducing the number of upscale retailers carrying Gucci in order to be more exclusive. De Sole visits stores in even the most distant locations to make sure they're up to Gucci quality.

"We are concentrating on control over each aspect of design, manufacturing, advertising, and distribution of Gucci merchandise," De Sole wrote in a recent half-year report. "This includes maintaining a rigorous policy of brand exclusivity, closing doors where necessary. We will continue to open new stores in important markets like Japan and Europe, as well as expanding and refurbishing existing stores in appropriate markets."

Gucci's inventories, receivables, and cash balances have never looked better, even in a difficult retailing environment in many regions of the world. At the same time, expansion, especially in emerging market nations, is an important part of De Sole's game plan. Gucci's recent fashion lines have been particularly well received around the world, thanks in great measure to the successful work of designer Tom Ford.

Most of Gucci's sales come from less than 100 of its stores around the world, and once they and others have been fully transformed to make the most of an expanding line of products, the prospects for the company will be even stronger. Future growth will come from these stores and well-chosen new locations. Gucci added 20 percent more floor space with new stores in 1998, with about 36 percent of those new stores in Japan. Aggressive and confident expansion in Asia during 1998 included six new Gucci stores, one men's boutique in Japan, and two stores in the new Hong Kong airport. A flagship location in Tokyo was set for spring 1999. Gucci acquired 51 percent of the stock of Shiatos Taiwan Company Limited, Gucci's franchisee in Taiwan, in a cash transaction in 1998 and renamed it Gucci Taiwan Limited. That operation has nine exclusive retail stores that sell Gucci products in Taiwan, including four in Taipei, one in Tainan, two in Taichung, two in Kaohsing, and a duty-free shop in downtown Taipei. Gucci opened seventeen new stores during its 1998 fiscal year.

In Europe, in 1998 it opened new stores in Zurich, Vienna, Monte Carlo, and a 10,000-square-foot flagship store in Milan.

New U.S. stores opened in Las Vegas and Kona. Major refurbishings in Paris, Beverly Hills, and Costa Mesa, California, also took place in 1998. In a $150 million cash transaction, Gucci purchased the operations of its watch licensee Severin Montres, now called Gucci Timepieces, in late 1997. This move enabled the company to control all aspects of design, production, marketing, and distribution of Gucci watches. It has closed a number of wholesale operations in order to maintain the long-term exclusivity and value of the Gucci brand—a goal it is pursuing for all its products these days.

Tight control of an enviable franchise that almost got away, that's what's behind the new and improved Gucci. A single-minded De Sole points to the company's benchmark principles: "Leadership in design, coupled with impeccable quality; focus on providing superior value to the consumer; tight control of distribution; striving for absolute consistency in image and presentation worldwide." All of which might sound corny, except that Gucci management believes it with a passion and is daily proving just how serious it is about boldly maintaining its name and special place in retailing.

20. GUCCI GROUP N.V.

Netherlands   Ticker symbol GUC

One New York registered share represents one ordinary share

Stock price $39 7/8 (9/16/98)   Dividend yield 1%

(Financial data from I/B/E/S International is in Netherland guilder)*

BUSINESS DESCRIPTION

LEATHER GOODS ACCOUNTED FOR 59% OF FISCAL 1997 REVENUES, SHOES 18%, READY-TO-WEAR 9%, ROYALTIES 4%, TIES AND SCARFS 5%, WATCHES, AND OTHER 5%

ADDRESS AND CONTACTS

Address	Rembrandt Toren
	Amstelplein 1 Netherlands
Telephone	31-20-462-1700
Fax	31-20-465-3569

Gucci Group N.V.

BASIC FINANCIAL INFORMATION

Capital Structure†
Long Term Debt:	NA
Total Debt:	NA
Common Sh. Equity:	NA

SALES BREAKDOWN

Product Segments†

Leather Goods	886.86
Royalties	65.51
Ready-to-wear	129.32
Shoes	263.74
Ties and Scarves	69.08

Geographic Segments†

USA	290.63
Asia	392.04
Europe	180.56
Other	17.44

Displayed Currency: Netherland Guilder (1.00:1)

*I/B/E/S and I/B/E/S Express are registered trademarks of I/B/E/S International Inc. Copyright 1993–1996 I/B/E/S International Inc. All rights reserved.

†Values are displayed in millions.

FINANCIAL STATEMENT DATA

INCOME STATEMENT	1998	1997	1996	1995	1994
Net Sales or Revenues	975.40	1498.52	937.12	474.17	378.27
EBITDA	NA	463.51	261.36	67.65	-3.17
Depreciation Depletion & Amort	NA	19.51	19.39	17.97	24.00
Operating Income	NA	406.86	225.11	56.62	7.94
Interest Expense	3.87	3.87	29.87	15.49	12.42
Pretax Income	NA	440.13	212.10	34.20	-39.59
Net Income	175.50	286.50	152.53	31.06	-42.52

BALANCE SHEET	1998	1997	1996	1995	1994
Assets					
Cash & Equivalents	NA	424.92	216.05	65.26	44.04
Receivables—Net	NA	126.82	43.92	23.22	21.84
Inventories	NA	248.39	124.56	86.06	84.93
Total Current Assets	NA	966.99	455.90	203.20	170.27
Property Plant & Eq.— Net	NA	115.31	116.28	115.16	156.90
Total Assets	NA	1128.70	595.42	334.61	351.75
Liabilities & Shareholders' Equity					
Total Current Liabilities	NA	491.54	230.34	168.21	280.94
Long Term Debt	NA	0.00	1.58	380.11	4.06
Preferred Stock	NA	0.00	0.00	0.00	0.00
Common Equity	NA	601.60	331.83	-241.39	29.22
Total Liabilities & Sh. Equity	NA	1128.70	549.42	334.61	351.75

CASH FLOW	1998	1997	1996	1995	1994
Funds from Operations	NA	313.14	175.26	55.22	-18.52
Total Sources	NA	99.30	455.33	11.21	44.16
Cash Dividends Paid—					
Total	NA	29.69	0.00	0.00	0.00
Total Uses	NA	99.30	455.33	11.21	44.16
Incr/Decr in Working					
Capital	NA	249.89	190.57	145.67	-39.44
Free Cash Flow	NA	408.27	232.69	59.55	-10.20

INTERNATIONAL BUSINESS	1998	1997	1996	1995	1994
Foreign Assets	NA	235.17	261.82	192.47	226.01
Foreign Sales	NA	1191.29	536.72	38.82	302.72
Foreign Income	NA	292.12	106.00	4.44	-28.19

SUPPLEMENTARY DATA	1998	1997	1996	1995	1994
Employees	NA	1504	1176	1096	1187
R&D Expenses	NA	NA	NA	NA	NA
Goodwill/Cost in					
Excess of Assets					
Purchased	NA	0.00	4.05	4.01	4.62
Extra Items & Gain/					
Loss in Sale of Assets	NA	0.00	0.00	0.00	0.00

Displayed Currency: Netherland Guilder (1.00:1)
All values are displayed in millions (except employees).

FINANCIAL RATIOS AND GROWTH RATES

PROFITABILITY	1998	1997	1996	1995	1994	5YR AVG
Operating Profit						
Margin %	NA	27.15	24.02	11.94	2.10	16.30
Tax Rate %	NA	34.91	28.09	9.16	NA	24.05
Net Margin %	17.99	19.12	16.28	6.55	-11.24	9.74
Return on Assets %	15.55	48.55	51.47	11.74	-8.80	23.70
Return on Equity—						
Total %	29.17	86.34	NA	106.30	-47.96	43.46
Cash Flow % Sales	NA	20.90	18.70	11.65	-4.90	11.59
Sales per Employee						
(in 000s)	NA	996	797	433	319	636

ASSET UTILIZATION	1998	1997	1996	1995	1994	5YR AVG
Total Asset Turnover	NA	1.33	1.57	1.42	1.08	1.35
Capital Exp % Gross						
Fixed Assets	NA	23.61	13.12	3.92	2.73	10.85
Acc Depreciation %						
Gross Fixed Assets	NA	50.72	46.76	44.27	38.98	45.18
Assets per Employee						
(in 000s)	NA	750	506	305	296	465

Gucci Group N.V.

LIQUIDITY	1998	1997	1996	1995	1994	5YR AVG
Current Ratio	NA	1.97	1.98	1.21	0.61	1.44
Quick Ratio	NA	1.12	1.13	0.53	0.23	0.75

LEVERAGE	1998	1997	1996	1995	1994	5YR AVG
Total Debt % Common Equity	NA	8.06	0.58	-173.39	572.91	102.04
Long Term Debt % Common Equity	NA	0.00	0.48	-157.47	13.89	-35.77
Common Equity % Total Assets	NA	53.30	55.73	-72.14	8.31	11.30
Long Term Debt % Total Capital	NA	0.00	0.47	274.01	12.20	71.67
Operating Cash/ Fixed Charges	NA	80.82	5.87	3.57	-1.49	22.19

GROWTH %	1998	1997	1996	1995	1994	5YR AVG
Net Sales	-34.91	59.91	97.63	25.35	8.13	22.76
Operating Income	NA	80.73	297.59	613.21	-+	NA
Total Assets	NA	89.56	77.94	-4.87	-9.86	NA
Earnings per Share*	-37.82	51.88	352.31	-+	N+	-+
Dividends per Share*	NA	50.15	-+	0.00	0.00	NA
Book Value per Share	NA	77.65	-+	-926.01	-67.04	NA

Displayed Currency: Netherland Guilder (1.00:1)
*Source: Worldscope. Value may differ from I/B/E/S.
Note: 5-Year Average calculations exclude NAs.

PER SHARE AND RELATED DATA

SOURCE: WORLDSCOPE	1998	1997	1996	1995	1994
Earnings per Share	2.92	4.70	3.09	0.68	-0.95
Dividends per Share	NA	0.77	0.51	0.00	0.00
Book Value per Share	NA	10.08	5.67	-5.36	0.65
Total Investment Return	NA	NA	NA	NA	NA
Market Price (Year-end)	82.00	124.20	68.80	NA	NA
Market Capitalization (in millions)	NA	7414.96	4024.81	NA	NA
Price/Earnings Ratio	28.08	26.45	22.25	NA	NA
Price/Book Value	NA	12.33	12.13	NA	NA
Dividend Yield	NA	0.62	0.74	NA	NA
Dividend Payout per Share	NA	16.35	16.54	0.00	0.00
Common Shares Outstanding (Year-end) in Millions	NA	59.70	58.50	45.00	45.00
Stock Split/Dividend Ratio	NA	NA	NA	NA	NA
Type of Share	Aandeel Op Naam				

Displayed Currency: Netherland Guilder (1.00:1)
Note: Data is sourced from Worldscope and may differ from I/B/E/S historical data.

21. Hewlett-Packard Company

Close, but no cigar. At least, not yet.

While Hewlett-Packard Company is considered the classiest company in the computer industry and merits an impressive number-five spot on *Fortune* magazine's list of America's Most Admired Companies, it has lately missed the lofty expectations Wall Street set for it. For example, despite rising printer and personal computer sales, the company acknowledged in the first half of fiscal 1998 that earnings fell "well short" of expectations. The reasons given were cutthroat PC pricing pressures and economic weakness in Asia that hurt divisions such as measurement systems. The earlier exuberance of analysts, who had expected Hewlett-Packard to rise above the competition and had strongly touted its stock, quickly turned to stinging criticism of the company for not keeping everyone well informed of its sales and bottom line. The company's strong increase in revenue wasn't enough to assuage their unhappiness. Chairman, President, and Chief Executive Officer Lewis Platt announced he would take bold steps to get rising expenses under control. For example, he imposed the latest of several pay cuts in August 1998, a three-month, 5 percent reduction for about 2,400 mid- to upper-level managers. He also said the firm would close its U.S. offices for four days between Christmas and the New Year, and ask its operations outside the United States to shut down for comparable four-day periods.

To believe in Hewlett-Packard as an investment is to believe in its long-term quality as a company and its ability to push itself to the next level. It has come a long way and has done so in a thoughtful, well-thought-out manner. It was started humbly in a garage in Palo Alto, California, in 1939 by Dave Packard and Bill Hewlett, where they built the audio oscillators used to provide sound for the Disney film *Fantasia*.

Hewlett-Packard is now the world's second-largest maker of personal computers behind IBM. It is famous for peripherals such as the HP LaserJet and HP DeskJet printers. Its new HP 4000 printers produce 1,200 dots per inch print equivalent at full engine speed—an important innovation over competitors who must cut engine speed by half to achieve the highest quality output possible on their printers. Its new HP DeskJet 722C printer, which has improved color through several new technologies offering better resolution and smaller ink dot size, supports Intel's MMX technology for fast performance.

In addition, it's the number-two worldwide maker of PC servers based on Windows NT and the number-one commercial UNIX server vendor by revenue. It has installed thousands of data center systems with its customers. For example, when Barnes & Noble launched its barnesandnoble.com Web site, it chose Hewlett-Packard NetServer LX Pro systems and Microsoft Windows NT for its front-end search-engine and e-commerce functions. Hewlett-Packard's ability to effectively integrate these system platforms is why it was chosen. The company also makes digital scanners and data-storage tapes. It's best known as a printer maker, with 80 percent of sales coming from computer peripherals and computer-related services. Hewlett-Packard has 121,900 employees and 600 sales and support offices worldwide.

Hewlett-Packard is counting on the rough-and-tumble PC business to serve as a growth vehicle now that the highly successful printer group, which had grown at a dramatic pace for years, may be slowing a bit due to competition. Thus far, computers have been a business with significant growth but one that has not produced profits due to the all-out price battles with competitors such as Compaq Computer. Hewlett-Packard, which introduced the world's first scientific handheld calculator back in 1972, also manufactures testing and measurement equipment and medical electronics. It is moving into new markets such as document copying and digital photography. The company entered into electronic commerce with its $1.3 billion acquisition of VeriFone, which makes small terminals that process credit- and debit-card transactions. Meanwhile, its new line of Internet commerce software called HP Domain Commerce lets big companies set up online express checkout lanes for their favorite customers. The company acquired Heartstream in 1998. Foreign sales account for more than half of Hewlett-Packard's revenues.

No company can go it alone these days, for alliances and agreements to use equipment have become critical. For example, four of the leading suppliers of the software that is used to control small electronic devices have licensed Hewlett-Packard's version of the Java programming language, a real boost to efforts by the company to create a version of Java to rival that of Sun Microsystems Incorporated. Hewlett-Packard intends to offer its own version of Java for use in printers, consumer-electronics products, and other devices that aren't traditional computers because it was unhappy about Sun's tight control of developing and licensing Java. In yet another venture, Hewlett-Packard and Cisco Systems Inc. agreed to a broad technology development, Internet solutions, and customer support alliance. This agreement expanded an ongoing relationship to more fully integrate computing, networking, and network management. Hewlett-Packard is hedging its bets by collaborating with Microsoft to "ruggedize" its Windows NT network operating system and is helping Intel design its next-generation chip to run operating systems other than Windows. There have been pressures beyond trouble meeting analyst estimates in today's high-tech world. Xerox Corp. filed suit in May 1998 against Hewlett-Packard, accusing the company of violating its patents related to ink-jet printers, seeking a permanent injunction barring it from manufacturing and selling color ink-jet printers and supplies.

With the customer the obvious linchpin to future efforts, Hewlett-Packard is working harder on developing stronger consumer branding. Early in fiscal year 1998, it began a strong push to become a household name in the consumer market. The theme "Expanding Possibilities," along with the HP logo, is the new signature for all consumer marketing. It appears on products and is supported by an aggressive consumer-advertising campaign and retail-communications program for the full spectrum of consumers. Also with customers in mind, Hewlett-Packard has moved its computer organization from a sales force organized strictly by its products to one organized by customers and sales channels so the company becomes easier for customers to work with.

As Hewlett-Packard gets its act together providing surprisingly good profits, the entire company intends to kick into high gear. "Amid the profound changes in our industry, we hear one consistent message from customers and partners: the importance of speed," Platt wrote in his letter in the most recent annual report. "Our customers and partners' success is increasingly dependent on their ability to bring products to market and deliver services rapidly and more efficiently. To help organizations accomplish this, we in turn have to move much more nimbly than in the past."

---

21. HEWLETT-PACKARD COMPANY

United States   Ticker symbol HWP

Stock price $51 (9/16/98)   Dividend yield 1.25%

(Financial data is from I/B/E/S International)*

BUSINESS DESCRIPTION

DESIGNS, MANUFACTURES, AND SERVICES PRECISION ELECTRONIC INSTRUMENTS AND SYSTEMS FOR MEASUREMENT, ANALYSIS, AND COMPUTATIONS

ADDRESS AND CONTACTS

Address   3000 Hanover Street
                     Palo Alto CA 94304
Telephone   1-415-857-1501

BASIC FINANCIAL INFORMATION

Capital Structure[†]	Long Term Debt:	3158.00
	Total Debt:	4304.00
	Common Sh. Equity:	16155.00

SALES BREAKDOWN

Product Segments[†]	Computer Products	35449.00
	Electronic Test	4297.00
	Medical Electronics	1265.00
	Electronic Components	975.00
	Chemical Analysis	909.00
Geographic Segments[†]	United States	19076.00
	Europe	14332.00
	Asia Pacific, Canada	9487.00

Displayed Currency: U.S. Dollar (1.00:1)

*I/B/E/S and I/B/E/S Express are registered trademarks of I/B/E/S International Inc. Copyright 1993–1996 I/B/E/S International Inc. All rights reserved.

[†]Values are displayed in millions.

FINANCIAL STATEMENT DATA

INCOME STATEMENT	1997	1996	1995	1994	1993
Net Sales or Revenues	42895.00	38420.00	31519.00	24991.00	20317.00
EBITDA	6226.00	5318.00	4977.00	3584.00	2750.00
Depreciation Depletion & Amort	1556.00	1297.00	1139.00	1006.00	846.00
Operating Income	4339.00	3726.00	3568.00	2549.00	1879.00
Interest Expense	327.00	327.00	206.00	155.00	121.00
Pretax Income	4455.00	3694.00	3632.00	2423.00	1783.00
Net Income	3229.00	2586.00	2433.00	1599.00	1177.00

BALANCE SHEET	1997	1996	1995	1994	1993
Assets					
Cash & Equivalents	4569.00	3327.00	2616.00	2478.00	1644.00
Receivables—Net	8173.00	7126.00	6735.00	5028.00	4208.00
Inventories	6763.00	6401.00	6013.00	4273.00	3691.00
Total Current Assets	20947.00	17991.00	16239.00	12509.00	10236.00
Property Plant & Eq.—Net	6312.00	5536.00	4711.00	4328.00	4180.00
Total Assets	31749.00	27699.00	24427.00	19567.00	16736.00
Liabilities & Shareholders' Equity					
Total Current Liabilities	11219.00	10623.00	10944.00	8230.00	6868.00
Long Term Debt	3158.00	2579.00	663.00	547.00	667.00
Preferred Stock	0.00	0.00	0.00	0.00	0.00
Common Equity	16155.00	13438.00	11839.00	9926.00	8511.00
Total Liabilities & Sh. Equity	31749.00	27699.00	24427.00	19567.00	16736.00

CASH FLOW	1997	1996	1995	1994	1993
Net Cash Flow— Operating	4321.00	3456.00	1613.00	2224.00	1142.00
Net Cash Flow— Investing	3012.00	2175.00	1175.00	1610.00	1604.00
Net Cash Flow— Financing	-1122.00	-369.00	178.00	-146.00	710.00
Incr/Decr in Working Capital	2360.00	2073.00	1016.00	911.00	783.00
Free Cash Flow	3888.00	3117.00	3376.00	2327.00	1345.00

INTERNATIONAL BUSINESS	1997	1996	1995	1994	1993
Foreign Assets	18259.00	15191.00	13022.00	9043.00	7508.00
Foreign Sales	23819.00	21379.00	17556.00	13522.00	14665.00
Foreign Income	2574.00	1942.00	2170.00	1484.00	1077.00

SUPPLEMENTARY DATA	1997	1996	1995	1994	1993
Employees	121900	112000	102300	98400	96200
R&D Expenses	3078.00	2718.00	2302.00	2027.00	1761.00
Goodwill/Cost in Excess of Assets Purchased	NA	NA	NA	NA	NA
Extra Items & Gain/ Loss in Sale of Assets	0.00	0.00	0.00	0.00	0.00

Displayed Currency: U.S. Dollar (1.00:1)
All values are displayed in millions (except employees).

FINANCIAL RATIOS AND GROWTH RATES

PROFITABILITY	1997	1996	1995	1994	1993	5YR AVG
Operating Profit Margin %	10.12	9.70	11.32	10.20	9.25	10.12
Tax Rate %	29.99	29.99	33.01	34.01	33.99	32.20
Net Margin %	7.27	6.73	7.72	6.40	5.79	6.78
Return on Assets %	11.77	11.47	13.13	10.17	9.17	11.14
Return on Equity— Total %	23.21	21.84	24.51	18.79	15.70	20.81
Cash Flow % Sales	9.78	9.12	10.31	9.80	9.28	9.66
Sales per Employee (in 000s)	352	343	308	254	211	294

ASSET UTILIZATION	1997	1996	1995	1994	1993	5YR AVG
Total Asset Turnover	1.35	1.39	1.29	1.28	1.21	1.30
Capital Exp % Gross Fixed Assets	19.85	21.58	18.30	15.84	18.67	18.85
Acc Depreciation % Gross Fixed Assets	46.40	45.71	46.14	45.48	44.47	45.64
Assets per Employee (in 000s)	260	247	239	199	174	224

LIQUIDITY	1997	1996	1995	1994	1993	5YR AVG
Current Ratio	1.87	1.69	1.48	1.52	1.49	1.61
Quick Ratio	1.14	0.98	0.85	0.91	0.85	0.95

LEVERAGE	1997	1996	1995	1994	1993	5YR AVG
Total Debt % Common Equity	27.14	35.01	32.75	30.38	33.57	31.77
Long Term Debt % Common Equity	19.55	19.19	5.60	5.51	7.84	11.54
Common Equity % Total Assets	50.88	48.51	48.47	50.73	50.85	49.89
Long Term Debt % Total Capital	16.35	16.10	5.30	5.22	7.27	10.05
Operating Cash/ Fixed Charges	19.51	10.72	15.78	15.80	15.59	15.48

GROWTH %	1997	1996	1995	1994	1993	5YR AVG
Net Sales	11.65	21.89	26.12	23.01	23.81	21.19
Operating Income	16.45	4.43	39.98	35.66	33.83	25.32
Total Assets	14.62	13.40	24.84	16.92	22.16	18.30
Earnings per Share*	19.92	6.26	50.81	32.04	33.24	27.59
Dividends per Share*	17.39	22.67	30.43	21.05	18.75	21.98
Book Value per Share	16.35	14.91	15.93	15.66	12.65	15.09

Displayed Currency: U.S. Dollar (1.00:1)
*Source: Worldscope. Value may differ from I/B/E/S.
Note: 5-Year Average calculations exclude NAs.

PER SHARE AND RELATED DATA

SOURCE: WORLDSCOPE	1997	1996	1995	1994	1993
Earnings per Share	2.95	2.46	2.32	1.54	1.16
Dividends per Share	0.54	0.46	0.38	0.29	0.24
Book Value per Share	15.09	12.97	11.29	9.74	8.42
Total Investment Return	NA	21.10	69.21	27.88	14.42
Market Price (Year-end)	62.38	50.25	41.88	24.97	19.75
Market Capitalization (in millions)	64934.99	50959.68	42708.73	25450.85	19964.33
Price/Earnings Ratio	21.14	20.43	18.09	16.27	16.99
Price/Book Value	4.13	3.87	3.71	2.56	2.35
Dividend Yield	0.87	0.92	0.90	1.15	1.20
Dividend Payout per Share	18.31	18.70	16.20	18.73	20.43
Common Shares Outstanding (Year-end) in Millions	1041.04	1014.12	1019.91	1019.31	1010.85
Stock Split/Dividend Ratio	NA	NA	0.50	0.25	0.25

Type of Share Common

Displayed Currency: U.S. Dollar (1.00:1)
Note: Data is sourced from Worldscope and may differ from I/B/E/S historical data.

22. Honda Motor Company

Although Asian economic woes exact a toll on its business, Honda Motor Company has maintained its cruising speed as it passed through that tollbooth.

Much-admired Honda is the number-three carmaker in Japan after Toyota and Nissan and the world's largest maker of motorcycles. From its beginnings in 1948, the youngest of Japan's carmakers has created a global network with eighty-nine production facilities in thirty-three countries that supply Honda products to most countries in the world. Popular car models that hold their resale value due to dependability and precision designs include the Honda Accord, Civic, and Prelude, as well as the upscale Acura line. Sales outside of Japan account for nearly 70 percent of total sales and cars make up about 80 percent of the company's profits. Best of all, worldwide sales continue to grow despite turmoil in the Pacific region. Honda also makes all-terrain vehicles, small engines, lawn mowers, portable generators, and outboard motors. In order to deal better with tough competition and currency fluctuations, Honda has significantly expanded its North American manufacturing operations, where its profitability per vehicle has been improving rapidly.

Honda's share price was driven down by fears about the effects of the Asian economic crisis on earnings, but that's all the more reason to buy, many analysts believe. Turmoil in the Asian market, especially Thailand and Indonesia, has had considerably more effect on Honda's extensive motorcycle operations, which range from small scooters to highway cruisers, than on its all-important motor vehicle sales. Still, in the spring of 1998 Honda cut its temporary work force to 2,800 from 3,600 the prior year, and overall, there's an uneasy tug-of-war between the difficult Asian business and the boost to profits from the United States.

In somewhat of a surprise, fifty-eight-year-old Hiroyuki Yoshino, president of Honda's research and development division, was named president and chief executive officer of the carmaker in 1998. He replaced Nobuhiko Kawamoto, who retired after eight successful years at the top. Record profits and the overtaking of Mitsubishi Motors Co. as Japan's number-three carmaker were some of his major accomplishments. Though no one expected the changing of the guard so soon and some analysts had expected a younger choice, Yoshino is expected to run Honda much as Kawamoto did. For example, both were on the project team that developed engine emission controls in the late 1960s and 1970s that gave Honda a boost in the U.S. market with the CVCC engine for the Honda Civic.

Engineering, manufacturing, and sales have all been components of Yoshino's background. His many challenges include not only holding on to the company's gained market share, but slicing vehicle development time from the current two years to twenty months. Upon being named to the new post by Kawamoto, Yoshino said he hoped to add value to the carmaker that will last through future generations. Another worrisome consideration is the economic trouble in Honda's home country. "The reasons for Japan's troubled economy are complicated and complex," said Kawamoto, who points out that ongoing cost cuts and successful new models have helped keep Honda profitable even in Japan. "We are prepared even if these conditions continue forever. We will survive."

Honda worked hard to "prime the pump" of sales in beleaguered Japan in 1998. For example, it began offering information on new models through personal computers at more than a thousand convenience stores in the Tokyo metropolitan area, targeting younger drivers in order to help improve the sluggish Japanese consumer market. In addition, Honda introduced its new Capa, a compact multipurpose wagon, in Japan in early 1998 with a belief it has strong sales potential despite the decline in that country's car demand. The vehicle has a large interior but is still capable of maneuvering narrow Japanese roads, and is designed to aim for young families. Meanwhile, in a production move, Honda has put into effect a new parts purchasing system at its Suzuka manufacturing plant in Mie Prefecture in which detailed production plans and parts lists are submitted to suppliers one week in advance. Shipments can then be made on a regular basis, rather than the many deliveries required with the existing just-in-time method. It hopes to put the new system into effect at other facilities in Japan and overseas. Meanwhile, Honda decided to stop making cars in New Zealand as of the fall of 1998 following a decision by that country's government to remove all import taxes on imported motor vehicles. The end of tariffs meant there was no longer an advantage to building cars locally when foreign-made vehicles could be brought in more cheaply.

To gain worldwide attention, Honda has been active in international automobile and motorcycle racing for decades. Its racing circuit at Suzuka is one of the world's major racetracks. In addition, its Twin Ring Motegi interactive motorsports facility, opened in 1997, features a European-style road course and American-style speedway. Besides motorsports events, it allows visitors to participate in motorsports on a variety of facilities and short courses, and offers safety instruction programs.

In explaining its international stance, Honda points to its commitment to local markets and economies. Its philosophy is to produce where there is market demand by integrating with local customs and cultures and making use of local management resources. It builds products that meet the specific needs in each world market region, including the Americas; Europe, the Middle East, and Africa; Asia and Oceania; and Japan. For example, the new Honda Accord features two designs: one tailored to the needs of the U.S. market and one suited to the Japanese. There's already a European version of that same Accord. In another example, the Acura 3.0CL, introduced in North America in 1996, comes equipped with a V-6 engine built exclusively in the United States. Honda's global network enables the exchange of ideas and information among employees to assure a higher level of creativity in its technology and products. It continues its worldview with production facilities in burgeoning countries. In 1998, Honda opened several new factories in emerging markets, including car plants in Turkey, India, and Brazil, as well as a motorcycle factory in Vietnam.

When you climb behind the wheel of any Honda automobile, it instills the same reassuring feel that its vehicles have for decades. It is a comfortable feel that, though tailored somewhat to each region of the world, is a bit like coming home again. Honda is a company with a strong corporate identity that continues to fascinate the world, even when some of its markets undergo hard times.

22. HONDA MOTOR COMPANY

Japan   Ticker symbol HMC

One American Depositary Receipt represents two ordinary shares

ADR price $65 1/2 (9/16/98)   Dividend yield .42%

(Financial data from I/B/E/S International is in Japanese yen)*

BUSINESS DESCRIPTION

AUTOMOBILE BUSINESS ACCOUNTED FOR 80% OF FISCAL 1997 REVENUES, MOTORCYCLE BUSINESS 13%, FINANCIAL SERVICES 2%, AND OTHER BUSINESS 5%

ADDRESS AND CONTACTS

Address	1-1, Minami-Aoyama 2-Chome
	Minato-ku Tokyo 107 Japan
Telephone	81-3-34231111
Fax	81-3-54121515

BASIC FINANCIAL INFORMATION

Capital Structure[†]	Long Term Debt:	NA
	Total Debt:	NA
	Common Sh. Equity:	NA

SALES BREAKDOWN

Product Segments[†]	Automobile Business	4229.06
	Motorcycle Business	689.46
	Power Products	280.78
	Financial Services	94.01

Honda Motor Company

Geographic Segments[†]		
	Japan	3372.31
	Outside Japan	3296.91
	Eliminations	-1375.92

Displayed Currency: Japanese Yen (1.00:1)

*I/B/E/S and I/B/E/S Express are registered trademarks of I/B/E/S International Inc. Copyright 1993–1996 I/B/E/S International Inc. All rights reserved.

[†]Values are displayed in billions.

FINANCIAL STATEMENT DATA

INCOME STATEMENT	1998	1997	1996	1995	1994
Net Sales or Revenues	6000.00	5293.30	4252.25	3966.16	3862.72
EBITDA	NA	559.59	270.74	253.78	225.50
Depreciation Depletion & Amort	NA	141.35	125.01	125.11	143.23
Operating Income	NA	401.45	143.63	107.92	78.33
Interest Expense	27.51	27.51	30.60	34.38	35.38
Pretax Income	443.30	390.72	115.13	94.29	46.89
Net Income	NA	NA	NA	NA	23.71

BALANCE SHEET	1998	1997	1996	1995	1994
Assets					
Cash & Equivalents	NA	359.15	299.16	202.99	186.76
Receivables—Net	NA	770.79	640.74	497.60	487.38
Inventories	NA	551.15	489.33	512.31	586.97
Total Current Assets	NA	1961.25	1636.70	1367.38	1420.09
Property Plant & Eq.— Net	NA	1036.48	926.95	886.65	919.61
Total Assets	NA	4176.62	3498.23	2994.73	2908.80
Liabilities & Shareholders' Equity					
Total Current Liabilities	NA	1808.70	1517.54	1262.28	1243.19
Long Term Debt	NA	734.25	656.46	589.54	612.51
Preferred Stock	NA	0.00	0.00	0.00	0.00
Common Equity	NA	1388.43	1144.54	1017.46	967.34
Total Liabilities & Sh. Equity	NA	4176.62	3498.23	2994.73	2908.80

CASH FLOW	1998	1997	1996	1995	1994
Funds from Operations	NA	344.21	186.28	170.05	183.84
Total Sources	NA	1849.24	1287.14	1044.61	933.44
Cash Dividends Paid—Total	NA	13.64	13.64	13.64	13.63
Total Uses	NA	1849.24	1287.14	1044.61	933.44
Incr/Decr in Working Capital	NA	33.39	14.06	-71.80	117.82
Free Cash Flow	NA	341.81	120.25	125.14	103.66

157

INTERNATIONAL BUSINESS	1998	1997	1996	1995	1994
Foreign Assets	NA	2227.91	1664.02	1026.07	1022.83
Foreign Sales	NA	3296.91	2520.45	2430.43	2295.48
Foreign Income	NA	202.47	61.70	54.00	17.41

SUPPLEMENTARY DATA	1998	1997	1996	1995	1994
Employees	NA	101100	96800	92800	91300
R&D Expenses	NA	251.13	220.57	203.00	188.81
Goodwill/Cost in Excess of Assets Purchased	NA	NA	NA	NA	NA
Extra Items & Gain/ Loss in Sale of Assets	NA	NA	NA	NA	0.00

Displayed Currency: Japanese Yen (1.00:1)
All values are displayed in billions (except employees).

FINANCIAL RATIOS AND GROWTH RATES

PROFITABILITY	1998	1997	1996	1995	1994	5YR AVG
Operating Profit Margin %	NA	7.58	3.38	2.72	2.03	3.93
Tax Rate %	NA	48.38	50.62	47.62	71.91	54.63
Net Margin %	NA	4.18	1.67	1.55	0.61	2.00
Return on Assets %	NA	6.84	3.04	2.90	1.56	3.58
Return on Equity— Total %	NA	19.32	6.96	6.36	2.29	8.73
Cash Flow % Sales	NA	6.50	4.38	4.29	4.76	4.98
Sales per Employee (in 000s)	NA	52357	43928	42739	42308	45333

ASSET UTILIZATION	1998	1997	1996	1995	1994	5YR AVG
Total Asset Turnover	NA	1.27	1.22	1.32	1.33	1.28
Capital Exp % Gross Fixed Assets	NA	8.11	6.16	5.66	5.40	6.33
Acc Depreciation % Gross Fixed Assets	NA	61.41	62.03	61.00	59.25	60.92
Assets per Employee (in 000s)	NA	41312	36139	32271	31860	35395

LIQUIDITY	1998	1997	1996	1995	1994	5YR AVG
Current Ratio	NA	1.08	1.08	1.08	1.14	1.10
Quick Ratio	NA	0.62	0.62	0.56	0.54	0.59

Honda Motor Company

LEVERAGE	1998	1997	1996	1995	1994	5YR AVG
Total Debt %						
Common Equity	NA	88.66	106.31	104.00	115.92	103.72
Long Term Debt %						
Common Equity	NA	52.88	57.36	57.94	63.32	57.88
Common Equity %						
Total Assets	NA	33.24	32.72	33.98	33.26	33.30
Long Term Debt %						
Total Capital	NA	34.03	35.98	36.26	38.16	36.11
Operating Cash/						
Fixed Charges	NA	12.51	6.09	4.95	5.20	7.19

GROWTH %	1998	1997	1996	1995	1994	5YR AVG
Net Sales	13.35	24.48	7.21	2.68	-6.53	7.74
Operating Income	NA	179.49	33.10	37.77	-27.98	NA
Total Assets	NA	19.39	16.81	2.95	-3.34	NA
Earnings per Share*	17.85	212.50	15.29	159.47	-37.95	46.88
Dividends per Share*	20.00	7.14	0.00	0.00	0.00	5.15
Book Value per Share	NA	21.31	12.48	5.13	-6.69	NA

Displayed Currency: Japanese Yen (1.00:1)
*Source: Worldscope. Value may differ from I/B/E/S.
Note: 5-Year Average calculations exclude NAs.

PER SHARE AND RELATED DATA

SOURCE: WORLDSCOPE	1998	1997	1996	1995	1994
Earnings per Share	267.5	227.0	72.6	63.0	24.3
Dividends per Share	18.0	15.0	14.0	14.0	14.0
Book Value per Share	NA	1425.0	1174.7	1044.4	993.5
Total Investment Return	NA	NA	58.38	-9.45	11.68
Market Price (Year-end)	4800.0	3690.0	2330.0	1480.0	1650.0
Market Capitalization					
(in billions)	NA	3595.26	2270.14	1441.78	1606.63
Price/Earnings Ratio	17.94	16.26	32.08	23.49	67.96
Price/Book Value	NA	2.59	1.98	1.42	1.66
Dividend Yield	0.38	0.41	0.60	0.95	0.85
Dividend Payout per					
Share	6.73	6.61	19.28	22.22	57.66
Common Shares					
Outstanding					
(Year-end) in					
Millions	NA	974.31	974.30	974.17	973.70
Stock Split/Dividend Ratio	NA	NA	NA	NA	NA
Type of Share	Common				

Displayed Currency: Japanese Yen (1.00:1)
Note. Data is sourced from Worldscope and may differ from I/B/E/S historical data.

159

23. Hutchison Whampoa Limited

Value and superior growth: That's what Hutchison Whampoa Limited, a giant Hong Kong–based international conglomerate, consistently creates. It has earned a reputation for stable earnings, flexible operations, and resilience in coping with changing economic conditions. Its stock is a bet on the future of Hong Kong and China, and opportunities that will abound throughout the rest of Asia once economic turmoil eases.

With origins dating back to the 1800s, Hutchison boasts extensive interests in shipping, food processing and distribution, retailing, and manufacturing. It is also involved in real estate as a major landholder and hotel operator in Hong Kong. The company's Asian telecommunications holdings are a part of subsidiary Hutchison Telecommunications and include cellular phone and paging businesses. Its shipping interests involve majority interests in container and other terminal facilities in Hong Kong, China, and the United Kingdom. The company also has energy, finance, and investment holdings. Its development of both residential and commercial properties has had a significant impact on the Hong Kong property market, one example being Whampoa Garden, an estate of eighty-eight residential towers containing more than 10,000 flats that was completed in 1991. That expansive development also includes schools, a transport terminal, and shopping arcades.

One of Hong Kong's largest blue-chip companies, with 30,000 employees worldwide, Hutchison is part of Cheung Kong Limited Group, whose chairman, Li Kashing, is also chairman of Hutchison. A successful tycoon ranked as one of the world's wealthiest men, Li and his family own a controlling

160

interest in the company. With more than forty years of involvement in major Hong Kong commercial developments, Li has been an advisor on Hong Kong affairs to the Chinese government and served on various high-level committees that coordinated the turnover of Hong Kong to mainland control.

Adding to the company's attractiveness, Hutchison has a number of independent operating units that have excellent spin-off potential, leaving the opportunity to create still more value. It has endless ways to obtain cash and improve its bottom line, such as it did when it sold its stakes in Asia Satellite Telecommunications Holdings Limited and Procter & Gamble–Hutchison Limited in 1997. The company is committed to a policy of maintaining controlled growth of existing businesses in Hong Kong and other major Chinese cities, while also looking toward the "prudent" expansion of those businesses into overseas markets. Its prospects reflect the tremendous importance of China's economy in the region and the potential for per-capita income there to grow dramatically.

This fascinating company's many divisions have unique histories. For example, its property group was originally established in 1863 to acquire docks and repair yards at Whampoa, on the Canton River in China. It ran one of the largest dry-docking, ship repair, and shipbuilding operations in the Far East for over a century, surviving two world wars. At its peak, it was handling an average of twenty-five vessels each week. In 1960, it was servicing the ships of more than twenty-three nations. The company ventured into property development in 1969 and, by the late 1970s, its business was mostly property-related, with the Aberdeen and Hung Hom docks being redeveloped into today's Aberdeen Centre, Hunghom Bay Centre, Whampoa Garden, and the Harbourfront. Meanwhile, the company's A.S. Watson & Co. Limited, one of the best-known trading names in Asia, began as a small dispensary in Guangzhou, China, in 1828 before being opened in Hong Kong in 1841. It became one of the first companies in the world to produce carbonated soft drinks. By the turn of the century, A.S. Watson had become a major trading force in Hong Kong, China, and the Philippines, with more than

100 retailing and dispensing branches. Today it has more than 700 stores and manufactures and markets more than twenty international food and beverage brands.

Hutchison's strong competitive position and influential contacts continue to help it obtain lucrative deals, such as telecommunications ventures in China. Since the implementation of the "one country–two systems" principle in the reunification of China, Hutchison's operations in Hong Kong, mainland China, and in more than twenty other countries around the globe have continued to grow steadily. As China further strengthens its reform policies, there should be greater expansion opportunities. The company intends to keep Hong Kong as its base of operations. Despite the Asian region's unprecedented financial turmoil, the impact on the group was nominal due to the diversification of its businesses both in industry and geographic terms, except for a property project in Hong Kong.

While the group's portfolio of investment properties recorded improved rental levels, financial turmoil in Hong Kong and Southeast Asia exerted some pressure on rental levels in 1998. Among its large commercial efforts, Cheung Kong Center is being built on the site of the former Hilton Hotel in Hong Kong. Part of the tower was opened for occupation by the end of 1998, with the second phase—underground parking and the rest of the development—to be completed in the year 2000.

The telecommunications business has made impressive gains in Hong Kong market share and the launch of its PCS network was well received by consumers. Internationally, the group increased cellular subscriber levels in India and Australia and acquired a cellular operator in Sri Lanka. The company also acquired an interest in a U.S.-based PCS business providing service to an area with total population of 66 million. In Europe, Orange Plc. passed the 1-million-subscribers mark to account for 25 percent of the United Kingdom's cellular market growth. Regarding its oil holdings, Husky Oil in Canada has substantially increased its earnings, along with significant growth in shareholder value, cash flow, and production volumes. In addition, Hutchison was given the contract to operate the Atlantic and

Pacific ports of the Panama Canal in 1997. (The United States turns over full control of the canal to Panama in 1999.)

Hutchison's long-term fundamentals and financial position remain strong. Steps have recently been taken to lengthen the term of the group's financing, to further strengthen its financial position, and to enhance its cash flow and liquidity. Chairman Li asserted in his letter in the most recent annual report: "With its solid base of recurrent quality income, strong cash flow, and financial position, the group is well-positioned to move forward to the next century with confidence."

23. HUTCHISON WHAMPOA LIMITED

Hong Kong   Ticker symbol HUWHY

One American Depositary Receipt represents five ordinary shares

ADR price $24 1/4 (9/16/98)   Dividend yield 2.12%

(Financial data from I/B/E/S International is in Hong Kong dollar)*

BUSINESS DESCRIPTION

RETAIL, MANUFACTURING, AND OTHER SERVICES ACCOUNTED FOR 49% OF 1996 REVENUES, PORTS AND RELATED SERVICES 21%, TELECOMMUNICATIONS 19%, AND OTHER 11%

ADDRESS AND CONTACTS

Address	Hutchison House
	22nd Floor
	Hong Kong
Telephone	852-25230161
Fax	852-28100705

BASIC FINANCIAL INFORMATION

Capital Structure[†]	Long Term Debt:	72719.50
	Total Debt:	83195.40
	Common Sh. Equity:	85589.00

SALES BREAKDOWN

Product Segments[†]	Retail, Manufacturing	18102.00
	Ports & Related Services	7813.00
	Telecommunications	7042.00
	Property	2156.00
	Energy, Finance	1549.00

SALES BREAKDOWN

Geographic
Segments†

Hong Kong	25563.00
Asia	6526.00
Europe	4254.00
North America	319.00

Displayed Currency: Hong Kong Dollar (1.00:1)
*I/B/E/S and I/B/E/S Express are registered trademarks of I/B/E/S International Inc. Copyright 1993–1996 I/B/E/S International Inc. All rights reserved.
†Values are displayed in millions.

FINANCIAL STATEMENT DATA

INCOME STATEMENT	1997	1996	1995	1994	1993
Net Sales or Revenues	44590.00	36662.00	35026.00	30168.00	24748.00
EBITDA	18763.70	15449.00	12770.00	7881.30	6848.00
Depreciation Depletion & Amort	2938.50	2529.90	2606.70	1493.10	1423.40
Operating Income	9050.40	8819.10	9407.30	6388.20	5903.60
Interest Expense	2818.30	2818.30	2896.60	1607.00	1148.50
Pretax Income	11180.00	10362.00	7279.00	5141.00	4408.00
Net Income	NA	12020.00	9567.00	8021.00	6304.00

BALANCE SHEET	1997	1996	1995	1994	1993
Assets					
Cash & Equivalents	NA	10839.70	16398.60	12513.10	6153.40
Receivables—Net	NA	5081.00	4570.60	3379.60	2313.60
Inventories	NA	2463.90	2688.80	1957.90	1584.00
Total Current Assets	NA	18385.00	23658.00	17850.60	10351.00
Property Plant & Eq.— Net	NA	63188.00	54508.00	52191.90	42292.00
Total Assets	202336.80	131873.70	119504.50	194618.00	81895.00
Liabilities & Shareholders' Equity					
Total Current Liabilities	30106.90	20288.00	28987.00	17489.50	17158.00
Long Term Debt	72719.50	34453.70	26152.70	26175.60	14235.20
Preferred Stock	0.00	0.00	0.00	0.00	0.00
Common Equity	85589.00	68899.00	58839.00	57156.90	49061.00
Total Liabilities & Sh. Equity	202336.80	131873.70	119504.50	194618.00	81895.00

CASH FLOW	1997	1996	1995	1994	1993
Funds from Operations	10609.30	9590.50	9808.20	8505.20	6044.00
Total Sources	NA	53524.70	29020.30	31713.30	20611.00
Cash Dividends Paid— Total	6043.00	4594.00	3614.00	2714.00	1996.00
Total Uses	NA	53524.70	29020.30	31713.30	20611.00

Incr/Decr in Working					
Capital	NA	3426.00	-5690.10	7168.10	-2877.00
Free Cash Flow	NA	2485.00	6459.00	719.30	3139.00

INTERNATIONAL BUSINESS	1997	1996	1995	1994	1993
Foreign Assets	NA	NA	NA	NA	NA
Foreign Sales	NA	11099.00	12625.00	9072.00	6302.00
Foreign Income	NA	1416.00	830.00	-595.00	264.00

SUPPLEMENTARY DATA	1997	1996	1995	1994	1993
Employees	NA	27733	29137	26855	22489
R&D Expenses	NA	NA	NA	NA	NA
Goodwill/Cost in Excess of Assets Purchased	NA	0.00	0.00	0.00	0.00
Extra Items & Gain/ Loss in Sale of Assets	NA	0.00	0.00	0.00	0.00

Displayed Currency: Hong Kong Dollar (1.00:1)
All values are displayed in millions (except employees).

FINANCIAL RATIOS AND GROWTH RATES

PROFITABILITY	1997	1996	1995	1994	1993	5YR AVG
Operating Profit Margin %	20.30	24.06	26.86	21.18	23.85	23.25
Tax Rate %	NA	7.32	8.18	18.51	20.25	13.57
Net Margin %	27.51	32.79	27.31	26.59	25.47	27.93
Return on Assets %	11.63	11.47	5.89	10.80	10.56	10.07
Return on Equity— Total %	NA	20.43	16.74	16.35	17.59	17.78
Cash Flow % Sales	23.79	26.16	28.00	28.19	24.42	26.11
Sales per Employee (in 000s)	NA	1322	1202	1123	1100	1187

ASSET UTILIZATION	1997	1996	1995	1994	1993	5YR AVG
Total Asset Turnover	0.22	0.28	0.29	0.16	0.30	0.25
Capital Exp % Gross Fixed Assets	NA	18.00	10.02	13.16	8.25	12.36
Acc Depreciation % Gross Fixed Assets	NA	12.27	13.47	4.12	5.92	8.94
Assets per Employee (in 000s)	NA	4755	4101	7247	3642	4936

LIQUIDITY	1997	1996	1995	1994	1993	5YR AVG
Current Ratio	NA	0.91	0.82	1.02	0.60	0.84
Quick Ratio	NA	0.78	0.72	0.91	0.51	0.73

LEVERAGE	1997	1996	1995	1994	1993	5YR AVG
Total Debt %						
Common Equity	97.20	58.94	68.77	56.88	46.75	65.71
Long Term Debt %						
Common Equity	84.96	50.01	44.45	45.80	29.02	50.85
Common Equity %						
Total Assets	42.30	52.25	49.24	29.37	59.91	46.61
Long Term Debt %						
Total Capital	42.64	30.99	28.95	29.58	22.06	30.85
Operating Cash/						
Fixed Charges	2.28	3.40	3.39	5.29	5.26	3.93

GROWTH %	1997	1996	1995	1994	1993	5YR AVG
Net Sales	21.62	4.67	16.10	21.90	17.68	16.22
Operating Income	2.62	-6.25	47.26	8.21	58.65	19.45
Total Assets	53.43	10.35	-38.60	137.64	23.97	25.09
Earnings per Share*	-3.31	25.28	19.37	24.02	79.00	26.27
Dividends per Share*	5.33	27.12	26.88	36.76	23.64	23.50
Book Value per Share	15.98	17.00	3.08	16.41	26.93	15.63

Displayed Currency: Hong Kong Dollar (1.00:1)
*Source: Worldscope. Value may differ from I/B/E/S.
Note: 5-Year Average calculations exclude NAs.

PER SHARE AND RELATED DATA

SOURCE: WORLDSCOPE	1997	1996	1995	1994	1993
Earnings per Share	3.210	3.320	2.650	2.220	1.790
Dividends per Share	1.580	1.500	1.180	0.930	0.680
Book Value per Share	22.088	19.044	16.277	15.791	13.564
Total Investment Return	NA	NA	54.25	-16.29	159.47
Market Price					
(Year-end)	48.600	60.750	47.100	31.300	38.500
Market Capitalization					
(in millions)	188319.83	219782.79	170259.89	113294.88	139249.98
Price/Earnings Ratio	15.14	18.30	17.77	14.10	21.51
Price/Book Value	2.20	3.19	2.89	1.98	2.84
Dividend Yield	3.25	2.47	2.51	2.97	1.77
Dividend Payout per					
Share	49.22	45.18	44.53	41.89	37.99
Common Shares					
Outstanding					
(Year-end) in					
Millions	3874.89	3617.82	3614.86	3619.64	3616.88
Stock Split/Dividend					
Ratio	NA	NA	NA	NA	1.00
Type of Share	*Ordinary*				

Displayed Currency: Hong Kong Dollar (1.00:1)
Note: Data is sourced from Worldscope and may differ from I/B/E/S historical data.

24. Intel Corporation

ntel inside" will never be quite the same. Intel Corporation, the world's number-one maker of microprocessors with 90 percent of the market, underwent a noteworthy changing of the guard on May 20, 1998, when the brilliant and passionate Andy Grove, *Time* magazine's 1997 Man of the Year, handed over his chief executive officer position to second-in-command Craig Barrett. Grove, who continues to provide advice as chairman, turned in an amazing 47 percent average annual return to shareholders during a CEO tenure that began in January 1987. No wonder the company ranked fourth on *Fortune* magazine's 1998 list of Most Admired Companies in America and Grove was *Chief Executive* magazine's 1997 Chief Executive of the Year.

Besides having to fill Grove's formidable shoes, President and CEO Barrett takes over at a time when this legendary company that always had the right answers must grapple with slower personal computer demand, declining computer prices, Asian economic woes, and federal antitrust scrutiny. Barrett certainly has the company background to deal with challenges. This detail-oriented metallurgist and former Stanford University professor was largely responsible for halting the onslaught of Japanese computer chips in the 1980s by working to successfully transform Intel's manufacturing operations into the world's most efficient. To keep on top of the business at the grassroots level, Barrett each year visits each of Intel's dozens of manufacturing facilities around the world.

Faced with declining profits that disappointed Wall Street analysts, Intel had cut 3,000 jobs through attrition and layoffs by year-end 1998 and informed PC makers of deep price cuts in coming quarters. Still, Wall Street's Intel "fans" believe this company, which was responsible for turning microprocessors into the brains of the computer world, can emerge impressively from a less-than-impressive period of declining earnings. After all, its ability to deliver PC technology gives it a competitive advantage, while effective marketing campaigns have made its name one of the best-known corporate monikers worldwide. In addition, it has a dynamic new strategy with streamlined manufacturing and an extensive product line that bridges the world of cheap computers and expensive servers. Critics, on the other hand, say the changing PC marketplace will continue to exert pressure on the firm's bottom line. Intel is especially feeling the heat from smaller competitors such as Advanced Micro Devices, National Semiconductor, and Cyrix, whose Pentium-compatible processors are getting a foothold in the market for under-$1,000 PCs. Yet Intel isn't rolling over and playing dead. Effective May 1, 1998, the company cut prices from 8.5 percent to as much as 42 percent on certain microprocessor chips for portable computers, reflecting a policy of changing pricing more frequently in today's highly competitive environment.

Intel microprocessors have been in IBM-compatible personal computers since the 1970s. It markets them under the Pentium, Pentium Pro, Pentium MMX, and Pentium II trademarks to original-equipment manufacturers in the United States and overseas. Intel also makes memory chips, graphics accelerator chips, computer modules and boards, network and communication products, and personal-conferencing products. New boss Barrett is expected to emphasize special PC chips for handling digital photography and video through a 1998 alliance with Eastman Kodak aimed at developing products and platforms. Networking equipment for smaller businesses and specialized efforts such as the company teaming up with SAP A.G. (see Chapter 41) to provide Internet transaction-processing services are also on his agenda. Entering the graphics chips market, Intel acquired Chips & Technologies in 1998. Intel has plants in Ireland, Israel, Malaysia, the Philippines, and the United States. Almost 60 percent of its sales are outside the United States. It will continue to upgrade products and facilities to work hard to maintain its dominant position.

Beyond providing strong returns to its investors, Intel itself is a smart investor. Many of the companies Intel has invested in went on to become hot Wall Street properties, among them Rambus Incorporated, Broadcom Corporation, Verisign Incorporated, At Home Corporation, and C Net Incorporated. In April 1998, Intel showed Wall Street about twenty of the smaller companies it has been investing in lately, such as eFusion Incorporated, which is developing a system to enable a single line to handle Internet and phone transmissions simultaneously, and Inktomi Corporation, which makes software to ease congestion on the overburdened Internet.

Industry and economic factors have weighed heavily on the company lately. Weaker-than-expected demand for products in early 1998 led to lower revenues in the Americas, Japan, and Europe, although revenue from the Asia-Pacific region was in fact stronger than it was at year-end 1997. The company expressed disappointment, pointing out that the PC industry seemed to have gotten ahead of itself, building more product than customers purchased. Yet corporate management continued to show its long-term confidence by investing in the future and approving an increase in its stock buyback program of 100 million additional shares.

Intel has introduced many new products, among them Pentium II processors running at 350 and 400 MHz, which are Intel's newest and highest performance processors for corporate and home users; and networking products such as the Express 8100 Router, Express 130T Standalone Hub, and the 82559 high-speed Ethernet controller. In addition, Dell Computer Corporation and Intel combined resources to devise initiatives to enable customers and software providers to transition their software applications to next-generation computing. However, Intel delayed by more than six months the delivery of its next generation Merced microprocessor because it had underestimated the testing involved. It now doesn't expect to make shipments of Merced until mid-2000.

In a sign of the times, dominant player Intel's name has come up in discussions about antitrust. The Federal Trade Commission during 1998 was looking at whether Intel illegally used monopoly power to harm rivals and punish anyone who didn't play by its rules. The FTC would first have to show that Intel is a monopoly, which means proving either that Intel could raise its prices without decreasing its market share, or that cutting its supply of chips would raise their market price. The FTC initially considered charges that Intel retaliated against three customers—Digital Equipment Corporation, Intergraph Corporation, and Compaq Computer Corporation—that sued the company in patent disputes. A U.S. District Court judge slapped an injunction on Intel to stop such behavior toward Intergraph. Intel appealed on the grounds that it has the right to withhold its technology from its customers. In addition, the FTC has been studying complaints that Intel discourages computer makers who buy processors from rivals, and that it increasingly holds sway on the basic design of PCs as well. Intel denies that it has a monopoly in the microprocessor market and does not believe that customers must have access to its advanced product information. The Intel suit is about complex patent disagreements with customers that may harm unspecified innovation in the future, and contends that Intel was tough on customers because they could become potential competitors. Critics of the government action believed it would have a hard time proving its case based on such vague charges and also that Intel is, in fact, facing growing competition from low-price rivals.

There's a lot of change under way in the PC industry and it is already affecting Intel. The greatest fear would be any major shift that opens the door to new competition or significantly changes the design of future systems, forcing Intel to dramatically alter its business model. As one of America's most savvy and adaptable companies, Intel is working hard to stay ahead of the game. In his book *Only the Paranoid Survive* (Doubleday, 1996), Andy Grove made a point about keeping pace: "Note that everywhere there are winners and losers. And note also that, to a large extent, whether a company became a winner or loser was related to its degree of adaptability. It is at such times of fundamental change that the cliché 'adapt or die' takes on its true meaning."

24. INTEL CORPORATION

United States   Ticker symbol INTC

Stock price $86 1/4   (9/16/98)   Dividend yield .14%

(Financial data is from I/B/E/S International)*

BUSINESS DESCRIPTION

DESIGNS, DEVELOPS, MANUFACTURES, AND MARKETS COMPUTER COMPONENTS AND RELATED PRODUCTS AT VARIOUS LEVELS OF INTEGRATION

ADDRESS AND CONTACTS

Address   2200 Mission College Boulevard
              Santa Clara CA 95052-8119
Telephone   1-408-765-8080

BASIC FINANCIAL INFORMATION

Capital Structure†	Long Term Debt:	448.00
	Total Debt:	770.00
	Common Sh. Equity:	19295.00

SALES BREAKDOWN

Product Segments†	Microcomputer Computers	25070.00
Geographic		
Segments†	United States	11053.00
	Europe	6774.00
	Asia Pacific	4754.00
	Japan	2489.00

Displayed Currency: U.S. Dollar (1.00:1)

*I/B/E/S and I/B/E/S Express are registered trademarks of I/B/E/S International Inc. Copyright 1993–1996 I/B/E/S International Inc. All rights reserved.

†Values are displayed in millions.

FINANCIAL STATEMENT DATA

INCOME STATEMENT	1997	1996	1995	1994	1993
Net Sales or Revenues	25070.00	20847.00	16202.00	11521.00	8782.00
EBITDA	12878.00	9847.00	7038.00	4688.00	4297.00
Depreciation Depletion & Amort	2192.00	1888.00	1371.00	1028.00	717.00

INCOME STATEMENT	1997	1996	1995	1994	1993
Operating Income	9887.00	7553.00	5252.00	3387.00	3392.00
Interest Expense	58.00	58.00	29.00	57.00	50.00
Pretax Income	10659.00	7934.00	5638.00	3603.00	3530.00
Net Income	6945.00	5157.00	3566.00	2288.00	2295.00

BALANCE SHEET	1997	1996	1995	1994	1993
Assets					
Cash & Equivalents	9927.00	7994.00	2458.00	2410.00	3136.00
Receivables—Net	3438.00	3723.00	3116.00	1978.00	1448.00
Inventories	1697.00	1293.00	2004.00	1169.00	838.00
Total Current Assets	15867.00	13684.00	8097.00	6167.00	5802.00
Property Plant & Eq.— Net	10666.00	8487.00	7471.00	5367.00	3996.0
Total Assets	28880.00	23735.00	17504.00	13816.00	11344.00
Liabilities & Shareholders' Equity					
Total Current Liabilities	6020.00	4863.00	3619.00	3024.00	2433.00
Long Term Debt	448.00	728.00	400.00	392.00	426.00
Preferred Stock	0.00	0.00	0.00	0.00	0.00
Common Equity	19295.00	16872.00	12140.00	9267.00	7500.00
Total Liabilities & Sh. Equity	28880.00	23735.00	17504.00	13816.00	11344.00

CASH FLOW	1997	1996	1995	1994	1993
Net Cash Flow— Operating	10008.00	8743.00	4026.00	2981.00	2801.00
Net Cash Flow— Investing	6859.00	5268.00	2687.00	2903.00	3337.00
Net Cash Flow— Financing	-3212.00	-773.00	-1056.00	-557.00	352.00
Incr/Decr in Working Capital	1026.00	4343.00	1335.00	-226.00	519.92
Free Cash Flow	8377.00	6823.00	3488.00	2247.00	2364.00

INTERNATIONAL BUSINESS	1997	1996	1995	1994	1993
Foreign Assets	4706.00	2496.00	4901.00	2940.00	2192.00
Foreign Sales	14017.00	15985.00	8280.00	5695.00	4366.00
Foreign Income	1789.00	4784.00	1937.00	1075.00	897.00

SUPPLEMENTARY DATA	1997	1996	1995	1994	1993
Employees	63700	48500	41600	32600	29500
R&D Expenses	2347.00	1808.00	1296.00	1111.00	970.00
Goodwill/Cost in Excess of Assets Purchased	NA	NA	NA	NA	NA
Extra Items & Gain/ Loss in Sale of Assets	0.00	0.00	0.00	0.00	0.00

Displayed Currency: U.S. Dollar (1.00:1)
All values are displayed in millions (except employees).

FINANCIAL RATIOS AND GROWTH RATES

PROFITABILITY	1997	1996	1995	1994	1993	5YR AVG
Operating Profit Margin %	39.44	36.23	32.42	29.40	38.62	35.22
Tax Rate %	34.84	35.00	36.75	36.50	34.99	35.62
Net Margin %	27.70	24.74	22.01	19.86	26.13	24.09
Return on Assets %	29.34	29.56	25.95	20.50	28.78	26.82
Return on Equity—Total %	41.16	42.48	38.48	30.51	42.15	38.96
Cash Flow % Sales	36.99	35.23	33.12	28.01	35.04	33.68
Sales per Employee (in 000s)	394	430	389	353	298	373

ASSET UTILIZATION	1997	1996	1995	1994	1993	5YR AVG
Total Asset Turnover	0.87	0.88	0.93	0.83	0.77	0.86
Capital Exp % Gross Fixed Assets	24.83	21.20	30.11	28.66	30.62	27.08
Acc Depreciation % Gross Fixed Assets	41.16	40.49	36.64	36.98	36.70	38.39
Assets per Employee (in 000s)	453	489	421	424	385	434

LIQUIDITY	1997	1996	1995	1994	1993	5YR AVG
Current Ratio	2.64	2.81	2.24	2.04	2.38	2.42
Quick Ratio	2.22	2.41	1.54	1.45	1.88	1.90

LEVERAGE	1997	1996	1995	1994	1993	5YR AVG
Total Debt % Common Equity	3.99	6.62	6.14	9.81	12.31	7.77
Long Term Debt % Common Equity	2.32	4.31	3.29	4.23	5.68	3.97
Common Equity % Total Assets	66.81	71.08	69.36	67.07	66.11	68.09
Long Term Debt % Total Capital	2.27	4.14	3.19	4.06	5.37	3.81
Operating Cash/ Fixed Charges	257.58	126.62	185.03	56.61	61.54	137.48

GROWTH %	1997	1996	1995	1994	1993	5YR AVG
Net Sales	20.26	28.67	40.63	31.19	50.27	33.81
Operating Income	30.90	43.81	55.06	-0.15	127.64	46.01
Total Assets	21.68	35.60	26.69	21.79	40.25	28.99
Earnings per Share*	33.22	44.17	53.82	0.77	109.26	44.17

GROWTH %	1997	1996	1995	1994	1993	5YR AVG
Dividends per Share*	21.05	26.67	30.43	-8.00	400.00	55.87
Book Value per Share	24.55	37.58	29.75	25.49	34.15	30.21

Displayed Currency: U.S. Dollar (1.00:1)
*Source: Worldscope. Value may differ from I/B/E/S.
Note: 5-Year Average calculations exclude NAs.

PER SHARE AND RELATED DATA

SOURCE: WORLDSCOPE	1997	1996	1995	1994	1993
Earnings per Share	3.87	2.91	2.02	1.31	1.30
Dividends per Share	0.12	0.10	0.08	0.06	0.06
Book Value per Share	11.86	9.52	6.92	5.34	4.25
Total Investment Return	NA	NA	78.16	3.40	43.10
Market Price (Year-end)	70.25	65.47	28.38	15.97	15.50
Market Capitalization (in millions)	114367.00	107500.10	46591.75	26380.37	25916.00
Price/Earnings Ratio	18.15	22.54	14.08	12.19	11.92
Price/Book Value	5.92	6.87	4.10	2.99	3.65
Dividend Yield	0.16	0.15	0.26	0.36	0.40
Dividend Payout per Share	2.97	3.27	3.72	4.39	4.81
Common Shares Outstanding (Year-end) in Millions	1628.00	1642.00	1642.00	1652.00	1672.00
Stock Split/Dividend Ratio	NA	0.50	0.50	0.25	0.25
Type of Share	Common				

Displayed Currency: U.S. Dollar (1.00:1)
Note: Data is sourced from Worldscope and may differ from I/B/E/S historical data.

25. Ito-Yokado Company

Whether you want a quick Slurpee drink, a family-size box of cereal, a sport shirt, or a set of golf clubs, Ito-Yokado Company is ready.

Japan's second-largest retailer is a sophisticated and innovative firm known for employing an efficient "just-in-time" point-of-sale inventory control system pioneered by Japan's auto industry. Ito-Yokado operates about 7,200 7-Eleven stores in Japan and 5,500 7-Eleven outlets in North America, where since 1991 it has owned 64 percent of 7-Eleven's parent company, Southland Corporation. Yet all of those convenience stores account for only about one-third of the company's sales. The majority of profits come from additional retail operations with more than 1,300 other stores, such as superstores that sell food, clothing, and household goods; supermarkets; discount outlets; and clothing stores. The company also owns restaurants. Ito-Yokado holds the Japanese franchises for Robinson's department stores, Oshman's sporting goods stores, and the Denny's restaurants. The company has additional operations in insurance and publishing.

Not only has it been Japan's most profitable retailer for nearly two decades, but Ito-Yokado returned Southland to profitability in the United States. U.S. pension fund managers and other long-term buyers have been big purchasers of Ito-Yokado shares, encouraged by the company's move to better its profit margins by improving its selection of products to sell. For the 1997 fiscal year, consolidated sales of Ito-Yokado exceeded those of competitor Daiei Incorporated for the first time. In addition, Ito-Yokado shares have been favored over those of another major rival, Jusco Company, which was hit by a larger than expected pretax profit fall due to sluggish consumer demand. Despite a strong business performance by 7-Eleven Japan, however, Ito-Yokado's results were pushed down by decreased profit at its U.S. unit Southland.

As one of the world's leading diversified retailing companies, Ito-Yokado has forty-nine subsidiaries and rules them with an iron hand. In Japan its strict discipline and control are behind its point-of-sale computerized cash registers, which let headquarters know each and every time a sale is made. This system, believed to double the profitability of a typical 7-Eleven, is earmarked for the North American market as well. The company monitors how much time the store managers spend using the analytical tools built into the cash register to follow product sales. Included within the information that can be flashed on the computer screen are not only sales data, but demographic trends and weather forecasts. Based on this system, delivery of fresh food such as sandwiches, box lunches, rice balls, and delicatessen dishes occurs three times daily in Japan to make sure no fresh food is wasted. The company also shares the information with suppliers and manufacturers.

Japan's ongoing economic troubles have led to changes in retailing. President and Chief Executive Officer Toshifumi Suzuki, in the firm's 1997 annual report, pointed to a gradual retailing shift from a seller's market to a buyer's market. Japan's 1997 increase in the consumption tax rate from 3 to 5 percent, along with the discontinuation of income tax rebates, further eroded consumer confidence and spending in that country. As a result of so many concerns and a lack of assurance that the government has the means to solve them, Japanese consumers not only expect high quality at reasonable prices, but products that show innovation, Suzuki believes. A low price alone will not prompt a purchase, since consumers demand products that offer lower prices without sacrificing value, Suzuki emphasized. Presentation, customer service, and a clear explanation of how specific merchandise offers value are key to succeeding in a difficult market. That, of course, is a philosophy that doesn't just fit the Japanese consumer, but consumers the world over.

Team merchandising, in which a retailer and a manufacturer work together in product development, is another concept that Ito-Yokado wants to expand in order to meet customer needs. The company has, for example, carried out team merchandising efforts with international partners such as Wal-Mart Stores and Europe's Metro Group. The best example of this was the company's "soft-fit" bra project in 1995 that brought together a team consisting of Ito-Yokado, textile maker Toray Industries, and apparel-maker Gunze. Identifying a desire among its customers for a bra with no wire that fit softly, the team was able to design and launch the product within six months. Despite having a higher price than the underwire bra, the new product was a great hit that significantly boosted sales.

Ito-Yokado management is convinced that Japan's retailing industry is lagging behind in merchandising compared to other retailers around the world, with major revamping required. In Japan, the head managers of all 158 Ito-Yokado stores meet weekly to confirm basic policies and exchange information about their stores' merchandise and marketing efforts. In addition, the manager of each store's section meets daily with sales personnel, or the sales personnel meet among themselves, to discuss the day's key targets, sales techniques, and sales data. A view of the store as a whole, beyond just one individual section, is a part of such discussions. Through its global merchandising network, Ito-Yokado comes up with items specifically geared to its customers, such as Galleria Europe's fashion items, Bodum of Europe kitchen utensils, Cannon towels, and outerwear produced in China. In one year, the company sold 70,000 coats and 250,000 sweaters. The company has worked with material and apparel makers to offer merchandise, including undergarments, that lets customers coordinate their wardrobes.

With a high-tech system that keeps it in direct contact with its customers and managers, Ito-Yokado feels it has the global retailing scene in hand and is capable of dealing with anything a regional economy can dish out.

A firm belief in a fast-moving, no-nonsense "top-down" management philosophy was related by Suzuki in a 1998 message to employees: "Yesterday's conventional wisdom is no longer valid today. The so-called bottom-up system is a decision-making process based on building consensus from the lowest echelon and has been considered a strong feature of Japanese-style management for many years. However, in today's business environment, in which problems that require immediate solutions are presented to us incessantly, building consensus from the bottom up does not result in quick responses. Unless the leader oversees the entire situation, and makes rational and courageous judgments, we cannot optimize the whole system or make needed innovations."

25. ITO-YOKADO COMPANY

Japan   Ticker symbol IYCOY

One American Depositary Receipt represents one ordinary share

ADR price $48 3/4 (9/16/98)   Dividend yield .46%

(Financial data from I/B/E/S International is in Japanese yen)*

BUSINESS DESCRIPTION

SUPERSTORES AND OTHER RETAIL OPERATIONS ACCOUNTED FOR 62% OF FISCAL 1997 REVENUES, CONVENIENCE STORES 34%, AND RESTAURANT OPERATIONS 4%

ADDRESS AND CONTACTS

Address	1-4, Shiba-koen 4-Chome
	Minato-ku Tokyo 105-8571 Japan
Telephone	81-3-34592111
Fax	81-3-34596873

BASIC FINANCIAL INFORMATION

Capital Structure[†]	Long Term Debt:	NA
	Total Debt:	NA
	Common Sh. Equity:	938.41

SALES BREAKDOWN

Product Segments[†]	Superstores & Other	1892.18
	Convenience Stores	1015.30
	Restaurant Operations	131.73
	Eliminations	-20.35

Ito-Yokado Company

Geographic
  Segments†   Japan   2258.24
                  North America   765.69
                  Eliminations   -5.08

Displayed Currency: Japanese Yen (1.00:1)
*I/B/E/S and I/B/E/S Express are registered trademarks of I/B/E/S International Inc. Copyright
1993–1996 I/B/E/S International Inc. All rights reserved.
†Values are displayed in billions.

FINANCIAL STATEMENT DATA

INCOME STATEMENT	1998	1997	1996	1995	1994
Net Sales or Revenues	3129.59	3018.86	2892.06	2878.90	2884.46
EBITDA	NA	306.72	303.38	300.06	288.18
Depreciation Depletion					
& Amort	85.47	81.16	78.79	79.24	82.32
Operating Income	221.32	220.41	218.60	211.40	196.60
Interest Expense	14.00	14.00	15.26	18.84	20.43
Pretax Income	212.67	212.21	209.48	202.22	185.78
Net Income	NA	NA	NA	NA	57.91

BALANCE SHEET	1998	1997	1996	1995	1994
Assets					
Cash & Equivalents	NA	445.95	393.58	373.20	325.79
Receivables—Net	NA	37.92	34.33	33.22	35.11
Inventories	NA	95.15	84.99	81.58	75.01
Total Current Assets	NA	616.36	544.06	516.35	469.21
Property Plant & Eq.—					
Net	NA	826.21	789.93	759.86	748.70
Total Assets	1974.29	1831.68	1719.87	1654.88	1577.17
Liabilities & Shareholders' Equity					
Total Current Liabilities	474.02	427.77	414.08	401.87	397.33
Long Term Debt	NA	183.18	169.93	214.54	295.52
Preferred Stock	0.00	0.00	0.00	0.00	0.00
Common Equity	938.41	881.25	821.78	755.29	679.24
Total Liabilities					
& Sh. Equity	1974.29	1831.68	1719.87	1654.88	1577.17

CASH FLOW	1998	1997	1996	1995	1994
Funds from Operations	155.94	189.99	188.50	185.91	176.37
Total Sources	NA	618.19	570.50	648.36	621.02
Cash Dividends Paid—					
Total	NA	13.86	13.84	13.82	13.80
Total Uses	NA	618.19	570.50	648.36	621.02
Incr/Decr in Working					
Capital	NA	58.61	15.51	42.60	32.77
Free Cash Flow	NA	208.46	202.52	191.36	191.24

INTERNATIONAL BUSINESS	1998	1997	1996	1995	1994
Foreign Assets	NA	343.39	311.48	293.22	337.87
Foreign Sales	NA	765.69	649.05	690.37	756.36
Foreign Income	NA	19.79	14.60	14.76	2.94

SUPPLEMENTARY DATA	1998	1997	1996	1995	1994
Employees	NA	15086	36932	34697	33629
R&D Expenses	NA	NA	NA	NA	NA
Goodwill/Cost in Excess of Assets Purchased	NA	97.42	89.38	90.77	105.68
Extra Items & Gain/	NA	0.00	0.08	0.00	0.90
Loss in Sale of Assets	NA	0.00	0.08	0.00	0.90

Displayed Currency: Japanese Yen (1.00:1)
All values are displayed in billions (except employees).

FINANCIAL RATIOS AND GROWTH RATES

PROFITABILITY	1998	1997	1996	1995	1994	5YR AVG
Operating Profit Margin %	7.07	7.30	7.56	7.34	6.82	7.22
Tax Rate %	NA	51.49	50.84	52.43	58.07	53.21
Net Margin %	2.25	2.46	2.65	2.48	2.04	2.38
Return on Assets %	3.85	4.83	5.24	5.30	4.58	4.76
Return on Equity— Total %	NA	9.04	10.15	10.50	9.27	9.74
Cash Flow % Sales	4.98	6.29	6.52	6.46	6.11	6.07
Sales per Employee (in 000s)	NA	200110	78308	82332	85773	111631

ASSET UTILIZATION	1998	1997	1996	1995	1994	5YR AVG
Total Asset Turnover	1.59	1.65	1.68	1.74	1.83	1.70
Capital Exp % Gross Fixed Assets	NA	6.82	7.48	8.52	7.94	7.69
Acc Depreciation % Gross Fixed Assets	NA	42.68	41.41	40.46	38.70	40.81
Assets per Employee (in 000s)	NA	121416	46569	47327	46899	65553

LIQUIDITY	1998	1997	1996	1995	1994	5YR AVG
Current Ratio	NA	1.44	1.31	1.28	1.18	1.31
Quick Ratio	NA	1.13	1.03	1.01	0.91	1.02

Ito-Yokado Company

LEVERAGE	1998	1997	1996	1995	1994	5YR AVG
Total Debt %						
Common Equity	NA	24.35	25.27	32.98	49.78	33.10
Long Term Debt %						
Common Equity	NA	20.79	20.68	28.40	43.51	28.34
Common Equity %						
Total Assets	47.53	48.11	47.78	45.64	43.07	46.43
Long Term Debt %						
Total Capital	NA	14.19	14.22	18.65	26.08	18.29
Operating Cash/						
Fixed Charges	NA	13.57	12.35	9.87	8.64	11.11

GROWTH %	1998	1997	1996	1995	1994	5YR AVG
Net Sales	3.67	4.38	0.46	-0.19	-4.96	0.62
Operating Income	0.41	0.83	3.41	7.53	-4.90	1.37
Total Assets	7.79	6.50	3.93	4.93	0.36	4.67
Earnings per Share*	-5.17	-2.98	7.42	23.21	-10.78	1.67
Dividends per Share*	0.00	0.00	0.00	0.00	0.00	0.00
Book Value per Share	NA	7.17	8.69	10.99	7.03	NA

Displayed Currency: Japanese Yen (1.00:1)
*Source: Worldscope. Value may differ from I/B/E/S.
Note: 5-Year Average calculations exclude NAs.

PER SHARE AND RELATED DATA

SOURCE: WORLDSCOPE	1998	1997	1996	1995	1994
Earnings per Share	172.5	181.9	187.5	174.6	141.7
Dividends per Share	34.0	34.0	34.0	34.0	34.0
Book Value per Share	NA	2161.2	2016.7	1855.4	1671.7
Total Investment Return	NA	NA	34.41	-25.35	72.16
Market Price (Year-end)	6900.0	5480.0	5880.0	4400.0	5940.0
Market Capitalization					
(in billions)	NA	2234.56	2396.08	1791.11	2413.57
Price/Earnings Ratio	40.00	30.12	31.36	25.21	41.93
Price/Book Value	NA	2.54	2.92	2.37	3.55
Dividend Yield	0.49	0.62	0.58	0.77	0.57
Dividend Payout per					
Share	19.71	18.69	18.13	19.48	24.00
Common Shares					
Outstanding					
(Year-end) in					
Millions	NA	407.77	407.50	407.07	406.32
Stock Split/Dividend Ratio	NA	NA	NA	NA	NA
Type of Share Common					

Displayed Currency: Japanese Yen (1.00:1)
Note: Data is sourced from Worldscope and may differ from I/B/E/S historical data.

26. Johnson & Johnson

With sixty-five consecutive years of sales increases and thirty-five consecutive years of dividend increases, Johnson & Johnson has proven to be an "ouchless" investment.

The world's largest and most diversified health care product maker boasts the famous products Band-Aid adhesive bandages; Johnson's baby products; Reach toothbrushes; Monistat-7 yeast-infection treatments; Neutrogena skin- and health-care products; Stayfree, Carefree, Sure & Natural, and o.b. women's sanitary products; Acuvue disposable contact lenses; Pediacare children's medications; and Tylenol medications. The company also makes prescription drugs such as Retin-A cream and Ortho-Novum oral contraceptives, as well as pharmaceuticals such as its Ergamisol cancer treatment and Hismanal antihistamine. Its professional products range from surgical instruments to replacement joints. The company's purchase of the 84 percent stake in leading orthopedic device maker DePuy Inc. held by Roche Holding A.G. for $3.5 billion, or $35 a share, in July 1998 made it the top player in the artificial joint and spinal implant business. It also underscored Johnson & Johnson's ongoing commitment to expansion of its professional products business, which has faced strong competition. More than one-third of the company's sales are derived from products introduced within the past five years. Drugs account for one-third of company sales, but represent more than half of operating income due to high margins.

A potential blockbuster drug for the firm is Regranex, a treatment for diabetic foot ulcers that went on the market in 1998. Clinical trials demonstrated that a daily topical application of Regranex Gel plus good ulcer care healed more diabetic ulcers than placebo gel plus good ulcer care. It has a potential market of $500 million to $1 billion a year after a ramp-up period of three years. Diabetic foot ulcers affect 2.4 million people worldwide and about 600,000 new cases must be treated each year. The company is also advancing in the women's health market. It acquired Gynecare Incorporated, maker of medical devices for treating uterine disorders, for $80 million and Biopsys Medical Incorporated, a maker of equipment used to diagnose breast cancer.

Innovative products are key to the company's future. For example, its McNeil subsidiary received approval from the U.S. Food and Drug Administration in 1998 to market sucralose, the only low-calorie sweetener that is made from sugar, tastes like sugar, and can be used virtually anywhere sugar is used, including in cooking and baking. The FDA granted approval for its use in fifteen food and beverage categories, including baked goods and baking mixes, beverages, dairy products, processed fruits, and fruit juices. That subsidiary also acquired from Finland's Raisio Group the exclusive worldwide marketing rights to the patented dietary ingredient stanol ester, which has been clinically proven to reduce cholesterol by inhibiting its absorption. In addition, the company signed a licensing agreement with Japan Tobacco for rights to a novel class of compounds for treatment of pain and inflammation. These licensed compounds are believed to selectively inhibit the activity of type-II cyclooxygenase, an enzyme involved in the activity of substances that mediate inflammation, pain, and fever. In 1998 the company's Cordis Corporation acquired the intellectual property and assets of IsoStent Incorporated, which included the BX Stent, a new flexible medical device in development for treating coronary artery disease. Meanwhile, also in 1998, the company's Indigo Medical Incorporated was cleared by the FDA to begin marketing a treatment for symptoms of an enlarged prostate in men.

Johnson & Johnson is the parent to more than 180 operating companies with operations in fifty countries worldwide and sales in 175 countries. It recently has focused attention on widening its presence in China and Eastern Europe. The company continues to expand its product line through an aggressive research and development program that cost more than $2.3 billion in 1998, and through acquisitions, with thirty-four acquisitions already made during the 1990s. At the same time, it divested businesses that no longer met its growth objectives. Of course, Johnson & Johnson is no diamond in the rough: It was ranked number nine on *Fortune* magazine's annual survey of America's Most Admired Companies in 1998.

The company has always had a solid-citizen, responsible image. Development of the first ready-made, ready-to-use surgical dressings by Johnson & Johnson in the mid-1880s marked the first practical application of the theory of antiseptic wound treatment. Company founder Robert Wood Johnson nurtured the concept of a practical application of British surgeon Sir Joseph Lister's teachings about airborne germs as "invisible assassins." Johnson's surgical dressings were wrapped and sealed in sterile individual packages and suitable for instant use without the risk of contamination. He joined with his two brothers, James Wood and Edward Mead Johnson, who formed a partnership in 1885. Operations began in New Brunswick, New Jersey, in 1886. The first products were improved medicinal plasters containing medical compounds mixed in an adhesive. Next came a soft, absorbent cotton and gauze dressing that could be mass produced and shipped in quantity to hospitals, physicians, and druggists. The company incorporated in 1887 and was on its way. Now it's poised to begin yet another century.

"We are convinced that long-term success in the new millennium will come only to those companies that value innovation and learn how to harness its power for growth," Chairman and Chief Executive Officer Ralph Larsen said in his letter in the company's most recent annual report. "We have set our sights on leadership in health care on a global basis and we believe that innovation will propel us forward, to realize our long-term vision."

Larsen has identified Johnson & Johnson's strongest "growth platforms" for the future as the following:

• Cardiology and the treatment of circulatory diseases, in which its Cordis affiliate is well positioned.

• Skin care, with the fastest-growing skin care portfolio worldwide.

• Wound care, from adhesive bandages to genetically engineered prescription products.

• Diabetes, with the introduction of Smartstrip test strips in markets outside the United States.

• Minimally invasive therapies, with its Ethicon Endo-Surgery continuing to set the pace.

• Urology, with the acquisition of Indigo Medical combining fiber-optics with diode laser technology in treatment.

• Vision care, in which Vistakon has emerged as the market leader in the disposable contact business.

• Pain management, its product lineup bolstered by the acquisition of adult Motrin Ibuprofen.

• Nutraceuticals, with Lactaid lactose-intolerance products posting strong double-digit gains.

• Central nervous system, with Ortho-McNeil's Topamax for the treatment of epilepsy a growing contributor.

• Gastrointestinal, including a Merck joint venture and category-leading brands Pepcid AC, Mylanta, and Imodium.

Legal decisions play an increasing role in big business these days and one went Johnson & Johnson's way in 1998. An arbitrator ordered Amgen Inc. to pay Johnson & Johnson $200 million, taking care of the primary disagreement in an arbitration battle between the companies over a popular anemia drug. The amount of the final order, including interest, was considerably more than Amgen had expected. The dispute involved the allocation of sales of the drug erythropoietin, which the companies sell in the United States under different names for different medical conditions. Amgen's Epogen provides about half its total revenue, and Procrit is one of the big sellers for Johnson & Johnson.

26. JOHNSON & JOHNSON

United States   Ticker symbol JNJ

Stock price $77 1/16 (9/16/98)   Dividend yield 1.30%

(Financial data is from I/B/E/S International)*

BUSINESS DESCRIPTION

PROFESSIONAL PRODUCTS ACCOUNTED FOR 37% OF 1997 REVENUES, PHARMACEUTICAL PRODUCTS 34%, AND CONSUMER PRODUCTS 29%

ADDRESS AND CONTACTS

Address	One Johnson & Johnson Plaza
	New Brunswick NJ 08933
Telephone	1-732-524-0400

BASIC FINANCIAL INFORMATION

Capital Structure[†]	Long Term Debt:	1126.00
	Total Debt:	1840.00
	Common Sh. Equity:	12359.00

SALES BREAKDOWN

Product Segments[†]	Professional Products	8435.00
	Pharmaceutical Products	7696.00
	Consumer Products	6498.00
Geographic Segments[†]	United States	11757.00
	Europe	5942.00
	Western Hemisphere	2034.00
	Asia Pacific	2896.00

Displayed Currency: U.S. Dollar (1.00:1)

*I/B/E/S and I/B/E/S Express are registered trademarks of I/B/E/S International Inc. Copyright 1993–1996 I/B/E/S International Inc. All rights reserved.

[†]Values are displayed in millions.

FINANCIAL STATEMENT DATA

INCOME STATEMENT	1997	1996	1995	1994	1993
Net Sales or Revenues	22629.00	21620.00	18842.00	15734.00	14138.00
EBITDA	5763.00	5167.00	4317.00	3547.00	3075.00
Depreciation Depletion & Amort	1067.00	1009.00	857.00	724.00	617.00
Operating Income	4622.00	4303.00	3511.00	2807.00	2394.00
Interest Expense	180.00	180.00	213.00	186.00	174.00
Pretax Income	4576.00	4033.00	3317.00	2681.00	2332.00
Net Income	3303.00	2887.00	2403.00	2006.00	1787.00

Johnson & Johnson

BALANCE SHEET	1997	1996	1995	1994	1993
Assets					
Cash & Equivalents	2899.00	2136.00	1364.00	704.00	476.00
Receivables—Net	4317.00	3251.00	2903.00	2601.00	2107.00
Inventories	2516.00	2498.00	2276.00	2161.00	1717.00
Total Current Assets	10563.00	9370.00	7938.00	6680.00	5217.00
Property Plant & Eq.—					
Net	5810.00	5651.00	5196.00	4910.00	4406.00
Total Assets	21121.00	20010.00	17873.00	15668.00	12242.00
Liabilities & Shareholders' Equity					
Total Current Liabilities	5283.00	5184.00	4388.00	4266.00	3212.00
Long Term Debt	1126.00	1410.00	2107.00	2199.00	1493.00
Preferred Stock	0.00	0.00	0.00	0.00	0.00
Common Equity	12359.00	10836.00	9045.00	7122.00	5568.00
Total Liabilities					
& Sh. Equity	21121.00	20010.00	17873.00	15668.00	12242.00

CASH FLOW	1997	1996	1995	1994	1993
Net Cash Flow—					
Operating	4343.00	3891.00	3382.00	2975.00	2168.00
Net Cash Flow—					
Investing	1614.00	1692.00	1096.00	2556.00	1261.00
Net Cash Flow—					
Financing	-1919.00	-1368.00	-1734.00	-188.00	-1244.00
Incr/Decr in Working					
Capital	1094.00	636.00	1136.00	409.00	9.00
Free Cash Flow	4372.00	3794.00	3061.00	2610.00	2100.00

INTERNATIONAL BUSINESS	1997	1996	1995	1994	1993
Foreign Assets	9542.00	9147.00	8188.00	6580.00	5380.00
Foreign Sales	10872.00	10721.00	9652.00	7922.00	6935.00
Foreign Income	1825.00	1849.00	1702.00	1421.00	1373.00

SUPPLEMENTARY DATA	1997	1996	1995	1994	1993
Employees	90500	89300	82300	81500	81600
R&D Expenses	2140.00	1905.00	1634.00	1278.00	1182.00
Goodwill/Cost in Excess of Assets Purchased	NA	NA	NA	NA	NA
Extra Items & Gain/	0.00	0.00	0.00	0.00	0.00
Loss in Sale of Assets	0.00	0.00	0.00	0.00	0.00

Displayed Currency: U.S. Dollar (1.00:1)
All values are displayed in millions (except employees).

FINANCIAL RATIOS AND GROWTH RATES

PROFITABILITY	1997	1996	1995	1994	1993	5YR AVG
Operating Profit						
Margin %	20.43	19.90	18.63	17.84	16.93	18.75
Tax Rate %	27.82	28.42	27.56	25.18	23.37	26.47
Net Margin %	14.60	13.35	12.75	12.75	12.64	13.22
Return on Assets %	16.90	16.61	15.94	17.15	15.74	16.47
Return on Equity—						
Total %	30.48	31.92	33.74	36.03	34.56	33.35
Cash Flow % Sales	18.78	18.01	16.97	16.93	16.87	17.51
Sales per Employee						
(in 000s)	250	242	229	193	173	217

ASSET UTILIZATION	1997	1996	1995	1994	1993	5YR AVG
Total Asset Turnover	1.07	1.08	1.05	1.00	1.15	1.07
Capital Exp % Gross						
Fixed Assets	14.73	15.22	15.36	12.24	14.37	14.38
Acc Depreciation %						
Gross Fixed Assets	38.48	37.37	36.44	35.86	35.04	36.64
Assets per Employee						
(in 000s)	233	224	217	192	150	203

LIQUIDITY	1997	1996	1995	1994	1993	5YR AVG
Current Ratio	2.00	1.81	1.81	1.57	1.62	1.76
Quick Ratio	1.37	1.04	0.97	0.77	0.80	0.99

LEVERAGE	1997	1996	1995	1994	1993	5YR AVG
Total Debt %						
Common Equity	14.89	21.06	26.84	43.50	43.25	29.91
Long Term Debt %						
Common Equity	9.11	13.01	23.29	30.88	26.81	20.62
Common Equity %						
Total Assets	58.52	54.15	50.61	45.46	45.48	50.84
Long Term Debt %						
Total Capital	8.35	11.51	18.89	23.59	21.14	16.70
Operating Cash/						
Fixed Charges	26.56	21.63	15.01	14.32	13.71	18.24

GROWTH %	1997	1996	1995	1994	1993	5YR AVG
Net Sales	4.67	14.74	19.75	11.29	2.80	10.47
Operating Income	7.41	22.56	25.08	17.25	5.14	15.21
Total Assets	5.55	11.96	14.07	27.99	3.01	12.19

Johnson & Johnson

Earnings per Share*	11.06	16.67	19.23	13.87	11.38	14.40
Dividends per Share*	15.65	14.84	13.27	11.88	13.48	13.82
Book Value per Share	10.04	16.46	26.09	27.90	9.76	17.80

Displayed Currency: U.S. Dollar (1.00:1)
*Source: Worldscope. Value may differ from I/B/E/S.
Note: 5-Year Average calculations exclude NAs.

PER SHARE AND RELATED DATA

SOURCE: WORLDSCOPE	1997	1996	1995	1994	1993
Earnings per Share	2.41	2.17	1.86	1.56	1.37
Dividends per Share	0.85	0.74	0.64	0.57	0.51
Book Value per Share	8.95	8.13	6.98	5.54	4.33
Total Investment Return	NA	NA	58.50	24.52	-9.14
Market Price (Year-end)	65.88	49.75	42.75	27.38	22.44
Market Capitalization (in millions)	88610.90	66291.08	55376.64	35204.80	28853.77
Price/Earnings Ratio	27.33	22.93	22.98	17.55	16.38
Price/Book Value	7.36	6.12	6.12	4.94	5.18
Dividend Yield	1.29	1.48	1.50	2.06	2.25
Dividend Payout per Share	35.27	33.87	34.41	36.22	36.86
Common Shares Outstanding (Year-end) in Millions	1345.14	1332.48	1295.36	1286.02	1285.96
Stock Split/Dividend Ratio	NA	NA	0.50	0.50	0.50
Type of Share	*Common*				

Displayed Currency: U.S. Dollar (1.00:1)
Note: Data is sourced from Worldscope and may differ from I/B/E/S historical data.

27. Eli Lilly & Company

Talk about a complete transformation from a quiet Midwestern firm to a global powerhouse. Sidney Taurel, who succeeded Randall Tobias as chief executive officer of U.S. drug company Eli Lilly & Company on July 1, 1998, and became chairman at year-end, is a Moroccan-born, former Spanish citizen whose native tongue is French. He's held a number of international positions since joining Lilly in 1971, among them head of its Brazilian affiliate, vice president of Lilly European operations, and president of Lilly International. As president of the pharmaceutical division and most recently company president and chief operating officer, he's been running wide-ranging Lilly operations for several years. That in turn freed up Tobias to give hundreds of speeches, raise the company's visibility, and meet with officials of foreign governments to open overseas markets. Tobias was recognized for his energetic efforts by *Business Week* magazine as one of the top twenty-five managers of the year for 1997, while the magazine named the new Lilly drug Zyprexa, a treatment for the symptoms of schizophrenia, as one of the top products of the year. Used in bipolar disorder involving episodes of severe mania and depression, Zyprexa is approved in more than fifty countries.

The result of this powerful one-two punch of Tobias and Taurel has been the best-performing big U.S. pharmaceutical company stock over the past five years. Taurel now predicts that Lilly, once a slowpoke among drug companies in expanding to foreign markets, will continue its international expansion of the past several years and increase its sales force. Japan is now a primary target. Research joint ventures will be expanded too, such as the one with Millennium Pharmaceuticals Inc. on potential atherosclerosis drugs. Emphasis on speeding up the entire process will continue. Since the early 1990s, the company has completely reorganized the way it does research, streamlined its processes, and set new priorities. As a result, it has cut in half— to about 2,500 days—the time it takes to move a compound through development to global markets.

Of course, Indianapolis, Indiana–based Eli Lilly wasn't exactly small potatoes before this international shift. It's a major company that employs 29,000 people worldwide and markets products in 156 countries and is perhaps best known for making Prozac, the world's best-selling antidepressant, which currently holds 20 percent of the market. The company doubled its marketing efforts for that drug in 1998 in the hopes of increasing global sales of the drug. The first potential patent expiration for Prozac occurs in the United States in February 2001, and it's expected that December 2003, when the sue patent expires, is the time when competition will likely arise. Other well-known Lilly products are the Humulin rapid-acting insulin, the Gemzar treatment for pancreatic cancer and associated pain, and the ReoPro blod-clot inhibitor used in angioplasties. Lilly's insulin business is under pressure as new oral diabetes drugs are being developed that would reduce the need for insulin. The firm also makes products for animal uses such as Tylan, an antibiotic for cattle, swine, and poultry. Eli Lilly's PCS Health Systems and Integrated Medical Systems provide health care management services. The company has about 7 percent of revenues in Asia, about 5 percent of those in Japan, so the effect of instability there has not been significant for it.

Eli Lilly has been in the forefront of women's health and drug research. It gained attention in 1998 when two years of clinical trials indicated its Evista osteoporosis preventive drug might prevent breast cancer without the higher rates of uterine cancer associated with tamoxifen, the other recent breast-cancer breakthrough. The great interest generated by these findings was hardly surprising, for breast cancer strikes an estimated 178,000 women annually in the United States and kills 43,500. Taurel says he sees "big pent-up demand" for the drug. In addition, two years of research in twenty-five countries involving the new Eli Lilly medication with the chemical name raloxifene indicated that it may offer postmenopausal women many of the bone-enhancing and cardiovascular benefits of estrogen therapy, yet doesn't seem to be associated with the cancers that usually accompany estrogen. It's no surprise that Lilly is a leader in women's health research, for its Lilly Center for Women's Health was established in early 1996 and has since awarded significant grants to support projects in gender-based health research. It has supported continuing education programs such as the post-menopausal Health Curriculum and has also partnered with organizations such as the European institute of Women's Health and the Society for the Advancement of Women's Health Research.

The company was founded in 1876 by Colonel Eli Lilly, a thirty-eight-year-old pharmaceutical chemist and Civil War Union Army officer who invented a process for coating pills with gelatin. He was frustrated by the poorly prepared, ineffective medicines of his day and made a commitment to manufacture high-quality medicines based on the best available science dispensed by physicians rather than sideshow hucksters. Lilly wants to keep its independence, and in 1998 received approval from its shareholders to increase the authorized number of its common shares to 3.2 billion from 1.6 billion. While Eli Lilly management said it didn't know of any effort to gain control of the firm or accumulate its shares, it could use the additional shares to try to avert a hostile takeover effort by countering the bid or selling them to dilute the bidder's voting power, according to a filing with the Securities and Exchange Commission. Lilly has been considered a likely takeover candidate in any industry consolidation because, despite its large size, it's still one of the smaller of the major drug makers.

Did someone say "whoops"? Even an inspired company with a world strategy can make a wrong move. For example, Lilly's $4.1 billion purchase of PCS Health Systems from McKesson Corporation in 1994 has turned out to be a painful venture, with a $2.4 billion charge against second-quarter 1997 results taken to write down the value of the investment by more than half. PCS is the largest pharmacy-benefits management business, processing prescription drug purchases for millions of Americans. However, other drug companies didn't buy minority stakes in PCS, which would have reduced Lilly's financial exposure, as Lilly had hoped. Furthermore, managed health care didn't take off as quickly as some had expected it to. Finally, PCS's lack of a mail-prescription business made it tough for PCS pharmacists to switch drug purchases toward Lilly drugs. Yet the one-time loss from the PCS charge was partly offset by the $900 million sale to Dow Chemical Company of Lilly's stake in the DowElanco agricultural joint venture.

Despite that miscue, which the company could conceivably turn around in the future, Eli Lilly continues to move aggressively into the world marketplace. As Taurel stated in his letter in the most recent annual report: "Our goal is to create an innovation engine that is open to the world, one that identifies the best sources of learning, improves everything it does, and seeks innovation wherever it's available—a research and development organization capable of consistently and rapidly discovering and developing truly innovative medicines."

27. ELI LILLY & COMPANY

United States   Ticker symbol LLY

Stock price $76 3/16 (9/16/98)   Dividend yield 1.05%

(Financial data is from I/B/E/S International)*

BUSINESS DESCRIPTION

DEVELOPS AND MARKETS HUMAN MEDICINES AND ANIMAL HEALTH PRODUCTS AND IS INVOLVED IN HEALTH CARE MANAGEMENT

ADDRESS AND CONTACTS

Address   Lilly Corporate Center
               Indianapolis IN 46285
Telephone   1-317-276-2000

BASIC FINANCIAL INFORMATION

Capital Structure†	Long Term Debt:	2326.10
	Total Debt:	2553.70
	Common Sh. Equity:	4645.60

SALES BREAKDOWN

Product Segments†	Central Nervous	3519.70
	Endocrine	1386.30
	Anti-Infectives	1272.50
	Animal Health	589.80
	Health Care MTG	548.50
Geographic Segments†	United States	5411.70
	Europe, Middle East	2298.10
	Other	807.80

Displayed Currency: U.S. Dollar (1.00:1)
*I/B/E/S and I/B/E/S Express are registered trademarks of I/B/E/S International Inc. Copyright
1993–1996 I/B/E/S International Inc. All rights reserved.
†Values are displayed in millions.

FINANCIAL STATEMENT DATA

INCOME STATEMENT	1997	1996	1995	1994	1993
Net Sales or Revenues	8517.60	7346.60	6763.80	5711.60	6452.40
EBITDA	1254.10	2863.60	2605.60	2234.60	1171.40
Depreciation Depletion & Amort	509.80	543.50	553.70	432.20	398.30
Operating Income	2458.30	2046.80	1981.80	1736.50	1825.30
Interest Expense	324.60	324.60	324.60	129.20	96.70
Pretax Income	510.20	2031.30	1765.60	1698.60	701.90
Net Income	-385.20	1523.50	1306.60	1286.10	491.10

BALANCE SHEET	1997	1996	1995	1994	1993
Assets					
Cash & Equivalents	2024.60	955.10	1084.10	746.70	987.10
Receivables—Net	1883.20	1737.10	1808.40	1834.60	950.10
Inventories	900.70	881.40	839.60	968.90	1103.00
Total Current Assets	5320.70	3891.30	4138.60	3962.30	3697.10
Property Plant & Eq.—Net	4101.70	4307.00	4239.30	4411.50	4200.20
Total Assets	12577.40	14307.20	14412.50	14507.40	9623.60
Liabilities & Shareholders' Equity					
Total Current Liabilities	4191.60	4222.20	4967.00	5669.50	2928.00
Long Term Debt	2326.10	2516.50	2592.90	2125.80	835.20
Preferred Stock	0.00	0.00	0.00	0.00	0.00
Common Equity	4645.60	6100.10	5432.60	5355.60	4568.80
Total Liabilities & Sh. Equity	12577.40	14307.20	14412.50	14507.40	9623.60

Eli Lilly and Company

CASH FLOW	1997	1996	1995	1994	1993
Net Cash Flow— Operating	2400.40	1991.40	1824.60	1532.30	1516.90
Net Cash Flow— Investing	-809.70	468.00	562.80	4405.00	866.70
Net Cash Flow— Financing	-1954.60	-1661.10	-813.70	2837.30	-523.10
Incr/Decr in Working Capital	1460.00	497.50	878.80	-2476.30	161.70
Free Cash Flow	887.80	2419.70	2054.30	1658.10	537.90

INTERNATIONAL BUSINESS	1997	1996	1995	1994	1993
Foreign Assets	3376.50	3923.30	3705.00	3714.40	2889.60
Foreign Sales	3105.90	3587.00	3301.60	2430.00	1919.10
Foreign Income	1753.20	831.00	789.20	657.10	260.10

SUPPLEMENTARY DATA	1997	1996	1995	1994	1993
Employees	31100	29200	26800	24900	32700
R&D Expenses	1382.00	1189.50	1042.30	897.10	954.60
Goodwill/Cost in Excess of Assets Purchased	NA	NA	NA	NA	NA
Extra Items & Gain/	0.00	0.00	-984.30	0.00	-10.90
Loss in Sale of Assets	0.00	0.00	-984.30	0.00	-10.90

Displayed Currency: U.S. Dollar (1.00:1)
All values are displayed in millions (except employees).

FINANCIAL RATIOS AND GROWTH RATES

PROFITABILITY	1997	1996	1995	1994	1993	5YR AVG
Operating Profit	28.86	27.86	29.30	30.40	28.29	28.94
Tax Rate %	175.48	25.00	26.00	30.23	30.03	57.35
Net Margin %	-4.52	20.74	4.77	22.52	7.44	10.19
Return on Assets %	-1.61	11.89	3.52	14.08	6.08	6.79
Return on Equity— Total %	-6.31	28.04	6.02	28.15	9.82	13.14
Cash Flow % Sales	22.54	29.63	30.42	34.20	25.34	28.43
Sales per Employee (in 000s)	274	252	252	229	197	241

ASSET UTILIZATION	1997	1996	1995	1994	1993	5YR AVG
Total Asset Turnover	0.68	0.51	0.47	0.39	0.67	0.54
Capital Exp % Gross Fixed Assets	5.21	6.26	8.07	8.20	9.65	7.48
Acc Depreciation % Gross Fixed Assets	41.69	39.31	37.92	37.22	36.04	38.43
Assets per Employee (in 000s)	404	490	538	583	294	462

LIQUIDITY	1997	1996	1995	1994	1993	5YR AVG
Current Ratio	1.27	0.92	0.83	0.70	1.26	1.00
Quick Ratio	0.93	0.64	0.58	0.46	0.66	0.65

LEVERAGE	1997	1996	1995	1994	1993	5YR AVG
Total Debt % Common Equity	54.97	61.14	82.86	90.56	29.77	63.86
Long Term Debt % Common Equity	50.07	41.25	47.73	39.69	18.28	39.41
Common Equity % Total Assets	36.94	42.64	37.69	36.92	47.47	40.33
Long Term Debt % Total Capital	32.62	29.21	32.31	28.41	15.46	27.60
Operating Cash/ Fixed Charges	7.54	6.71	6.34	15.12	16.91	10.52

GROWTH %	1997	1996	1995	1994	1993	5YR AVG
Net Sales	15.94	8.62	18.42	-11.48	4.62	6.67
Operating Income	20.10	3.28	14.13	-4.86	6.05	7.39
Total Assets	-12.09	-0.73	-0.65	50.75	10.96	7.72
Earnings per Share*	-125.18	20.87	3.37	166.47	-40.57	-100.00
Dividends per Share*	9.55	4.32	5.56	3.28	8.20	6.16
Book Value per Share	-24.63	10.11	6.93	17.24	-6.63	-0.58

Displayed Currency: U.S. Dollar (1.00:1)
*Source: Worldscope. Value may differ from I/B/E/S.
Note: 5-Year Average calculations exclude NAs.

PER SHARE AND RELATED DATA

SOURCE: WORLDSCOPE	1997	1996	1995	1994	1993
Earnings per Share	-0.35	1.39	1.15	1.11	0.42
Dividends per Share	0.76	0.69	0.67	0.63	0.61
Book Value per Share	4.04	5.36	4.87	4.55	3.88
Total Investment Return	NA	NA	75.48	14.77	1.75
Market Price (Year-end)	69.63	36.50	28.13	16.41	14.84
Market Capitalization (in millions)	77320.09	40356.06	30979.83	19158.31	17381.94
Price/Earnings Ratio	NM	26.26	24.46	14.75	35.55
Price/Book Value	17.23	6.81	5.78	3.60	3.82
Dividend Yield	1.09	1.90	2.36	3.84	4.11
Dividend Payout per Share	-217.14	49.91	57.83	56.63	146.11
Common Shares Outstanding (Year-end) in Millions	1110.52	1105.65	1101.51	1167.74	1170.99
Stock Split/Dividend Ratio	1.00	0.50	0.50	0.25	0.25
Type of Share	*Common*				

Displayed Currency: U.S. Dollar (1.00:1)
Note: Data is sourced from Worldscope and may differ from I/B/E/S historical data.

28. Manpower Incorporated

Get me a temp!" is the battle cry of many lean-and-mean down-sized 1990s corporations.

Manpower Incorporated is benefiting from the growing trend of companies keeping employment rolls to a minimum while using temporary employees during busy periods. In light of changing trends, there's less stigma attached to being a temp these days. A tight labor market, demand for white-collar workers, and increased outsourcing have left employment services like Manpower sitting pretty. The company's quarterly hiring outlook survey has lately found a steady increase in the number of additional workers companies say they'd be hiring and very few anticipated decreases in their staffs. There has even been a 25 percent increase in the number of available summer jobs. Best of all, demand is worldwide, making it possible to reduce exposure to any one country because different economies run on different cycles. Companies today prefer to retain one or two companies with the ability to manage their needs globally, rather than doling out contracts to local firms, giving a giant international operation like Manpower a definite edge. It has had an edge for quite some time, turning its fiftieth consecutive year of revenue growth in 1997.

Manpower is the largest nongovernment employment services organization in the world, with more than 2,776 owned and franchised offices in forty-eight countries. It places more than 1.6 million workers worldwide, supplying temporary office and clerical, industrial, trade, and technical employees, while working with more than 250,000 businesses worldwide on an ongoing basis. Manpower also provides permanent employee services, including employee testing and training. The goal is a seamless, systematic approach to placing individuals in office or industrial

197

assignments, providing the best workers for the jobs. Its fastest-growing division is Manpower Technical, which works with businesses engaged in state-of-the-art technological projects. Its employees are assigned to many of the world's leading high-technology firms. Another fast-growing area is customer service center staffing; the company now has more than 30,000 call center specialists at work each day across the globe. The firm was named tops in the field of temporary help in *Fortune* magazine's 1998 America's Most Admired Companies list.

Manpower's top three markets are the United States, France, and the United Kingdom, with additional offices in continental Europe, Canada, Japan, Israel, Colombia, Costa Rica, Guatemala, Australia, Malaysia, and Morocco. Southeast Asia accounts for less than 1 percent of revenues. The company has elected to grow by adding offices, rather than through acquisitions. The long-term objective is a well-balanced global network to eliminate exposure to economic fluctuations in any particular geographic region. There is risk that a strengthening U.S. dollar against the currencies of the nations in which Manpower does business can hurt earnings, but currency fluctuations don't have much impact, because Manpower's prices and expenses are denominated in the same local currencies. France had a dramatic impact on the firm's bottom line in early 1998 with tremendous growth despite the loss of government tax subsidies, which some had feared would hurt results. Europe, Asia, and Latin America showed strong gains, while U.S. operations were roughly in line with expectations. Another plus for Manpower is that no client represents more than 1 percent of its annual revenue.

"We have created what I consider to be a well-balanced business—geographically, segment-wise, and on the basis of the size of our account portfolio—and I believe we now have the innovative tools to maintain both our growth and our profitability in the years ahead," Mitchell Fromstein, chairman, president, and chief executive officer, said in his most recent letter in the company's annual report.

Manpower offers its employees many ongoing training opportunities, at no charge, to increase their marketability and wage-earning potential. This, along with paid holidays, vacation, and comprehensive major medical coverage, helps attract quality workers. The company's Manpowernet is a massive Internet-based global training capability and an intranet-based system linking major customer sites to all Manpower sites. It provides up-to-date account information and service knowledge on a real-time basis. Manpower has also introduced an Internet training facility known as the Manpower Global Learning Center through which current and prospective contract workers receive the latest in training, with a goal of reaching a million people. This teaching capacity should allow the company to accomplish both recruitment and growth objectives to give it a clear competitive advantage in the years to come. With demand soaring for qualified high-tech contract professionals, Manpower has already been providing free training to its technical services employees worldwide. Its training course includes thirteen main curricula covering 200 courses in applications such as Lotus Notes, Microsoft Office, and Windows. After the coursework, professionals can become certified in various applications, which makes them more marketable and able to command higher salaries.

The Predictable Performance System is a proven system that lets Manpower make a realistic prediction of just how a person will perform on the job—before he or she even goes on assignment. The company prides itself on its comprehensive interview. Structured to be identical for all office and industrial applicants, it goes in-depth to profile work experience, interests, and preferences. It probes for details about training and work experience. It also reveals personal likes and dislikes. These findings help make an accurate match of an individual to the type of work for which that person is fully qualified, as well as jobs that he or she is most interested in doing, which translates to better productivity.

The ongoing concerns of building a long-term workforce are taken seriously by Manpower. Lately, it has targeted urban poor as the next labor pool by opening offices to attract inner-city workers. Placing offices in poorer areas, Manpower can direct them toward full-time employment. No other staffing company has come up with as aggressive a strategy as Manpower's, which avoids the typical public-private partnership, strictly using the private sector. It dropped out of a welfare collaboration with government agencies in Milwaukee, at a cost to Manpower of $100,000, because it didn't like the politics of how it was being handled. While it may reach primarily the most motivated of welfare recipients, so far its go-it-alone policy has been successful.

28. MANPOWER INCORPORATED

United States   Ticker symbol MAN

Stock price $21 7/8 (9/16/98)   Dividend yield .82%

(Financial data is from I/B/E/S International)*

BUSINESS DESCRIPTION

HOLDING COMPANY WITH SUBSIDIARIES THAT PROVIDE EMPLOYMENT SERVICES, INCLUDING TEMPORARY HELP, CONTRACT SERVICES, AND TRAINING AND TESTING OF TEMPORARY AND PERMANENT WORKERS

ADDRESS AND CONTACTS

Address   5301 North Ironwood Road
                   Milwaukee WI 53217-4910
Telephone   1-414-961-1000

GENERAL INFORMATION

Mkt Cap (in Millions):   3295.00
Shares Outstanding: 81597000

*I/B/E/S and I/B/E/S Express are registered trademarks of I/B/E/S International Inc. Copyright 1993–1996 I/B/E/S International Inc. All rights reserved.

FINANCIAL STATEMENT DATA

INCOME STATEMENT	1997	1996	1995	1994	1993
Net Sales or Revenues	7258.50	6079.90	5484.17	4296.44	3180.39
Cost of Goods Sold	5948.31	4931.94	4483.34	3499.83	2555.21
Total Operating Expenses	7003.12	5852.95	5272.52	4144.70	3175.66
Depreciation and Amortization	41.62	35.62	27.82	20.74	18.71
Operating Income	255.39	226.96	211.65	151.75	4.73
EBIT	249.21	242.31	211.65	151.75	-15.27
Interest Expense	NA	NA	7.86	15.26	12.25
Income Tax Provisions	85.33	80.01	75.75	52.56	21.42
Net Income	163.88	162.30	128.04	83.93	-48.93

200

Manpower Incorporated

BALANCE SHEET	1997	1996	1995	1994	1993
Assets					
Cash	142.25	180.55	142.77	82.05	63.27
Total Current Assets	1686.90	1439.09	1277.31	987.34	651.34
Total Assets	2047.03	1752.26	1517.79	1191.20	833.28
Liabilities & Shareholders' Equity					
Total Current Liabilities	1004.68	811.26	776.32	668.42	440.75
Long Term Debt	189.79	100.85	61.78	30.87	30.05
Total Liabilities	1429.47	1151.56	1062.79	987.72	730.60
Shareholders' Equity	617.59	600.71	454.99	203.47	102.68
Total Liabilities & Sh. Equity	2047.03	1752.26	1517.79	1191.20	833.28

CASH FLOW	1997	1996	1995	1994	1993
Cash from Operations	36.10	102.62	102.22	36.46	105.49
Cash from Financing	42.12	13.97	-0.68	4.62	-77.53
Cash from Investing	-112.21	-67.37	-44.77	-24.73	-15.18
Cash Dividends	-13.84	-12.30	-10.17	-8.15	NA
Change in Working Capital	54.39	126.84	182.07	108.33	-2.35
Free Cash Flow	90.21	120.45	119.17	40.45	101.95

PER SHARE DATA*	1997	1996	1995	1994	1993
Earnings per Share	2.02	1.98	1.70	1.13	-0.66
Dividends per Share	0.17	0.15	0.13	0.11	NA
Book Value per Share	7.61	7.32	6.05	2.75	1.39
Price/Earnings Ratio	17.45	16.44	16.53	24.82	NM
Price/Book Ratio	4.63	4.44	4.65	10.24	12.64

Displayed Currency: U.S. Dollar (1.00:1)
All values are displayed in millions.
*Data is sourced from Disclosure and may differ from I/B/E/S historical per share information.

FINANCIAL RATIOS AND GROWTH RATES

PROFITABILITY	1997	1996	1995	1994	1993	5YR AVG
Operating Profit Margin %	3.52	3.73	3.86	3.53	0.15	2.96
Net Margin %	2.26	2.67	2.33	1.95	-1.54	1.54
Cash Flow % Sales	0.50	1.69	1.86	0.85	3.32	1.64
Return on Assets %	8.01	9.26	8.44	7.05	-5.87	5.38
Return on Equity— Total %	26.54	27.02	28.14	41.25	-47.66	15.06

UTILIZATION	1997	1996	1995	1994	1993	5YR AVG
Asset Turnover	3.55	3.47	3.61	3.61	3.82	3.61
Inventory Turnover	NA	NA	NA	NA	NA	NA

LIQUIDITY	1997	1996	1995	1994	1993	5YR AVG
Current Ratio	1.68	1.77	1.65	1.48	1.48	1.61
Quick Ratio	NA	NA	NA	NA	NA	NA

LEVERAGE	1997	1996	1995	1994	1993	5YR AVG
Long Term Debt % Common Equity	30.73	16.79	13.58	15.17	29.26	21.11
Total Liability % Common Equity	231.47	191.70	233.58	485.43	711.52	370.74
Times Interest Earned	NA	NA	26.92	9.95	-1.25	11.87
Long Term Debt % Total Capital	20.34	14.76	12.91	14.45	22.68	17.03
Total Liability % Total Capital	153.19	168.53	222.03	462.38	551.50	311.52

GROWTH %	1997	1996	1995	1994	1993	5YR AVG
Net Sales	19.39	10.86	27.64	35.09	-0.19	17.94
Operating Income	0.97	26.75	52.56	-+	N-	-+
Total Assets	16.82	15.45	27.42	42.95	-9.66	19.69
Earnings per Share*	2.15	16.20	50.17	-+	NA	-+
Dividends per Share*	13.33	15.38	18.18	NA	NA	NA
Book Value per Share	4.00	21.03	120.12	97.06	NA	40.42

*Source: Disclosure. Value may differ from I/B/E/S.
Note: 5-Year Average calculations exclude NAs.

DISCLOSURE AND I/B/E/S QUARTERLY FINANCIAL INFORMATION

SEC QUARTERLY FINANCIALS	Mar 98	Dec 97	Sep 97	Jun 97	Mar 97
Revenues	1872.87	1972.27	1973.02	1792.22	1521.00
Cost of Goods	1545.51	1608.80	1622.09	1473.07	1244.35
EBIT	33.62	64.58	83.91	61.03	39.69
Net Income	21.69	43.70	52.69	40.89	26.60

SEC QUARTERLY GROWTH RATES	Mar 98	Dec 97	Sep 97	Jun 97	
Revenues	-17.51	-8.07	-0.38	5.11	
Cost of Goods	24.20	24.06	17.61	23.65	
Net Income	-18.46	-9.12	0.52	5.93	

SEC QUARTERLY PER SHARE DATA	Mar 98	Dec 97	Sep 97	Jun 97	Mar 97
Earnings per Share	0.27	0.54	0.64	0.50	0.32
Dividends per Share	NA	0.09	NA	0.08	NA

Displayed Currency: U.S. Dollar (1.00:1)
Values are displayed in millions.
*Growth versus the same quarter in the prior year.

29. Mattel Incorporated

A toy is a toy, no matter what the country. That's why Mattel Incorporated, the number-one U.S. toymaker, plans to aggressively double its international sales over the next four years, increasing them from the current 35 percent of total sales to a dramatic 60 percent. While world economies will play a role, two-thirds of that growth should come from Japan and Europe, and less than a quarter from the United States and Latin America, it projects.

However, while Mattel designs products with worldwide appeal and markets them globally to more than 140 countries, it is now developing some toys based on how much they will cost when translated into a specific foreign currency. In the past, a number of toys, especially premium Barbie dolls, were simply too expensive when they were transplanted in their original form to foreign markets. Mattel is now introducing lower-priced Barbies in foreign markets through a line called "Global Friends" that features a different doll for each major global city. In addition, each Mattel product category has been given its own managers for marketing and product development in Europe, the United States, Latin America, and Asia.

Speaking of global issues, the company has also been in the forefront of establishing manufacturing principles for all of its facilities around the world, a process monitored by Dr. S. Prakash Sethi of Baruch College, City University of New York, an international expert on corporate governance and ethics. Included in its guidelines is a provision that no one under the age of sixteen may work in a facility that produces its products. Sanitation, lighting, ventilation, and servicing of machinery are all tracked. The far-flung manufacturing efforts of the company continue to grow. Primary manufacturing outside the United States is in China, Italy, Malaysia, Indonesia, and Mexico. The company has been a beneficiary of the Asian currency devaluations, as its best-selling fashion doll and toy car brands are produced in Malaysia, Indonesia, and Thailand.

Leading the company into this worldwide whirlwind is the highest-ranking female executive in the United States, Jill Barad, who became president and chief executive officer January 1, 1997, and assumed the additional post of chairman on October 8 of that year. She began with Mattel in 1981 as a product manager and became president of Mattel USA by 1990. This hard-driving executive is credited with boosting the Barbie brand from $200 million in sales in 1981 to $1.7 billion and for successfully integrating Tyco Toys Incorporated, with its Sesame Street characters and Matchbox toys, into Mattel following the $755 million acquisition of the number-three toymaker in 1996. The company realized $100 million of incremental savings in 1998 from that merger. Barad's goal is to inject the company with the sort of nonfaddish predictability that Wall Street and investors crave and the toy industry historically has not exemplified. Analysts also note that the majority of sales occur in the final two months of the year. An emphasis on its powerful core brands lessens volatility and means stable long-term growth in the United States and overseas. Barad has also been willing to take tough steps to strengthen the company. She took a significant charge and announced the layoff of 2,700 employees, or 10 percent of its workforce, after the Tyco merger.

Barad acts quickly and shrewdly. For example, inventory reductions by Toys "R" Us Inc., the biggest toy chain in the United States and one that accounts for about one-fifth of all Mattel sales, put pressure on Mattel revenues in 1998. As part of an effort to reduce reliance on toy chains, Barad decided to pay $700 million to buy direct marketer Pleasant Co., maker of the American Girls doll collection, books, and accessories. She also announced plans to open a new flagship Barbie store in Beverly Hills, California, and to begin using the Internet to market its toys.

Mattel's major brands, known to kids everywhere, include Barbie, Disney entertainment lines, Hot Wheels and Matchbox cars, and Cabbage Patch Kids. Its Fisher-Price line dominates the market for toys for preschool children, although it has been a drag on company results lately. The company also produces family and education games, such as Uno, Scrabble, and Skip-bo. Most sales are from toys aimed at girls, though the company is expanding its line of toys for boys and was aided in that regard by the acquisition of Tyco, with a stable of boy-oriented items. Nearly 90 percent of Mattel sales and about 99 percent of profits come from its core Barbie, Hot Wheels, Fisher-Price, and Disney licenses. Two animated Disney films, *Mulan,* a Chinese folktale, and *A Bug's Life,* the second film from the makers of *Toy Story,* were released in 1998, and there were, of course, new toys based on the characters in these films. Toys are definitely high-tech. Mattel signed a letter of intent with Intel Corp. in 1998 to collaborate on the next generation of interactive toys. Mattel toy designers will work with a team of Intel engineers at the chip company's Portland, Oregon, architecture lab to develop advanced interactive toys. The first toys from this venture will be unveiled in one to two years. The Barbie interactive business has quadrupled from $20 million in sales to $80 million. Through the acquisition of PrintPaks, an interactive arts and crafts company, Barbie has gone digital with a Barbie digital camera that lets girls take photos of themselves and friends and download them onto their personal computers.

Over the past ten years, Mattel has made eleven acquisitions, including Fisher-Price, Kransco, Spear, and Tyco. With strong cash flow and low debt on its balance sheet, Mattel is likely to continue to make acquisitions a part of its future in the rapidly consolidating toy industry. The company also sold one break-even division, its sports business, which included the Frisbee and Hula Hoop brands, to Wham-O Incorporated of San Francisco for about $20 million in early 1998. Mattel beat out rival Hasbro Incorporated to sign an exclusive licensing deal with the National Basketball Association, with a new Women's National Basketball Association Barbie being an example of what will come from that deal. In addition, Avon Products Incorporated has joined with Mattel to launch Barbie in China, while U.S. Avon ladies will sell three kinds of Barbies, Barbie cosmetics, Cabbage Patch Dolls, Hot Wheels cars, and talking Sesame Street characters.

Mattel's 25,000 employees can feel confident that the company doesn't merely toy with them. *Fortune* magazine named Mattel one of the 100 Best Companies to Work For, while *Working Mother* magazine has honored it for several years running. The company's LifeWorks Resources program provides employees with the tools and time to meet the needs of their children, aging parents, and other family members. It also offers programs that help employees address job-related issues, health and fitness, personal finances, and even the needs of pets. The company offers sixteen weeks of unpaid maternity leave, plus flex-time, job sharing, and compressed work weeks. An on-site Child Development Center at its El Segundo, California, headquarters provides full-time care for children through age six, including a fully accredited kindergarten class.

"We continue to target earnings growth of at least 15 percent on an ongoing basis," Barad wrote in her letter in the most recent annual report. "Our business is all about kids, their dreams, and our incredible portfolio of time-tested brands."

29. MATTEL INCORPORATED

United States   Ticker symbol MAT

Stock price $34 15/16 (9/16/98)   Dividend yield .92%

(Financial data is from I/B/E/S International)*

BUSINESS DESCRIPTION

DESIGNS, DEVELOPS, MANUFACTURES, MARKETS, AND DISTRIBUTES A WIDE VARIETY OF TOY PRODUCTS ON A WORLDWIDE BASIS

ADDRESS AND CONTACTS

Address   333 Continental Boulevard
                 El Segundo CA 90245-5012
Telephone   1-310-252-2000

Mattel Incorporated

BASIC FINANCIAL INFORMATION

Capital Structure[†]	Long Term Debt:	808.30
	Total Debt:	839.42
	Common Sh. Equity:	1821.30

SALES BREAKDOWN

Product Segments[†]	Toys	4834.62
Geographic Segments[†]	United States	2959.77
	Asia & Latin America	804.08
	Europe & Canada	1070.77

Displayed Currency: U.S. Dollar (1.00:1)

*I/B/E/S and I/B/E/S Express are registered trademarks of I/B/E/S International Inc. Copyright 1993–1996 I/B/E/S International Inc. All rights reserved.

[†]Values are displayed in millions.

FINANCIAL STATEMENT DATA

INCOME STATEMENT	1997	1996	1995	1994	1993
Net Sales or Revenues	4834.62	3785.96	3638.81	3205.03	2704.45
EBITDA	705.12	770.33	739.48	573.35	391.23
Depreciation Depletion & Amort	189.91	149.06	132.98	124.27	91.97
Operating Income	823.91	668.88	601.60	548.57	426.18
Interest Expense	75.53	75.53	73.59	55.45	62.61
Pretax Income	425.08	545.74	532.90	393.63	236.65
Net Income	279.29	377.64	354.46	251.14	131.02

BALANCE SHEET	1997	1996	1995	1994	1993
Assets					
Cash & Equivalents	694.95	500.62	483.46	259.68	523.58
Receivables—Net	1091.42	732.31	679.28	762.02	580.31
Inventories	428.84	372.69	350.84	339.14	219.99
Total Current Assets	2461.74	1770.84	1690.82	1543.52	1470.75
Property Plant & Eq.— Net	601.60	579.61	499.31	415.92	326.88
Total Assets	3803.79	2893.52	2695.51	2459.03	2000.08
Liabilities & Shareholders' Equity					
Total Current Liabilities	1173.42	960.37	847.68	915.88	783.33
Long Term Debt	808.30	485.37	572.66	457.46	398.94
Preferred Stock	0.77	0.00	0.00	33.80	30.30
Common Equity	1821.30	1447.79	1275.17	1051.89	787.51
Total Liabilities & Sh. Equity	3803.79	2893.52	2695.51	2459.03	2000.08

CASH FLOW	1997	1996	1995	1994	1993
Net Cash Flow— Operating	481.85	515.22	405.49	343.44	303.34
Net Cash Flow— Investing	205.96	219.11	180.08	526.50	88.80
Net Cash Flow— Financing	-116.23	-260.93	-0.12	-86.05	-16.37
Incr/Decr in Working Capital	477.84	-32.66	211.50	-59.78	228.42
Free Cash Flow	483.55	561.32	532.59	409.97	290.36

INTERNATIONAL BUSINESS	1997	1996	1995	1994	1993
Foreign Assets	1364.82	1163.84	1148.34	1111.12	836.16
Foreign Sales	1874.85	2957.64	2767.30	2353.85	1901.03
Foreign Income	473.72	398.45	396.51	273.90	165.19

SUPPLEMENTARY DATA	1997	1996	1995	1994	1993
Employees	25000	26000	25000	22000	21000
R&D Expenses	156.35	126.24	111.28	93.15	75.42
Goodwill/Cost in Excess of Assets Purchased	534.13	397.82	411.26	418.90	124.4
Extra Items & Gain/ Loss in Sale of Assets	-4.61	0.00	0.00	0.00	-18.70

Displayed Currency: U.S. Dollar (1.00:1)
All values are displayed in millions (except employees).

FINANCIAL RATIOS AND GROWTH RATES

PROFITABILITY	1997	1996	1995	1994	1993	5YR AVG
Operating Profit Margin %	17.04	17.67	16.53	17.12	15.76	16.82
Tax Rate %	31.83	30.80	32.86	35.01	42.57	34.61
Net Margin %	5.90	9.97	9.83	7.98	4.33	7.60
Return on Assets %	11.91	15.86	16.53	14.62	12.58	14.30
Return on Equity— Total %	18.97	29.61	33.70	31.89	22.43	27.32
Cash Flow % Sales	13.12	14.21	13.46	12.46	6.70	11.99
Sales per Employee (in 000s)	193	146	146	146	129	152

ASSET UTILIZATION	1997	1996	1995	1994	1993	5YR AVG
Total Asset Turnover	1.27	1.31	1.35	1.30	1.35	1.32
Capital Exp % Gross Fixed Assets	23.61	23.95	27.04	24.58	18.14	23.46

Mattel Incorporated

Acc Depreciation %						
Gross Fixed Assets	35.90	33.59	34.75	37.42	41.21	36.57
Assets per Employee						
(in 000s)	152	111	108	112	95	116

LIQUIDITY	**1997**	**1996**	**1995**	**1994**	**1993**	**5YR AVG**
Current Ratio	2.10	1.84	1.99	1.69	1.88	1.90
Quick Ratio	1.52	1.28	1.37	1.12	1.41	1.34

LEVERAGE	**1997**	**1996**	**1995**	**1994**	**1993**	**5YR AVG**
Total Debt %						
Common Equity	46.09	42.27	48.73	43.78	63.97	48.97
Long Term Debt %						
Common Equity	44.38	33.52	44.91	43.49	50.66	43.39
Common Equity %						
Total Assets	47.88	50.04	47.31	42.78	39.37	45.47
Long Term Debt %						
Total Capital	30.73	25.11	30.99	29.64	32.79	29.85
Operating Cash/						
Fixed Charges	5.97	7.12	6.22	6.38	2.59	5.66

GROWTH %	**1997**	**1996**	**1995**	**1994**	**1993**	**5YR AVG**
Net Sales	27.70	4.04	13.53	18.51	46.35	21.21
Operating Income	23.18	11.18	9.67	28.72	63.12	25.82
Total Assets	31.46	7.35	9.62	22.95	58.70	24.72
Earnings per Share*	-30.88	34.92	40.63	45.45	-32.69	5.12
Dividends per Share*	12.50	25.00	25.00	30.43	38.01	25.91
Book Value per Share	17.14	41.89	22.05	2.89	6.48	17.32

Displayed Currency: U.S. Dollar (1.00:1)
*Source: Worldscope. Value may differ from I/B/E/S.
Note: 5-Year Average calculations exclude NAs.

PER SHARE AND RELATED DATA

SOURCE: WORLDSCOPE	**1997**	**1996**	**1995**	**1994**	**1993**
Earnings per Share	0.94	1.36	1.01	0.72	0.49
Dividends per Share	0.27	0.24	0.19	0.15	0.12
Book Value per Share	6.08	5.19	3.66	3.00	2.91
Total Investment Return	NA	NA	54.18	14.77	9.77
Market Price (Year-end)	37.25	27.75	24.60	16.08	14.14
Market Capitalization					
(in millions)	10862.10	7520.25	6688.74	4440.09	3696.63

Global Investing 1999 Edition

SOURCE: WORLDSCOPE	1997	1996	1995	1994	1993
Price/Earnings Ratio	39.63	20.40	24.40	22.43	28.70
Price/Book Value	6.12	5.34	6.72	5.36	4.85
Dividend Yield	0.72	0.86	0.78	0.96	0.83
Dividend Payout per Share	28.72	17.65	19.05	21.43	23.90
Common Shares Outstanding (Year-end) in Millions	291.60	271.00	271.90	276.12	261.36
Stock Split/Dividend Ratio	NA	NA	0.80	0.64	0.51
Type of Share Common					

Displayed Currency: U.S. Dollar (1.00:1)
Note: Data is sourced from Worldscope and may differ from I/B/E/S historical data.

30. Medtronic Incorporated

Medtronic gets the world's hearts up to speed. It's the largest maker of implantable biomedical devices, including the most-prescribed pacemaker, which accounts for 44 percent of its revenues. These coin-sized implantable pace generators with extended battery life are vital lifesaving devices. To acknowledge their importance, the company that many consider to be the best medical device company in the world gives each new employee a bronze medallion inscribed with the words, "Toward man's full life." It also invites patients to an annual holiday party to tell employees how Medtronic saved or changed their lives.

Although the pacemaker market has lately been rather flat, the company holds 45 percent of the worldwide market for these devices and its earnings outlook is strong based on an impressive pipeline of new products. One example is the Kappa 400 Series next-generation pacemaker with extensive self-programming capabilities and improved diagnostic features. It allows physicians to streamline their implant procedures, fine-tune pacing therapy quickly and easily, and simplify follow-up routines. Medtronic Vision, the pacemaker industry's first icon-based programming software is an integral part of the system. Powerful diagnostic capabilities in the pacemaker collect data between patient follow-up visits and provide clinically relevant information that can help physicians make faster and more informed decisions. Pacing products, constituting nearly two-thirds of sales, include bradycardia devices, which pace slow or irregular heartbeats, and tachyarrhythmia devices, which correct rapid heartbeats.

This innovative company has had a remarkable run in the 1990s. Chairman and Chief Executive Officer William George was named one of the Top 25 Managers of the Year by *Business Week* magazine in 1998, and was credited for "pumping Medtronic into high gear" since taking over in 1991. New products, greater research and development spending, and tight financial discipline have added up to excellent returns for shareholders during his tenure.

The firm's therapeutic medical products focus on improving cardiovascular and neurological health. Medtronic makes mechanical and tissue heart valves, implantable neurostimulation and drug delivery systems, perfusion blood systems, and catheters used in angioplastics. Its dual-chamber implantable cardiac defribrillator (ICD), the Gem DR, released in 1998, is an important step: Analysts expect dual-chamber devices to snare a larger portion of the ICD market because they can distinguish between different types of arrythmias and help reduce the number of inappropriate shocks delivered when a defibrillator misdiagnoses an arrythmia in the lower chambers as an irregular heartbeat in the upper chambers of the heart. Another important product will be the Jewel AF defibrillator used to treat atrial fibrillation, an abnormally fast heartbeat in the upper chambers. Lagging sales of angioplasty devices have hurt revenues, with a restructuring charge taken and a consolidation of administration and manufacturing in Europe and Japan that is helping the company's bottom line.

Medtronic's fastest-growing business has been its neurological division, which should grow at a 30 percent clip for the next decade, producing implantable drug-delivery systems to control pain and reduce severe muscle rigidity associated with cerebral palsy and other neurological conditions. It also has been developing neurostimulation products based on electrical-stimulation technology used in the firm's pacemakers and defibrillators, such as the Activa tremor-control device and another to control incontinence. Others will target epilepsy and loss of muscle movement from Parkinson's disease. It is also developing products for minimally invasive cardiac surgery and sleep apnea. Monitoring the heart less expensively has been a major consideration. The company recently introduced its Remote Assistant cardiac monitor, a handheld patient–activated diagnostic tool that records important heart rate information associated with a patient's symptoms or exercise response. It's a convenient alternative to large, expensive cardiac monitors. Another recent product is the Reveal Insertable Loop Recorder, the world's first cardiac monitor designed to be inserted under the skin. This unique product offers hope to patients who have been frustrated by expensive and often inconclusive testing for unexplained fainting spells.

Medtronic's devices serve more than 1.4 million individuals worldwide each year. It sells its products in more than 120 countries and foreign sales account for about one-third of sales. The company operates research and manufacturing facilities in the United States and overseas, employing 13,500. Sales have been constrained by the strength of the dollar. Negative currency translation and foreign exchange fluctuations have had an impact on its bottom line, and it has begun a program to protect those results.

The company was formed as a partnership in 1949 by Earl Bakken and Palmer Hermundslie from an idea they came up with while talking about Earl's part-time work at Northwestern Hospital in Minneapolis. They realized that while hospital engineers could service heavy machinery, they were not trained to repair more delicate laboratory equipment. Earl left his graduate studies, Palmer quit his job with a local lumber firm, and together they formed a medical equipment repair company named Medtronic in a 600-square-foot garage. In the mid-1950s, Medtronic became acquainted with Dr. C. Walton Lillehei, a pioneer in open heart surgery at the University of Minnesota Medical School. Medtronic engineers got closely involved in his work, which led to the development of the wearable, external, battery-powered pacemaker. It was gradually revised until the first implantable pacemaker debuted in 1960.

Medtronic has actively acquired related businesses and technologies to establish new platforms for growth. It most recently made acquisitions or minority investments in an automated autotransfusion system from perHop of Switzerland; Vista Medical Technologies' visualization system and Computer Motion's robotics microsurgery system for minimally invasive therapies; Somnus Medical Technologies' ablation therapy for conditions affecting the upper airway; and Inverventional Innovations' technology for delivering radiation within the body's blood vessels.

Its efforts have gained attention. The company was also chosen one of The 100 Best Companies to Work For by *Fortune* magazine in 1998. In addition, Medtronic received the award for general excellence in ethics from *Business Ethics* magazine for programs such as its compliance program. Each of approximately 4,000 employees who work directly with customers are required each year to fill out a twelve-page ethics questionnaire and sign the company's code of conduct. There's a telephone hotline directly into the general counsel's office to enable employees to anonymously report ethics problems. It also has an initiative to establish uniform codes of conduct in foreign countries. The company has also gained attention for its Medtronic Foundation, which awards grants focusing on education, health, and community, with priority given to programs that benefit those who are disadvantaged. For example, the foundation's STAR (Science and Technology Are Rewarding) program stimulates young people's interest in science, health, and technology.

"We envision rapid increases in revenues outside the United States, through increased educational and service offerings for customers in developing markets," the company's top three executives stated in their letter in the most recent annual report. "We face growing global competition in all of our businesses, but we believe the dedication of our employees to customer-focused quality and medical innovation will enable Medtronic to continue to gain market share in all our businesses around the world."

30. MEDTRONIC INCORPORATED

United States   Ticker symbol MDT

Stock price $57 1/16 (9/16/98)   Dividend yield .46%

(Financial data is from I/B/E/S International)*

BUSINESS DESCRIPTION

ENGAGED IN MANUFACTURING BIOMEDICAL DEVICES TO IMPROVE CARDIO-VASCULAR AND NEUROLOGICAL HEALTH

ADDRESS AND CONTACTS

Address	7000 Central Avenue N.E.
	Minneapolis MN 55432
Telephone	1-612-514-4000
Fax	1-612-514-4879

BASIC FINANCIAL INFORMATION

Report Dates	Last Quarter: Jan 98	Reported On: Feb 18, 1998
	Next Quarter: April 98	Expected On: May 22, 1998
Capital Structure†	Long Term Debt:	13.98
	Total Debt:	120.36
	Common Sh. Equity:	1746.22

SALES BREAKDOWN

Product Segments†	Medical Instruments	2438.22
Geographic Segments†	United States	1619.93
	Europe	770.19
	Asia Pacific	268.38
	Other Americas	69.63
	Eliminations	-289.91

Displayed Currency: U.S. Dollar (1.00:1)
*I/B/E/S and I/B/E/S Express are registered trademarks of I/B/E/S International Inc. Copyright 1993–1996 I/B/E/S International Inc. All rights reserved.
†Values are displayed in millions.

FINANCIAL STATEMENT DATA

INCOME STATEMENT	1997	1996	1995	1994	1993
Net Sales or Revenues	2438.22	2169.11	1742.39	1390.92	1328.21
EBITDA	935.41	788.14	557.61	433.59	393.53
Depreciation Depletion & Amort	116.89	111.78	106.50	78.58	69.93

INCOME STATEMENT	1997	1996	1995	1994	1993
Operating Income	784.47	647.17	436.34	332.67	295.12
Interest Expense	7.96	7.96	9.01	8.21	10.45
Pretax Income	809.14	668.40	442.10	346.80	313.46
Net Income	NA	437.80	294.00	232.36	211.58

BALANCE SHEET	1997	1996	1995	1994	1993
Assets					
Cash & Equivalents	250.57	460.85	323.65	181.41	155.98
Receivables—Net	516.98	456.77	413.94	340.93	349.99
Inventories	282.55	257.35	221.93	213.30	189.07
Total Current Assets	1237.91	1343.23	1103.91	845.86	774.69
Property Plant & Eq.— Net	487.22	415.29	331.06	301.78	282.78
Total Assets	2409.21	2503.30	1946.73	1623.25	1286.45
Liabilities & Shareholders' Equity					
Total Current Liabilities	518.69	525.05	456.13	439.44	348.10
Long Term Debt	13.98	15.34	14.20	20.23	10.85
Preferred Stock	0.00	0.00	0.00	0.00	0.00
Common Equity	1746.22	1789.30	1335.01	1053.49	841.48
Total Liabilities & Sh. Equity	2409.21	2503.30	1946.73	1623.25	1286.45

CASH FLOW	1997	1996	1995	1994	1993
Net Cash Flow— Operating	463.62	500.50	387.18	356.86	291.51
Net Cash Flow— Investing	-78.00	429.92	240.00	258.06	162.79
Net Cash Flow— Financing	-491.10	-58.35	-159.72	-66.92	-152.64
Incr/Decr in Working Capital	-98.97	170.41	241.37	-20.18	39.25
Free Cash Flow	764.08	624.37	460.75	372.79	316.45

INTERNATIONAL BUSINESS	1997	1996	1995	1994	1993
Foreign Assets	678.98	582.77	365.27	404.90	388.17
Foreign Sales	1035.06	932.12	765.80	593.53	557.55
Foreign Income	270.44	276.01	202.04	121.08	108.95

SUPPLEMENTARY DATA	1997	1996	1995	1994	1993
Employees	13719	10526	8896	8709	9247
R&D Expenses	280.21	236.68	191.35	156.31	132.96

Goodwill/Cost in Excess of Assets Purchased	394.24	386.05	278.72	279.51	109.58
Extra Items & Gain/ Loss in Sale of Assets	0.00	0.00	0.00	0.00	-14.36

Displayed Currency: U.S. Dollar (1.00:1)
All values are displayed in millions (except employees).

FINANCIAL RATIOS AND GROWTH RATES

PROFITABILITY	1997	1996	1995	1994	1993	5YR AVG
Operating Profit Margin %	32.17	29.84	25.04	23.92	22.22	26.64
Tax Rate %	34.50	34.50	33.50	33.00	32.50	33.60
Net Margin %	21.74	20.18	16.87	16.71	14.85	18.07
Return on Assets %	21.42	22.76	18.48	18.48	17.54	19.74
Return on Equity— Total %	29.62	32.79	27.91	27.61	24.76	28.54
Cash Flow % Sales	26.61	23.81	23.03	21.99	19.86	23.06
Sales per Employee (in 000s)	178	206	196	160	144	177

ASSET UTILIZATION	1997	1996	1995	1994	1993	5YR AVG
Total Asset Turnover	1.01	0.87	0.90	0.86	1.03	0.93
Capital Exp % Gross Fixed Assets	17.75	19.64	13.54	9.97	14.00	14.98
Acc Depreciation % Gross Fixed Assets	49.51	50.19	53.73	50.52	48.63	50.52
Assets per Employee (in 000s)	176	238	219	186	139	192

LIQUIDITY	1997	1996	1995	1994	1993	5YR AVG
Current Ratio	2.39	2.56	2.42	1.92	2.23	2.30
Quick Ratio	1.48	1.75	1.62	1.19	1.45	1.50

LEVERAGE	1997	1996	1995	1994	1993	5YR AVG
Total Debt % Common Equity	6.89	4.24	3.57	7.44	12.21	6.87
Long Term Debt % Common Equity	0.80	0.86	1.06	1.92	1.29	1.19
Common Equity % Total Assets	72.48	71.48	68.58	64.90	65.41	68.57
Long Term Debt % Total Capital	0.79	0.85	1.05	1.88	1.27	1.17
Operating Cash/ Fixed Charges	69.22	64.88	44.54	37.26	25.25	48.23

GROWTH %	1997	1996	1995	1994	1993	5YR AVG
Net Sales	12.41	24.49	25.27	4.72	12.86	15.68
Operating Income	21.22	48.32	31.16	12.73	19.94	26.10
Total Assets	-3.76	28.59	19.93	26.18	10.57	15.67
Earnings per Share*	14.56	-8.85	0.44	61.87	71.60	23.85
Dividends per Share*	21.43	42.13	25.48	20.78	20.37	25.78
Book Value per Share	-1.52	45.61	16.94	30.30	2.68	17.54

Displayed Currency: U.S. Dollar (1.00:1)
*Source: Worldscope. Value may differ from I/B/E/S.
Note: 5-Year Average calculations exclude NAs.

PER SHARE AND RELATED DATA

SOURCE: WORLDSCOPE	1997	1996	1995	1994	1993
Earnings per Share	1.18	1.03	1.13	1.13	0.70
Dividends per Share	0.21	0.18	0.12	0.10	0.08
Book Value per Share	4.14	4.21	2.89	2.47	1.90
Total Investment Return	NA	22.33	101.78	36.42	-13.10
Market Price (Year-end)	52.50	34.00	27.94	13.91	10.27
Market Capitalization (in millions)	24550.42	15933.61	12908.18	6466.82	4748.45
Price/Earnings Ratio	44.49	33.01	24.72	12.36	14.77
Price/Book Value	12.67	8.08	9.67	5.63	5.41
Dividend Yield	0.40	0.51	0.44	0.71	0.79
Dividend Payout per Share	18.01	16.99	10.90	8.72	11.69
Common Shares Outstanding (Year-end) in Millions	467.63	468.64	462.04	465.03	462.56
Stock Split/Dividend Ratio	1.00	0.50	0.50	0.25	0.13
Type of Share Common					

Displayed Currency: U.S. Dollar (1.00:1)
Note: Data is sourced from Worldscope and may differ from I/B/E/S historical data.

31. MGIC Investment Corporation

Home sweet home can mean sweet profits for investors. Immigration has pushed U.S. population growth in the 1990s to its highest level in forty years, with continued strong growth projected for the next two decades. This should drive the market for homes, with mortgage originations approaching $4 trillion. Sixty-six percent of U.S. households now own homes—the highest percentage since 1980—and the U.S. government wants to see home ownership hit 70 percent by the year 2000.

MGIC Investment Corporation, the parent company of Mortgage Guaranty Insurance, is the nation's leading private mortgage insurance company. It often speaks of its contributions to home ownership in reverential tones that evoke thoughts of Mom, apple pie, and the American flag. But beyond doing the right thing, it has turned in record earnings in each of its seven years as a public company and given a powerful boost to its stock. The company provides mortgage insurance coverage to protect against loss from defaults to mortgage bankers, savings institutions, commercial banks, mortgage brokers, credit unions, and other lenders. Private mortgage insurance covers residential first mortgage loans and enables people to purchase homes with less than 20 percent down. It reduces its risk by providing support and educational programs for new homeowners and by keeping a close watch on their payments. MGIC insures more than 1.33 million home mortgages totaling more than $138.5 billion. It's the undisputed leader with a 27 percent chunk of the market. Northwestern Mutual Life Insurance Company is MGIC's largest shareholder, with an 18 percent ownership position.

219

Potential risks to MGIC's future include the possibility that interest rates may increase rather than remain stable or decrease, and that demand for housing may grow less than projected or decrease. There's also the chance that government housing may change, perhaps including adjustments in Federal Housing Administration loan limits and in the statutory charters and coverage requirements of Freddie Mac and Fannie Mae. There's also the possibility that delinquencies, incurred losses, or paid losses may increase faster than projected as a result of adverse changes in regional or national economies affecting borrowers' incomes or housing values.

William Lacy, chairman and chief executive of Mortgage Guaranty Insurance Corporation and the president and chief executive officer of MGIC Investment Corporation, has effectively focused the company on strong risk management and customer relations while building its public image. Lacy sees the home buyer as MGIC's real customer, rather than the lending institutions, and has therefore initiated programs to promote 3 percent down payments for selected buyers, eliminate most closing-time insurance costs, and distribute first-time home buyer video workbooks to lenders. He has also developed a training and counseling program to help lenders effectively serve borrowers and to help financially distressed borrowers avoid foreclosure.

For each year of new insurance writings since it came into being in 1985, MGIC has experienced fewer losses than the rest of the private mortgage insurance industry. Thanks to its MGIC Mortgage Score software, which estimates default risk, its loss ratio since 1992 has been 35 percent, versus an industry average of 56 percent. This program analyzes credit history, real estate market conditions, and other borrrower information. The higher the score, the less likely a foreclosure will take place. Its claims-paying ability receives an AA+ rating from Standard & Poor's Insurance Rating Analysis and Fitch Research, while it gets another high mark of Aa2 from Moody's Investors Service. Such high rankings reflect MGIC's market leadership position among the nine private mortgage insurers, its underwriting and pricing expertise, depth of management, and sound capital adequacy. It counts on geographic diversification of the insurance in force to ease volatility, strong profitability, and sophisticated technology applications. Potential factors affecting the rating include susceptibility to economic changes, market competition, and the market's increased use of structured transactions such as captive reinsurance and pool insurance. MGIC's continued focus on conservatively underwriting mortgage default risk is key to its success.

MGIC's insurance also makes possible the sale of low down payment mortgage loans in the secondary mortgage market, principally to the Federal Home Loan Mortgage Corporation. In particular, it helps young families buy their first home. Some homeowners also use it to trade up to larger homes. Since 1990, the portion of the overall mortgage origination market that is privately insured has more than doubled. The company has other noninsurance subsidiaries that provide various services for the home mortgage finance industry, such as secondary marketing of mortgage-related assets, real estate valuation, contract underwriting, real estate disposition, and consulting. Freddie Mac and MGIC have joined forces to produce EarlyIndicator, software that studies late payments. It determines which borrowers are least likely to pay and offers ways to bring balances current. Collection attempts focus on these accounts.

MGIC was formed through a series of transactions undertaken after its predecessor's parent, Baldwin United Corporation, declared bankruptcy in 1983. There had been heavy losses due to lax underwriting standards, especially for homeowners with reduced down payments in energy-producing states such as Texas. There was too much optimism on the company's part that housing market inflation could go on indefinitely covering losses, an assumption that had to change. MGIC began writing new business on March 1, 1985. It now has more than 1,000 full- and part-time employees, with more than half assigned to its Milwaukee headquarters and the rest to its field offices. The company retains exposure to 65 percent of the book of business written by MGIC's predecessor company, Wisconsin Mortgage

Assurance Corp., and earnings prospects have been significantly improved by the reduced relevance of problems associated with that WMAC business. Management's primary objectives are to balance the quality of MGIC's insured risk with production volume and efficiency, while improving service to financial institutions. One plus is its compensation plan, which is partially based on productivity and the performance of business written.

This low-key company that's on a mission to put Americans into homes combined its annual report to shareholders with its proxy statement in 1998 to reduce the cost of annual meeting materials. No bright colors, no shiny paper, just black-and-white type relating the fact that the company had enjoyed a 25 percent increase in earnings and reached yet another record high.

In the company's letter to shareholders, management stated its belief that continued low interest rates, a steady increase in the home ownership rate, and demand for housing from the immigrant population would fuel further MGIC growth: "MGIC's leadership role in insuring low down payment mortgages, coupled with our programs designed to meet the needs of the underserved population, positions us well to capitalize on these market opportunities."

31. MGIC INVESTMENT CORPORATION

United States   Ticker symbol MTG

Stock price $40 7/16 (9/16/98)   Dividend yield .25%

(Financial data is from I/B/E/S International)*

BUSINESS DESCRIPTION

PROVIDER OF PRIVATE MORTGAGE INSURANCE COVERAGE TO MORTGAGE BANKERS, SAVINGS INSTITUTIONS, AND OTHER LENDERS

ADDRESS AND CONTACTS

Address   MGIC Plaza
               250 East Kilbourn Avenue
               Milwaukee WI 53202
Telephone   1-414-347-6480

MGIC Investment Corporation

BASIC FINANCIAL INFORMATION

Report Dates	Last Quarter: Mar 98	Reported On: Apr 09, 1998
	Next Quarter: Jun 98	Expected On: Jul 13, 1998
Capital Structure[†]	Long Term Debt:	212.50
	Total Debt:	237.50
	Common Sh. Equity:	1402.80

SALES BREAKDOWN

Product Segments[†]	NA
Geographic Segments[†]	NA

Displayed Currency: U.S. Dollar (1.00:1)
*I/B/E/S and I/B/E/S Express are registered trademarks of I/B/E/S International Inc. Copyright 1993–1996 I/B/E/S International Inc. All rights reserved.
[†]Values are displayed in millions.

FINANCIAL STATEMENT DATA

INCOME STATEMENT	1997	1996	1995	1994	1993
Net Sales or Revenues	868.28	745.63	617.89	502.23	403.52
Investment Income	123.60	105.36	87.54	75.23	64.69
Total Claim and Loss Expense	242.36	234.35	189.98	153.08	107.13
Operating Income	471.77	368.82	295.23	220.94	178.70
Interest Expense	6.40	3.79	3.82	3.86	3.89
Pretax Income	465.37	365.03	291.41	217.08	174.82
Net Income	323.75	257.99	207.57	159.52	127.27

BALANCE SHEET	1997	1996	1995	1994	1993
Assets					
Cash	4.89	3.86	9.69	3.49	4.19
Total Investments	2416.74	2036.23	1687.22	1292.96	1099.64
Total Assets	2617.69	2222.32	1874.72	1476.27	1343.20
Liabilities & Shareholders' Equity					
Total Insurance Reserves	796.99	733.35	622.20	561.38	532.27
Total Debt	237.50	35.42	45.57	48.41	51.40
Preferred Stock	0.00	0.00	0.00	0.00	0.00
Common Equity	1402.80	1325.43	1066.65	862.38	712.07
Total Liabilities & Sh. Equity	2617.69	2222.32	1874.72	1476.27	1343.21

CASH FLOW	1997	1996	1995	1994	1993
Net Cash Flow— Operating	363.96	367.76	286.54	239.45	212.70
Net Cash Flow— Investing	344.00	314.46	359.92	155.10	169.07

CASH FLOW	1997	1996	1995	1994	1993
Net Cash Flow— Financing	-44.31	0.41	-3.64	-7.50	-7.98

SUPPLEMENTARY DATA	1997	1996	1995	1994	1993
Fixed Income Secs— Total	2185.95	1892.08	1602.81	1125.52	1010.01
Equity Securities— Total	116.05	4.04	3.84	3.65	3.39
Real Estate Assets	0.00	0.00	0.00	0.00	0.00
Mortgage Policy and Other Loans	0.00	0.00	0.00	0.00	0.00
Benefit and Loss Reserves	0.00	0.00	0.00	0.00	0.00
Unearned Premiums	198.31	219.31	251.16	281.14	306.85
Policy and Contract Claims	598.68	514.04	371.02	274.47	213.60
Employees	1090	1026	1066	1121	1195
Goodwill/Cost in Excess of Assets Purchased	NA	NA	NA	NA	NA
Extra Items & Gain/ Loss in Sale of Assets	0.00	0.00	0.00	0.00	0.00

Displayed Currency: U.S. Dollar (1.00:1)
All values are displayed in millions (except employees).

FINANCIAL RATIOS AND GROWTH RATES

PROFITABILITY	1997	1996	1995	1994	1993	5YR AVG
Return on Assets %	14.76	13.90	14.23	12.07	12.69	13.53
Return on Equity— Total %	24.43	24.19	24.07	22.40	21.49	23.31
Tax Rate %	30.43	29.32	28.77	26.52	27.20	28.45
Net Premiums Written % Equity	52.22	55.21	55.70	57.62	57.87	55.72
Combined Ratio	56.91	62.85	66.15	71.05	74.32	66.25
Investment Income % Inv Assets	6.07	6.24	6.77	6.84	7.22	6.63

LEVERAGE	1997	1996	1995	1994	1993	5YR AVG
Total Capital % Total Assets	64.92	63.07	61.72	59.19	55.70	60.92
Common Equity % Total Assets	53.59	59.64	56.90	58.42	53.01	56.31

LIQUIDITY	1997	1996	1995	1994	1993	5YR AVG
Benefit & Loss Res % Tot Cap	0.00	0.00	0.00	0.00	0.00	0.00

MGIC Investment Corporation

ASSET UTILIZATION	1997	1996	1995	1994	1993	5YR AVG
Assets per Employee (in 000s)	2402	2166	1759	1317	1124	1753

OTHER	1997	1996	1995	1994	1993	5YR AVG
Invested Assets % Total Liab	198.93	227.03	208.80	210.62	174.23	203.92
Invested Assets % Total Assets	92.32	91.63	90.00	87.58	81.87	88.68
Eq Secs % Real Estate % Inv Assets	4.80	0.20	0.23	0.28	0.31	1.16

GROWTH %	1997	1996	1995	1994	1993	5YR AVG
Total Assets	17.79	18.54	26.99	9.91	31.29	20.67
Total Insurance Reserves	8.68	17.86	10.83	5.47	56.97	18.64
Net Sales or Revenues	16.45	20.67	23.03	24.46	25.43	21.97
Operating Income	27.91	24.93	33.63	23.63	22.76	26.51
Earnings per Share*	27.02	23.71	29.63	25.00	24.14	25.88
Dividends per Share*	18.75	0.00	0.00	10.34	3.57	6.30
Book Value per Share	5.59	28.21	22.64	21.05	19.24	19.10

Displayed Currency: U.S. Dollar (1.00:1)
*Source: Worldscope. Value may differ from I/B/E/S.
Note: 5-Year Average calculations exclude NAs.

PER SHARE AND RELATED DATA

SOURCE: WORLDSCOPE	1997	1996	1995	1994	1993
Earnings per Share	2.75	2.17	1.75	1.35	1.08
Dividends per Share	0.10	0.08	0.08	0.08	0.07
Book Value per Share	12.08	11.44	8.92	7.28	6.01
Total Investment Return	NA	NA	64.26	13.79	15.56
Market Price (Year-end)	66.50	38.00	27.13	16.56	14.63
Market Capitalization (in millions)	7567.14	4358.26	3164.37	1934.33	1704.49
Price/Earnings Ratio	24.18	17.55	15.50	12.27	13.54
Price/Book Value	5.50	3.32	3.04	2.28	2.43
Dividend Yield	0.14	0.21	0.29	0.48	0.50
Dividend Payout per Share	3.45	3.70	4.57	5.93	6.71
Common Shares Outstanding (Year-end) in Millions	113.79	144.69	116.66	116.79	116.55
Stock Split/Dividend Ratio	NA	0.50	0.50	0.50	0.50

Type of Share   Common

Displayed Currency: U.S. Dollar (1.00:1)
Note. Data is sourced from Worldscope and may differ from I/B/E/S historical data.

32. Microsoft Corporation

Though many of the headlines with Microsoft Corporation's name in them have centered on government antitrust actions, the company nonetheless remains king of its domain: Its software is installed in more than 155 million personal computers—which is why high-visibility founder and Chief Executive Officer Bill Gates, who owns about 22 percent of the company's shares, remains America's richest individual. And it is also why he's not willing to concede anything without a fight. That encompasses both the fight in court and the fight for a positive public image, the latter emphasizing a smiling Gates appearing in national magazines wearing casual sweaters and talking in a low-key style about threats to innovation. One mutual fund manager put it this way: "Microsoft may not be as dominant as it would have been had the government stayed out, but its stock only becomes more interesting on any price weakness."

The world's number-one independent software company includes the proprietary industry standard operating systems Windows 95, Windows 98, and Windows NT. That's in addition to its Word, Excel, and Office suite applications; processing programs; games; and reference works—all of which have been designed to work easily with its operating systems. The Microsoft Network offers proprietary online content, and its Internet Explorer web browser has battled Netscape for market share. With NBC, the company operates innovative cable news channel MSNBC. It also offers electronic arts-and-entertainment guides, development software for creating Web pages, and other online services. Microsoft agreed to acquire an 11 percent stake in Comcast and invest in Apple Computer in 1997.

Microsoft was founded as a partnership in 1975 by Bill Gates and Paul Allen, and incorporated in 1981. Its early vision of a computer on every desk and in every home is today coupled with a commitment to Internet-related technologies that expand the power and reach of the PC and its users. Microsoft boasts more than 300 products and technologies. Though many "techies," young and old, rail against Microsoft's overwhelming power in the industry, it has apparently captured the hearts of the portion of the youth culture that admires business achievement. Gates was near the top of the list of individuals most admired by 1998 graduating M.B.A. students, according to a survey of prestigious U.S. business schools, while Microsoft was the most admired company. That biennial survey looking at soon-to-be graduates' goals, attitudes, and career plans included students from Duke, Dartmouth, Northwestern, University of Chicago, and University of Pennsylvania.

Antitrust action has often targeted stock market leaders, starting with railroads and industrial trusts at the turn of the century, and continuing with IBM and AT&T in the modern era. Antitrust concerns about Microsoft have been ongoing. After settlement talks failed, the federal government and twenty state attorneys general filed two broad antitrust suits against the company in May 1998, initiating the government's most direct attack on a company in a generation. The suits, announced by United States Attorney General Janet Reno, accused the company of leveraging a monopoly in PC operating systems to win control of other software markets, primarily for the browsers used for access to the World Wide Web. The suits asked that the company either leave out its Internet Explorer software or include a rival, Netscape Navigator. A federal appeals panel struck down an earlier preliminary injuction in June 1998, thereby permitting shipment of Windows 98 with the Internet software included. The federal and state suits were consolidated and a fall 1998 trial date set. The court considered whether Microsoft bundled its software for anticompetitive reasons, and whether the bundling created any benefit to the consumer. In addition, federal investigators have scrutinized areas such as the pricing of Microsoft Office, the bundling of software for receiving video over the Internet, and the advantage it gains through its Web TV PC software that links television with the Internet.

Windows 98, which had been considered by experts to be just a minor improvement over Windows 95, enjoyed a blaze of publicity thanks to the government's actions. It got off to a rousing sales start, with retail sales exceeding a million copies soon after its introduction on June 25, 1998. Designed to make a computer work better by integrating tightly with the Internet and providing better system performance and easier system diagnostics and maintenance, Windows 98 is expected to provide a strong boost to the company's bottom line. However, the company postponed delivery of its important Windows NT 5.0 Workstation, with analysts now expecting shipment in late summer or early fall 1999 instead of the first quarter of the year as originally planned. This major overhaul of Windows NT for networked computers is considered crucial in winning corporate customers away from mainframe computers or systems running Unix operating systems for their basic business systems. Meanwhile, a move toward Office 97 by large and small customers worldwide has been another recent positive for Microsoft. While the company has remained concerned about its business in the Far East, there is evidence its business there isn't getting weaker. There has also been sales momentum in the existing Windows NT Service and BackOffice suite of products.

Microsoft has announced new or expanded alliances with Amdahl, Digital Equipment, NCR, and Wang to assist these firms in building their Microsoft technology skills and to jointly offer new products. Windows NT Workstation continues to grow significantly in sales, with workstations equipped with Windows NT more than doubling in 1997. The versatile Windows NT is becoming popular in factories where it can run and link a wide range of operations. According to a 1997 study conducted by Deloitte & Touche for Digital Equipment Corporation, the average three-year total cost of ownership for technical workstations running Windows NT Workstation is 37 percent less than for comparable machines. The findings indicated that for a group of twenty-five technical workstations, three-year savings would amount to nearly $1 million. Microsoft and Sony Corporation announced plans to begin collaboration to create a convergence between the PC and consumer audio visual electronics platforms. The firms plan to cross-license key technologies, including Microsoft's Windows CE operating system and Sony's Home Networking Module.

Thinking small is also a part of Microsoft's future. It hopes to achieve with palm-top computers, car information systems, and set-top boxes that turn a television into an Internet terminal what it has already accomplished with PCs. Hosting a Windows CE strategy day in Paris in early 1998, Microsoft executives expressed strong confidence that palm-tops will be as big as the PC market in a few years. Windows CE was originally launched in 1996 and there are now more than 600,000 palm-top computers in the world. Large European manufacturers that have aligned behind Windows CE are Philips Electronics N.V., Siemens A.G., and Ericsson A.B., while P.S.A. Peugeot Citroën is developing a PC information and entertainment system in the car.

Besides antitrust regulatory pressure, there's the chance that slowing PC unit growth could erode Microsoft's share price. Competition from Oracle, Lotus/IBM, and Netscape in the enterprise software market, and the momentum of Internet and Java computing products, could also slow Microsoft's advance. Yet Wall Street still believes in Microsoft, and, as Gates acknowledged in his letter in the most recent annual report: "Our business is one of risks and challenges and great potential rewards."

---

32. MICROSOFT CORPORATION

United States   Ticker symbol MSFT

Stock price $108 3/16 (9/16/98)   No dividend

(Financial data is from I/B/E/S International)*

BUSINESS DESCRIPTION

DEVELOPS AND MARKETS OPERATING SYSTEM FOR PC AND SERVER. SOFTWARE FOR BUSINESS PRODUCTIVITY, INTERNET, AND HARDWARE

ADDRESS AND CONTACTS

Address   One Microsoft Way
                 Richmond WA 98052-6399
Telephone   1-425-882-8080

BASIC FINANCIAL INFORMATION

Report Dates	Last Quarter: Mar 98	Reported On: Apr 22, 1998
	Next Quarter: Jun 98	Reported On: Jul 20, 1998
Capital Structure†	Long Term Debt:	0.00
	Total Debt:	0.00
	Common Sh. Equity:	9797.00

SALES BREAKDOWN

Product Segments†	Platforms	5969.00
	Application and C	5389.00
Geographic Segments†	United States	8877.00
	European Operations	2770.00
	Other International	1757.00
	Eliminations	-2046.00

Displayed Currency: U.S. Dollar (1.00:1)
*I/B/E/S and I/B/E/S Express are registered trademarks of I/B/E/S International Inc. Copyright
1993–1996 I/B/E/S International Inc. All rights reserved.
†Values are displayed in millions.

FINANCIAL STATEMENT DATA

INCOME STATEMENT	1997	1996	1995	1994	1993
Net Sales or Revenues	11358.00	8671.00	5937.00	4649.00	3753.00
EBITDA	5871.00	3859.00	2436.00	1959.00	1552.00
Depreciation Depletion & Amort	557.00	480.00	269.00	237.00	151.00
Operating Income	5130.00	3078.00	2038.00	1726.00	1326.00
Interest Expense	0.00	0.00	0.00	0.00	0.00
Pretax Income	5314.00	3379.00	2167.00	1722.00	1401.00
Net Income	NA	2195.00	1453.00	1146.00	953.00

BALANCE SHEET	1997	1996	1995	1994	1993
Assets					
Cash & Equivalents	8966.00	6940.00	4750.00	3614.00	2290.00
Receivables—Net	980.00	639.00	581.00	475.00	338.00
Inventories	NA	NA	88.00	102.00	127.00
Total Current Assets	10373.00	7839.00	5620.00	4312.00	2850.00
Property Plant & Eq.—Net	1465.00	1326.00	1192.00	930.00	867.00
Total Assets	14387.00	10093.00	7210.00	5363.00	3805.00
Liabilities & Shareholders' Equity					
Total Current Liabilities	3610.00	2425.00	1347.00	913.00	563.00
Long Term Debt	0.00	0.00	0.00	0.00	0.00
Preferred Stock	980.00	0.00	0.00	0.00	0.00
Common Equity	9797.00	6908.00	5333.00	4450.00	3242.00
Total Liabilities & Sh. Equity	14387.00	10093.00	7210.00	5363.00	3805.00

CASH FLOW	1997	1996	1995	1994	1993
Net Cash Flow— Operating	4689.00	3719.00	1990.00	1593.00	1074.00
Net Cash Flow— Investing	3089.00	2670.00	1376.00	1202.00	976.00
Net Cash Flow— Financing	-501.00	-405.00	-138.00	83.00	186.00
Incr/Decr in Working Capital	1349.00	1141.00	874.00	1112.00	964.24
Free Cash Flow	5372.00	3365.00	1941.00	1681.00	1316.00

INTERNATIONAL BUSINESS	1997	1996	1995	1994	1993
Foreign Assets	4100.00	3322.00	2495.00	1789.00	1443.00
Foreign Sales	4527.00	3206.00	2133.00	1776.00	1684.00
Foreign Income	1482.00	1056.00	503.00	377.00	378.00

SUPPLEMENTARY DATA	1997	1996	1995	1994	1993
Employees	22232	20561	17801	15257	14430
R&D Expenses	1925.00	1432.00	860.00	610.00	470.00
Goodwill/Cost in Excess of Assets Purchased	NA	NA	NA	NA	NA
Extra Items & Gain/ Loss in Sale of Assets	0.00	0.00	0.00	0.00	0.00

Displayed Currency: U.S. Dollar (1.00:1)
All values are displayed in millions (except employees).

FINANCIAL RATIOS AND GROWTH RATES

PROFITABILITY	1997	1996	1995	1994	1993	5YR AVG
Operating Profit Margin %	45.17	35.50	34.33	37.13	35.33	37.49
Tax Rate %	35.00	35.04	32.95	33.45	31.98	33.68
Net Margin %	30.41	25.31	24.47	24.65	25.39	26.05
Return on Assets %	34.22	30.44	27.09	30.12	36.10	31.60
Return on Equity— Total %	49.78	41.16	32.65	35.35	43.46	40.48
Cash Flow % Sales	42.87	30.85	29.00	29.75	29.42	32.38
Sales per Employee (in 000s)	511	422	334	305	260	366

ASSET UTILIZATION	1997	1996	1995	1994	1993	5YR AVG
Total Asset Turnover	0.79	0.86	0.82	0.87	0.99	0.87
Capital Exp % Gross Fixed Assets	17.97	21.06	25.96	19.24	19.98	20.84
Acc Depreciation % Gross Fixed Assets	47.25	43.18	37.49	35.64	26.59	38.09
Assets per Employee (in 000s)	647	491	405	352	264	432

231

LIQUIDITY	1997	1996	1995	1994	1993	5YR AVG
Current Ratio	2.87	3.23	4.17	4.72	5.06	4.01
Quick Ratio	2.76	3.13	3.96	4.48	4.67	3.80

LEVERAGE	1997	1996	1995	1994	1993	5YR AVG
Total Debt % Common Equity	0.00	0.00	0.00	0.00	0.00	0.00
Long Term Debt % Common Equity	0.00	0.00	0.00	0.00	0.00	0.00
Common Equity % Total Assets	68.10	68.44	73.97	82.98	85.20	75.74
Long Term Debt % Total Capital	0.00	0.00	0.00	0.00	0.00	0.00
Operating Cash/ Fixed Charges	210.99	NA	NA	NA	NA	210.99

GROWTH %	1997	1996	1995	1994	1993	5YR AVG
Net Sales	30.99	46.05	27.70	23.87	36.04	32.71
Operating Income	66.67	51.03	18.08	30.17	33.14	38.79
Total Assets	42.54	39.99	34.44	40.95	44.13	40.37
Earnings per Share*	53.52	32.53	36.32	24.34	22.22	33.34
Dividends per Share*	0.00	0.00	0.00	0.00	0.00	0.00
Book Value per Share	54.03	24.83	34.39	12.69	35.82	31.65

Displayed Currency: U.S. Dollar (1.00:1)
*Source: Worldscope. Value may differ from I/B/E/S.
Note: 5-Year Average calculations exclude NAs.

PER SHARE AND RELATED DATA

SOURCE: WORLDSCOPE	1997	1996	1995	1994	1993
Earnings per Share	1.47	0.96	0.72	0.53	0.43
Dividends per Share	0.00	0.00	0.00	0.00	0.00
Book Value per Share	4.43	2.87	2.30	1.71	1.52
Total Investment Return	NA	NA	43.56	51.63	-5.56
Market Price (Year-end)	64.63	41.31	21.94	15.28	10.08
Market Capitalization (in millions)	155617.00	98654.25	51597.00	35513.63	22736.25
Price/Earnings Ratio	43.96	43.15	30.36	28.83	23.64
Price/Book Value	14.60	14.38	9.53	8.92	6.63
Dividend Yield	0.00	0.00	0.00	0.00	0.00
Dividend Payout per Share	0.00	0.00	0.00	0.00	0.00
Common Shares Outstanding (Year-end) in Millions	2408.00	2388.00	2352.00	2324.00	2256.00
Stock Split/Dividend Ratio	0.50	0.50	0.25	0.25	0.13
Type of Share	*Common*				

Displayed Currency: U.S. Dollar (1.00:1)
Note: Data is sourced from Worldscope and may differ from I/B/E/S historical data.

33. National Australia Bank Limited

Not just an Aussie bank, mate. More than half the assets of National Australia Bank Limited, Australia's largest banking group, are located well beyond the Land Down Under, with its most recent giant step being the one it took into the United States mortgage servicing industry.

Founded in the Australian state of Victoria in 1858, "the National" quickly gained a reputation, still enjoyed today, as one of the more prudent banking institutions in the country. A long line of mergers has added to its size. Now, through about 2,360 offices, National Australia Bank offers banking, asset management, financial management, and other financial services to individuals and businesses. It was ranked in a recent edition of *Fortune* magazine's Global Top 500 survey as the fifty-third largest bank in the world by total revenue and ninth most profitable.

The holding company also owns the United Kingdom's Clydesdale Bank and Yorkshire Bank, Ireland's National Irish Bank and Northern Ireland's Northern Bank, the Bank of New Zealand, and National Australia Bank Asia. It acquired the investment management company County NatWest Australia Investment Management Limited in early 1998. This was a significant step by the bank in building a new force in Australian and international funds management, and part of the overall strategy of building noninterest income. In addition, its National Australia Financial Management division and the German insurance firm Gerling-Konzern Group have now joined forces to develop group life and disability insurance products to market to Australian businesses. The financial management division has been turning in strong gains in its protection insurance, pension, retirement income, and retail investment products, sold through the bank and by external financial advisors.

The bank has taken big international steps. In the United States, National Australia Bank acquired residential mortgage loan producer and servicer HomeSide Incorporated in a $1.2 billion deal in 1998. It also owns Michigan National Corporation, the holding company for the 190-branch Michigan National Bank. Its revenue breakdown, beyond the more than 50 percent of its assets in Australia, includes 23 percent in Europe, 10 percent in New Zealand, 8 percent in the United States, and less than 5 percent in Asia. Uncertainty about Asian economies was expected to depress immediate prospects in the region, but Managing Director and CEO Don Argus said, "Our credit exposure in Asia is modest and well-diversified. Over 70 percent of our Asian exposure is short-term in nature with a maturity of less than twelve months."

It's getting its global house in order. The bank spent $207 million in 1998 on the restructuring of its worldwide business to speed up its entry into a worldwide integrated financial service group. That's a cost it expects to recoup within two years. Staff cuts and other personnel costs were included, as were closings and remodeling of its network of Australian branches to reflect the growing preference of customers for carrying out transactions by telephone and electronically. There will be a single central hub dealing with premium customers and high value, complex sales, surrounded by a network of smaller, differentiated outlets. Management was similarly restructured, splitting into three tiers covering global, regional, and individual business unit operations, while operations were grouped into three regions: Asia Pacific, Europe, and the United States.

Specialization is the key to the financial future. Indicative of that is National Australia Bank's acquisition of HomeSide. In an increasingly competitive U.S. market, HomeSide has continued to perform well by emphasizing strict cost controls and risk management. It is the number-two mortgage servicer behind Norwest, with $206 billion in loans, and has boosted its size through the purchase of Banc One's $19 billion mortgaging servicing portfolio. The top six mortgage servicers control only one-third of the U.S. mortgage servicing industry, which is a business driven by economies of scale, so efficient large players have considerable opportunity to increase their operations by acquisitions. HomeSide leads competitors in efficiency with an impressive $40 cost per loan and 1,500 loans per employee. A combination of technology and strategic use of subservers—niche players paid a fee to service an aspect of a loan without owning the servicing rights—are behind its success. Management of interest rate risk is conducted through its hedge portfolio, with the objective of offsetting changes in the value of the servicing portfolio. Over the last five years, it has maintained a 97 percent correlation between the value of the mortgage servicing portfolio and the hedge portfolio. Importantly, HomeSide operates as a wholesaler, preferring to buy mortgages from smaller firms to avoid having to maintain a more costly retail presence. Using this strategy, it can better handle volume flows, especially when interest rates increase and volumes decline.

There was embarrassment in early 1998. Subsidiary National Irish Bank, Ireland's fourth-largest bank, ran advertisements in March 1998 in national newspapers offering customer-advice telephone numbers after the bank admitted it knowingly overcharged customers in the late 1980s and early 1990s. The Irish government had launched an investigation following Irish television reports that customers had been overcharged at a number of branches. National Australia Bank in a statement said current depositors have no reason to be concerned about the overcharging and that the practices don't reflect today's operations.

Growth is planned for the future. For example, the bank has expressed an interest in acquiring a credit card business outside Australia, to build up its network of merchants in the United States and Europe. While the bank has a competitive advantage over its local competitors in its card-based business because of its relationship with merchants, outside of Australia there's a gap in its operations, management concedes.

Besides its global ventures, National Australia Bank has been concerned about the possibility of a major Australian bank falling to a foreign institution. It has urged the Australian government to relax a prohibition on mergers between Australia's four biggest banks, allowing them to build the mass required to venture overseas themselves or fight off challenges at home. The government has previously said it might relax the ban on major bank mergers if competition increased in the business lending market. The announcement of the gigantic Citicorp/Travelers Group merger raised the real possibility that point might now be reached. The changing world and the changing face of financial services means taking an entirely new approach, this prudent but aggressive banking company is convinced.

"The group has been consistent in its view that globalization will lead to the gradual erosion of national geographic boundaries in trade, capital, and technology flows, government economic policies, and corporate growth strategies," Argus wrote in the most recent Australia National Bank annual report. "It heightens the need for highly effective capital management and cost containment."

33. NATIONAL AUSTRALIA BANK LIMITED

Australia   Ticker symbol NAB

One American Depository Receipt represents five ordinary shares

Stock price $61 5/8 (9/16/98)   Dividend yield 4.70%

(Financial data from I/B/E/S International is in Australian dollar)*

BUSINESS DESCRIPTION

COMMERCIAL BANKING ACCOUNTED FOR 98% OF FISCAL 1997 REVENUES, MERCHANT AND INVESTMENT BANKING 1%, AND FINANCE AND LIFE INSURANCE 1%

ADDRESS AND CONTACTS

Address	500 Bourke Street
	Melbourne Victoria 3001 Australia
Telephone	61-3-96413500
Fax	61-3-96414916

BASIC FINANCIAL INFORMATION

Capital Structure†	Long Term Debt:	23945.00
	Total Debt:	34046.00
	Common Sh. Equity:	12579.00

National Australia Bank Limited

SALES BREAKDOWN

Product Segments†	Commercial Banking	15908.00
	Finance & Life Insurance	154.00
	Merchant & Investment Banking	109.00
Geographic Segments†	Australia	8728.00
	Europe	3982.00
	New Zealand	2017.00
	United States	1228.00
	Asia	516.00

Displayed Currency: Australian Dollar (1.00:1)

*I/B/E/S and I/B/E/S Express are registered trademarks of I/B/E/S International Inc. Copyright 1993–1996 I/B/E/S International Inc. All rights reserved.

†Values are displayed in millions.

FINANCIAL STATEMENT DATA

INCOME STATEMENT	1997	1996	1995	1994	1993
Net Sales or Revenues	16171.00	14937.00	12769.00	10237.00	10485.90
Interest Income—Net	5316.00	5092.00	4579.00	4245.00	4117.20
Total Non-Interest Income	3277.00	2887.00	2296.00	2252.00	2058.10
Net Income	2223.00	2102.00	1969.00	1708.00	1128.80

BALANCE SHEET	1997	1996	1995	1994	1993
Assets					
Cash & Due from Banks	16405.00	15251.00	13882.00	12958.00	12130.70
Total Investments	19530.00	15617.00	13044.00	11589.00	12816.90
Loans—Net	130218.00	111413.00	92514.00	78500.00	72008.70
Total Assets	201968.99	173710.00	147077.01	125883.00	117251.30
Liabilities & Shareholders' Equity					
Deposits—Total	118368.00	101834.00	84166.00	71710.00	67704.90
Total Debt	34046.00	27515.00	22530.00	20997.00	22023.40
Preferred Stock	0.00	0.00	0.00	0.00	0.00
Common Equity	12579.00	12519.00	11381.00	9852.00	8815.80
Total Liabilities & Sh. Equity	201968.99	173710.00	147077.01	125883.00	117251.30

CASH FLOW	1997	1996	1995	1994	1993
Funds from Operations	2190.00	2581.00	1496.00	3538.00	3248.90
Total Sources	33918.00	31266.00	27275.00	17693.00	22540.10
Cash Dividends Paid—Total	895.00	760.00	535.00	314.00	261.50
Total Uses	33918.00	31206.00	27275.00	17693.00	22540.10
Free Cash Flow	4324.00	3959.00	3587.00	3167.00	2735.60

SUPPLEMENTARY DATA	1997	1996	1995	1994	1993
Provision for Loan					
Losses	332.00	333.00	116.00	179.00	604.20
Non-Interest Expense	4945.00	4587.00	3913.00	3699.00	3679.70
Interbank Loans	NA	NA	NA	NA	NA
Consumer and					
Installment Loans	1817.00	1624.00	1374.00	1135.00	1019.70
Real Estate					
Mortgage Loans	33420.00	28111.00	23472.00	19441.00	15176.10
Reserve for Loan					
Losses	1354.00	1286.00	1086.00	1302.00	1848.70
Foreign Assets	94396.00	79712.00	61764.00	54809.00	55826.30
Demand Deposits	30818.00	26719.00	22777.00	22335.00	20757.50
Savings/Other Time					
Deposits	21004.00	21031.00	20680.00	13667.00	11678.30
Consumer Liability					
on Acceptances	19605.00	17283.00	16657.00	16031.00	14036.10
Employees	46392	47178	45585	43871	43053
Goodwill/Cost in					
Excess of Assets					
Purchased	2122.00	2218.00	1385.00	1478.00	1569.00
Extra Items & Gain/	0.00	0.00	0.00	0.00	0.00
Loss in Sale of					
Assets	0.00	0.00	0.00	0.00	0.00

Displayed Currency: Australian Dollar (1.00:1)
All values are displayed in millions (except employees).

FINANCIAL RATIOS AND GROWTH RATES

PROFITABILITY	1997	1996	1995	1994	1993	5YR AVG
Return on Assets %	2.04	2.26	2.40	2.14	1.94	2.16
Return on Equity—						
Total %	17.76	18.47	19.99	19.37	14.12	17.94
Tax Rate %	33.02	31.32	31.47	35.71	41.58	34.64
Efficiency of Earning						
Assts	10.24	11.69	11.89	9.68	11.89	11.08
Total Interest						
Income % Earning						
Assets	10.15	11.42	11.63	9.41	11.55	10.83
Total Interest Exp %						
Interest Bearing						
Liabilities	5.86	6.52	6.36	4.17	5.46	5.67
Non-Interest Income %						
Total Revenues	20.26	19.33	17.98	22.00	19.63	19.84
Return on Earning						
Assets	1.75	1.99	2.19	2.01	1.55	1.90

LIQUIDITY	1997	1996	1995	1994	1993	5YR AVG
Total Deposits %						
Total Assets	64.91	65.10	64.53	65.28	65.60	65.08
Total Loans %						
Total Deposits	111.16	110.67	111.21	111.28	109.09	110.68

National Australia Bank Limited

Cash & Secs %						
Total Deposits	30.36	30.31	31.99	34.23	36.85	32.75
Reserve for Loan Losses %Total						
Loans	1.03	1.14	1.16	1.63	2.50	1.49

LEVERAGE	1997	1996	1995	1994	1993	5YR AVG
Common Equity %						
Total Assets	6.90	8.00	8.73	8.97	8.54	8.23
Loan Loss Coverage						
Ratio	10.48	12.26	9.24	4.95	2.45	7.88

OTHER	1997	1996	1995	1994	1993	5YR AVG
Earning Assets %						
Total Assets	82.11	81.21	80.94	82.01	82.18	81.69

GROWTH %	1997	1996	1995	1994	1993	5YR AVG
Total Assets	16.27	18.11	16.84	7.36	14.09	14.47
Net Sales or Revenues	8.26	16.98	24.73	-2.37	2.39	9.57
Earnings per Share*	4.70	2.70	10.76	45.65	35.29	35.29
Dividends per Share*	8.05	4.82	12.16	48.00	11.11	15.87
Book Value per Share	4.79	6.41	10.72	7.30	6.00	7.02

*Source: Worldscope. Value may differ from I/B/E/S.
Note: 5-Year Average calculations exclude NAs.

PER SHARE AND RELATED DATA

SOURCE: WORLDSCOPE	1997	1996	1995	1994	1993
Earnings per Share	1.516	1.448	1.410	1.273	0.874
Dividends per Share	0.940	0.870	0.830	0.740	0.500
Book Value per Share	8.882	8.476	7.966	7.194	6.705
Total Investment Return	NA	NA	21.41	-8.44	73.76
Market Price (Year-end)	21.220	13.340	11.700	10.320	12.080
Market Capitalization					
(in millions)	30051.38	19703.18	16716.41	14132.59	15882.78
Price/Earnings Ratio	14.00	9.21	8.30	8.11	13.82
Price/Book Value	2.39	1.57	1.47	1.43	1.80
Dividend Yield	4.43	6.52	7.09	7.17	4.14
Dividend Payout per					
Share	62.01	60.08	58.87	58.13	57.21
Common Shares Outstanding (Year-end) in					
Millions	1416.18	1477.00	1428.75	1369.44	1314.80
Stock Split/Dividend					
Ratio	NA	NA	NA	NA	1.00
Type of Share	Ordinary				

Displayed Currency: Australian Dollar (1.00:1)
Note: Data is sourced from Worldscope and may differ from I/B/E/S historical data.

34. Novartis A.G.

Novartis A.G., the life sciences giant created by the $27 billion merger of Ciba-Geigy Limited and Sandoz Limited in late 1996, isn't running like a Swiss watch just yet. It still has to get its timing down. Yet, despite ongoing skepticism about whether bigger really *is* better when it results in such an immense company, Novartis's growth, consistency, and potential for improving its pharmaceutical profit margins should help it command a premium stock price. This company with more than 100,000 employees worldwide ranks second in health care behind Glaxo Wellcome, second in nutrition behind Abbott Labs, first in jarred baby foods with its Gerber products division, and first in agriproducts. Its pharmaceutical division, providing more than 40 percent of total company sales, makes prescription and generic drugs, over-the-counter products, contact lenses, and ophthalmic medications. Famous brand names such as athlete's foot treatment Desenex, laxative ExLax, antacid Maalox, and allergy treatment Tavist are in its product line. Ciba, the second-largest provider of contact lenses and lens care, is a worldwide leader in the research, development, and manufacturing of optical and ophthalmic products and service. Novartis's nutrition division manufactures medical nutrition supplements. Over-the-counter drugs were moved into the nutrition division in 1998.

Its agribusiness division produces herbicides, insecticides, and fungicides for crop protection. The company also makes parasite-control products and medicines for pets and farm animals, as well as seeds for hardier, higher-yield crops. Novartis acquired Young's Animal Health business in Australia and New Zealand from the

British-based Grampian Pharmaceuticals Group in 1998. Young's product line includes treatments against parasite infestations and other medications for farm and domesticated animals. Novartis obtained approval from European regulatory authorities in 1998 to market Clomicalm, a new oral treatment for behavioral disorders in dogs, which became the first small-animal veterinary pharmaceutical approved for all states of the European Union through centralized registration. The medication offers veterinarians a fast-acting way of easing anxiety in dogs separated from their owners, a condition affecting about 15 percent of dogs.

The name Novartis comes from the Latin term *novae artes*, or new arts and new skills. Novartis specifically means utilizing scientific research, imagination, and new technologies to provide benefits for mankind. The company had a solid first full year of operation, although it suffered from stagnating sales in early 1998 due in part to weak pharmaceutical sales in Japan and Brazil despite a pickup in sales in Europe. Price cuts for seven Novartis drugs in Switzerland, imposed on the Federal Bureau for Social Insurance, weren't expected to have a major impact on overall sales. General and administrative costs have decreased as a result of the merger and the number of employees was reduced by 9,100. However, research and development costs are up as a necessary part of doing business, while marketing expenses have increased in order to support some important product launches.

Pharmaceuticals are expected to continue to lead the firm's profitability, despite the recent negative impact of Japanese price cuts. An annual compound growth rate of about 15 percent is projected through the year 2002. Novartis's key growth drugs are Lamisil for fungal nail and skin infections, Lescol to lower cholesterol, Aredia for cancer, Miacalcic for osteoporosis, Foradil for asthma, and Cibacen/Lotensin for hypertension. In the United States, Lescol sales may be under pressure, but Lamisil and the Aredia treatment for Paget's disease and hypercalcemia are expected to experience strong growth. More recent drugs that have been received well include the antihypertensive Diovan, Apligraf to improve wound healing, and Exelon for Alzheimer's.

In 1998, Novartis received marketing clearance from the U.S. Food and Drug Administration for Simulect, which prevents acute rejection episodes in renal transplant recipients. The company also completed a definitive agreement with Noven Pharmaceuticals Incorporated for a joint venture that initially will concentrate on marketing an estrogen-replacement therapy patch developed by Noven.

Its generic drug business has also done fairly well, due in part to the 1996 acquisition of Azupharma, Germany's third-largest generic drug company, and also strong growth of its penicillin and cephalosporin businesses. The U.S. generics market, however, still faces heavy price erosion from fierce competition. Nutrition profit margins are expected to improve, while agribusiness should see continued positive volume and profitability driven by new products and further cost synergies.

Speeding up the genetics research race, Novartis formed the Novartis Institute for Functional Genomics near San Diego, California, in 1998 for the purpose of working simultaneously on a large number of known genetic links. Hundreds of links have been made between genetic characteristics and many of today's major diseases, such as Alzheimer's disease, diabetes, asthma, depression, and cancer. However, to derive a therapeutic benefit, more needs to be learned about the functional relationship between a particular genotype and a disease state. The company will invest $250 million over the next decade in the center, funded by a private foundation affiliated with the company known as the Novartis Research Foundation.

As big and accomplished as Novartis is, perhaps it has yet to discover a cure for acquisition fever. President and Chief Executive Officer Daniel Vasella stressed in 1998 that Novartis's primary objective is internal growth, but he didn't exclude altogether the possibility of another merger in the future. Asked by a Swiss journalist if he might not be tempted to repeat the merger process, Vasella answered "maybe."

In the meantime, Novartis is busy overcoming indigestion from its massive merger as its progress is carefully monitored by critics waiting for it to stumble. In the most recent company report, Chairman Alex Krauer and Vasella expressed optimism: "We believe that our know-how and our comprehensive port-folio of products and services will provide lasting solutions to challenges and will help protect and ensure the well-being of animals, plants, crops, and people of all ages all over the world."

34. NOVARTIS A.G.

Switzerland   Ticker symbol NVTSY

One American Depositary Receipt represents 1/20th of a share

ADR price $85 3/8 (9/16/98)   Dividend yield .98%

(Financial data from I/B/E/S International is in Swiss franc)*

BUSINESS DESCRIPTION

HEALTH CARE PRODUCTS ACCOUNTED FOR 69% OF 1997 REVENUES, AGRI-CULTURAL CHEMICALS 27%, AND NUTRITION PRODUCTS 13%

ADDRESS AND CONTACTS

Address	Lichtstrasse 35
	CH-4002 Basel, Switzerland
Telephone	41-61-324-8000
Fax	41-61-324-2744

BASIC FINANCIAL INFORMATION

Capital Structure[†]	Long Term Debt:	3611.00
	Total Debt:	11076.00
	Common Sh. Equity:	26801.00

SALES BREAKDOWN

Product Segments[†]	Health care Products	18742.00
	Agricultural Chemicals	8327.00
	Nutrition Products	4111.00
Geographic Segments[†]	Europe	11665.00
	The Americas	14572.00
	Asia, Africa & Australia	4943.00

Displayed Currency: Swiss Franc (1.00:1)
*I/B/E/S and I/B/E/S Express are registered trademarks of I/B/E/S International Inc. Copyright 1003 1990 I/B/E/S International Inc. All rights reserved.
†Values are displayed in millions.

FINANCIAL STATEMENT DATA

INCOME STATEMENT	1997	1996	1995	1994	1993
Net Sales or Revenues	31180.00	36233.00	35943.00	37919.00	37747.00
EBITDA	9063.00	5143.00	8029.00	7386.00	7200.00
Depreciation Depletion & Amort	1292.00	1934.00	1877.00	1869.00	1909.00
Operating Income	6783.00	5410.00	5494.00	4861.00	4228.00
Interest Expense	835.00	835.00	811.00	883.00	927.00
Pretax Income	6903.00	2374.00	5341.00	4634.00	4364.00
Net Income	5211.00	2304.00	4216.00	3647.00	3485.00

BALANCE SHEET	1997	1996	1995	1994	1993

Assets

	1997	1996	1995	1994	1993
Cash & Equivalents	18486.00	19043.00	15374.00	12586.00	13393.00
Receivables—Net	8570.00	6763.00	7930.00	9273.00	8976.00
Inventories	6545.00	7961.00	7357.00	8203.00	8634.00
Total Current Assets	34170.00	36298.00	31343.00	30792.00	31338.00
Property Plant & Eq.— Net	11589.00	16026.00	15465.00	17780.00	18308.00
Total Assets	51828.00	58027.00	50888.00	51409.00	51966.00

Liabilities & Shareholders' Equity

	1997	1996	1995	1994	1993
Total Current Liabilities	17056.00	16450.00	14162.00	19322.00	14304.00
Long Term Debt	3611.00	5595.00	5589.00	3732.00	4000.00
Preferred Stock	0.00	0.00	0.00	0.00	0.00
Common Equity	26801.00	27677.00	25526.00	22367.00	27637.00
Total Liabilities & Sh. Equity	51828.00	58027.00	50888.00	51409.00	51966.00

CASH FLOW	1997	1996	1995	1994	1993
Funds from Operations	5741.00	5604.00	5769.00	5766.00	5855.00
Total Sources	6794.00	1802.00	3895.00	8807.00	3965.00
Cash Dividends Paid— Total	1377.00	1158.00	934.00	852.00	732.00
Total Uses	6794.00	1802.00	3895.00	8807.00	3965.00
Incr/Decr in Working Capital	-2734.00	2667.00	5711.00	-5564.00	NA
Free Cash FLow	7509.00	3266.00	6178.00	5169.00	4451.00

INTERNATIONAL BUSINESS	1997	1996	1995	1994	1993
Foreign Assets	7698.00	NA	NA	NA	NA
Foreign Sales	19515.00	21736.00	21564.00	23001.00	22433.00
Foreign Income	2787.00	NA	NA	NA	NA

Novartis A.G.

SUPPLEMENTARY DATA	1997	1996	1995	1994	1993
Employees	87239	116178	133959	144284	140030
R&D Expenses	3693.00	3656.00	3527.00	3786.00	3946.00
Goodwill/Cost in Excess of Assets Purchased	1182.00	1224.00	501.00	NA	NA
Extra Items & Gain/ Loss in Sale of Assets	0.00	0.00	0.00	0.00	0.00

Displayed Currency: Swiss Franc (1.00:1)
All values are displayed in millions (except employees).

FINANCIAL RATIOS AND GROWTH RATES

PROFITABILITY	1997	1996	1995	1994	1993	5YR AVG
Operating Profit Margin %	21.75	14.93	15.29	12.82	11.20	15.20
Tax Rate %	24.25	2.86	20.84	20.24	19.55	17.55
Net Margin %	16.71	6.36	11.73	9.62	9.23	10.73
Return on Assets %	9.97	5.61	9.24	8.14	NA	8.24
Return on Equity— Total %	18.83	9.03	18.85	13.20	NA	14.97
Cash Flow % Sales	18.41	15.47	16.05	15.21	15.51	16.13
Sales per Employee (in 000s)	357	312	268	263	270	294

ASSET UTILIZATION	1997	1996	1995	1994	1993	5YR AVG
Total Asset Turnover	0.60	0.62	0.71	0.74	0.73	0.68
Capital Exp % Gross Fixed Assets	7.19	6.25	6.45	6.99	8.56	7.09
Acc Depreciation % Gross Fixed Assets	46.37	46.67	46.08	43.98	42.99	45.22
Assets per Employee (in 000s)	594	499	380	356	371	440

LIQUIDITY	1997	1996	1995	1994	1993	5YR AVG
Current Ratio	2.00	2.21	2.21	1.59	2.19	2.04
Quick Ratio	1.59	1.57	1.65	1.13	1.56	1.50

LEVERAGE	1997	1996	1995	1994	1993	5YR AVG
Total Debt % Common Equity	41.33	46.45	46.05	56.93	37.59	45.67
Long Term Debt % Common Equity	13.47	20.22	21.90	16.69	14.47	17.35
Common Equity % Total Assets	51.71	47.70	50.16	43.51	53.18	49.25

LEVERAGE	1997	1996	1995	1994	1993	5YR AVG
Long Term Debt %						
Total Capital	11.79	16.65	17.75	14.06	12.47	14.54
Operating Cash/						
Fixed Charges	6.61	6.71	7.11	6.53	6.32	6.66

GROWTH %	1997	1996	1995	1994	1993	5YR AVG
Net Sales	-13.95	0.81	-5.21	0.46	NA	NA
Operating Income	25.38	-1.53	13.02	14.97	NA	NA
Total Assets	-10.68	14.03	-1.01	-1.07	NA	NA
Earnings per Share*	130.30	-46.16	13.12	3.26	NA	NA
Dividends per Share*	25.00	NA	NA	NA	NA	NA
Book Value per Share	-2.64	8.32	11.67	-20.14	NA	NA

Displayed Currency: Swiss Franc (1.00:1)
*Source: Worldscope. Value may differ from I/B/E/S.
Note: 5-Year Average calculations exclude NAs.

PER SHARE AND RELATED DATA

SOURCE: WORLDSCOPE	1997	1996	1995	1994	1993
Earnings per Share	76.0	33.0	61.3	54.2	52.5
Dividends per Share	25.0	20.0	NA	NA	NA
Book Value per Share	391.3	401.9	371.1	332.3	416.1
Total Investment					
Return	NA	NA	NA	NA	NA
Market Price					
(Year-end)	2370.0	1533.0	NA	NA	NA
Market Capitalization					
(in millions)	162310.70	105557.57	NA	NA	NA
Price/Earnings Ratio	31.18	46.45	NA	NA	NA
Price/Book Value	6.06	3.81	NA	NA	NA
Dividend Yield	1.05	1.30	NA	NA	NA
Dividend Payout per					
Share	32.89	60.61	NA	NA	NA
Common Shares					
Outstanding					
(Year-end) in					
Millions	68.49	68.86	68.79	67.31	66.42
Stock Split/Dividend Ratio	NA	NA	NA	NA	NA
Type of Share	*Namenaktie*				

Displayed Currency: Swiss Franc (1.00:1)
Note: Data is sourced from Worldscope and may differ from I/B/E/S historical data.

35. Pfizer Incorporated

Pfizer Incorporated—more than just sex. The dramatic introduction of the Viagra pill for the treatment of male impotence made it the most celebrated new drug in history, featured on the cover of *Time* magazine, lampooned nightly by Jay Leno on *The Tonight Show*, copied by unauthorized Indian pharmaceutical labs, and heartily endorsed as effective by former U.S. presidential candidate Bob Dole. Within weeks after Viagra's introduction, Pfizer's unsolicited name recognition went from 8 percent to more than 34 percent. The very day I began writing this chapter, a fellow at a restaurant table next to mine loudly asked the server for "the Viagra salad, please" to the sustained guffaws of his fellow tablemates.

Pfizer, already emerging as the premier U.S. pharmaceutical company as rival Merck & Company sees some of its key patents expiring, has been deftly using Viagra as a pedestal to expound on the strength of its entire health care line. Everyone seems to be listening and, after all, many of the patients in need of Viagra have additional ailments that require additional drugs. Pfizer, long famous for its unparalleled drug pipeline, invested $2.2 billion in research and development in 1998, one of the largest amounts of any company in the world, and it has 6,000 researchers hard at work on three continents. Its drug discovery teams need less than one-third the industry's average 190 person-years of work to advance a compound from conception to clinical trials. The company has eighteen major products in development, including one drug in Phase I testing for cancer therapy.

This is a quick, flexible company whose well-known and

profitable drugs include Norvasc for cardiovascular disease, antidepressant Zoloft, antibiotic Zithromax, the antidiabetic agent Glucotrol XL, and the new broad-spectrum antibiotic Trovan. It is a preferred partner as well, comarketing the cholesterol-lowering drug Lipitor with its developer, Warner-Lambert Company; colaunching with Japan's Eisai the first important drug to offset symptoms of Alzheimer's disease, Aricept, in 1997; and comarketing G.D. Searle's Celebra, the first significant new arthritis medicine in more than a decade, in summer 1998. Because of its celebrated marketing know-how, which highlights the uniqueness of each and every drug and gets out the word through an impressive army of 14,500 sales representatives worldwide who call on doctors, Pfizer is the clear partner of choice for smaller drug firms seeking to realize the full potential of any key drug.

Pfizer also makes consumer health products, such as BenGay muscle rub, Visine eyedrops, Plax dental rinse, Barbasol shaving products, and Bain de Soleil sunscreens. Health care products account for 85 percent of sales. The firm is also the world's number-one producer of veterinary medicine for farm and domestic animals. While it also manufactures medical equipment, such as prosthetic implants, catheters, ultrasonic cutting devices, and monitoring systems, it may sell these off because they don't quite fit in with its other product lines. This is a major company dedicated to building from within, not going the major merger and acquisition route. It sold its Howmedica orthopedic instrument business to Stryker Corp. in the fall of 1998.

The Viagra phenomenon has been powerful, especially for a drug originally pursued as heart medication but unexpectedly found in 1992 to boost erections in clinical tests. Less than three months after its introduction, prescriptions in the United States totaled 2.7 million. Sales were $409 million in its first quarter in the market, even before the drug was officially launched worldwide. The drug, which costs $10 a pill in the United States, was selling for $59 on the black market in Taiwan before it even passed clinical tests there.

Yet any new drug also brings with it concerns. Sixty-nine

Viagra users died in the first several months it was offered, and there were additional reports of serious adverse reactions such as heart attacks, strokes, blackouts, and vision problems. Pfizer and the Food and Drug Administration emphasized, however, that users are often elderly with additional health problems and taking other medication. They contend there's no evidence any of the patients would have died if they took the drug as directed. The FDA convened a team of seven specialists to study reports on Viagra, but found no indication that anything unusual had occurred. Both Pfizer and the FDA said they had no concerns about the safety of the drug.

Some insurers have refused to cover Viagra, giving as their reasons either the drug's significant cost or their concerns about its long-term safety. Pfizer mounted a high-profile offensive against insurers who criticized the drug, saying that their challenges were factually and medically incorrect, causing unnecessary fear. There have also been lawsuits from users or families of users who say its use led to death, heart attacks, or other complications. Viagra includes a warning against its use in combination with nitrates, such as nitroglycerin, used to treat chest pain, a consideration the company has alerted the nation's emergency room doctors and paramedics about. It has also advised doctors to consider the cardiovascular health of their patients before prescribing the drug.

"Our worst fear, which is the fear of anyone introducing a new drug, is that there will be some rare but serious side effect," William Steere, Jr., Pfizer chairman and chief executive officer, told me in an interview in his Manhattan office. "We haven't seen that, the only concern being the low chance of having a heart attack during sex." Meanwhile, the sales potential is tremendous, with a Merrill Lynch survey of fifty urologists predicting a 95 percent compounded annual growth rate in the number of patients treated with Viagra for its first three years of availability. Merrill Lynch forecast that sales of the drug would reach $1.3 billion in 1999. It's now available in fifty countries.

"Whether at the turn of the century we're the number-one drug company depends on our maintaining our focus, continuing to manage our research well, and marketing to point out the differences in our drugs," emphasized Steere, who spends half of his time traveling both to get the word out on the company and to inspect its ongoing efforts, all as part of his efforts to ensure double-digit growth for the foreseeable future. "This is the golden age of science in which research has gone down to the atomic level, and, as Viagra points out, we're working to find answers to the many examples of human frailty we encounter as we grow older."

The entire area of "lifestyle" drugs, ranging from sexual concerns to baldness, from weight loss to arthritis, is a major growth area as baby boomers grow older. Pfizer is positioning itself to be in the catbird's seat for years to come as it leads the way worldwide in asking and answering the important health questions affecting aging populations worldwide.

35. PFIZER INCORPORATED

United States   Ticker symbol PFE

Stock price $102 (9/16/98)   Dividend yield .75%

(Financial data is from I/B/E/S International)*

BUSINESS DESCRIPTION

PHARMACEUTICAL AND HEALTH CARE PRODUCTS ACCOUNTED FOR 88% OF 1997 REVENUES, ANIMAL HEALTH 11%, AND CONSUMER PRODUCTS 1%

ADDRESS AND CONTACTS

Address	235 East 42nd Street
	New York NY 10017-5755
Telephone	1-212-573-2323

BASIC FINANCIAL INFORMATION

Capital Structure[†]	Long Term Debt:	729.00
	Total Debt:	2984.00
	Common Sh. Equity:	7933.00

SALES BREAKDOWN

Product Segments[†]	Health Care	10689.00
	Animal Health Care	1329.00
	Consumer Health Care	486.00

Pfizer Incorporated

Geographic
   Segments[†]

United States	6867.00
Europe	2853.00
Asia	1675.00
Canada/Latin America	849.00
Africa/Middle East	260.00

Displayed Currency: U.S. Dollar (1.00:1)
*I/B/E/S and I/B/E/S Express are registered trademarks of I/B/E/S International Inc. Copyright 1993–1996 I/B/E/S International Inc. All rights reserved.
[†]Values are displayed in millions.

FINANCIAL STATEMENT DATA

INCOME STATEMENT	1997	1996	1995	1994	1993
Net Sales or Revenues	12504.00	11306.00	10021.40	8281.30	7477.70
EBITDA	3739.00	3399.00	2911.30	2280.40	1216.10
Depreciation Depletion & Amort	502.00	430.00	419.60	292.00	258.20
Operating Income	3278.00	3014.00	2514.60	1972.50	1665.30
Interest Expense	170.00	170.00	204.90	141.60	106.50
Pretax Income	3088.00	2804.00	2299.20	1861.50	851.50
Net Income	2213.00	1929.00	1572.90	1298.40	657.50

BALANCE SHEET	1997	1996	1995	1994	1993
Assets					
Cash & Equivalents	1589.00	1637.00	1512.00	2018.60	1176.50
Receivables—Net	2527.00	2252.00	2024.00	1665.00	1468.70
Inventories	1773.00	1589.00	1384.10	1264.90	1093.50
Total Current Assets	6820.00	6468.00	6152.40	5788.40	4733.20
Property Plant & Eq.— Net	4137.00	3850.00	3472.60	3073.20	2632.50
Total Assets	15106.00	14370.00	12729.30	11098.50	9330.90
Liabilities & Shareholders' Equity					
Total Current Liabilities	5305.00	5640.00	5187.20	4825.90	3443.60
Long Term Debt	729.00	687.00	833.00	604.20	570.50
Preferred Stock	0.00	0.00	0.00	0.00	0.00
Common Equity	7933.00	6954.00	5506.60	4323.90	3865.50
Total Liabilities & Sh. Equity	15106.00	14370.00	12729.30	11098.50	9330.90

CASH FLOW	1997	1996	1995	1994	1993
Net Cash Flow— Operating	1629.00	2067.00	1821.40	1488.50	1263.00
Net Cash Flow— Investing	1022.00	937.00	2342.80	840.30	196.90
Net Cash Flow— Financing	-848.00	-382.00	-519.10	61.90	-1567.00

251

CASH FLOW	1997	1996	1995	1994	1993
Incr/Decr in Working Capital	687.00	-137.20	2.70	-327.10	-877.80
Free Cash Flow	2796.00	2625.00	2215.00	1608.90	581.90

INTERNATIONAL BUSINESS	1997	1996	1995	1994	1993
Foreign Assets	6240.00	6130.00	5694.70	4352.90	3755.40
Foreign Sales	5637.00	5365.00	4898.00	3870.10	4008.60
Foreign Income	1294.00	1287.00	1099.80	707.00	428.00

SUPPLEMENTARY DATA	1997	1996	1995	1994	1993
Employees	49200	46500	43800	40800	40500
R&D Expenses	1928.00	1684.00	1442.00	1139.40	974.40
Goodwill/Cost in Excess of Assets Purchased	1294.00	1424.00	1243.00	325.70	231.10
Extra Items & Gain/ Loss in Sale of Assets	0.00	0.00	0.00	0.00	0.00

Displayed Currency: U.S. Dollar (1.00:1)
All values are displayed in millions (except employees).

FINANCIAL RATIOS AND GROWTH RATES

PROFITABILITY	1997	1996	1995	1994	1993	5YR AVG
Operating Profit Margin %	26.22	26.66	25.09	23.82	22.27	24.81
Tax Rate %	28.01	30.99	32.10	30.00	22.47	28.71
Net Margin %	17.70	17.06	15.70	15.68	8.79	14.99
Return on Assets %	16.08	16.01	15.32	14.81	7.59	13.96
Return on Equity— Total %	31.82	35.03	36.38	33.59	13.93	30.15
Cash Flow % Sales	21.90	21.65	20.07	19.53	17.95	20.22
Sales per Employee (in 000s)	254	243	229	203	185	223

ASSET UTILIZATION	1997	1996	1995	1994	1993	5YR AVG
Total Asset Turnover	0.83	0.79	0.79	0.75	0.80	0.79
Capital Exp % Gross Fixed Assets	14.60	12.89	12.74	13.45	14.75	13.69
Acc Depreciation % Gross Fixed Assets	35.94	35.89	36.44	38.45	38.79	37.10
Assets per Employee (in 000s)	307	309	291	272	230	282

Pfizer Incorporated

LIQUIDITY	1997	1996	1995	1994	1993	5YR AVG
Current Ratio	1.29	1.15	1.19	1.20	1.37	1.24
Quick Ratio	0.78	0.69	0.68	0.76	0.77	0.74

LEVERAGE	1997	1996	1995	1994	1993	5YR AVG
Total Debt % Common Equity	37.62	42.02	52.09	65.32	45.25	48.46
Long Term Debt % Common Equity	9.19	9.88	15.13	13.97	14.76	12.59
Common Equity % Total Assets	52.52	48.39	43.26	38.96	41.43	44.91
Long Term Debt % Total Capital	8.42	8.93	13.04	12.16	12.75	11.06
Operating Cash/ Fixed Charges	18.14	14.40	9.82	11.42	12.61	13.28

GROWTH %	1997	1996	1995	1994	1993	5YR AVG
Net Sales	10.60	12.82	21.01	10.75	3.42	11.58
Operating Income	8.76	19.86	27.48	18.45	15.37	17.83
Total Assets	5.12	12.89	14.69	18.94	-2.70	9.51
Earnings per Share*	13.71	19.60	19.33	104.39	-36.92	15.91
Dividends per Share*	13.33	15.38	10.64	11.90	13.51	12.94
Book Value per Share	13.73	29.14	23.81	13.58	-16.64	11.48

Displayed Currency: U.S. Dollar (1.00:1)
*Source: Worldscope. Value may differ from I/B/E/S.
Note: 5-Year Average calculations exclude NAs.

PER SHARE AND RELATED DATA

SOURCE: WORLDSCOPE	1997	1996	1995	1994	1993
Earnings per Share	1.70	1.50	1.25	1.05	0.51
Dividends per Share	0.68	0.60	0.52	0.47	0.42
Book Value per Share	6.13	5.39	4.17	3.37	2.97
Total Investment Return	NA	NA	65.80	14.68	-2.51
Market Price (Year-end)	74.56	41.50	31.50	19.31	17.25
Market Capitalization (in millions)	96484.52	53535.00	40147.80	24273.96	22143.65
Price/Earnings Ratio	43.86	27.76	25.20	18.44	33.66
Price/Book Value	12.16	7.70	7.55	5.73	5.81
Dividend Yield	0.91	1.45	1.65	2.43	2.43
Dividend Payout per Share	40.00	40.13	41.60	44.87	81.95
Common Shares Outstanding (Year-end) in Millions	1294.00	1290.00	1274.53	1256.90	1283.69
Stock Split/Dividend Ratio	1.00	0.50	0.50	0.25	0.25
Type of Share	Common				

Displayed Currency: U.S. Dollar (1.00:1)
Note: Data is sourced from Worldscope and may differ from I/B/E/S historical data.

36. Procter & Gamble Company

No task is too tough: A 6,700-gallon spill of animal fat had kept a stretch of Interstate 74 in Ohio closed for more than three days in May 1998. After shoveling, scrubbing, sand-blasting, and using solvents, highway crews weren't able to remove the five-acre mess until they used Procter & Gamble Company's Dawn dishwashing liquid. That unexpected success became yet another public relations coup for P&G, the world's marketing leader.

Procter & Gamble is both the number-one maker of household products and the world's largest advertiser. It has nearly 5 billion customers these days, versus 1 billion a decade ago, an indication of its future growth potential. P&G generates loads of cash and offers a mind-boggling array of 300 products used daily by its customers. Half of its sales come from outside the United States, and about one-third of those come from Europe. Research and development, along with distribution, are important attributes of this worldwide packaged-goods company providing products in laundry and cleaning, paper goods, beauty care, food and beverage, and health care. Its Tide was the world's first heavy-duty synthetic detergent. Pampers created the disposable diaper business, and Pert Plus was the first two-in-one shampoo and conditioner. P&G also produces the soap operas *As the World Turns, Another World*, and *Guiding Light*.

The company's famous North American brands include Noxzema, Pampers, Camay, Ivory, Folgers, Cover Girl cosmetics, Cascade, Joy, Bounce, Downy, Tampax, Giorgio and Hugo Boss fragrances, Old Spice, Metamucil, Head & Shoulders, Comet, Hawaiian Punch, Crest, Cheer, Jif, Bounty, Charmin, Crisco, Pringles, and Vicks Cough Drops. It also makes many prescription drugs and physician-selected products.

William Procter and James Gamble began making and selling soap and candles in 1837, formalizing their business relationship by pledging $3,596 apiece and calling the resulting company Procter & Gamble. Their forward-looking and optimistic approach to business was reflected in their decision, for example, to build a new plant to sustain their growing business in the 1850s despite rumors of an impending civil war. Management's current goals are to hold top market shares in its core businesses, while moving into emerging countries and working to develop new global businesses. Acquisitions are expected to be one tool in its strategy to double sales from its 1997 figure by the year 2006, and its acquisition of Tambrands is a good example of its growth path. It will use specialized programs such as its "efficient consumer response" initiative, which is expected to bring in $1 billion in savings over the next few years. To achieve all of its goals, P&G must continue to be both disciplined and aggressive. It must use hedging contracts to protect its income from foreign exchange fluctuations. It has expanded to cover virtually all countries in economically troubled Asia and the headquarters for its Asian operations is in Japan. Its stock price was under pressure in 1998, but this top-tier firm with world-beating products is a long-term player.

"We are setting out to double our business in the next decade," John Pepper, chairman and chief executive, explained in the company's most recent annual report. "About 40 percent of this growth will come from our strongest core businesses—laundry, hair care, feminine protection, and diapers. An additional 20 to 25 percent will be generated by our growth in key developing markets, including Eastern Europe, China, and the Southern cone of Latin America. The balance will come from totally new categories, which we are working at record levels to create."

Innovation remains key at P&G. For example, its brand-new product Febreze, a household product that uses a unique odor removal technology to clean away odors from fabrics, was introduced in the spring of 1998. It also launched ThermaCare Heat Wraps, which are portable, long-lasting therapeutic heat wraps designed to relieve temporary muscle and joint pain, and received marketing approval along with Hoechst Marion Roussel for Actonel, a risodronate sodium tablet for treatment of Paget's disease of the bone. It reached agreement with Empresas CMPC to acquire 100 percent ownership of the disposable diaper and feminine pad venture called Prosan that the companies operate in Argentina and Chile. The company developed Olestra, a fat substitute used in snacks and crackers that gained some attention due to publicity over some potential side effects that the company says have been overblown.

P&G's products are sold in more than 140 countries. It has operations in more than seventy countries with more than 103,000 employees. Although price increases that had been a long time in coming helped the company's returns in the United States and Europe in 1998, actual unit volume was down. It cut prices on tissue and paper towel products by 4 to 7 percent, tied mostly to pulp costs, in early 1998, and had raised some detergent prices by 10 percent in the fall of 1997. Double-digit growth in Central and Eastern Europe, the Middle East, Africa, and Latin America has lately contributed greatly to its bottom line. Economic woes in Asia, especially Japan, led to lower consumption in that region, although unit volume grew due in part to P&G's purchase of South Korea's Ssangyong Paper Company.

The company has promised to remain consistently among the top one-third of its peer companies in total shareholder return. It believes it can continue to build profit margins through steps such as "regionalizing" its North American business with common packages and marketing programs. It has already gained notoriety for paring down unnecessary operations in order to keep everything simple. Standardizing product formulas, reducing store discounts and rebates, and issuing fewer coupons have also been a part of its plan. It has profited the past several years by selling off second-tier brands such as Aleve, Lava, Bain de Soleil, and Lestoil, and said in the spring of 1998 that it was considering the sale of the North American portion of its Attends adult diaper business because it's too small for a company of P&G's size. That market is dominated by Kimberly-Clark's Depends, Poise, and Overnight products, which make up more than half the total market. P&G

continues to develop its product lines and is only launching new products with strong chances for success. From now on, it's more of the same but on a worldwide stage. Looking forward, P&G most recently began a corporate restructuring and named Durk Jager, chief operating officer, as CEO.

36. PROCTER & GAMBLE COMPANY

United States   Ticker symbol PG

Stock price $69 9/16 (9/16/98)   Dividend yield 1.64%

(Financial data is from I/B/E/S International)*

BUSINESS DESCRIPTION

LAUNDRY/CLEANING PRODUCTS ACCOUNTED FOR 31% OF FISCAL 1997 REVENUES, PAPER 29%, BEAUTY CARE 20%, FOOD/BEVERAGES 12%, AND HEALTH CARE 8%

ADDRESS AND CONTACTS

Address	One Procter & Gamble Plaza
	Cincinnati OH 45202
Telephone	1-513-983-1100

BASIC FINANCIAL INFORMATION

Report Dates	Last Quarter: Mar 98	Reported On: Apr 23, 1998
	Next Quarter: Jun 98	Expected On: Aug 05, 1998
Capital Structure[†]	Long Term Debt:	4143.00
	Total Debt:	4992.00
	Common Sh. Equity:	11821.00

SALES BREAKDOWN

Product Segments[†]	Laundry and Cleaning	10933.00
	Paper	10113.00
	Beauty Care	7108.00
	Food and Beverage	4108.00
	Health Care	2897.00
Geographic Segments[†]	North America	17702.00
	Europe, Middle East	11581.00
	Asia	3572.00
	Latin America	2304.00

Displayed Currency: U.S. Dollar (1.00:1)
*I/B/E/S and I/B/E/S Express are registered trademarks of I/B/E/S International Inc. Copyright 1003 1990 I/B/E/S International Inc. All rights reserved.
[†]Values are displayed in millions.

FINANCIAL STATEMENT DATA

INCOME STATEMENT	1997	1996	1995	1994	1993
Net Sales or Revenues	35764.00	35284.00	33434.00	30296.00	30433.00
EBITDA	7193.00	6511.00	5741.00	4962.00	2041.00
Depreciation Depletion & Amort	1487.00	1358.00	1253.00	1134.00	1140.00
Operating Income	5488.00	4815.00	4179.00	3580.00	3161.00
Interest Expense	484.00	484.00	488.00	482.00	577.00
Pretax Income	5249.00	4669.00	4000.00	3346.00	349.00
Net Income	NA	2943.00	2543.00	2109.00	167.00

BALANCE SHEET	1997	1996	1995	1994	1993
Assets					
Cash & Equivalents	3110.00	2520.00	2178.00	2656.00	2322.00
Receivables—Net	2738.00	2841.00	3562.00	3115.00	3111.00
Inventories	3087.00	3130.00	3453.00	2877.00	2903.00
Total Current Assets	10786.00	10807.00	10842.00	9988.00	9975.00
Property Plant & Eq.— Net	11376.00	11118.00	11026.00	10024.00	9485.00
Total Assets	27544.00	27730.00	28125.00	25535.00	24935.00
Liabilities & Shareholders' Equity					
Total Current Liabilities	7798.00	7825.00	8648.00	8040.00	8287.00
Long Term Debt	4143.00	4670.00	5161.00	4980.00	5174.00
Preferred Stock	225.00	210.00	179.00	155.00	133.00
Common Equity	11821.00	11512.00	10410.00	8677.00	7308.00
Total Liabilities & Sh. Equity	27544.00	27730.00	28125.00	25535.00	24935.00

CASH FLOW	1997	1996	1995	1994	1993
Net Cash Flow— Operating	5882.00	4158.00	3568.00	3649.00	3338.00
Net Cash Flow— Investing	2068.00	2466.00	2363.00	2008.00	1630.00
Net Cash Flow— Financing	-3507.00	-1583.00	-1600.00	-1591.00	-1043.00
Incr/Decr in Working Capital	6.00	788.00	246.00	260.00	-36.00
Free Cash Flow	5064.00	4332.00	3595.00	3121.00	130.00

INTERNATIONAL BUSINESS	1997	1996	1995	1994	1993
Foreign Assets	10653.00	11222.00	12062.00	10688.00	10157.00
Foreign Sales	17457.00	17682.00	16822.00	16058.00	15856.00
Foreign Income	1348.00	1207.00	1105.00	767.00	87.00

Procter & Gamble Company

SUPPLEMENTARY DATA

	1997	1996	1995	1994	1993
Employees	106000	103000	99200	96500	103500
R&D Expenses	1282.00	1221.00	1257.00	1059.00	956.00
Goodwill/Cost in Excess of Assets Purchased	3949.00	4175.00	4474.00	3564.00	957.00
Extra Items & Gain/ Loss in Sale of Assets	NA	NA	NA	0.00	-925.00

Displayed Currency: U.S. Dollar (1.00:1)
All values are displayed in millions (except employees).

FINANCIAL RATIOS AND GROWTH RATES

PROFITABILITY	1997	1996	1995	1994	1993	5YR AVG
Operating Profit Margin %	15.35	13.65	12.50	11.82	10.39	12.74
Tax Rate %	34.94	34.76	33.88	33.92	22.92	32.08
Net Margin %	9.55	8.63	7.91	7.30	-2.16	6.25
Return on Assets %	13.40	11.97	11.62	10.14	-1.21	9.18
Return on Equity— Total %	28.76	28.27	29.31	28.86	-8.45	21.35
Cash Flow % Sales	13.65	14.23	12.20	11.69	9.95	12.34
Sales per Employee (in 000s)	337	343	337	314	294	325

ASSET UTILIZATION	1997	1996	1995	1994	1993	5YR AVG
Total Asset Turnover	1.30	1.27	1.19	1.19	1.22	1.23
Capital Exp % Gross Fixed Assets	11.43	12.03	12.10	11.58	12.85	12.00
Acc Depreciation % Gross Fixed Assets	38.92	38.62	37.84	36.94	36.24	37.71
Assets per Employee (in 000s)	260	269	284	265	241	264

LIQUIDITY	1997	1996	1995	1994	1993	5YR AVG
Current Ratio	1.38	1.38	1.25	1.24	1.20	1.29
Quick Ratio	0.75	0.69	0.66	0.72	0.66	0.69

LEVERAGE	1997	1996	1995	1994	1993	5YR AVG
Total Debt % Common Equity	42.23	50.26	58.90	73.24	95.59	64.04
Long Term Debt % Common Equity	35.05	40.57	49.58	57.39	70.80	50.68

LEVERAGE	1997	1996	1995	1994	1993	5YR AVG
Common Equity % Total Assets	42.92	41.51	37.01	33.98	29.31	36.95
Long Term Debt % Total Capital	25.59	28.49	32.77	36.06	41.01	32.78
Operating Cash/ Fixed Charges	7.91	7.82	6.32	5.56	4.14	6.35

GROWTH %	1997	1996	1995	1994	1993	5YR AVG
Net Sales	1.36	5.53	10.36	-0.45	3.65	4.02
Operating Income	13.98	15.22	16.73	13.26	10.25	13.87
Total Assets	-0.67	-1.40	10.14	2.41	3.79	2.77
Earnings per Share*	6.33	15.08	17.06	359.46	-70.46	14.22
Dividends per Share*	12.35	13.33	13.64	12.82	8.84	12.18
Book Value per Share	12.41	-7.39	17.98	18.30	-13.76	4.62

Displayed Currency: U.S. Dollar (1.00:1)
*Source: Worldscope. Value may differ from I/B/E/S.
Note: 5-Year Average calculations exclude NAs.

PER SHARE AND RELATED DATA

SOURCE: WORLDSCOPE	1997	1996	1995	1994	1993
Earnings per Share	2.44	2.29	1.99	1.70	0.37
Dividends per Share	0.96	0.85	0.75	0.66	0.59
Book Value per Share	8.63	7.68	8.29	7.03	5.94
Total Investment Return	NA	NA	36.29	11.09	8.48
Market Price (Year-end)	79.81	53.81	41.50	31.00	28.50
Market Capitalization (in millions)	107811.40	73787.70	56985.65	42429.60	38859.99
Price/Earnings Ratio	32.78	23.50	20.85	18.24	77.03
Price/Book Value	9.24	7.01	5.00	4.41	4.80
Dividend Yield	1.20	1.58	1.81	2.13	2.05
Dividend Payout per Share	39.22	37.12	37.69	38.82	158.11
Common Shares Outstanding (Year-end) in Millions	1350.80	1371.20	1373.15	1368.70	1363.51
Stock Split/Dividend Ratio	1.00	0.50	0.50	0.50	0.50
Type of Share	*Common*				

Displayed Currency: U.S. Dollar (1.00:1)
Note: Data is sourced from Worldscope and may differ from I/B/E/S historical data.

37. Quilmes Industrial S.A.

Beer is a universal language, and in South America the translation is Quilmes. Brewer Quilmes International (Quinsa) S.A. is a leader in its beer markets, holding more than 75 percent of the market in Paraguay, 70 percent in Argentina, and 50 percent in Uruguay. It also sells beer in Chile and Bolivia. Total beer consumption in those countries has grown more than 35 percent in the 1990s. The beer business in each of Quilmes's countries of operation is characterized by strong competition among major brewers, with extensive advertising and promotional campaigns, new brands, and new forms of packaging. The Quilmes strategy is to focus on its basic business while seeking growth through geographical expansion and product diversification. Following the purchase of the brand Cerveceria Bieckert in 1997, for example, the company acquired several smaller brewers in South America in early 1998. Compared with North America and Western Europe, the age of beer consumers in South America is younger and beer consumption is lower. In light of the strong competition among brewers, future growth in beer consumption in the region seems assured.

Besides twenty-four brands of beer that include three Heineken imports, Quilmes sells soft drinks and bottled water. Through its Coca-Cola franchise, it is responsible for nearly 90 percent of soft-drink sales in Paraguay. Its bottled water, sold under the Eco de los Andes label, has been enjoying dramatic growth since its introduction in 1994. The company's stock is undervalued compared to its peers, based mostly on a lagging core business in Argentina ever since El Niño hit, and emerging market turmoil added to its discount. Stronger sales in Chile,

261

Paraguay, and Bolivia have offset that, however, and the company actually gained market share in Argentina in early 1998 thanks to newly offered brands Quilmes Light and Bieckert. It had previously introduced the new Iguana premium brand, repositioned Heineken to compete better in the premium market, and rounded out its position in the market with the acquired Bieckert brand. Still, its rising revenues haven't been fully exhibited in its bottom line and currency devaluations and economic fluctuations in many of the countries it serves have made managing its business more demanding. Giving the stock some added punch is the fact that Quilmes is sometimes mentioned as an attractive takeover target for a larger brewing company.

Quinsa, a holding company based in Luxembourg, owns 85 percent of Quilmes International Limited in Bermuda, while strong global brewer Heineken International Beheer B.V. has owned the remaining 15 percent since 1984. As part of this relationship, Heineken provides the company with technical advice regarding its brewing facilities and beer products. The company has invested more than $530 million in the construction of new plant and modernization in the 1990s, while reducing employee rolls from 5,900 to 5,400. Management is convinced that technologically advanced, less labor intensive production capacity represents a significant advantage in the region.

In Argentina, the company operates five breweries with a nationwide distribution system for several beer brands, including Quilmes Cristal, the country's leading brand; Quilmes Bock, a dark beer; Andes; Norte; Palermo; Imperial; and a nonalcoholic beer, Liberty. It also imports and distributes Heineken, Amstel, and Buckler. Its Iguana 100 percent malted barley beer in a clear glass bottle competes in the premium segment. Most Argentine beer is sold in returnable bottles, most of which are one-liter size. Its beer products are sold in more than 200,000 points of sale in Argentina, reaching a 94 percent physical distribution.

In Brazil, Quilmes, following several acquisitions there, is the number-two brewer in the country. It has two brewing facilities there and a malting plant. Incesa beer and liquid malt brands sold in Bolivia include Taquina Export, Cerveceria Taquina's principal brand; Ducal, Cerveceria Santa Cruz's principal brand; Imperial, Taquina Pilsner; Malta; Ricomalt; Pilsener; Crucena; and alcohol-free Maltin. Sixty percent of Bolivia's population is under twenty-five years of age. Quilmes entered the Chilean market in 1991 because it offered good potential and was dominated by a single company. It has a modern brewery and provides three locally brewed brands, while importing and distributing Heinekin as well. Seventy-five percent of sales come from the Becker brand, positioned as a quality but affordable product. It also brews Baltica, a dry beer with a slightly higher alcoholic content. The Quilmes brand was launched in late 1995.

Its products in Paraguay constitute a strong, diversified product line whose principal brand, Pilsen, is a leader in rural areas and gaining market share elsewhere. Pilsen Dorado is strong in urban markets, while Baviera is a premium beer. It also sells the imports Baltica from Chile and Heineken from Holland. Beer is distributed from its two plants, as well as from three key distribution centers. In addition, the company produces, distributes, and sells Coca-Cola brands and is the only Coke bottler in the country. Finally, in Uruguay, Quilmes's main brand and market leader is Pilsen, positioned as a standard-price, quality beer for young people. It also markets premium brand Zillertal and Baltica. In late 1996, the company discontinued the brand Uruguaya, which previously had been a market leader. There is a main brewery and thirty distribution centers.

The company's strong cash flow permits it to finance new investments with relatively little long-term debt. This brewer does things carefully and does them right. For example, it started a new company, Quilmes do Brasil, to coordinate exports of its beer from plants in Argentina, Paraguay, and Uruguay to Southern Brazil and also began exporting its Quilmes Cristal brand there as well. The company's strategy is to introduce its brands in that region, consolidate their positions through exports, and then eventually to consider the possibility of constructing a brewery in Brazil.

"In our existing markets, Quinsa has maintained its strategy of investing significantly in its brands in order to capitalize on the potential of what are still comparatively low per capita consumption levels in the region," Jacques–Louis de Montalembert, chairman of the board, said in his letter in the company's most recent annual report. "Quinsa has also continued to invest in product development, plant modernization, and personnel training to ensure further improvement in its already high standards of quality, productivity, and service."

37. QUILMES INDUSTRIAL S.A.

Luxembourg   Ticker symbol LQU

One American Depositary Receipt represents one nonvoting preferred share

ADR price $6 15/16 (9/16/98)   Dividend yield 3.19%

(Financial data from I/B/E/S International is in Argentine peso)*

BUSINESS DESCRIPTION

LEADING BREWERS IN SOUTH AMERICA, ALSO PRODUCES SOFT DRINKS, MINERAL WATER, MALT, HOPS, AND CROWN CAPS. NO SALES BREAKDOWN AVAILABLE

ADDRESS AND CONTACTS

Address	84, Grand-Rue
	1660 Luxembourg City, Luxembourg
Telephone	352-47-38-84-OR +35
Fax	352-22-60-56

BASIC FINANCIAL INFORMATION

Capital Structure[†]	Long Term Debt:	76.22
	Total Debt:	172.23
	Common Sh. Equity:	411.09

SALES BREAKDOWN

Product Segments[†]		NA
Geographic		
Segments[†]	Argentina	514.98
	Paraguay	185.85
	Uruguay	76.52
	Chile	27.62
	Intersegment Sale	-11.03

Displayed Currency: Argentine Peso (1.00:1)
*I/B/E/S and I/B/E/S Express are registered trademarks of I/B/E/S International Inc. Copyright 1993–1996 I/B/E/S International Inc. All rights reserved.
[†]Values are displayed in millions.

Quilmes Industrial S.A.

FINANCIAL STATEMENT DATA

INCOME STATEMENT	1996	1995	1994	1993	1992
Net Sales or Revenues	812.00	796.80	753.80	643.80	440.15
EBITDA	194.92	188.31	208.00	159.89	88.61
Depreciation Depletion & Amort	64.62	52.15	35.90	30.59	NA
Operating Income	123.57	133.87	183.80	139.19	82.47
Interest Expense	13.29	13.29	9.10	6.34	4.16
Pretax Income	117.32	122.88	163.00	122.96	84.45
Net Income	58.96	60.24	86.70	64.75	43.66

BALANCE SHEET	1996	1995	1994	1993	1992
Assets					
Cash & Equivalents	97.70	58.44	55.50	58.41	31.28
Receivables—Net	92.71	75.72	71.20	59.80	39.50
Inventories	111.09	118.18	90.30	64.45	58.91
Total Current Assets	326.87	285.01	235.00	198.69	143.85
Property Plant & Eq.—Net	547.35	473.63	465.40	325.81	199.58
Total Assets	936.36	818.38	751.60	545.99	411.15
Liabilities & Shareholders' Equity					
Total Current Liabilities	256.04	254.95	224.00	153.65	121.18
Long Term Debt	76.22	77.82	85.90	54.15	35.24
Preferred Stock	0.00	0.00	0.00	0.00	0.00
Common Equity	411.09	331.87	298.90	225.42	169.59
Total Liabilities & Sh. Equity	936.36	818.38	751.60	545.99	411.15

CASH FLOW	1996	1995	1994	1993	1992
Funds from Operations	118.98	108.39	128.30	97.12	70.59
Total Sources	148.66	136.59	229.50	125.93	157.31
Cash Dividends Paid—Total	20.20	20.48	15.50	8.91	5.45
Total Uses	148.66	136.56	229.50	125.93	157.31
Incr/Decr in Working Capital	42.94	18.18	-40.69	24.20	-46.72
Free Cash Flow	132.16	112.09	12.00	47.82	-5.64

INTERNATIONAL BUSINESS	1996	1995	1994	1993	1992
Foreign Assets	920.15	824.68	751.60	NA	NA
Foreign Sales	812.00	796.80	753.80	643.80	440.15
Foreign Income	144.95	166.33	NA	NA	NA

265

SUPPLEMENTARY DATA	1996	1995	1994	1993	1992
Employees	5400	5200	5500	5600	5200
R&D Expenses	0.49	0.50	NA	NA	NA
Goodwill/Cost in Excess of Assets Purchased	NA	NA	NA	NA	NA
Extra Items & Gain/ Loss in Sale of Assets	0.00	0.00	0.00	0.00	0.00

Displayed Currency: Argentine Peso (1.00:1)
All values are displayed in millions (except employees).

FINANCIAL RATIOS AND GROWTH RATES

PROFITABILITY	1996	1995	1994	1993	1992	5YR AVG
Operating Profit Margin %	15.22	16.80	24.38	21.62	18.74	19.35
Tax Rate %	33.44	33.33	30.61	30.76	33.88	32.41
Net Margin %	7.26	7.56	11.50	10.06	9.92	9.26
Return on Assets %	8.90	8.49	14.80	18.23	16.08	13.30
Return on Equity— Total %	19.16	18.64	33.52	41.52	35.34	29.64
Cash Flow % Sales	14.65	13.60	17.02	15.09	16.04	15.28
Sales per Employee (in 000s)	150	153	137	115	85	128

ASSET UTILIZATION	1996	1995	1994	1993	1992	5YR AVG
Total Asset Turnover	0.87	0.97	1.00	1.18	1.07	1.02
Capital Exp % Gross Fixed Assets	7.86	11.53	32.02	24.99	33.76	22.03
Acc Depreciation % Gross Fixed Assets	31.43	28.34	23.97	27.33	28.51	27.92
Assets per Employee (in 000s)	173	157	137	97	79	129

LIQUIDITY	1996	1995	1994	1993	1992	5YR AVG
Current Ratio	1.28	1.12	1.05	1.29	1.19	1.18
Quick Ratio	0.74	0.53	0.57	0.77	0.58	0.64

LEVERAGE	1996	1995	1994	1993	1992	5YR AVG
Total Debt % Common Equity	41.90	53.25	50.25	43.30	46.82	47.10
Long Term Debt % Common Equity	18.54	23.45	28.74	24.02	20.78	23.11
Common Equity % Total Assets	43.90	40.55	39.77	41.29	41.25	41.35

Quilmes Industrial S.A.

	1996	1995	1994	1993	1992	5YR AVG
Long Term Debt %						
Total Capital	11.87	14.88	17.82	15.37	13.72	14.73
Operating Cash/						
Fixed Charges	9.17	8.16	14.10	15.33	16.98	12.75

GROWTH %	1996	1995	1994	1993	1992	5YR AVG
Net Sales	1.91	5.70	17.09	46.27	21.98	17.61
Operating Income	-7.69	-27.17	32.05	68.79	59.50	19.04
Total Assets	14.42	8.89	37.66	32.80	33.98	25.00
Earnings per Share*	-2.72	-30.46	33.84	48.37	11.84	8.48
Dividends per Share*	-27.81	33.20	34.68	70.45	64.92	29.49
Book Value per Share	19.23	11.62	32.61	32.91	29.01	24.79

Displayed Currency: Argentine Peso (1.00:1)
*Source: Worldscope. Value may differ from I/B/E/S.
Note: 5-Year Average calculations exclude NAs.

PER SHARE AND RELATED DATA

SOURCE: WORLDSCOPE	1996	1995	1994	1993	1992
Earnings per Share	0.571	0.587	0.845	0.631	0.425
Dividends per Share	0.192	0.266	0.200	0.149	0.087
Book Value per Share	3.877	3.252	2.913	2.197	1.653
Total Investment Return	NA	-35.43	9.30	133.43	NA
Market Price (Year-end)	8.086	10.437	15.335	12.388	5.840
Market Capitalization					
(in millions)	857.37	1065.22	1573.36	1270.97	599.20
Price/Earnings Ratio	14.15	17.77	18.15	19.63	13.73
Price/Book Value	2.09	3.21	5.26	5.64	3.53
Dividend Yield	2.38	2.55	1.30	1.20	1.49
Dividend Payout per					
Share	33.65	45.35	23.68	23.53	20.48
Common Shares					
Outstanding					
(Year-end) in					
Millions	106.03	102.06	102.60	102.60	102.60
Stock Split/Dividend					
Ratio	NA	0.67	0.67	NA	NA
Type of Share	Registered				

Displayed Currency: Argentine Peso (1.00:1)
Note: Data is sourced from Worldscope and may differ from I/B/E/S historical data.

38. Roche Holding A.G.

Although Switzerland's Roche Holding A.G. spent more than a century developing into one of the world's leading research-based health care groups and one of the largest producers of vitamins, fragrances, and flavors, it is still growing and changing. Its majority interest in Genentech, one of the world's largest biotechnology firms, solidifies its prominent international health care position. Pharmaceuticals, accounting for two-thirds of Roche's sales, include the U.S. injectable antibiotic Rocephin, AIDS drug Invirase, stroke medicine Ticlid, and acne treatment Roaccutane/Accutane. Its over-the-counter products include vitamins, the analgesic Aleve, and Femstat 3 antifungal for vaginal yeast infections. The stock looks especially attractive following a period in which its income was off a bit, due in part to the $11 billion acquisition of Corange Limited. That 1997 purchase, which included the products of Behringer Mannheim Group and DePuy Inc., made Roche the world's number-one diagnostics company. Because leading orthopedic device maker DePuy didn't fit in with its other lines, Roche agreed to sell its 84 percent stake in DePuy to Johnson & Johnson for $3.5 billion, or $35 a share, in July 1998. Prior acquisitions in the 1990s included Sara Lee Corporation's European-based over-the-counter drug business in 1991 and Syntex Corporation in 1994. The economic slowdown in Southeast Asia has affected demand and pricing, but hasn't had a significant effect on overall results.

Founded as a drug-manufacturing business in 1896 by Fritz Hoffmann-LaRoche, today's Roche Holding boasts a number-one or -two position in all of its core businesses except retail pharmaceuticals, where reaching a top-five position probably won't be achieved without another acquisition. For the company to reach the next level, it must take some important steps, including expansion of that business. While pharmaceuticals had strong returns in the first half of 1998, Ticlid's patent expired during the year, to be followed by high gross margin drugs Roaccutane and Versed. It's generally believed high revenues and profit from Xenical and Posicor can help take up the slack from those expirations. Overall revenue growth was strong in early 1998, boosted by products brought into the Roche portfolio by Boehringer Mannheim, such as antianemic Recormon, lipid lowerer Bezalip, and cardiovascular drug Coreg/Dilatrend. The U.S. Food and Drug Administration approved the anti–Parkinson's disease treatment Tasmar.

Franz Humor was appointed chief executive officer in January 1998 and also retained his role as the head of the pharmaceuticals division. Fritz Gerber, who stepped down as chairman of the executive committee and CEO at the end of 1997, but continued on as executive chairman, said of Roche's future in the most recent annual report: "The ability and the will to see change as opportunity, to be open to the new, will remain decisive. Our history is characterized by a commitment to innovation, and this will continue to be the key to our future success."

Building that future, Roche has a number of new drugs and comarketing deals in its pipeline. For example, the Xeloda drug of Hoffmann–LaRoche, a unit of Roche, reduced tumor size by more than 50 percent in eleven of forty-three patients tested with hard-to-treat tumors that didn't respond to standard chemotherapy. The U.S. Food & Drug Administration used this data in its decision to accelerate approval of the drug in the United States for 1998 availability. The FDA issued a letter of approvability for Xenical, the company's weight management drug to treat obesity by blocking the absorption of fat in the gastrointestinal tract. Meanwhile, Roche and T.O.A. Medical Electronics of Japan agreed in 1998 on global cooperation in sales and marketing, as well as in joint research and development for future products. Roche's Hoffmann–LaRoche unit and Smith Kline Beecham Plc. are copromoting Coreg, which combines beta-blockade and alpha-blocade in one drug for the treatment of heart failure. Roche and the Icelandic research firm DeCode Genetics Incorporated are to collaborate in genetic research with the aim of developing new therapeutic and diagnostic products to combat disease. Genentech, in which Roche owns a 66 percent stake, experienced strong earnings growth in early 1998 driven by sales of Rituxan for treatment of patients with non-Hodgkin's lymphoma.

The company's fragrances and flavors division makes ingredients for luxury perfumes, toilet waters, cosmetics, soaps, and other household products, as well as natural and synthetic flavor additives for beverages, foods, tobacco products, pharmaceuticals, oral hygiene products, and animal feeds. The vitamin business makes vitamins such as A, E, C, B-complex, beta-carotene, astaxanthin, citric acid, and chloratetracycline; carotenoids, which are coloring agents found in plants and animals; and fine chemicals such as citric acid, polyunsaturated fatty acids, medicinal feed additives, feed enzymes, sunscreen agents, and emulsifiers. Exceptional sales growth in Latin America, China, Europe, and Africa have been a boost to this division. Use of more efficient manufacturing technologies is helping to lay the foundation for sustained cost leadership in production, including chemical and biotechnological processes. The search for new coloring agents for the food and feed industries has led to the development of carotenoids with an expanded range of uses.

Understanding and utilizing molecular structure will be key to the coming century. With more than fifty years of experience in biochemistry, Roche's molecular biochemicals business is one of the world's leading producers of research reagents and systems for the advancement of medical science and industrywide use. Each year it introduces more than 100 products into the market. The company features a strong emphasis on polymerase chain reaction (PCR) technology, a Nobel Prize–winning discovery that permits virtually unlimited copies of genetic material made in a test tube. Since acquiring the rights to PCR technology in 1991, Roche has made it the leading DNA probe technology in the world in a wide range of applications. This makes it possible to diagnose infectious agents early and to monitor disease progression and responses to therapy. New applications will make it possible to predict predisposition to diseases and individualize patient therapy. The company also offers a wide range of products to doctors and patients for professional testing and patient self-monitoring. Besides diagnostic tools such as meters and test strips, it offers comprehensive education and training materials as well.

All of which means that a global company well steeped in the past can be well positioned for the future if it keeps making smart acquisitions and developing competitive products.

38. ROCHE HOLDING A.G.

Switzerland   Ticker symbol ROHHY

One ADR represents 1/100th of an ordinary share

ADR price $114 (9/16/98)   Dividend yield .49%

(Financial data from I/B/E/S International is in Swiss franc)*

BUSINESS DESCRIPTION

PHARMACEUTICALS ACCOUNTED FOR 65% OF 1997 REVENUES, VITAMINS AND FINE CHEMICALS 20%, DIAGNOSTICS 5%, AND FRAGRANCES, FLAVORS, AND OTHER 10%

ADDRESS AND CONTACTS

Address	Postfach
	Ch-4002 Basel, Switzerland
Telephone	41-61-6888888
Fax	41-61-6882775

BASIC FINANCIAL INFORMATION

Capital Structure[†]	Long Term Debt:	11321.00
	Total Debt:	12942.00
	Common Sh. Equity:	18250.00

SALES BREAKDOWN

Product Segments[†]	Pharmaceuticals	12070.00
	Vitamins & Fine Chemicals	3803.00
	Fragrances and Flavors	1928.00
	Diagnostics	966.00

SALES BREAKDOWN

Geographic
   Segments†

Switzerland	320.00
European Union	5588.00
Other European	841.00
North America	6974.00
Asia	2333.00
Other	2711.00

Displayed Currency: Swiss Franc (1.00:1)
*I/B/E/S and I/B/E/S Express are registered trademarks of I/B/E/S International Inc. Copyright 1993–1996 I/B/E/S International Inc. All rights reserved.

†Values are displayed in millions.

FINANCIAL STATEMENT DATA

INCOME STATEMENT	1997	1996	1995	1994	1993
Net Sales or Revenues	18767.00	15966.00	14722.00	14748.00	14315.00
EBITDA	165.00	6871.00	6015.00	5220.00	4588.00
Depreciation Depletion & Amort	1486.00	1209.00	1119.00	979.00	930.00
Operating Income	2424.00	2624.00	2510.00	2112.00	2348.00
Interest Expense	953.00	953.00	774.00	649.00	524.00
Pretax Income	-2259.00	4709.00	4122.00	3592.00	3134.00
Net Income	-2031.00	3899.00	3372.00	2860.00	2478.00

BALANCE SHEET	1997	1996	1995	1994	1993
Assets					
Cash & Equivalents	9306.00	15028.00	14499.00	14298.00	14588.00
Receivables—Net	5734.00	4296.00	3924.00	3706.00	3143.00
Inventories	5845.00	4318.00	3966.00	3690.00	3127.00
Total Current Assets	22323.00	24289.00	22932.00	22684.00	21296.00
Property Plant & Eq.— Net	12716.00	9375.00	7885.00	8050.00	6789.00
Total Assets	54776.00	39776.00	35564.00	36233.00	30926.00
Liabilities & Shareholders' Equity					
Total Current Liabilities	14158.00	5434.00	5657.00	8916.00	4466.00
Long Term Debt	11321.00	8524.00	7518.00	5210.00	4498.00
Preferred Stock	0.00	0.00	0.00	0.00	0.00
Common Equity	18250.00	20780.00	17554.00	16422.00	17914.00
Total Liabilities & Sh. Equity	54776.00	39776.00	35564.00	36233.00	30926.00

CASH FLOW	1997	1996	1995	1994	1993
Funds from Operations	3965.00	5309.00	4630.00	3574.00	3174.00
Total Sources	6410.00	5265.00	3400.00	9666.00	4169.00
Cash Dividends Paid— Total	647.00	863.00	474.00	404.12	311.51

Roche Holding A.G.

	1997	1996	1995	1994	1993
Total Uses	6410.00	5265.00	3400.00	9666.00	4196.00
Incr/Decr in Working Capital	-10690.00	1580.00	3507.00	-3062.00	2687.00
Free Cash Flow	-1637.00	5247.00	4525.00	3865.00	3181.00

INTERNATIONAL BUSINESS	1997	1996	1995	1994	1993
Foreign Assets	19200.00	17192.00	NA	NA	NA
Foreign Sales	18447.00	15675.00	14432.00	14447.00	14000.00
Foreign Income	NA	NA	NA	NA	NA

SUPPLEMENTARY DATA	1997	1996	1995	1994	1993
Employees	73348	48972	50497	61381	56082
R&D Expenses	2903.00	2446.00	2290.00	2332.00	2163.00
Goodwill/Cost in Excess of Assets Purchased	5692.00	252.00	238.00	NA	NA
Extra Items & Gain/ Loss in Sale of Assets	0.00	0.00	0.00	0.00	0.00

Displayed Currency: Swiss Franc (1.00:1)
All values are displayed in millions (except employees).

FINANCIAL RATIOS AND GROWTH RATES

PROFITABILITY	1997	1996	1995	1994	1993	5YR AVG
Operating Profit Margin %	12.92	16.43	17.05	14.32	16.40	15.42
Tax Rate %	NA	16.10	16.74	18.76	19.85	17.86
Net Margin %	-10.82	24.42	22.90	19.39	17.31	14.64
Return on Assets %	-3.55	12.73	10.72	10.63	10.24	8.15
Return on Equity— Total %	-9.77	22.21	20.53	15.97	15.44	12.88
Cash Flow % Sales	21.13	33.25	31.45	24.23	22.17	26.45
Sales per Employee (in 000s)	256	326	292	240	255	274

ASSET UTILIZATION	1997	1996	1995	1994	1993	5YR AVG
Total Asset Turnover	0.34	0.40	0.41	0.41	0.46	0.41
Capital Exp % Gross Fixed Assets	8.56	9.48	10.20	9.07	10.34	9.53
Acc Depreciation % Gross Fixed Assets	39.59	45.28	46.02	46.14	50.10	45.43
Assets per Employee (in 000s)	747	812	704	590	551	681

LIQUIDITY	1997	1996	1995	1994	1993	5YR AVG
Current Ratio	1.58	4.47	4.05	2.54	4.77	3.48
Quick Ratio	1.06	3.56	3.26	2.02	3.97	2.77

LEVERAGE	1997	1996	1995	1994	1993	5YR AVG
Total Debt %						
Common Equity	70.92	47.92	47.44	55.88	29.69	50.37
Long Term Debt %						
Common Equity	62.03	41.02	42.83	31.73	25.11	40.54
Common Equity %						
Total Assets	33.32	52.24	49.36	45.32	57.93	47.63
Long Term Debt %						
Total Capital	36.81	28.28	29.06	23.16	19.53	27.37
Operating Cash/						
Fixed Charges	4.23	5.57	5.98	5.51	6.06	5.47

GROWTH %	1997	1996	1995	1994	1993	5YR AVG
Net Sales	17.54	8.45	-0.18	3.02	10.51	7.70
Operating Income	-7.62	4.54	18.84	-10.05	16.64	3.97
Total Assets	37.71	11.84	-1.85	17.16	12.12	14.71
Earnings per Share*	-151.99	15.60	17.77	12.80	29.33	-100.00
Dividends per Share*	10.67	17.19	16.36	14.58	29.73	17.54
Book Value per Share	-12.18	18.38	6.89	-10.52	11.64	2.11

Displayed Currency: Swiss Franc (1.00:1)
*Source: Worldscope. Value may differ from I/B/E/S.
Note: 5-Year Average calculations exclude NAs.

PER SHARE AND RELATED DATA

SOURCE: WORLDSCOPE	1997	1996	1995	1994	1993
Earnings per Share	-235.0	452.0	391.0	332.0	294.3
Dividends per Share	83.0	75.0	64.0	55.0	48.0
Book Value per Share	2115.8	2409.1	2035.1	1903.9	2127.7
Total Investment					
Return	NA	NA	46.08	1.27	53.39
Market Price					
(Year-end)	14505.0	10415.0	9125.0	6335.0	6310.0
Market Capitalization					
(in millions)	125114.72	89835.91	78708.84	54643.35	53125.53
Price/Earnings Ratio	NM	23.04	23.34	19.08	21.44
Price/Book Value	6.86	4.32	4.48	3.33	2.97
Dividend Yield	0.57	0.72	0.70	0.87	0.76
Dividend Payout per					
Share	-35.32	16.59	16.37	16.57	16.31
Common Shares					
Outstanding					
(Year-end) in					
Millions	8.63	8.63	8.63	8.63	8.42
Stock Split/Dividend Ratio	NA	NA	NA	NA	1.00
Type of Share	Genussschein				

Displayed Currency: Swiss Franc (1.00:1)
Note: Data is sourced from Worldscope and may differ from I/B/E/S historical data.

39. Safeway Incorporated

What a difference five years makes. The second-largest food retailer in the United States, once a less than efficient operation, continues to show remarkable improvement in profitability as it gradually shrinks its operating and administration expenses. This consistent grocer's results regularly beat expectations, something that Wall Street analysts and investors find irresistible. Expected compound earnings-per-share returns of 15 percent, strong cash flow, and a dedication to shareholder value don't hurt either.

Safeway Incorporated operates approximately 1,370 stores in the West, Rocky Mountain, Southwest, and Midatlantic regions of the United States and Western Canada. Included in that total are more than 300 stores of the Vons Companies, the largest supermarket chain in southern California. Following its acquisition by Safeway in 1997, with its stores continuing to operate under the Vons name, Vons has been an addition with substantial synergistic benefits. Safeway also has a 49 percent interest in Casa Ley, which operates food/variety stores in western Mexico. Bottom line–conscious Kohlberg Kravis Roberts, involved in the 1986 acquisition of Safeway by a partnership formed by KKR and company senior management, owns about one-third of Safeway. Boasting a total of 147,000 employees, an aggressive Safeway spent $950 million in 1998 to open forty-five new stores, complete more than 200 remodeling jobs, and finish construction of its Maryland distribution center. It has most recently streamlined the administrative structure at Vons and combined Vons's previously outsourced processing operations into the Safeway information technology group.

The company has continued to consolidate its private label

manufacturing by closing two plants, yet has introduced more than 200 new Safeway Select items, bringing its total offerings close to 1,000 items, including soft drinks, pasta, salsa, whole bean coffee, cookies, ice cream, yogurt, pet food, and laundry detergent. The line also includes Safeway Select "Healthy Advantage" items such as low-fat ice cream and low-fat cereal bars, and Safeway Select "Gourmet Club" frozen entrees and hors d'oeuvres. The company also offers a wide selection of private label products under the brand names of Safeway, Vons, Lucerne, Jerseymaid, and Mrs. Wright's. Safeway manufactures more than one-half of its private label merchandise in company-owned plants and purchases the remainder from third parties.

Hard-nosed Steven Burd, forty-eight-year-old president and chief executive officer of the chain who is depicted in company photographs in down-to-business shirtsleeves, additionally assumed the chairman's title in May 1998 when Peter Magowan retired. Magowan, who had relinquished the CEO post to Burd in 1993 when he became president and managing partner of the San Francisco Giants baseball team, has remained a board member since his retirement. Burd's hard work and fervent belief in the company has not gone unnoticed monetarily, for he was featured in *Fortune* magazine's Fortunes in the Future special report in 1998 as having one of the top personal CEO "treasure chests," holding $120.5 million worth of nonexercised company stock options. Burd proclaimed Safeway's recent progress this way in his letter in the most recent annual report: "In 1992 Safeway was an industry laggard, trailing its peers in almost every key measure of operating and financial performance. Today it ranks among the best. We are committed to growing our business for our customers, our employees, and our stockholders."

On the labor front, Safeway signed major union contracts early in several key markets to help it achieve competitive labor costs. These included employees represented by the United Food and Commercial Workers Union in northern California and Spokane, Washington, as well as union members in British Columbia. While Safeway is in a highly competitive business facing the likes of Kroger (the nation's largest grocer), Lucky,

Albertsons, Cub Foods, Great Atlantic & Pacific, Food Lion, American Stores, Fred Meyer, and Thriftway, its operations are so geographically diverse that no one battleground should significantly affect its bottom line in a given year. Furthermore, it has proven adept at cutting costs sufficiently to take on all comers in any market. It is a company to be reckoned with.

Disciplined spending is a keystone of this revived grocery chain. Before a major capital spending project is approved, it is reviewed by the real estate committee, whose seven members include the chief executive officer and the chief financial officer. At Safeway, capital spending is a carefully planned, disciplined process. It requires a 22.5 percent pretax return on investment for all new store and remodeling projects. Projects are tracked over an extended period to measure actual results against targeted rates of return. By concentrating the majority of its capital spending in areas where it already commands strong market positions, Safeway believes it can enhance prospects for long-term sales growth and operating margin improvement. More than half of its stores have been built or remodeled in the past five years, leaving significant opportunities to continue improving the store base. Safeway, which owns more than one-third of its stores and leases the rest, operates stores ranging in size from 6,900 square feet to more than 89,000 square feet, determining the size of a store based on needs of the community, the location and site plan, and the estimated return on capital invested. Most stores offer a wide selection of both food and general merchandise and include specialty departments such as bakery, delicatessen, floral, and pharmacy. In most of the larger stores, specialty departments are showcased in each corner and along the perimeter walls of the store. The company's primary new store prototype is 55,000 square feet, but it continues to operate a number of smaller stores designed for smaller communities and areas where there are space limitations.

Emphasizing that it would have "no significant effect" on its earnings, Safeway said its Vons business contributed to a $58.5 million payment in 1998 to Foodmaker Incorporated, which operates and franchises Jack in the Box restaurants, to settle all claims in a lawsuit from the 1993 E. coli–related illnesses at some Jack in the Box restaurants. The net cash payment by Vons was a small portion of the total settlement.

Safeway, which authorized a two-for-one stock split in early 1998, has taken the basic concept of the neighborhood grocery store to new levels of efficiency. And it plans to improve even more.

39. SAFEWAY INCORPORATED

United States   Ticker symbol SWY

Stock price $44 3/4 (9/16/98)   No dividend

(Financial data is from I/B/E/S International)*

BUSINESS DESCRIPTION

AN INTERNATIONAL CHAIN OF RETAIL STORES THAT HAS AN EXTENSIVE NETWORK OF DISTRIBUTION, MARKETING, AND FOOD PROCESSING FACILITIES

ADDRESS AND CONTACTS

Address	5918 Stoneridge Mall Road
	Pleasanton CA 94588
Telephone	1-925-467-3000

BASIC FINANCIAL INFORMATION

Capital Structure[†]	Long Term Debt:	3040.90
	Total Debt:	3340.30
	Common Sh. Equity:	2149.00

SALES BREAKDOWN

Product Segments[†]	Retailing household	22483.80
Geographic		
Segments[†]	United States	19075.90
	Canada	3407.90

Displayed Currency: U.S. Dollar (1.00:1)
*I/B/E/S and I/B/E/S Express are registered trademarks of I/B/E/S International Inc. Copyright 1993–1996 I/B/E/S International Inc. All rights reserved.
[†]Values are displayed in millions.

FINANCIAL STATEMENT DATA

INCOME STATEMENT	1997	1996	1995	1994	1993
Net Sales or Revenues	22483.80	17269.00	16397.50	15626.60	15214.50
EBITDA	1740.10	1236.40	1063.10	947.90	782.30
Depreciation Depletion & Amort	457.50	340.30	333.70	329.40	334.00
Operating Income	1279.70	891.70	727.40	612.10	441.50
Interest Expense	182.80	182.80	199.80	221.70	265.50
Pretax Income	1041.40	717.60	529.60	396.80	182.80
Net Income	621.50	460.60	326.30	239.70	123.30

BALANCE SHEET	1997	1996	1995	1994	1993
Assets					
Cash & Equivalents	77.20	79.70	74.80	60.70	118.40
Receivables—Net	180.80	160.90	152.70	147.90	119.50
Inventories	1613.20	1283.30	1191.80	1136.00	1128.10
Total Current Assets	2029.70	1654.40	1514.80	1437.60	1464.00
Property Plant & Eq.— Net	4115.30	2756.40	2592.90	2506.40	2560.10
Total Assets	8493.90	5545.20	5194.30	5022.10	5074.70
Liabilities & Shareholders' Equity					
Total Current Liabilities	2538.60	2030.00	1939.00	1823.60	1711.40
Long Term Debt	3040.90	1728.50	1949.80	2024.30	2481.30
Preferred Stock	0.00	0.00	0.00	0.00	0.00
Common Equity	2149.00	1186.80	795.50	643.80	382.90
Total Liabilities & Sh. Equity	8493.90	5545.20	5194.30	5022.10	5074.70

CASH FLOW	1997	1996	1995	1994	1993
Net Cash Flow— Operating	1221.60	825.20	657.70	753.30	599.40
Net Cash Flow— Investing	607.70	482.30	425.70	331.60	227.90
Net Cash Flow— Financing	-614.60	-337.50	-218.40	-478.50	-353.90
Incr/Decr in Working Capital	-133.30	48.60	-38.20	-138.60	-274.70
Free Cash Flow	981.90	694.60	612.20	608.00	537.00

INTERNATIONAL BUSINESS	1997	1996	1995	1994	1993
Foreign Assets	880.20	919.80	932.80	850.80	990.70
Foreign Sales	3407.90	3471.50	3495.10	3386.50	3458.50
Foreign Income	110.10	138.90	137.30	121.20	5.20

SUPPLEMENTARY DATA	1997	1996	1995	1994	1993
Employees	147000	119000	114000	110000	105900
R&D Expenses	NA	NA	NA	NA	NA
Goodwill/Cost in Excess of Assets Purchased	1824.70	312.50	323.80	331.10	347.60
Extra Items & Gain/ Loss in Sale of Assets	-64.10	0.00	-2.00	-10.50	0.00

Displayed Currency: U.S. Dollar (1.00:1)
All values are displayed in millions (except employees).

FINANCIAL RATIOS AND GROWTH RATES

PROFITABILITY	1997	1996	1995	1994	1993	5YR AVG
Operating Profit Margin %	5.69	5.16	4.44	3.92	2.90	4.42
Tax Rate %	43.67	42.78	43.09	43.83	50.88	44.85
Net Margin %	2.48	2.67	1.99	1.53	0.81	1.90
Return on Assets %	12.92	11.14	9.12	7.61	5.71	9.30
Return on Equity— Total %	46.97	57.90	50.68	62.60	50.72	53.77
Cash Flow % Sales	4.87	4.82	4.05	3.64	2.52	3.98
Sales per Employee (in 000s)	153	145	144	142	144	146

ASSET UTILIZATION	1997	1996	1995	1994	1993	5YR AVG
Total Asset Turnover	2.65	3.11	3.16	3.11	3.00	3.01
Capital Exp % Gross Fixed Assets	11.35	10.69	9.62	7.77	5.83	9.05
Acc Depreciation % Gross Fixed Assets	38.41	45.63	44.68	42.71	39.15	42.12
Assets per Employee (in 000s)	58	47	46	46	48	49

LIQUIDITY	1997	1996	1995	1994	1993	5YR AVG
Current Ratio	0.80	0.81	0.78	0.79	0.86	0.81
Quick Ratio	0.10	0.12	0.12	0.11	0.14	0.12

Safeway Incorporated

LEVERAGE	1997	1996	1995	1994	1993	5YR AVG
Total Debt %						
Common Equity	155.44	167.19	275.32	341.12	702.32	328.28
Long Term Debt %						
Common Equity	141.50	145.64	245.10	314.43	648.03	298.94
Common Equity %						
Total Assets	25.30	21.40	15.31	12.82	7.55	16.48
Long Term Debt %						
Total Capital	58.59	59.29	71.02	75.87	86.63	70.28
Operating Cash/						
Fixed Charges	4.43	4.56	3.32	2.57	1.45	3.27

GROWTH %	1997	1996	1995	1994	1993	5YR AVG
Net Sales	30.20	5.31	4.93	2.71	0.41	8.21
Operating Income	43.51	22.59	18.84	38.64	-0.02	23.71
Total Assets	53.18	6.76	3.43	-1.04	-2.89	10.20
Earnings per Share*	28.87	185.29	-33.66	100.98	22.89	43.21
Dividends per Share*	0.00	0.00	0.00	0.00	0.00	0.00
Book Value per Share	-84.81	51.35	25.68	68.43	51.81	-5.87

Displayed Currency: U.S. Dollar (1.00:1)
*Source: Worldscope. Value may differ from I/B/E/S.
Note: 5-Year Average calculations exclude NAs.

PER SHARE AND RELATED DATA

SOURCE: WORLDSCOPE	1997	1996	1995	1994	1993
Earnings per Share	1.25	0.97	0.34	0.51	0.26
Dividends per Share	0.00	0.00	0.00	0.00	0.00
Book Value per Share	0.38	2.51	1.66	1.32	0.78
Total Investment Return	NA	NA	61.57	50.00	63.46
Market Price (Year-end)	31.63	21.38	12.88	7.97	5.31
Market Capitalization					
(in millions)	16995.27	9464.85	5502.77	3340.50	2156.88
Price/Earnings Ratio	25.30	22.04	37.87	15.55	20.83
Price/Book Value	82.87	8.5	17.76	6.03	6.78
Dividend Yield	0.00	0.00	0.00	0.00	0.00
Dividend Payout per					
Share	0.00	0.00	0.00	0.00	0.00
Common Shares					
Outstanding					
(Year-end) in					
Millions	537.40	442.80	427.40	418.20	406.00
Stock Split/Dividend					
Ratio	0.50	0.50	0.25	0.25	0.25
Type of Share	Common				

Displayed Currency: U.S. Dollar (1.00:1)
Note: Data is sourced from Worldscope and may differ from I/B/E/S historical data.

281

40. Sandvik A.B.

Known for its cutting tools, strong track record, and global strategy, Sweden's Sandvik A.B. is a materials technology engineering company with business activities worldwide. Under the company theme "Sandvik makes it possible," its efforts are conducted in more than 130 countries through 300 companies with more than 38,000 employees.

Sandvik's background in steel production contributes to its manufacture of sophisticated tools that effectively use the latest metals. It holds world-leading positions in cemented-carbide and high-speed tools for chip-forming metalworking; machinery, equipment, and tools for mining and construction; and stainless steels, special alloys, and resistance heating materials. It is also a leading manufacturer of cemented-carbide blanks, saws, and other hand tools and process systems. Sandvik's resources for research and development have increased 50 percent over 1997-98, with the number of patents up 70 percent. Company management has financial objectives of 6 percent sales growth and 20 percent return on net assets, with a dividend at least 50 percent of earnings per share and dividend-plus-share-value growth above the average of its peers.

Sandvik can customize its technology. With a reputation for making the finest saws in the world, regardless of what they're used for, the firm long ago noted the tradition of concert saw-playing by tuxedoed musicians who coax melodies out of the tool. So it annually manufactures several hundred "Stadivarius" saws, which are guaranteed to produce the sweetest melodies possible from shiny sharp-edged metal.

Strong sales for Sandvik in the United States and Europe—

especially Sweden, France, Italy, Germany—and Eastern Europe, boosted its bottom line in 1998, and the future upgrading of European manufacturing facilities should be a big plus for the company. It has worked hard over the years to build a strong presence in regions such as Eastern Europe, Southeast Asia, and Japan. Management considers Southeast Asia and Korea to be important growth areas for the company, and while sales declined there and in South America, Australia, and Brazil in early 1998, there was considerable relief that overall damage to profits wasn't worse. In addition, demand in China continues to be favorable and Sandvik's new carbide inserts plant in Langfang City is the most modern of its kind in that country. However, low international inflation has made it difficult to increase prices, and there's the ongoing concern about the Swedish krona becoming too strong, since the firm has a large Swedish manufacturing presence and must engage in hedging. A slump in steel prices have also taken a bite out of its profits. While Sandvik is not among the world's largest steel manufacturers in terms of tonnage, it is a leader in high-quality steel.

Founded in 1862 by technical genius Goran Fredrik Goransson as a small provincial Swedish steel mill that even then operated in market niches in which it was the best, this acquisition-minded company is today eyeing future purchases of companies in advanced materials technology to meet its long-term growth target of 6 percent annual sales volume. For example, in mid-1998 it acquired the German tube manufacturer Poppe & Pothoff's unit for stainless steel precision tubes. It manufactures seamless small-size, thick-walled tubes and coiled tubing for instrumentation and high pressure applications; capillary and medical implant tubes; and tubes with special surface finishes. Following the purchase of Finland's Tamrock in late 1997, the company meshed it and Sandvik Rock Tools into one business area under the name Sandvik Mining & Construction. The company also acquired Sweden's Kanthal, the world's leading manufacturer of high-temperature materials, and precision Twist Drill, an American company that ranks as one of the world's leading manufacturers of high-speed steel twist drills.

"Our expansion strategy is based on assumptions of increased sales in emerging new markets and more mature markets," President and Chief Executive Officer Clas Ake Hedstrom emphasized in his letter in the most recent annual report. "Today there are no signs of reversal in the group's highly favorable business development. The European Union will continue to be Sandvik's largest market region, driven primarily by Germany's production industry. Because of the present economic situation in Southeast Asia, operations in the region are being consolidated with a view toward the future growth potential this market area can offer."

Sandvik's historic strengths have been its marketing in close cooperation with worldwide customers and its continuous product renewal with an emphasis on advanced technology. Customers operate in many different industrial groups, including automotive and aerospace industries, mining and civil engineering, chemicals, oil and gas, power, pulp and paper, household appliances, electronics, medical technology, pharmaceuticals, and other engineering industries. The overall corporate strategy is to conduct sophisticated and comprehensive research and development to improve productivity and quality; create time savings and reduce costs for customers and the group's own operations in materials and surface-coating technology; product and application solutions; production and process technology; and information, communications, and logistics systems.

Business divisions consist of (1) Sandvik Tooling, with tools and tooling systems for metalworking applications, and the world's leading manufacturer of cemented-carbide tools in Sandvik Coromant, and high-speed tool firm CTT Tools; (2) Sandvik Mining and Construction, comprising Tamrock and Sandvik Rock Tools; (3) Sandvik Specialty Steels with Sandvik Steel and Kanthal; (4) Sandvik Hard Materials, which is active in the full spectrum from cemented carbide to diamond, including special ceramics for biotechnical applications; (5) Sandvik Saws and Tools, one of the world's largest manufacturers of handsaws and metal saw blades and many other tools; and (6) Sandvik Process Systems, which manufactures and markets complete systems for automatic goods sorting and process plants for the chemical and food processing industries.

Sandvik A.B.

In terms of thinking globally, Sandvik was a pioneer. It established its first representative outside Sweden on the European continent in the 1860s with expansion into Norway, Denmark, the United Kingdom, Russia, Germany, and France. The first subsidiary outside Europe was established in the United States after World War I, and in 1931 a company was established in Argentina. Africa gained a subsidiary in 1947, India in 1960, and Australia in 1961, with others in Japan, Singapore, Korea, and China to follow. It's expected that the non–European markets will provide Sandvik with its strongest future growth.

40. SANDVIK A.B.

Sweden   Ticker symbol SAVKY

One American Depositary Receipt represents one Series "B" share

ADR price $20 7/8 (9/16/98)   Dividend yield 4.30%

(Financial data from I/B/E/S International is in Swedish krona)*

BUSINESS DESCRIPTION

TOOLING ACCOUNTED FOR 33% OF 1997 REVENUES, STEEL 32%, SAWS AND TOOLS 9%, OTHER TOOLS 9%, ROCK TOOLS 7%, PROCESS SYSTEMS 6%, AND OTHER 4%

ADDRESS AND CONTACTS

Address	Vastra Verken
	Sandviken Sweden S-811 81
Telephone	46-26-260000
Fax	46-26-261022

BASIC FINANCIAL INFORMATION

Capital Structure†	Long Term Debt:	819.00
	Total Debt:	7268.00
	Common Sh. Equity:	17414.00

SALES BREAKDOWN

Product Segments†	Tooling	9211.00
	Steel	8980.00
	Saws & tools	2517.00
	Other tools	2475.00
	Rock tools	2003.00

285

SALES BREAKDOWN

Geographic
Segments†

Sweden	2036.00
EU (excl. Sweden)	12780.00
Rest of Europe	1485.00
NAFTA	5769.00
South America	1293.00
Other	4902.00

Displayed Currency: Swedish Krona (1.00:1)
*I/B/E/S and I/B/E/S Express are registered trademarks of I/B/E/S International Inc. Copyright 1993–1996 I/B/E/S International Inc. All rights reserved.
†Values are displayed in millions.

FINANCIAL STATEMENT DATA

INCOME STATEMENT	1997	1996	1995	1994	1993
Net Sales or Revenues	34119.00	28265.00	29700.00	25285.00	21770.00
EBITDA	NA	5696.00	6761.00	4982.00	3171.00
Depreciation Depletion & Amort	1486.00	1159.00	1071.00	1003.00	1104.00
Operating Income	3744.00	3937.00	4998.00	3390.00	1726.00
Interest Expense	256.00	256.00	266.00	287.00	348.00
Pretax Income	4205.00	4281.00	5424.00	3692.00	1719.00
Net Income	2725.00	3114.00	3727.00	2436.00	1069.00

BALANCE SHEET	1997	1996	1995	1994	1993
Assets					
Cash & Equivalents	NA	5400.00	5368.00	5653.00	4686.00
Receivables—Net	NA	6771.00	7073.00	6345.00	5558.00
Inventories	NA	7306.00	7097.00	6141.00	5724.00
Total Current Assets	NA	19923.00	19787.00	18435.00	16290.00
Property Plant & Eq.— Net	NA	9548.00	7908.00	7397.00	7182.00
Total Assets	40061.00	32774.00	30562.00	28368.00	25127.00
Liabilities & Shareholders' Equity					
Total Current Liabilities	15049.00	6936.00	6907.00	7539.00	5827.00
Long Term Debt	819.00	312.00	155.00	251.00	377.00
Preferred Stock	0.00	0.00	0.00	0.00	0.00
Common Equity	17414.00	20035.00	18503.00	16013.00	14364.00
Total Liabilities & Sh. Equity	40061.00	32774.00	30562.00	28368.00	25127.00

CASH FLOW	1997	1996	1995	1994	1993
Funds from Operations	4528.00	4680.00	5238.00	3249.00	2775.00
Total Sources	NA	6174.00	3315.00	2421.00	2102.00
Cash Dividends Paid— Total	1810.00	1640.00	1025.00	615.00	519.00
Total Uses	NA	6174.00	3315.00	2421.00	2102.00

Sandvik A.B.

	1997	1996	1995	1994	1993
Incr/Decr in Working Capital	NA	107.00	1984.00	433.00	368.00
Free Cash Flow	NA	3210.00	4711.00	3753.00	2285.00

INTERNATIONAL BUSINESS	1997	1996	1995	1994	1993
Foreign Assets	NA	NA	NA	NA	NA
Foreign Sales	NA	26229.00	27330.00	23515.05	20276.00
Foreign Income	NA	NA	NA	NA	NA

SUPPLEMENTARY DATA	1997	1996	1995	1994	1993
Employees	NA	30362	29946	29450	26869
R&D Expenses	NA	849.00	769.00	684.00	659.00
Goodwill/Cost in Excess of Assets Purchased	NA	287.00	259.00	327.00	311.00
Extra Items & Gain/ Loss in Sale of Assets	NA	0.00	0.00	0.00	0.00

Displayed Currency: Swedish Krona (1.00:1)
All values are displayed in millions (except employees).

FINANCIAL RATIOS AND GROWTH RATES

PROFITABILITY	1997	1996	1995	1994	1993	5YR AVG
Operating Profit Margin %	10.97	13.93	16.83	13.41	7.93	12.61
Tax Rate %	NA	26.09	29.54	33.23	33.45	30.58
Net Margin %	7.99	11.02	12.55	9.63	4.91	9.22
Return on Assets %	8.31	10.74	13.76	10.45	5.38	9.73
Return on Equity— Total %	13.60	16.83	23.27	16.96	7.82	15.70
Cash Flow % Sales	13.27	16.56	17.64	12.85	12.75	14.61
Sales per Employee (in 000s)	NA	931	992	859	810	898

ASSET UTILIZATION	1997	1996	1995	1994	1993	5YR AVG
Total Asset Turnover	0.85	0.86	0.97	0.89	0.87	0.89
Capital Exp % Gross Fixed Assets	NA	12.60	11.80	7.24	5.44	9.27
Acc Depreciation % Gross Fixed Assets	NA	51.61	54.50	56.42	55.87	54.60
Assets per Employee (in 000s)	NA	1079	1021	963	935	1000

LIQUIDITY	1997	1996	1995	1994	1993	5YR AVG
Current Ratio	NA	2.87	2.86	2.45	2.80	2.74
Quick Ratio	NA	1.75	1.80	1.59	1.76	1.73

LEVERAGE	1997	1996	1995	1994	1993	5YR AVG
Total Debt %						
Common Equity	41.74	6.79	4.62	7.77	8.90	13.96
Long Term Debt %						
Common Equity	4.70	1.56	0.84	1.57	2.62	2.26
Common Equity %						
Total Assets	43.47	61.13	60.54	56.45	57.17	55.75
Long Term Debt %						
Total Capital	3.76	1.32	0.72	1.33	2.17	1.86
Operating Cash/						
Fixed Charges	NA	18.28	19.69	11.32	7.97	14.32

GROWTH %	1997	1996	1995	1994	1993	5YR AVG
Net Sales	20.71	-4.83	17.46	16.15	26.44	14.66
Operating Income	-4.90	-21.23	47.43	96.41	65.80	29.17
Total Assets	22.23	7.24	7.73	12.90	4.16	10.68
Earnings per Share*	-9.38	-16.42	45.65	87.76	7.69	17.41
Dividends per Share*	7.69	8.33	60.00	66.67	18.42	29.80
Book Value per Share	-5.70	8.28	15.55	11.48	3.05	6.27

Displayed Currency: Swedish Krona (1.00:1)
*Source: Worldscope. Value may differ from I/B/E/S.
Note: 5-Year Average calculations exclude NAs.

PER SHARE AND RELATED DATA

SOURCE: WORLDSCOPE	1997	1996	1995	1994	1993
Earnings per Share	10.2	11.2	13.4	9.2	4.9
Dividends per Share	7.0	6.5	6.0	3.8	2.3
Book Value per Share	67.8	71.9	66.4	57.5	51.6
Total Investment Return	NA	NA	2.51	7.17	41.27
Market Price (Year-end)	227.0	185.0	116.5	119.5	115.0
Market Capitalization					
(in millions)	58723.99	51518.13	32442.50	33277.93	32024.78
Price/Earnings Ratio	22.36	16.52	8.69	12.99	23.47
Price/Book Value	3.35	2.57	1.75	2.08	2.23
Dividend Yield	3.08	3.51	5.15	3.14	1.96
Dividend Payout per					
Share	68.97	58.04	44.78	40.76	45.92
Common Shares					
Outstanding					
(Year-end) in					
Millions	258.70	278.48	278.48	278.48	278.48
Stock Split/Dividend					
Ratio	NA	NA	NA	NA	NA
Type of Share	B Fri Aktie				

Displayed Currency: Swedish Krona (1.00:1)
Note: Data is sourced from Worldscope and may differ from I/B/E/S historical data.

41. SAP A.G.

Blue jeans worn in a casual office environment, an innovative high-tech product that is wildly successful, and founders who are millionaires many times over. Sounds like a story line from Silicon Valley, but this one was scripted in Germany.

SAP A.G., the world's fourth-largest independent software firm, helps companies of all sizes worldwide become more efficient and flexible. It dominates the worldwide market for corporate client/server enterprise resource planning programs, controlling about one-third of the market for software used to integrate and process information in corporate product distribution, finance, human resources, and manufacturing. Its R/3 software, which draws together companies' back office processes through a fully integrated, modular structure featuring more than 1,000 business processes, is used by more than 7,000 firms that include Microsoft, Chevron, Colgate-Palmolive, and General Motors. Chevron, for example, credits SAP software for a 15 percent decrease in its purchasing costs, which may become as much as 25 percent once that installation is fully completed, and has found speedier transaction handling to be an attractive by-product. The average time to implement an R/3 package is between six and nine months, while the average time to implement R/3's accounting component is between one and three months.

Although SAP has been conservative in its revenues and earnings estimates, increased popularity of client/server systems in the corporate world has been a catalyst for powerful sales growth. It has also led to impressive stock-price gains, a pleasant relief following a nosedive that SAP shares took in 1996. Information-technology spending on the Year 2000 problem and new Euro currency conversions sent software sales skyrocketing in early 1998, with an added boost from the strength of key currencies against the German mark. Meanwhile, the company continued to snare lucrative contracts in 1998 to supply software to major firms such as German utility RWE A.G., Italy's state-owned energy holding company ENI SpA, Phillips Petroleum Company, and OfficeMax. It also opened several solution-center locations with Andersen Consulting for the utilities industry, to be called SolutionWorks, in London; Madrid; Manila; Walldorf, Germany; St. Petersburg, Florida; and Cincinnati. It will include important industry objectives such as personnel safety, maintenance and construction, and regulatory reporting. SAP is also increasingly targeting small and midsize companies, with 20 percent of its worldwide revenues now coming from such companies. While big-company enterprise resource planning systems can cost tens of millions of dollars to install, it licenses its software to efficiency-conscious smaller companies at an average cost of $250,000.

Founded in 1972 by five former IBM engineers, SAP (which stands for Systems, Applications, and Products in Data Processing) today has more than 7,500 customers in more than ninety countries using its applications. It has more than 15,000 employees in more than fifty countries worldwide and spends 20 percent of annual revenues on research and development. Three of SAP's founders control about two-thirds of the company. Principal operations are in Germany, the United States, and Japan, with substantial sales in Switzerland and Austria. The company has said slowing growth in Asia due to economic turmoil there isn't a significant factor in its overall corporate revenue forecast. Companies deciding to use SAP software are thinking long-term, and unlikely to pull the plug based on short-term economic concerns. In fact, SAP created nearly 5,000 new jobs in 1998.

A new, friendlier face was named to lead the company in May 1998. Fifty-year-old Henning Kagermann, who left a tenured position teaching theoretical physics at Braunschweig University to join SAP in 1982, is the first executive outside of SAP's five founders to hold a senior position at the company. His more open nature is needed, since steely predecessor Dietmar Hopp didn't project a positive image during a 1997 insider-trading scandal that hit the company, even though SAP's board members and employees were eventually cleared of suspicion by state prosecutors and federal supervisors. Kagermann shares the co-chairmanship with Hasso Plattner, the firm's technology visionary, while Hopp is retiring from the executive board to become chairman of the supervisory board. Kagermann must deal with an inevitable slowdown in the 60 percent quarterly sales gains of its flagship software, R/3. In addition, some competitors claim they've been catching up with SAP in new product areas such as Internet-related software.

Marketing is a major thrust of SAP, and the focus in the hiring of many new employees. Its Accelerated SAP program involves rapid implementation of the company's core R/3 product, while Team SAP includes more than 2,800 consultants and 15,000 partner consultants to support R/3 customers. There's also a new SAP America Public Sector subsidiary to provide planning, administrative, and information management systems for government, education, and nonprofit organizations in the United States.

The Pandesic joint venture between SAP and Intel Corporation will offer the first one-stop shop for all components required for electronic commerce on the Internet. For $25,000, small and midsize companies get everything they need to put their businesses on the Net in six weeks. Pandesic charges a small up-front price, but takes a fee of 1 to 6 percent of a customer's monthly sales. The product range includes partners Compaq, Hewlett-Packard, Cyber Cash, Citicorp, Smith Barney, Inacom, Taxware, UPS, and Yahoo! Pandesic, which can be installed within two weeks, will give SAP access to a new market that's independent of its previous R/3 business and probably has greater growth potential than the enterprise resource planning business, although the ultimate potential of the electronic commerce market remains the subject of speculation. SAP introduced "for the masses," as a top official put it, its Employee Self-Service Intranet Application Components 2.0 to provide Web-accessible and Web-based business applications. It's compatible with R/3 3.0 and higher, requiring Web-based Windows

NT Server 4.0, which supports both Internet Explorer and Netscape Navigator browsers running on any supported client system.

Finally, the firm's R/3 Release 4.0 introduced in 1998 permits its existing customers to introduce the latest version of SAP's personnel solution without having to upgrade its other R/3 applications, saving the customer time and money. Texas Instruments' storage products group, one of the initial forty customers, went live with Release 4.0 in just thirty days. This new product will also take SAP into a broad range of new market segments such as retail, financial services, and public administration.

Accelerated worldwide expansion of its turf is the goal at this uniquely European version of software success, proof positive that you don't have to be named Gates to make it happen.

41. SAP A.G.

Germany   Ticker symbol SAP

One American Depositary Receipt represents 1/12th of a preferred share

ADR price $46 7/8 (9/16/98)   Dividend yield .28%

(Financial data from I/B/E/S International is in German mark)*

BUSINESS DESCRIPTION

STANDARD APPLICATION SOFTWARE ACCOUNTED FOR 68% OF 1997 REVENUES, CONSULTING AND TRAINING 31%, AND OTHER, 1%

ADDRESS AND CONTACTS

Address	Neurottstrasse 16
	D-69190 Walldorf, Germany
Telephone	49-6227-747474
Fax	46-6227-757575

BASIC FINANCIAL INFORMATION

Report Dates	Last Annual: Dec 97	Reported On: Jan 29, 1998	
Capital Structure†	Long Term Debt:		5.12
	Total Debt:		168.26
	Common Sh. Equity:		3047.82

SAP A.G.

SALES BREAKDOWN

Product
Segments†

	Standard Applications	4097.00
	Consulting	1251.00
	Training	580.00
	Other	89.00
Geographic Segments†	Germany	1263.00
	Other European	1370.00
	America	2558.00
	Asia/Australia	746.00
	Africa	80.00

Displayed Currency: German Mark (1.00:1)
*I/B/E/S and I/B/E/S Express are registered trademarks of I/B/E/S International Inc. Copyright 1993–1996 I/B/E/S International Inc. All rights reserved.
†Values are displayed in millions.

FINANCIAL STATEMENT DATA

INCOME STATEMENT	1997	1996	1995	1994	1993
Net Sales or Revenues	6017.47	3722.15	2696.38	1831.14	1101.73
EBITDA	1832.81	1117.16	813.19	547.75	310.68
Depreciation Depletion & Amort	195.32	164.59	144.46	88.66	61.79
Operating Income	1582.33	881.25	610.47	417.58	184.21
Interest Expense	2.62	2.62	5.24	1.75	1.27
Pretax Income	1633.71	949.95	663.49	457.33	247.63
Net Income	922.98	566.22	403.32	280.25	145.77

BALANCE SHEET	1997	1996	1995	1994	1993
Assets					
Cash & Equivalents	1164.51	902.28	397.76	347.22	433.87
Receivables—Net	2355.00	1465.03	937.36	623.18	374.72
Inventories	7.52	7.80	5.56	4.94	5.50
Total Current Assets	3725.20	2456.82	1378.91	1006.56	837.53
Property Plant & Eq.— Net	853.31	621.90	575.01	514.48	419.39
Total Assets	5070.26	3367.10	2218.16	1749.73	1306.18
Liabilities & Shareholders' Equity					
Total Current Liabilities	836.65	510.21	332.48	246.40	141.06
Long Term Debt	5.12	8.83	20.55	21.95	1.00
Preferred Stock	NA	NA	NA	NA	NA
Common Equity	3047.82	2207.07	1526.47	1233.80	1007.82
Total Liabilities & Sh. Equity	5070.26	3367.10	2218.16	1749.73	1306.18

CASH FLOW	1997	1996	1995	1994	1993
Funds from Operations	1134.81	756.39	551.39	372.07	211.13
Total Sources	897.96	381.59	380.46	403.09	193.34
Cash Dividends Paid—					
Total	240.19	133.62	88.92	47.06	37.60
Total Uses	897.96	381.59	380.46	403.09	193.34
Incr/Decr in Working					
Capital	941.94	900.18	286.27	63.69	115.30
Free Cash Flow	1345.45	900.94	561.87	369.71	168.76

INTERNATIONAL BUSINESS	1997	1996	1995	1994	1993
Foreign Assets	NA	NA	NA	NA	NA
Foreign Sales	4754.00	2807.87	1897.84	1192.03	528.73
Foreign Income	874.00	NA	NA	NA	NA

SUPPLEMENTARY DATA	1997	1996	1995	1994	1993
Employees	12856	9202	6857	5229	3648
R&D Expenses	813.00	588.90	438.00	369.60	267.70
Goodwill/Cost in Excess of Assets Purchased	50.97	0.00	0.00	0.00	0.00
Extra Items & Gain/ Loss in Sale of Assets	0.00	0.00	0.00	0.00	0.00

Displayed Currency: German Mark (1.00:1)
All values are displayed in millions (except employees).

FINANCIAL RATIOS AND GROWTH RATES

PROFITABILITY	1997	1996	1995	1994	1993	5YR AVG
Operating Profit Margin %	26.30	23.68	22.64	22.80	16.72	22.43
Tax Rate %	43.36	40.26	38.99	38.52	40.91	40.41
Net Margin %	15.34	15.21	14.96	15.30	13.23	14.81
Return on Assets %	27.49	25.60	23.25	21.54	13.57	22.29
Return on Equity— Total %	41.82	37.09	32.69	27.81	16.25	31.13
Cash Flow % Sales	18.86	20.32	20.45	20.32	19.16	19.82
Sales per Employee (in 000s)	468	404	393	350	302	384

ASSET UTILIZATION	1997	1996	1995	1994	1993	5YR AVG
Total Asset Turnover	1.19	1.11	1.22	1.05	0.84	1.08
Capital Exp % Gross Fixed Assets	33.48	19.78	26.41	21.51	21.39	24.51
Acc Depreciation % Gross Fixed Assets	41.38	43.11	39.57	37.85	36.78	39.74
Assets per Employee (in 000s)	394	366	323	335	358	355

SAP A.G.

LIQUIDITY	1997	1996	1995	1994	1993	5YR AVG
Current Ratio	4.45	4.82	4.15	4.09	5.94	4.69
Quick Ratio	4.21	4.64	4.02	3.94	5.73	4.51

LEVERAGE	1997	1996	1995	1994	1993	5YR AVG
Total Debt % Common Equity	5.52	4.49	5.26	5.60	2.62	4.70
Long Term Debt % Common Equity	0.17	0.40	1.35	1.78	0.10	0.76
Common Equity % Total Assets	60.11	65.55	68.82	70.51	77.16	68.43
Long Term Debt % Total Capital	0.17	0.40	1.33	1.74	0.10	0.75
Operating Cash/ Fixed Charges	300.05	288.92	105.29	212.73	165.98	214.59

GROWTH %	1997	1996	1995	1994	1993	5YR AVG
Net Sales	61.67	38.04	47.25	66.21	32.55	48.57
Operating Income	79.55	44.36	46.19	126.68	65.66	70.07
Total Assets	50.58	51.80	26.77	33.96	20.93	36.24
Earnings per Share*	61.77	37.30	43.91	89.92	15.38	47.59
Dividends per Share*	54.05	37.04	50.00	87.50	20.00	48.10
Book Value per Share	37.04	41.41	23.72	20.93	12.38	26.65

Displayed Currency: German Mark (1.00:1)
*Source: Worldscope. Value may differ from I/B/E/S.
Note: 5-Year Average calculations exclude NAs.

PER SHARE AND RELATED DATA

SOURCE: WORLDSCOPE	1997	1996	1995	1994	1993
Earnings per Share	8.8	5.5	4.0	2.8	1.5
Dividends per Share	2.9	1.9	1.4	0.9	0.5
Book Value per Share	29.2	21.3	15.1	12.2	10.1
Total Investment Return	NA	NA	149.60	172.42	19.28
Market Price (Year-end)	588.5	215.0	217.8	87.8	32.6
Market Capitalization (in millions)	61380.55	22254.10	22048.04	8888.05	3256.00
Price/Earnings Ratio	66.50	39.30	54.67	31.71	22.34
Price/Book Value	20.14	10.08	14.44	7.20	3.23
Dividend Yield	0.48	0.86	0.62	1.03	1.47
Dividend Payout per Share	32.21	33.82	33.88	32.51	32.93
Common Shares Outstanding (Year-end) in Millions	104.30	103.51	101.23	101.23	100.00
Stock Split/Dividend Ratio	NA	NA	NA	0.10	0.02
Type of Share	Vorzugsaktie				

Displayed Currency: German Mark (1.00:1)
Note: Data is sourced from Worldscope and may differ from I/B/E/S historical data.

42. Schlumberger Limited N.V.

Performed by Schlumberger" is a new branded phrase that may remind you of the slogan "Intel inside." But perhaps that's not a bad comparison for this energy technology leader founded in 1927 by the French brothers Conrad and Marcel Schlumberger. They immediately built a worldwide reputation for scientific leadership by employing a new method of using electrical measurements taken inside an oil well's bore hole to predict future activity. Ever since, Schlumberger's commitment to research and development has surpassed that of its competitors.

Schlumberger Limited N.V. today is an advanced and innovative oil field services and electronic measurement product firm that has consistently expanded its oil field business faster and more profitably than its peers. It plays some role in half of every barrel of oil now produced, and the energy industry wouldn't be nearly as efficient if the company didn't exist. Operating in 930 facilities in more than 100 countries with 51,000 employees, Schlumberger is capable of dramatic earnings growth even in quarters when oil prices have taken a tumble. It provides oil field services and electronic measurement products of significant help to operators seeking to identify and profit from opportunities. Its oil field services businesses offers wireline logging, well testing, seismic surveying, geoscience software and computing services, drilling and pumping services, and cementing and stimulation services designed to boost well productivity. Its measurement and systems unit makes products such as utility meters, automatic testing equipment for the semiconductor industry, fuel-dispensing systems for gas stations, point-of-sale payment systems, and parking management systems.

By paying a hefty $2.97 billion in shares for Camco International Inc. in June 1998, Schlumberger filled a significant void in its oil services offerings. Although the price was deemed too rich by many investment analysts at the time, Schlumberger was banking on oil prices rising from their depressed levels. The Camco purchase, which includes assuming $160 million of its debt, is expected to add to Schlumberger earnings in 1999.

Oil field services revenue, especially from the company's fleet of deep-water drilling rigs, was up significantly in early 1998. However, oil prices falling to nine-year lows undoubtedly will mean a slowdown in subsequent quarters. The company's software and data management revenues were also up in early 1998. However, measurement and systems grew more modestly because gains in automated test equipment and smart cards was offset by a decline in metering activities in Europe and Asia, and by unfavorable currency exchange rates. Improved profitability in measurement and systems may take a while as European economies show fiscal austerity, but it should be kept in mind that this unit makes up only about 10 percent of Schlumberger profits. Sales outside the United States account for more than 70 percent of this French-American firm's total revenues.

"We are convinced that Schlumberger is only at the beginning of a long and favorable business cycle," Euan Baird, chairman and chief executive officer, said in his letter in the most recent annual report. "This optimism is based on three factors. First, demand for oil and gas is expected to keep rising at a brisk pace. Secondly, significant service opportunities in new frontiers, such as Russia, are starting to open up. Lastly, the potential for new technology to enhance the value of our services to our clients continues to increase."

Boosting efficiency is the key to Schlumberger's future. The oil industry today recovers only about one-third of the oil it finds. To make a significant improvement in productivity in which recovery rates regularly exceed 50 percent, the process by which oil and gas reservoirs are managed must change. Schlumberger's solution is to monitor the behavior of a producing reservoir through the use of permanent sensors of all types so that past and current knowledge will help evaluate the risks of a range of strategies. That way, problems will be detected and corrected before they become expensive or impossible to repair. Information technology would be deployed to make all relevant knowledge available to the user when and where it is needed, with a goal of "learning faster and learning forever."

Since 1995 the company has had a joint venture called Omnes with Cable & Wireless Plc. to provide information technology such as Internet communications to energy industry customers. It permits information technology systems to communicate anywhere in the world. The first phase of this is the Schlumberger Information Network (SINet), a global communications network providing data and voice communications to Schlumberger locations in more than thirty-five countries. With more than 1,000 portable computers in use by employees, dial-up connectivity for portables is an important new capability. Meanwhile, the company's GeoQuest unit is one of its fastest-growing businesses, designed to help customers optimize the value of oil and gas reservoirs by providing integrated software systems, data management, and interpretive services.

Schlumberger management decided to make a number of changes after its Forum 2005 initiative in which a group of thirty-six young, diverse Schlumberger workers imagined what they thought the company should become by the year 2005. Changes adopted by the company from the group's recommendations include: (1) Splitting each business group into Solutions and Products organizations. Solutions, organized along geographic markets, will be the primary contact with customers, while Products is responsible for technology, service delivery, and support. (2) Expanding and innovating the use of information technology. (3) Promoting flexibility in career planning and development to put more emphasis on personal needs. (4) Creating image-building programs to position the company more clearly as a global solutions provider.

There was plenty of deal-making in 1998. Schlumberger signed an agreement to provide oil field services to Russian oil giant Yuksi, which should begin adding to Schlumberger earnings in 1999. With the alliance, Yuksi became the first Russian oil firm to outsource some of its oil services. The company was also awarded a contract by Mobil Canada for three 3D seismic survey programs off Nova Scotia's shore. In addition, it was selected by Shell as one of its suppliers for state-of-the-art dispensing pumps, options, upgrade kinds, and parts, with Schlumberger to serve as a designated petroleum products provider for Canada, South America, Europe, and the United States.

In all of its reports, news releases, and speeches, Schlumberger stresses the importance of technology and has embraced all forms of it from the oil field to the Internet. Which is why Chairman Baird emphasizes the importance of being able to "challenge the status quo at all levels of the organization with fresh ideas" and why the founding Schlumberger brothers could easily identify their company even today based on its continuing passion for science and innovation.

42. SCHLUMBERGER LIMITED N.V.

France–United States   Ticker symbol SLB

Stock price $53 5/16 (9/16/98)   Dividend yield 1.41%

(Financial data is from I/B/E/S International)*

BUSINESS DESCRIPTION

OILFIELD SERVICES ACCOUNTED FOR 72% OF 1997 REVENUES, AND MEASUREMENT AND SYSTEMS 28%

ADDRESS AND CONTACTS

Address   277 Park Avenue
                 New York NY 10172
Telephone   1-212-350-9400

BASIC FINANCIAL INFORMATION

Capital Structure†	Long Term Debt:	1069.06
	Total Debt:	1923.60
	Common Sh. Equity:	6694.92

SALES BREAKDOWN

Product Segments[†]	Oilfield Services	7663.00
	Measurement & Systems	2985.00
Geographic Segments[†]	United States	2696.00
	Other Western Hemisphere	1508.00
	Europe	3093.00
	Other Eastern Hemisphere	3351.00

Displayed Currency: U.S. Dollar (1.00:1)
*I/B/E/S and I/B/E/S Express are registered trademarks of I/B/E/S International Inc. Copyright 1993–1996 I/B/E/S International Inc. All rights reserved.
[†]Values are displayed in millions.

FINANCIAL STATEMENT DATA

INCOME STATEMENT	1997	1996	1995	1994	1993
Net Sales or Revenues	10647.59	8956.15	7621.69	6696.84	6705.47
EBITDA	2727.73	1633.02	1672.19	1456.97	1522.94
Depreciation Depletion & Amort	972.54	885.20	820.20	776.17	790.17
Operating Income	1648.37	1058.40	760.46	596.90	633.97
Interest Expense	72.02	72.02	81.62	63.33	68.89
Pretax Income	1668.35	675.81	770.37	617.47	663.88
Net Income	1295.70	851.48	649.16	536.08	582.76

BALANCE SHEET	1997	1996	1995	1994	1993
Assets					
Cash & Equivalents	1761.08	1358.95	1120.53	1231.89	1185.63
Receivables—Net	2819.90	2260.09	1939.87	1761.02	1545.95
Inventories	1094.07	938.97	782.17	696.27	621.39
Total Current Assets	6071.22	5042.62	4023.70	3823.75	3476.17
Property Plant & Eq.— Net	3768.64	3358.58	3118.46	2857.49	2818.95
Total Assets	11893.96	10121.07	8910.10	8322.10	7916.95
Liabilities & Shareholders' Equity					
Total Current Liabilities	3629.90	3474.31	2764.27	2786.65	2568.34
Long Term Debt	1069.06	637.20	613.40	394.17	446.94
Preferred Stock	0.00	0.00	0.00	0.00	0.00
Common Equity	6694.92	5626.38	4964.02	4582.95	4406.34
Total Liabilities & Sh. Equity	11893.99	10121.07	8910.10	8322.10	7916.95

CASH FLOW	1997	1996	1995	1994	1993
Net Cash Flow— Operating	1707.99	1402.14	1194.34	943.06	1455.48
Net Cash Flow— Investing	2060.05	1392.50	941.05	799.09	1367.16
Net Cash Flow— Financing	331.50	55.11	-238.45	-150.04	-64.86
Incr/Decr in Working Capital	873.12	308.78	222.33	129.27	-334.41
Free Cash Flow	1231.75	475.07	733.34	674.13	831.84

Schlumberger Limited N.V.

INTERNATIONAL BUSINESS	1997	1996	1995	1994	1993
Foreign Assets	6.77	6.19	5.63	4.96	4919.00
Foreign Sales	7.95	6.85	5.44	4796.00	5214.00
Foreign Income	1.27	0.20	0.63	416.00	533.00

SUPPLEMENTARY DATA	1997	1996	1995	1994	1993
Employees	63500	57000	51000	48000	48000
R&D Expenses	486.20	452.61	427.85	418.87	450.18
Goodwill/Cost in Excess of Assets Purchased	1167.62	1225.34	1330.49	1204.69	1109.05
Extra Items & Gain/ Loss in Sale of Assets	0.00	0.00	0.00	0.00	248.00

Displayed Currency: U.S. Dollar (1.00:1)

All values are displayed in millions (except employees).

FINANCIAL RATIOS AND GROWTH RATES

PROFITABILITY	1997	1996	1995	1994	1993	5YR AVG
Operating Profit Margin %	15.48	11.82	9.98	8.91	9.45	11.13
Tax Rate %	22.34	NA	15.73	13.18	12.22	15.87
Net Margin %	12.17	9.51	8.52	8.00	12.39	10.12
Return on Assets %	13.37	10.09	8.45	7.30	12.51	10.34
Return on Equity— Total %	23.03	17.15	14.16	12.17	19.64	17.23
Cash Flow % Sales	21.92	19.41	19.45	19.86	20.59	20.25
Sales per Employee (in 000s)	168	157	149	140	140	151

ASSET UTILIZATION	1997	1996	1995	1994	1993	5YR AVG
Total Asset Turnover	0.90	0.88	0.86	0.80	0.85	0.86
Capital Exp % Gross Fixed Assets	14.65	12.09	10.31	9.17	8.45	10.93
Acc Depreciation % Gross Fixed Assets	63.09	64.93	65.76	66.53	65.51	65.17
Assets per Employee (in 000s)	187	178	175	173	165	176

LIQUIDITY	1997	1996	1995	1994	1993	5YR AVG
Current Ratio	1.67	1.45	1.46	1.37	1.35	1.46
Quick Ratio	1.26	1.04	1.11	1.07	1.06	1.11

Schlumberger Limited N.V.

LEVERAGE	1997	1996	1995	1994	1993	5YR AVG
Total Debt % Common Equity	28.73	25.79	24.43	24.03	19.22	24.44
Long Term Debt % Common Equity	15.97	11.33	12.36	8.60	10.14	11.68
Common Equity % Total Assets	56.29	55.59	55.71	55.07	55.66	55.66
Long Term Debt % Total Capital	13.77	10.17	11.00	7.92	9.21	10.41
Operating Cash/ Fixed Charges	26.88	24.13	18.16	21.00	20.04	22.04

GROWTH %	1997	1996	1995	1994	1993	5YR AVG
Net Sales	18.89	17.51	13.81	-0.13	5.91	10.96
Operating Income	55.74	39.18	27.40	-5.85	-9.68	18.62
Total Assets	17.52	13.59	7.07	5.12	12.99	11.16
Earnings per Share*	45.24	29.00	21.72	-7.92	-12.73	12.88
Dividends per Share*	0.00	5.26	18.75	0.00	0.00	4.56
Book Value per Share	14.87	11.78	7.91	4.57	3.42	8.42

Displayed Currency: U.S. Dollar (1.00:1)
*Source: Worldscope. Value may differ from I/B/E/S.
Note: 5-Year Average calculations exclude NAs.

PER SHARE AND RELATED DATA

SOURCE: WORLDSCOPE	1997	1996	1995	1994	1993
Earnings per Share	2.52	1.74	1.35	1.11	1.20
Dividends per Share	0.75	0.75	0.71	0.60	0.60
Book Value per Share	13.11	11.41	10.21	9.46	9.05
Total Investment Return	NA	NA	40.30	-12.77	5.37
Market Price (Year-end)	80.50	49.94	34.63	25.19	29.56
Market Capitalization (in millions)	40091.91	24622.90	16837.31	12202.44	14399.84
Price/Earnings Ratio	31.94	28.78	25.74	22.79	24.64
Price/Book Value	6.14	4.38	3.39	2.66	3.27
Dividend Yield	0.93	1.50	2.06	2.38	2.03
Dividend Payout per Share	29.76	43.23	52.97	54.30	50.00
Common Shares Outstanding (Year-end) in Millions	498.04	493.07	486.28	484.46	487.10
Stock Split/Dividend Ratio	NA	0.50	0.50	0.50	0.50
Type of Share	Common				

Displayed Currency: U.S. Dollar (1.00:1)
Note: Data is sourced from Worldscope and may differ from I/B/E/S historical data.

43. Siebe Plc.

Siebe Plc. is a sophisticated global company trying to keep everything under control. For example, a Siebe Environmental Controls management system handles the energy and environmental controls regulating the locker rooms and luxury boxes of the Ball Park at Arlington, home of the Texas Rangers of professional baseball. The company is also responsible for the building management systems at London's Heathrow airport.

The United Kingdom's largest diversified engineering group with more than 200 companies and 50,000 employees operating worldwide is involved in the business of control systems, industrial equipment, and temperature and appliance controls. Sometimes you see the Siebe name on its products and sometimes you don't, but many of its operating companies are famous brand names in their respective markets and all have the advantage of advanced manufacturing facilities. Products range from appliance controls on Jenn-Air ranges to NASA safety gloves to environmental controls at sports stadiums. Obtaining about 90 percent of its revenues outside the U.K., Siebe has significant operations in the United States, Europe, and Asia, while enjoying rapid growth in emerging markets including the Middle East, South America, and Eastern Europe. During 1998, Asian growth slowed, but the region still showed solid overall growth. Serving a broad set of industries balanced between early, middle, and late economic cycle exposure, Siebe is not entirely dependent upon any specific industries or geographic regions for its returns.

Its strong technology backed by a large research and development budget has made it a leader in product innovation and customer satisfaction. Siebe has a long history of innovation. It was founded in London in 1819 by Augustus Siebe, an immigrant

303

Austrian artillery officer whose inventive genius created the world's first diving suit, a revolutionary rotary water pump, breech-loading rifles, screw cutting machines, carbon arc lamps, and some of the world's first ice-making machines. From the late nineteenth century to the early 1970s, the company's core business was marine engineering and breathing apparatus. Products included submarine escape equipment and high altitude breathing apparatus for pilots. In 1972, the company acquired James North & Sons, Europe's largest manufacturer of safety equipment. The first half of the 1980s saw expansion into Continental Europe and North America, followed by the acquisition of the Tecalemit garage equipment and automotive tubing company. It added the CompAir compressed air group in 1985 that also brought with it three pneumatic controls companies. These together with two small controls companies from the Tecalemit acquisition foreshadowed the company's future. It acquired Robertshaw appliance controls in 1986 and began building a truly global controls business.

Company management is dedicated to providing its shareholders with the best long-term return on their investment when compared to its peer group. Its future currently looks especially bright in electronic process controls and software, as well as in air-conditioning. This is another company, along with AlliedSignal Incorporated and General Electric Company, that has embraced the Six Sigma approach to improving efficiency and quality in its lean manufacturing operations in order to build a sustainable cost advantage over competitors. Its management, corporate strategy, cash flow, and financial controls are all strong. Its stated strategies for growth include new product development, globalization that penetrates the Far Eastern and emerging markets, acquisitions, and an aggressive growth culture within its employee ranks. As company management puts it, "Key strategies are often similar to competitors', but the difference is intensity of implementation." Its biggest potential concerns are competition from Honeywell, the possibility of a decline in demand for some products, and extended problems in the Far East.

Wheeling and dealing is a part of the Siebe strategy. In 1997, the company bought Eaton Corporation's appliance control operations, the Ram Electronics Corporation electronic controls maker, the APV Plc. automation technology business, the Predictive Control Limited Advanced Control software line, the tube production line of Carl Froh GmbH, the P. J. King Pty. Limited automotive engineering company, and the Satchwell Controls Systems automation systems business of General Electric Company Plc. It had intended to divest some noncore businesses, then sold its RFI Shielding Limited electronic shielding materials firm to Cirqual Plc. and its Wells Electronics semiconductor burn-in and test socket business to PCD Incorporated. Siebe then cleared the antitrust waiting period to buy industrial software house Wonderware Corp. and software-provider Simulation Sciences Inc. in 1998, while making an agreed-upon takeover bid for control-maker Eurotherm Plc. Clearly, this is not a company that rests on its laurels.

"A major part of our acquisition strategy is to build a strong global market position in each of our core businesses," Barrie Stephens, who retired as chairman in early 1998 to be replaced at mid-year by British Airways Plc. Chairman Sir Colin Marshall, stated in his letter in the company's most recent annual report. "Major acquisitions, together with the smaller companies which we acquired, demonstrate our determination to remain focused on our core businesses. This strategy will continue into the future."

New Siebe Chairman Marshall has quite a pedigree. He was appointed chairman of British Airways in 1993 after ten years with the airline, initially as chief executive officer, and then as deputy chairman and CEO. He previously had a career in international business. He served as president of the Confederation of British Industry until mid-1998 and has been a board director of the New York Stock Exchange.

Big long-term contracts are the name of the game. For example, the company and Dow Chemical Company signed an agreement by which Siebe will become the sole preferred supplier to Dow for its advanced automation systems and will provide lifetime support of Dow's installed base of more than 1,000 plant automation systems worldwide. It also entered into global partnership agreements as the preferred supplier of plant automation solutions to both Shell International B. V. and Owens Corning. Siebe is a big, aggressive, technologically advanced company well positioned to profit from the stiff competition of the future, with a stock price humbled by recent world economic woes.

43. SIEBE PLC.

United Kingdom   Ticker symbol SIBEY

One American Depositary Receipt represents two ordinary shares

ADR price $7 1/4 (9/16/98)   Dividend yield 4%

(Financial data from I/B/E/S International is in British pence)*

BUSINESS DESCRIPTION

CONTROL SYSTEMS, TEMPERATURE AND APPLIANCE CONTROLS, AND INDUSTRIAL EQUIPMENT ARE THE MAIN PRODUCTS OF THE GROUP

ADDRESS AND CONTACTS

Address	Saxon House
	2-4 Victoria Street
	Windsor Berkshire SL4 1 United Kingdom
Telephone	44-1753-8554411
Fax	44-1753-840638

BASIC FINANCIAL INFORMATION

Capital Structure[†]	Long Term Debt:	69800.00
	Total Debt:	77520.00
	Common Sh. Equity:	101660.00

SALES BREAKDOWN

Product Segments[†]	Temperature & Appliance	139260.00
	Control Systems	107280.00
	Industrial Equipment	53990.00
Geographic Segments[†]	United Kingdom	32940.00
	North America	133530.00
	Rest of Europe	81560.00
	Pacific	39160.00
	South America	7850.00
	Other	5490.00

Displayed Currency: British Pence (1.00:1)
*I/B/E/S and I/B/E/S Express are registered trademarks of I/B/E/S International Inc. Copyright 1993–1996 I/B/E/S International Inc. All rights reserved.
[†]Values are displayed in millions.

Siebe Plc.

FINANCIAL STATEMENT DATA

INCOME STATEMENT	1997	1996	1995	1994	1993
Net Sales or Revenues	300530.01	259909.99	214620.00	186349.99	161859.99
EBITDA	63550.00	50910.00	43180.00	37460.00	32720.00
Depreciation Depletion & Amort	14660.00	12140.00	9970.00	9390.00	7650.00
Operating Income	47040.00	37360.00	28990.00	22550.00	21660.00
Interest Expense	5710.00	5710.00	5700.00	6350.00	6630.00
Pretax Income	42380.00	33060.00	27510.00	21720.00	18440.00
Net Income	25380.00	19300.00	16030.00	12740.00	10560.00

BALANCE SHEET	1997	1996	1995	1994	1993
Assets					
Cash & Equivalents	21080.00	28230.00	28010.00	39790.00	20540.00
Receivables—Net	72800.00	61140.00	53090.00	43690.00	37590.00
Inventories	50070.00	48930.00	46310.00	47730.00	42770.00
Total Current Assets	154209.99	145110.01	132460.00	135770.00	104520.00
Property Plant & Eq.—Net	108360.00	95410.00	85650.00	81830.00	70620.00
Total Assets	311110.01	290259.99	256260.00	257910.00	214190.00
Liabilities & Shareholders' Equity					
Total Current Liabilities	95040.00	83250.00	80930.00	73630.00	50850.00
Long Term Debt	69800.00	63140.00	44630.00	54370.00	61790.00
Preferred Stock	0.00	0.00	0.00	0.00	0.00
Common Equity	101660.00	106230.00	96620.00	95010.00	81110.00
Total Liabilities & Sh. Equity	311110.01	290259.99	256260.00	257910.00	214190.00

CASH FLOW	1997	1996	1995	1994	1993
Funds from Operations	47210.00	36750.00	30700.00	24920.00	20740.00
Total Sources	62290.00	116570.00	70380.00	30490.00	18560.00
Cash Dividends Paid—Total	5400.00	4850.00	4360.00	2290.00	3510.00
Total Uses	62290.00	116570.00	70380.00	30490.00	18560.00
Incr/Decr in Working Capital	-2690.00	10330.00	-10610.00	8470.00	21580.00
Free Cash Flow	39380.00	32000.00	29330.00	25650.00	23510.00

INTERNATIONAL BUSINESS	1997	1996	1995	1994	1993
Foreign Assets	209200.01	193340.00	166170.00	155960.00	146680.00
Foreign Sales	267589.99	234660.00	193100.01	167360.00	143180.01
Foreign Income	39290.00	31640.00	26610.00	22710.00	20300.00

307

SUPPLEMENTARY DATA	1997	1996	1995	1994	1993
Employees	42103	35825	32309	29938	29644
R&D Expenses	14090.00	11490.00	8690.00	7640.00	6550.00
Goodwill/Cost in					
Excess of Assets					
Purchased	0.00	0.00	0.00	0.00	0.00
Extra Items & Gain/					
Loss in Sale of Assets	0.00	0.00	0.00	0.00	0.00

Displayed Currency: British Pence (1.00:1)
All values are displayed in millions (except employees).

FINANCIAL RATIOS AND GROWTH RATES

PROFITABILITY	1997	1996	1995	1994	1993	5YR AVG
Operating Profit						
Margin %	15.65	14.37	13.51	12.10	13.38	13.80
Tax Rate %	37.00	38.32	39.51	39.46	40.62	38.98
Net Margin %	8.45	7.43	7.47	6.84	6.52	7.34
Return on Assets %	10.22	9.00	7.67	7.90	7.91	8.54
Return on Equity—						
Total %	23.89	19.98	16.87	15.71	16.02	18.49
Cash Flow % Sales	15.71	14.14	14.30	13.37	12.81	14.07
Sales per Employee						
(in 000s)	7138	7255	6643	6225	5460	6544

ASSET UTILIZATION	1997	1996	1995	1994	1993	5YR AVG
Total Asset Turnover	0.97	0.90	0.84	0.72	0.76	0.84
Capital Exp % Gross						
Fixed Assets	15.66	13.68	11.38	10.30	9.27	12.06
Acc Depreciation %						
Gross Fixed Assets	29.79	30.96	29.63	28.60	28.90	29.58
Assets per Employee						
(in 000s) .	7389	8102	7932	8615	7225	7853

LIQUIDITY	1997	1996	1995	1994	1993	5YR AVG
Current Ratio	1.62	1.74	1.64	1.84	2.06	1.78
Quick Ratio	0.99	1.07	1.00	1.13	1.14	1.07

LEVERAGE	1997	1996	1995	1994	1993	5YR AVG
Total Debt %						
Common Equity	76.25	67.27	61.18	70.49	90.84	73.21
Long Term Debt %						
Common Equity	68.66	59.44	46.19	57.23	76.18	61.54

Siebe Plc.

Common Equity % Total Assets	32.68	36.60	37.70	36.84	37.87	36.34
Long Term Debt % Total Capital	37.81	35.62	29.92	34.92	41.78	36.01
Operating Cash/ Fixed Charges	7.25	6.44	5.39	3.92	3.13	5.23

GROWTH %	1997	1996	1995	1994	1993	5YR AVG
Net Sales	15.63	21.10	15.17	15.13	-0.58	13.04
Operating Income	25.91	28.87	28.56	4.11	0.19	16.82
Total Assets	7.18	13.27	-0.64	20.41	13.48	10.51
Earnings per Share*	20.22	20.00	19.43	17.08	14.28	18.18
Dividends per Share*	10.44	10.00	10.00	11.56	10.19	10.44
Book Value per Share	-13.30	9.76	1.55	17.76	12.51	5.07

Displayed Currency: British Pence (1.00:1)
*Source: Worldscope. Value may differ from I/B/E/S.
Note: 5-Year Average calculations exclude NAs.

PER SHARE AND RELATED DATA

SOURCE: WORLDSCOPE	1997	1996	1995	1994	1993
Earnings per Share	54.10	45.00	37.50	31.40	26.82
Dividends per Share	14.70	13.31	12.10	11.00	9.86
Book Value per Share	214.70	247.62	225.61	222.17	188.66
Total Investment Return	NA	60.78	-5.05	35.30	52.98
Market Price (Year-end)	986.50	871.00	550.00	592.00	445.69
Market Capitalization (in millions)	467103.51	373656.68	235541.22	253165.60	175430.04
Price/Earnings Ratio	18.23	19.36	14.67	18.85	16.62
Price/Book Value	4.59	3.52	2.44	2.66	2.36
Dividend Yield	1.49	1.53	2.20	1.86	2.21
Dividend Payout per Share	27.17	29.58	32.27	35.03	36.67
Common Shares Outstanding (Year-end) in Millions	473.50	429.00	428.26	427.64	393.62
Stock Split/Dividend Ratio	NA	NA	NA	NA	0.99
Type of Share	Ordinary				

Displayed Currency: British Pence (1.00:1)
Note: Data is sourced from Worldscope and may differ from I/B/E/S historical data.

44. Sony Corporation

S ony Playstation rules. Any teenager will confirm that simple fact. This cutting-edge 32-bit game machine has captured the imagination of the world's home video game market with a wide array of sports stars, cartoon characters, and fast action. Sorry, Nintendo and Sega, but Playstation has posted sales gains of better than 70 percent for its game consoles and CDs. This four-year-old business already accounts for 10 percent of Sony Corporation's worldwide revenues. Though home video games are a fickle market segment and this particular product too will peak, Playstation and a weak yen helped Sony turn in record profits in the fiscal year that ended March 31, 1998, making it one of the few Japanese multinational firms to sidestep the consequences of that nation's recession. Most importantly, Sony hopes to transfer the amazing success of Playstation to the marketing and distribution of its music, film, TV, and games on the Internet. Sony and Microsoft Corporation are offering a set-top box upgrade of Playstation in 1999 that delivers interactive services to consumers over cable television and the two firms say they hope to collaborate on global digital home entertainment well into the next century.

Not that everything's as easy as playing a game for Sony. Besides the uncertainty surrounding Asia, ongoing concerns that will limit the company's profit growth include the expected decline in demand for Playstation, higher development costs for the next-generation game player, anticipated losses in new businesses such as digital satellite broadcasting, and intense price pressure from its competitors. And, of course, its future results will always face tough comparisons to stellar past results.

The history of Sony began in May 1946, with the founding of Tokyo Tsushin Kogyo (Tokyo Telecommunications Engineering) by Masaru Ibuka and Akio Morita, who worked to put together an "ideal" factory for building unique and exciting products. World-famous Sony, the most-respected brand sold in the United States, continues to increase its market share in consumer electronics, and has been gradually increasing its emphasis on entertainment operations. Since assuming his position in 1995, President and Chief Operating Officer Nobuyuki Idei has had an important role in a strong turnaround in the company's financial performance. Both he and Chairman and Chief Executive Officer Norio Ohga, who also began his tenure in 1995, are demanding that the company focus on youth-driven markets such as the Internet and digital communications.

Those top two executives believe, for example, that once the company can provide a steady supply of movies, software, and other content on a global scale, the performance of its pictures group should be more stable. After all, Sony helped pioneer the development of digital formats for audiovisual products. In 1982, it introduced the world's first CD player and was the first with a MiniDisc system in 1992. A digital camcorder joined the digital lineup in 1995. With the introduction of a DVD video player in 1997, Sony continued to be a leader in the development of new digital technologies and markets. Meanwhile, the company's High Definition Center has been busy converting the company's movie library into high-quality video formats as Sony prepares to meet the demand for DVDs, digital satellite broadcasts, and other digital applications on the verge of rapid growth. It is uniquely positioned to provide both hardware and software for a multimedia age, and has retained investment-banking firm Blackstone Group to consider potential related acquisitions in this regard.

"We are committed to remaining close to our customers and bringing new meaning to the word 'fun' in electronics and entertainment," Ohga and Idei stated in their joint letter in the most recent annual report. "Guided by this commitment, we will strive to develop new business fields involving hardware, software, and the electronic distribution of contents—all part of the never-ending challenge of creating and realizing new dreams."

Electronic products such as televisions, VCRs, camcorders, CD players, CD-ROM drives, and the Playstation home video game system currently account for more than three-fourths of total revenues. Its semiconductor and computer-related products include liquid crystal displays, electronic components, and rechargeable lithium batteries. Entertainment assets include Columbia Pictures Entertainment, TriStar Pictures, Columbia Records, Epic Records, Merv Griffin Enterprises, Loews Theater Management, and Cineplex Odeon. Sony, Softbank, and Fuji Television have agreed to jointly develop with Rupert Murdoch's News Corp. the JskyB digital broadcasting venture, which could be a boost for Sony's hardware and software businesses. The company also has insurance and finance businesses. For the company as a whole, sales outside of Japan account for nearly 65 percent of sales. Strongest returns have recently come from the United States, Europe, and Japan.

In electronics, Sony has lately suffered from weak market conditions in Brazil and in Asia, especially China, but this was more than offset by the fall in the yen's value and hit products that included MiniDisc players, digital video cameras, the Wega series flat-screen TVs, new Vaio series notebook personal computers, digital cellular telephones, and optical pickups. The company's music business is in the midst of a turnaround under the leadership of Sony Music Entertainment President Thomas Mottola, owing to a big boost from the success of releases such as Celine Dion's *Let's Talk About Love*, the *Titanic* soundtrack, Mariah Carey's *Butterfly*, Oasis's *Be Here Now*, and Savage Garden's self-titled album. Although *Godzilla* wasn't quite the monster hit of 1998 that Sony had hoped for, the film business runs in cycles among the major studios and the the prior year Sony enjoyed a record sales increase from blockbusters *Men in Black*, *My Best Friend's Wedding*, and *Air Force One*. Meanwhile, insurance group revenues have also been strong.

Sony has also put together a string of shrewd real estate deals in the United States, with its name currently on about 20 million square feet of office, industrial, and retail space. Much of the retail and office space is held on long-term leases. In San Diego, it erected two new buildings at its Rancho Bernardo campus for $46 million in 1997 and completed a $60 million expansion of its computer picture-tube manufacturing facility in 1998. It also has significant property in Culver City, California, and in New York. In addition, Sony Retail Entertainment is the major tenant of the new four-story, 350,000-square-foot Metreon entertainment center in Yerba Buna Gardens in San Francisco. Obviously, this is a company with long-range plans both on land and in cyberspace that will extend into the multimedia age and into whatever age will one day follow that.

44. SONY CORPORATION

Japan   Ticker symbol SNE

One American Depositary Receipt represents one ordinary share

ADR price $75 1/2 (9/16/98)   Dividend yield .49%

(Financial data from I/B/E/S International is in Japanese yen)*

BUSINESS DESCRIPTION

TV/VIDEO ACCOUNTED FOR 33% OF FISCAL 1997 REVENUES, AUDIO EQUIPMENT 18%, OTHER ELECTRONICS 27%, ENTERTAINMENT 18%, AND INSURANCE AND FINANCE 4%

ADDRESS AND CONTACTS

Address	7-35, Kitashinagawa 6-Chome
	Shinagawa-ku Tokyo 141 Japan
Telephone	81-3-54482180
Fax	81-2-54482244

BASIC FINANCIAL INFORMATION

Report Dates	Last Annual: Mar 98	Reported On: May 07, 1998
Capital Structure[†]	Long Term Debt:	1104.42
	Total Debt:	1303.83
	Common Sh. Equity:	1815.55

SALES BREAKDOWN

Product Segments[†]	Electronics	4410.40
	Entertainment	1043.99
	Insurance and Finance	269.35

SALES BREAKDOWN

Geographic
Segments†

Japan	3434.83
United States	1798.81
Europe	1143.34
Other	1445.11
Eliminations/Corp	-2158.96

Displayed Currency: Japanese Yen (1.00:1)
*I/B/E/S and I/B/E/S Express are registered trademarks of I/B/E/S International Inc. Copyright
1993–1996 I/B/E/S International Inc. All rights reserved.
†Values are displayed in billions.

FINANCIAL STATEMENT DATA

INCOME STATEMENT	1998	1997	1996	1995	1994
Net Sales or Revenues	6755.49	5663.13	4592.57	3983.44	3733.72
EBITDA	817.94	649.85	432.57	68.17	410.50
Depreciation Depletion & Amort	301.66	266.53	227.32	219.84	239.13
Operating Income	520.21	370.33	235.32	94.55	99.67
Interest Expense	70.89	70.89	67.09	69.28	69.22
Pretax Income	453.75	312.43	138.16	-220.95	102.16
Net Income	NA	NA	NA	NA	17.59

BALANCE SHEET	1998	1997	1996	1995	1994
Assets					
Cash & Equivalents	NA	601.13	520.36	558.35	565.08
Receivables—Net	NA	972.58	854.80	626.93	547.29
Inventories	NA	869.80	856.64	723.38	671.99
Total Current Assets	NA	2795.46	2523.99	2146.70	2023.73
Property Plant & Eq.— Net	NA	1481.64	1306.77	1170.95	1217.55
Total Assets	6403.04	5653.18	5027.37	4209.38	4259.78
Liabilities & Shareholders' Equity					
Total Current Liabilities	2116.32	1951.87	1707.60	1608.96	1407.64
Long Term Debt	1104.42	1088.11	1197.33	900.86	983.71
Preferred Stock	0.00	0.00	0.00	0.00	0.00
Common Equity	1815.55	1459.43	1169.17	1007.81	1329.57
Total Liabilities & Sh. Equity	6403.04	5653.18	5027.37	4209.38	4259.78

CASH FLOW	1998	1997	1996	1995	1994
Funds from Operations	523.73	520.35	441.40	265.21	322.00
Total Sources	NA	1123.92	915.78	757.83	862.83
Cash Dividends Paid— Total	NA	18.66	18.77	18.68	18.64
Total Uses	NA	1123.92	915.78	757.83	862.83
Incr/Decr in Working Capital	NA	27.21	278.65	-78.35	249.08
Free Cash Flow	NA	351.67	182.41	-154.69	212.37

Sony Corporation

INTERNATIONAL BUSINESS	1998	1997	1996	1995	1994
Foreign Assets	NA	2905.34	2413.98	1825.66	NA
Foreign Sales	NA	4387.26	3476.97	3029.49	2785.98
Foreign Income	NA	171.38	136.76	-201.98	NA

SUPPLEMENTARY DATA	1998	1997	1996	1995	1994
Employees	NA	163000	151000	138000	130000
R&D Expenses	NA	282.57	257.33	239.16	229.88
Goodwill/Cost in Excess of Assets Purchased	NA	161.84	148.73	121.38	424.48
Extra Items & Gain/ Loss in Sale of Assets	NA	0.00	0.00	0.00	0.00

Displayed Currency: Japanese Yen (1.00:1)
All values are displayed in billions (except employees).

FINANCIAL RATIOS AND GROWTH RATES

PROFITABILITY	1998	1997	1996	1995	1994	5YR AVG
Operating Profit Margin %	7.70	6.54	5.12	2.37	2.67	4.88
Tax Rate %	47.35	52.35	55.85	NA	76.95	58.13
Net Margin %	3.29	2.46	1.18	-7.36	0.41	-0.00
Return on Assets %	4.66	3.70	2.34	-5.81	1.35	1.25
Return on Equity— Total %	NA	11.93	5.38	-22.06	1.07	-0.92
Cash Flow % Sales	7.75	9.19	9.61	6.66	8.62	8.37
Sales per Employee (in 000s)	NA	34743	30414	28865	28721	30686

ASSET UTILIZATION	1998	1997	1996	1995	1994	5YR AVG
Total Asset Turnover	1.06	1.00	0.91	0.95	0.88	0.96
Capital Exp % Gross Fixed Assets	NA	9.56	9.06	8.99	8.10	8.93
Acc Depreciation % Gross Fixed Assets	NA	52.49	52.68	52.78	50.25	52.05
Assets per Employee (in 000s)	NA	34682	33294	30503	32768	32812

LIQUIDITY	1998	1997	1996	1995	1994	5YR AVG
Current Ratio	NA	1.43	1.48	1.33	1.44	1.42
Quick Ratio	NA	0.81	0.81	0.74	0.79	0.78

LEVERAGE	1998	1997	1996	1995	1994	5YR AVG
Total Debt %						
Common Equity	71.81	97.04	138.87	135.44	101.53	108.94
Long Term Debt %						
Common Equity	60.83	74.56	102.41	89.39	73.99	80.23
Common Equity %						
Total Assets	28.35	25.82	23.26	23.94	31.21	26.52
Long Term Debt %						
Total Capital	36.26	40.87	48.40	44.87	40.83	42.24
Operating Cash/						
Fixed Charges	NA	7.34	6.58	3.83	4.65	5.60

GROWTH %	1998	1997	1996	1995	1994	5YR AVG
Net Sales	19.29	23.31	15.29	6.69	-6.49	11.09
Operating Income	40.47	57.37	148.90	-5.14	-21.19	32.69
Total Assets	13.26	12.45	19.43	-1.18	-5.96	7.17
Earnings per Share*	56.34	130.75	-+-1755.34		-54.34	39.29
Dividends per Share*	9.09	10.00	0.00	0.00	0.00	3.71
Book Value per Share	NA	21.54	15.96	-24.24	-7.05	NA

Displayed Currency: Japanese Yen (1.00:1)
*Source: Worldscope. Value may differ from I/B/E/S.
Note: 5-Year Average calculations exclude NAs.

PER SHARE AND RELATED DATA

SOURCE: WORLDSCOPE	1998	1997	1996	1995	1994
Earnings per Share	483.4	309.2	134.0	-696.9	42.1
Dividends per Share	60.0	55.0	50.0	50.0	50.0
Book Value per Share	NA	3798.9	3125.6	2695.3	3557.7
Total Investment					
Return	NA	NA	48.05	-24.79	33.18
Market Price					
(Year-end)	11300.0	8650.0	6390.0	4350.0	5850.0
Market Capitalization					
(in billions)	NA	3323.10	2390.29	1626.51	2186.31
Price/Earnings Ratio	23.38	27.98	47.69	NM	138.95
Price/Book Value	NA	2.28	2.04	1.61	1.64
Dividend Yield	0.53	0.64	0.78	1.15	0.85
Dividend Payout per Share	12.41	17.79	37.31	-7.17	118.76
Common Shares					
Outstanding					
(Year-end) in					
Millions	NA	384.17	374.06	373.91	373.72
Stock Split/Dividend Ratio	NA	NA	NA	NA	NA
Type of Share Common					

Displayed Currency: Japanese Yen (1.00:1)
Note: Data is sourced from Worldscope and may differ from I/B/E/S historical data.

45. Total S.A.

No guts, no glory. Total S.A. is not only one of the world's largest oil and gas companies, but a bold one at that. It's willing to include political trouble spots such as Iran, Libya, and Burma among the more than 100 countries in which it operates. Chairman and Chief Executive Officer Thierry Desmarest isn't afraid to take such calculated risks because he enjoys the enviable financial safety net of running one of the most profitable, efficient, and fastest-growing of energy companies. Its exploration and development costs are among the industry's lowest at $4 a barrel. Total boasts a quality exploration and production portfolio in the Middle East, Latin America, the North Sea, and Asia. If the United States complains and threatens retaliation for aggressive moves such as the South Pars gas project in Iran scheduled for production in June 2001, so be it. Desmarest contends that he entered into the contract with the National Iranian Oil Co. because no long-term strategy would be complete without seeking growth in the Middle East. He remains defiant, seeming to like grabbing headlines for Total's aggressive exploits.

This French company that actually began its operations in that same Middle East region in 1924 does exploration, development, and production of crude oil and gas; refining and marketing of petroleum products; and trading and transport of both crude and finished products. Through its wholly owned Hutchinson subsidiary Total also makes specialty chemicals such as paints, inks, rubbers, resins, and adhesives. It runs approximately 10,000 Premier service stations, primarily in Europe and Africa. Sales outside France account for about three-quarters of Total's sales. In 1997 the company merged its refining and marketing businesses in the United States with those of Ultramar

Diamond Shamrock (UDS) through a stock swap, with Total now holding approximately 8 percent of UDS. Total's development of its Kuito oil field is on a fast track that may make it the first deep water West African field onstream in 1999, and its latest Landana field appears to be a second giant discovery there.

"Over the next years, and based on a constant reference environment, Total should be able to increase its net result by 15 percent per year," Desmarest told shareholders at the company's May 1998 annual meeting in Paris. "Ongoing growth as well as productivity efforts should compensate for the global environment deterioration, in which more favorable exchange rates and refining margins only partially offset the negative impact of lower crude prices."

Total stock ranks as an excellent long-term core investment with solid growth potential that also features defensive characteristics capable of withstanding anything the topsy-turvy world oil markets can dish out. In early 1998, the company made an ambitious upward revision in its 1997 three-year plan, setting a target of increasing its operating income to 20 percent, the improvement coming from productivity gains and growth in its business segments. About 70 percent of Total's capital expenditures are currently being allocated to upstream (which includes the Middle East, coal, gas, electricity, exploration, and production) development for projects with low break-even points that are resistant to a decline in crude oil prices. Within five years, the share of the upstream segment in capital invested should reach more than 50 percent, with chemicals remaining steady at 20 percent, and downstream (which includes trading, shipping, refining, and marketing) at around 30 percent. This new structure is designed to make the company a much stronger competitor.

The negative impact of lower oil prices has been compensated for to a large extent by a stable dollar and stronger European refining margins, with continued productivity gains and increasing oil and gas production also helping out. As far as the economic woes of Asia are concerned, Total's gas production is sold to state-owned companies or to quality industrial buyers under long-term contracts with prices linked to the dollar. That means gas production in Asia should continue to grow, despite the current economic trauma there. Importantly, Total's downstream and chemicals segments have limited exposure in Asia, with about 3 percent of capital invested downstream and 2 percent of chemical sales.

Most of Total's fields brought on recently in countries such as Colombia, Libya, Quatar, Thailand, and Indonesia began reaching their peak levels from 1998 on. Starting in the year 2000, new projects in Norway, Algeria, Iran, and Myanmar should come on stream as well. The company is concentrating on larger fields with better economies of scale and long production lives. Total's production in the Middle East is primarily located in the United Arab Emirates, Oman, and Quatar, while its production in the rest of the world in addition to those previously mentioned nations is primarily in the United Kingdom, Norway, the Netherlands, Argentina, Venezuela, the United States, Algeria, and Angola. The company conducts its refining and marketing operations through fourteen refineries in which it has an interest in France, the United Kingdom, the Netherlands, Germany, the French West Indies, Africa, and China.

Besides an impressive portfolio of projects and industry leadership in production growth prospects, Total can point to three main assets that ensure further growth:

• A strong balance sheet that allows for additional growth without the need to issue more shares, thus passing on maximum value to shareholders. Total also has a shareholders consulting committee, chaired by Desmarest, which meets regularly with representatives from management. Composed of twelve individual shareholders, the committee is consulted about financial communication from the group and offers its opinion on content of information. The committee is invited to make proposals to improve communication between company and shareholders.

• Technological expertise in a business where technology is increasingly proving to be a key factor in effective competition. The use of technology is an ongoing company priority and it has been a leader in areas ranging from new seismic methods to extended-reach drilling, including multidrain wells and deep offshore exploration.

• Well–trained, highly motivated employees who have achieved ambitious goals under a wide range of working environments.

The results bear out the success of Desmarest, who has no qualms about rubbing anyone the wrong way so long as it spells profit for Total and its shareholders.

45. TOTAL S.A.

France   Ticker symbol TOT

Two American Depositary Receipts represent one Class "B" share

ADR price $59 13/16 (9/16/98)   Dividend yield 1.81%

(Financial data from I/B/E/S International is in French franc)*

BUSINESS DESCRIPTION

REFINING, DISTRIBUTION, AND TRADING ACCOUNTED FOR 76% OF 1997 REVENUES, CHEMICALS 14%, EXPLORATION, PRODUCTION, AND TRADING 9%, AND OTHER 1%

ADDRESS AND CONTACTS

Address	Tour Total
	24, Cours Michelet
	92800 Puteaux, France
Telephone	33-1-41-35-40-00
Fax	33-1-41-35-42-91

BASIC FINANCIAL INFORMATION

Capital Structure[†]	Long Term Debt:	21742.00
	Total Debt:	30439.00
	Common Sh. Equity:	66632.00

SALES BREAKDOWN

Product Segments[†]	Refining, Distribution	145947.00
	Chemicals	28576.00
	Exploration, Production	36838.00
	Corporate	-20276.00
Geographic Segments[†]	France	51167.00
	Other European	47890.00
	North America	18098.00
	Africa	15834.00
	Far East & Other	80399.00

Displayed Currency: French Franc (1.00:1)

*I/B/E/S and I/B/E/S Express are registered trademarks of I/B/E/S International Inc. Copyright 1993–1996 I/B/E/S International Inc. All rights reserved.

[†]Values are displayed in millions.

FINANCIAL STATEMENT DATA

INCOME STATEMENT	1997	1996	1995	1994	1993
Net Sales or Revenues	191085.00	176577.00	135829.00	136743.00	135478.00
EBITDA	24334.00	19408.00	13516.00	14019.00	13417.00
Depreciation Depletion & Amort	8958.00	7925.00	6409.00	5963.00	5756.00
Operating Income	11679.00	8759.00	6064.00	4936.00	5345.00
Interest Expense	3274.00	3274.00	2948.00	2806.00	2940.00
Pretax Income	12142.00	8393.00	4269.00	5437.00	4974.00
Net Income	7611.00	5646.00	2248.00	3385.00	2965.00

BALANCE SHEET	1997	1996	1995	1994	1993
Assets					
Cash & Equivalents	14425.00	32971.00	29229.00	24513.00	24841.00
Receivables—Net	30835.00	30004.00	26902.00	25611.00	23567.00
Inventories	14550.00	15014.00	11704.00	11867.00	11732.00
Total Current Assets	61146.00	79519.00	69089.00	63215.00	60870.00
Property Plant & Eq.— Net	61400.00	54308.00	47881.00	46495.00	43937.00
Total Assets	150703.00	157458.01	138370.01	134298.00	131534.00
Liabilities & Shareholders' Equity					
Total Current Liabilities	44623.00	56710.00	43536.00	41358.00	38964.00
Long Term Debt	21742.00	20332.00	24208.00	22789.00	25495.00
Preferred Stock	1497.00	1309.00	1225.00	1337.00	1474.00
Common Equity	66632.00	59258.00	52398.00	51348.00	49439.00
Total Liabilities & Sh. Equity	150703.00	157458.01	138370.01	134298.00	131534.00

CASH FLOW	1997	1996	1995	1994	1993
Funds from Operations	15053.00	16488.00	11442.00	11795.00	10095.00
Total Sources	25462.00	18974.00	13489.00	15885.00	19618.00
Cash Dividends Paid—Total	2554.00	602.00	689.00	752.00	561.00
Total Uses	25462.00	18974.00	13489.00	15885.00	19618.00
Incr/Decr in Working Capital	-6286.00	-2744.00	3696.00	-49.00	3099.00
Free Cash Flow	8083.00	7687.00	3798.00	4145.00	2981.00

INTERNATIONAL BUSINESS	1997	1996	1995	1994	1993
Foreign Assets	NA	NA	NA	NA	NA
Foreign Sales	139918.00	131985.00	97882.00	82468.00	94635.00
Foreign Income	NA	NA	NA	NA	NA

SUPPLEMENTARY DATA	1997	1996	1995	1994	1993
Employees	54391	57555	53536	51803	49772
R&D Expenses	1289.00	1157.00	1099.00	1053.00	1108.00
Goodwill/Cost in Excess of Assets Purchased	7994.00	7855.00	6792.00	7046.00	7389.00
Extra Items & Gain/ Loss in Sale of Assets	0.00	0.00	0.00	0.00	0.00

Displayed Currency: French Franc (1.00:1)
All values are displayed in millions (except employees).

FINANCIAL RATIOS AND GROWTH RATES

PROFITABILITY	1997	1996	1995	1994	1993	5YR AVG
Operating Profit Margin %	6.11	4.96	4.46	3.61	3.95	4.62
Tax Rate %	33.58	31.24	47.39	31.82	33.07	35.42
Net Margin %	4.01	3.23	1.70	2.51	2.22	2.73
Return on Assets %	6.23	5.59	3.11	3.92	4.13	4.60
Return on Equity— Total %	12.84	10.78	4.38	6.85	7.27	8.42
Cash Flow % Sales	7.88	9.34	8.42	8.63	7.45	8.34
Sales per Employee (in 000s)	3513	3068	2537	2640	2722	2896

ASSET UTILIZATION	1997	1996	1995	1994	1993	5YR AVG
Total Asset Turnover	1.27	1.12	0.98	1.02	1.03	1.08
Capital Exp % Gross Fixed Assets	12.74	10.08	9.63	10.41	11.68	10.91
Acc Depreciation % Gross Fixed Assets	51.85	53.29	52.54	50.99	50.82	51.90
Assets per Employee (in 000s)	2771	2736	2585	2592	2643	2665

LIQUIDITY	1997	1996	1995	1994	1993	5YR AVG
Current Ratio	1.37	1.40	1.59	1.53	1.56	1.49
Quick Ratio	1.01	1.11	1.29	1.21	1.24	1.17

LEVERAGE	1997	1996	1995	1994	1993	5YR AVG
Total Debt % Common Equity	45.68	72.69	73.82	70.96	77.35	68.10
Long Term Debt % Common Equity	32.63	34.31	46.20	44.38	51.57	41.82

Total S.A.

Common Equity % Total Assets	44.21	37.63	37.87	38.23	37.59	39.11
Long Term Debt % Total Capital	23.77	24.46	30.18	29.26	32.43	28.02
Operating Cash/ Fixed Charges	4.08	4.92	3.74	4.10	3.37	4.04

GROWTH %	1997	1996	1995	1994	1993	5YR AVG
Net Sales	8.22	30.00	-0.67	0.93	-0.83	6.94
Operating Income	33.34	44.44	22.85	-7.65	-13.09	13.69
Total Assets	-4.29	13.79	3.03	2.10	13.78	5.45
Earnings per Share*	31.91	144.79	-34.25	8.15	0.00	18.09
Dividends per Share*	23.81	20.69	8.75	6.67	7.14	13.18
Book Value per Share	NA	9.68	-1.22	0.80	5.49	NA

Displayed Currency: French Franc (1.00:1)
*Source: Worldscope. Value may differ from I/B/E/S.
Note: 5-Year Average calculations exclude NAs.

PER SHARE AND RELATED DATA

SOURCE: WORLDSCOPE	1997	1996	1995	1994	1993
Earnings per Share	31.00	23.50	9.60	14.60	13.50
Dividends per Share	13.00	10.50	8.70	8.00	7.50
Book Value per Share	NA	243.65	222.15	224.90	223.12
Total Investment Return	NA	NA	9.35	-1.39	41.90
Market Price (Year-end)	655.00	422.00	330.50	310.20	322.70
Market Capitalization (in millions)	160038.22	102177.00	76150.05	69501.49	70525.66
Price/Earnings Ratio	21.13	17.96	34.43	21.25	23.90
Price/Book Value	NA	1.73	1.49	1.38	1.45
Dividend Yield	1.98	2.49	2.63	2.58	2.32
Dividend Payout per Share	41.94	44.68	90.62	54.79	55.56

Common Shares
  Outstanding
  (Year-end) in
  Millions
	244.33	242.13	230.41	224.05	218.55

Stock Split/Dividend Ratio	NA	NA	NA	NA	1.00
Type of Share	*B Actions Ordinaires*				

Displayed Currency: French Franc (1.00:1)
Note: Data is sourced from Worldscope and may differ from I/B/E/S historical data.

46. Unibanco

Unibanco—Uniao de Bancos Brasileiros—has had to be as quick on its feet as an agile Brazilian soccer player in World Cup competition to prosper over the decades in a volatile Brazilian market that had exhibited little or no discipline.

Brazil's third-largest private-sector bank with more than a thousand branches is an aggressive, acquisition-minded institution in step with the times. Its stock has lately been pressured by worldwide trends running against emerging markets. It should therefore benefit significantly as Brazil, under the anti-inflation directives of President Fernando Henrique Cardoso, reins in many past economic excesses, and spirited competition for market share provides the driving force behind all Brazilian industries. Unibanco's stock price tends to be tied to the general perception of Brazil's country risk, so periods of stumbling can provide an opportunity to buy a long-term investment at a lower price. But make no mistake: This stock is a calculated bet not just on bank management's ability, but on Brazil's future and the conviction that its tremendous resources can at long last be mustered effectively into an efficient modern economy. While Brazil is notching successes and gaining positive press clippings for its progress, it's hardly out of the woods yet.

Besides traditional retail and commercial banking, Unibanco offers money management services and import/export credit lines. Its insurance subsidiary, which is the sixth largest in Brazil, formed a joint venture American International Group, one of the world's largest insurance businesses, to sell insurance in Brazil. Through other subsidiaries, Unibanco provides telemarketing, credit card, and leasing services. Outside Brazil, it serves customers through offices in the Bahamas, the Cayman Islands, Luxembourg, Paraguay, the United Kingdom, Uruguay, and the United States. It doubled its customer base in late 1995 with the purchase of Banco Nacional and currently has more than 2 million customers. In 1997, the bank acquired a portion of the second-largest private pension fund in the country in assets and premiums, Prever Seguros e Previdencia, and bought 45 percent of Quatro/A, the leading telemarketing company in Brazil. Along with other Brazilian financial institutions, that year it created the Brazilian Securitization Company, which under government reform measures was to become Brazil's main mortgage securitization institution.

In 1998 Unibanco bought 51 percent of the common shares of Banco Dibens S.A., a full-service bank in São Paulo involved in automotive financing, and with its own network of car dealerships that represent Mercedes-Benz, Toyota, Volkswagen, and General Motors. This put Unibanco in second place in the non-manufacturer automotive financing market after ABN Amro and in an excellent position to compete for market leadership. Despite a downturn tied to emerging market woes in Asia and a defensive doubling of Brazil's interest rates in 1997, subsequent rate cuts have improved the situation and many in the financial community consider Brazil's financial system to be in much better shape than originally projected. There should therefore be lower loan loss provisions and higher loan growth, both of which will contribute to earnings.

Unibanco traces its history to 1924 when its founders obtained a license for establishing a banking division in the Moreira Salles and Company commercial firm. It expanded over the next decades through a variety of acquisitions and focused on financing foreign trade activities of a variety of Brazilian import and export businesses. It finally evolved in 1967 into the Union of Brazilian Banks, or Unibanco. It began growing through a number of acquisitions, such as Banco Predial do Rio de Janeiro S.A. in 1970 and Banco Mineiro S.A. in 1981. The bank in 1986 reorganized to focus primarily on mid- to high-income individuals. It merged with its affiliated companies in

1989 to form a multiple-service bank to directly offer banking and nonbanking financial products and services.

To broaden its middle- and high-income and high net-worth individual customer base, Unibanco is marketing a broad range of products and services to that segment, such as mutual funds, insurance, lease financing, savings, and retirement plans. Its "thirty-hours" phone, personal computer banking, and the "Banco 1" virtual bank are specifically targeted to the needs of this customer segment. For the lower income customer segment, Unibanco acquired a 48.8 percent interest in Banco Fininvest, a consumer finance company serving lower-income individuals. Management believes the opportunity for growth in this segment of the retail market is significant, based on increased purchasing power and demand for consumer credit resulting from the stabilization of the Brazilian economy and the relaxing of credit restrictions by the Central Bank. This banking strategy includes increasing credit card offerings to all three retail customer segments.

Unibanco expects that as the Brazilian economy grows and inflation moderates, its wholesale banking customers will require more comprehensive credit and noncredit financing services. It will likely expand investment banking services as Brazilian companies rely more on the domestic and international capital markets for their funding needs. In the large corporate segment, Unibanco is emphasizing specialized lending products, treasury, and cash management services. For the middle market, it will significantly increase lending activities and expand offerings of fee-based services such as electronic banking, investment banking, automated teller machines, credit cards, and management services. In the wholesale business, it will actively market fee-based services such as receivables collection, payroll services, supplier payments, investment advisory services, and cash management.

Unibanco put into effect a significant organizational restructuring in which it now has two presidents, for the retail and wholesale banking groups respectively, and one chief financial officer who is also responsible for risk management. All report directly to Chairman of the Board Pedro Moreira Salles. The separation into retail and wholesale banking groups is designed to maintain focus in each market while simplifying its overall structure. In addition, the bank has been involved in a comprehensive reengineering program to increase operating efficiencies. It managed, for example, to reduce and consolidate its fifty-seven back-office centers for processing of branch documents and accounts to five during the course of 1997. Its significant investments in technology, particularly automated banking services and information systems, should allow it to improve customer service, operating efficiency, and profitability.

Unibanco is a well-run financial institution that made the right moves in the past and should score big in the future if the Brazilian government is able to maintain a more stable economic environment.

46. UNIBANCO

Brazil   Ticker symbol UBB

Each American Depositary Receipt represents 500 units of one preferred share of Unibanco and one preferred "B" share of Unibanco Holdings S.A.

ADR price $16 5/8 (9/16/98)   Dividend yield 8.59%

(Financial data is from I/B/E/S International)*

BUSINESS DESCRIPTION

MULTIPLE BANK OFFERING A WIDE VARIETY OF BANKING SERVICES SUCH AS ASSET MANAGEMENT, LENDING, BROKERAGE, AND FOREIGN EXCHANGE

ADDRESS AND CONTACTS

Address	Av Euzebio Matoso, 891-2 Andar
	São Paulo SP 05423-901 Brazil
Telephone	55-11-8674322
Fax	55-11-8155084

BASIC FINANCIAL INFORMATION

Report Dates	Last Annual: Dec 97	Reported On: Feb 12, 1998
Capital Structure†	Long Term Debt:	3.40
	Total Debt:	9.27
	Common Sh. Equity:	2.63

SALES BREAKDOWN

Product Segments[†]   NA
Geographic Segments[†]   NA

Displayed Currency: U.S. Dollars/1000 Shares (1.00:1)
*I/B/E/S and I/B/E/S Express are registered trademarks of I/B/E/S International Inc. Copyright
1993–1996 I/B/E/S International Inc. All rights reserved.
[†]Values are displayed in millions.

FINANCIAL STATEMENT DATA

INCOME STATEMENT	1997	1996	1995	1994	1993
Net Sales or Revenues	8.24	8.53	3.66	1.74	0.54
Interest Income—Net	1.80	1.20	1.16	0.45	-0.17
Total Non-Interest Income	3.94	4.46	1.20	0.97	0.25
Net Income	0.43	0.29	0.15	`0.12	0.01

BALANCE SHEET	1997	1996	1995	1994	1993
Assets					
Cash & Due from Banks	1.68	2.92	2.64	1.33	0.04
Total Investments	10.46	8.24	7.90	1.65	0.29
Loans—Net	10.64	10.22	7.73	6.27	0.44
Total Assets	28.14	26.27	22.80	11.05	0.94
Liabilities & Shareholders' Equity					
Deposits—Total	6.45	7.57	9.38	4.92	0.44
Total Debt	9.27	8.86	8.63	3.21	0.31
Preferred Stock	NA	NA	NA	NA	NA
Common Equity	2.63	2.15	1.97	0.94	0.08
Total Liabilities & Sh. Equity	28.14	26.27	22.80	11.05	0.94

CASH FLOW	1997	1996	1995	1994	1993
Funds from Operations	1.14	0.48	0.15	0.12	0.02
Total Sources	5.98	7.78	8.45	2.97	0.82
Cash Dividends Paid— Total	0.14	0.09	0.05	0.04	0.00
Total Uses	5.98	7.78	8.45	2.97	0.82
Free Cash Flow	0.86	0.40	-0.07	-0.01	0.11

SUPPLEMENTARY DATA	1997	1996	1995	1994	1993
Provision for Loan Losses	0.90	0.79	0.70	0.12	0.01
Non-Interest Expense	4.41	4.45	1.47	1.03	0.05
Interbank Loans	0.40	0.22	0.08	1.00	0.05
Consumer and Installment Loans	NA	NA	NA	NA	NA

Real Estate Mortage Loans	NA	NA	NA	NA	NA
Reserve for Loan Losses	0.72	0.59	0.61	0.11	0.00
Foreign Assets	NA	NA	NA	NA	NA
Demand Deposits	1.03	0.83	1.01	0.45	0.02
Savings/Other Time Deposits	5.39	6.69	8.34	4.19	0.32
Consumer Liability on Acceptances	NA	NA	NA	NA	NA
Employees	NA	NA	29468	16879	19234
Goodwill/Cost in Excess of Assets Purchased	NA	NA	NA	NA	NA
Extra Items & Gain/ Loss in Sale of Assets	0.00	0.00	0.00	0.00	0.00

Displayed Currency: U.S. Dollars/1000 Shares (1.00:1)
All values are displayed in millions (except employees).

FINANCIAL RATIOS AND GROWTH RATES

PROFITABILITY	1997	1996	1995	1994	1993	5YR AVG
Return on Assets %	3.16	3.18	2.08	2.32	NA	2.68
Return on Equity— Total %	20.00	14.49	16.38	158.90	378.39	117.63
Tax Rate %	22.37	29.58	39.44	60.52	19.73	34.33
Efficiency of Earning Assets	30.48	38.53	38.64	162.45	3731.08	800.24
Total Interest Income % Earning Assets	23.31	26.05	31.01	105.88	2151.60	467.57
Total Interest Exp % Interest Bearing Liabilities	15.24	15.96	15.95	42.47	2025.78	423.08
Non-Interest Income % Total Revenues	47.79	52.27	32.91	55.69	46.55	47.04
Return on Earning Assets	2.33	1.82	1.95	16.54	76.48	19.83

LIQUIDITY	1997	1996	1995	1994	1993	5YR AVG
Total Deposits % Total Assets	22.92	28.81	41.15	44.51	47.43	36.96
Total Loans % Total Deposits	176.13	142.91	88.92	129.74	100.07	127.55
Cash & Secs % Total Deposits	188.20	147.43	112.43	60.53	74.01	116.50
Reserve for Loan Losses % Total Loans	6.57	5.57	7.40	2.02	1.13	4.54

LEVERAGE	1997	1996	1995	1994	1993	5YR AVG
Common Equity %						
Total Assets	9.35	8.20	8.63	8.54	8.08	8.56
Loan Loss Coverage						
Ratio	2.96	2.42	2.97	NA	NA	2.78

OTHER	1997	1996	1995	1994	1993	5YR AVG
Earning Assets %						
Total Assets	74.97	70.28	68.58	71.67	77.59	72.62

GROWTH %	1997	1996	1995	1994	1993	5YR AVG
Total Assets	7.12	15.23	106.36	1077.86	2978.97	291.85
Net Sales or Revenues	-3.42	133.14	110.50	221.22	3375.81	250.53
Earnings per Share*	45.37	84.00	-14.47	981.76	1739.16	1739.16
Dividends per Share*	46.71	34.30	28.05	13861.19	85.59	265.66
Book Value per Share	16.35	9.10	39.23	1032.04	1293.77	208.37

*Source: Worldscope. Value may differ from I/B/E/S.
Note: 5-Year Average calculations exclude NAs.

PER SHARE AND RELATED DATA

SOURCE: WORLDSCOPE	1997	1996	1995	1994	1993
Earnings per Share	0.00	0.00	0.00	0.00	0.00
Dividends per Share	0.00	0.00	0.00	0.00	0.00
Book Value per Share	0.03	0.02	0.02	0.02	0.00
Total Investment Return	NA	NA	55.22	844.28	2705.71
Market Price (Year-end)	0.05	0.03	0.02	0.01	0.00
Market Capitalization					
(in millions)	4.56	3.20	1.79	0.80	0.08
Price/Earnings Ratio	10.58	11.34	11.69	6.71	8.05
Price/Book Value	1.73	1.49	0.91	0.85	1.07
Dividend Yield	3.35	3.10	4.12	4.80	0.31
Dividend Payout per					
Share	35.49	35.17	48.19	32.18	2.49
Common Shares					
Outstanding					
(Year-end) in					
Millions	99122.64	94444.18	94142.98	62848.20	57129.38
Stock Split/Dividend Ratio	NA	NA	0.50	0.50	NA
Type of Share	*Preferencial*				

Displayed Currency: U.S. Dollars/1000 Shares (1.00:1)
Note: Data is sourced from Worldscope and may differ from I/B/E/S historical data.

47. Unilever

Anglo-Dutch Unilever, one of the world's largest companies and the second-biggest packaged consumer goods company behind Procter & Gamble, is as international as an organization can be. Through its food division and its home and personal care business, it offers more than 1,000 brands, many of them market leaders, although it's best known for Lipton tea, Bird's Eye frozen desserts, Ragu spaghetti sauce, Wisk laundry detergent, Dove soap, Vaseline petroleum jelly, Q-tips, Helene Curtis hair care, and Calvin Klein cosmetics. The company specifically describes itself as "international," not "global," because it does not attempt to enter all markets with the same product. For example, only a few food products such as ice cream, tea, and olive oil can effectively cross international boundaries, and the formulation for detergents will vary by country based on washing habits, machines, clothes, and water quality.

Enjoying an encouraging acceleration of its volume growth despite a weak outlook in Southeast Asia that is slowing things down a bit, Unilever continues to be a long-term growth stock of a company firmly committed to shareholder value through sustained growth. Management's objective is to deliver a total return to shareholders which is in the top one-third of its peers. This strong cash generator is well equipped to pay for its future expansion moves. Management remains confident in the longer-term outlook for Asia, given its young, well-educated, and hard-working populations eager for a higher standard of living. Conditions in Europe are improving, and both it and the United States should see reasonable growth. Developing and emerging countries now account for more than 30 percent of Unilever profits, the firm's priority regions for investment being Central and Eastern Europe, China, India, Southeast Asia, and south Latin America. While progress in China has thus far fallen short of the corporate plan, Unilever believes it simply requires taking a long-term perspective and intends to stick with its ambitious goals there. One reason behind Unilever's fast growth in today's emerging markets, especially in home and personal care, is its combination of historic presence and local understanding. For example, it has had companies for more than sixty years in Brazil, Chile, Côte d'Ivoire, India, Indonesia, Nigeria, the Philippines, South Africa, and Thailand.

In a unique arrangement, Netherlands-based Unilever N.V. owns half of Unilever and U.K.-based Unilever Plc. owns the other half. How did that happen? Unilever was created in 1929 from the merger of Margarine Unie of the Netherlands and Lever Brothers Limited of the United Kingdom. While the two firms had competed for supplies of oils and fats which they put to different uses, both were in the business of supplying goods for household needs, and they saw an advantage in joining forces.

As the result of a relatively recent management structure change, the companies have a seven-member executive committee headed by the chairmen of Unilever Plc. and Unilever N.V., with the responsibility for operations placed in the hands of fourteen newly defined business groups. The annual report, for example, has a "chairmen's statement" with the smiling faces of Niall FitzGerald (Unilever Plc.) and Morris Tabaksblat (Unilever N.V.) identified by the caption "Chairmen of Unilever." The two firms list their stock separately and the corporate center has offices in London and Rotterdam. Both Unilever N.V. and Unilever Plc. present the consolidated accounts of Unilever as their respective consolidated accounts. The companies together operate in more than ninety countries and sell products through third parties in an additional seventy. There are approximately 500 operating companies worldwide with 270,000 employees. As further evidence of its international bent, Unilever has introduced Total Productive Maintenance (TPM), the Japanese productivity program, in eighty of its factories. Like the Six Sigma quality program used by companies such as AlliedSignal and General Electric, it is geared to active involvement of employees in raising efficiency. For example, a sustained program at its Elais food company in Greece over six years increased employee production by 50 percent and helped double profit per employee.

The company sold its specialty chemicals division to Imperial Chemical Industries in 1997, a year in which it disposed of nineteen other businesses around the world that included the Cutex nail polish remover business in the United States. Its recent acquisitions have included Kibron ice cream in Brazil, the Helados Holanda and Bing ice cream businesses in Mexico, Monthelado ice cream in Argentina, Iberia margerine in Mexico, Poett detergents in Argentina, and Darenas industrial cleaning products in Denmark.

Half of Unilever's business is in food, where it is often essential to take a local view. The company focuses on five main areas of margarine, tea, ice cream, culinary products, and frozen foods, which make up 70 percent of food sales. Unilever is essentially a local company in all of the countries in which it operates and day-to-day operations are organized accordingly. There is a common Unilever approach to safety standards and personnel policies, whatever the country. In contrast, Unilever's attention to customers and consumers is explicitly local. As a result, innovation can happen everywhere, not just at the center of the company. Some of these initiatives later travel the world. For example, Magnum ice cream came from Germany, while Organics shampoo was developed in France and Thailand.

The major categories in Unilever's home care business are laundry and household care products for consumers. Unilever also has a strong professional cleaning business to meet the needs of industrial and institutional customers called DiverseyLever. In personal care, Unilever covers the spectrum from mass market toiletries like personal wash and skin-care products, deodorants, dental products, hair care, and home diagnostics products to prestige fragrances and cosmetics. Laundry is the largest category of this business and includes products ranging from hard soap bars for washing by hand to sophisticated concentrated detergents for washing machines. In the personal wash market, Unilever is a world leader with strong international brands such as Lux toilet soap and Dove. Unilever quickly grasped new opportunities in this area and is now a global leader in shower gels, a market that didn't exist ten years ago.

The products, the philosophy, and the international ability are all there in mighty Unilever. The primary challenge of such a monolithic corporation is to show that it can pull its forces together to provide the type of growth that is usually the domain of smaller companies.

47. UNILEVER

Netherlands   Ticker symbol UL

One American Depositary Receipt represents four ordinary shares

ADR price $35 13/16 (9/16/98)   Dividend yield 2.55%

(Financial data from I/B/E/S International is in Netherland guilder)*

BUSINESS DESCRIPTION

FOOD ACCOUNTED FOR 50% OF 1997 REVENUES, HOME AND PERSONAL CARE PRODUCTS 44%, SPECIALTY CHEMICALS 4%, AND PLANTATIONS/PLANT SCIENCE/TRADE 2%

ADDRESS AND CONTACTS

Address	Weena 455
	NL-3013 Al Rotterdam, Netherlands
Telephone	31-10-2174000
Fax	31-10-2174798

BASIC FINANCIAL INFORMATION

Capital Structure†	Long Term Debt:	5766.00
	Total Debt:	8905.00
	Common Sh. Equity:	24469.00

SALES BREAKDOWN

Product Segments†	Food Products	47216.00
	Home & Personal Care	41152.00
	Specialty Chemicals	3997.00
	Plantations, Plant	2232.00

Unilever

Geographic Segments[†]		
	Europe	43331.00
	North America	19613.00
	Africa & Middle East	6327.00
	Asia & Pacific	14613.00
	Latin America	10713.00

Displayed Currency: Netherland Guilder (1.00:1)

*I/B/E/S and I/B/E/S Express are registered trademarks of I/B/E/S International Inc. Copyright 1993–1996 I/B/E/S International Inc. All rights reserved.

[†]Values are displayed in millions.

FINANCIAL STATEMENT DATA

INCOME STATEMENT	1997	1996	1995	1994	1993
Net Sales or Revenues	94597.00	87795.00	79703.00	82590.00	77626.00
EBITDA	18757.00	10153.00	8834.00	9647.00	8287.00
Depreciation Depletion & Amort	2336.00	2224.00	2012.00	2037.00	1880.00
Operating Income	7576.00	7582.00	6389.00	7012.00	5397.00
Interest Expense	969.00	969.00	958.00	976.00	995.00
Pretax Income	15429.00	6960.00	5864.00	6634.00	5412.00
Net Income	10921.00	4200.00	3710.00	4324.00	3597.00

BALANCE SHEET	1997	1996	1995	1994	1993
Assets					
Cash & Equivalents	19530.00	5003.00	3707.00	4903.00	3364.00
Receivables—Net	10677.00	11407.00	10174.00	10858.00	10651.00
Inventories	10378.00	11573.00	10683.00	10168.00	9901.00
Total Current Assets	41424.00	28840.00	25342.00	25893.00	24720.00
Property Plant & Eq.—Net	20047.00	23509.00	21862.00	22156.00	21923.00
Total Assets	63319.00	54040.00	48189.00	49309.00	48061.00
Liabilities & Shareholders' Equity					
Total Current Liabilities	21681.00	21076.00	18699.00	19151.00	19817.00
Long Term Debt	5766.00	6365.00	5460.00	5610.00	4230.00
Preferred Stock	265.00	265.00	265.00	265.00	265.00
Common Equity	24469.00	15085.00	13724.00	14222.00	13239.00
Total Liabilities & Sh. Equity	63319.00	54040.00	48189.00	49309.00	48061.00

CASH FLOW	1997	1996	1995	1994	1993
Funds from Operations	7119.00	7420.00	6627.00	6608.00	6669.00
Total Sources	8716.00	8412.00	10855.00	11372.00	10147.00
Cash Dividends Paid— Total	2090.00	1811.00	1555.00	1526.00	1429.00

CASH FLOW	1997	1996	1995	1994	1993
Total Uses	8716.00	8736.00	10855.00	11372.00	10147.00
Incr/Decr in Working Capital	11979.00	1121.00	-99.00	1839.00	-137.00
Free Cash Flow	15719.00	7092.00	5764.00	5672.00	4457.00

INTERNATIONAL BUSINESS	1997	1996	1995	1994	1993
Foreign Assets	12124.00	13742.00	11995.00	11460.00	10617.00
Foreign Sales	51266.00	45089.00	37617.00	38121.00	31193.00
Foreign Income	4664.00	4147.00	3613.00	3354.00	3033.00

SUPPLEMENTARY DATA	1997	1996	1995	1994	1993
Employees	287000	306000	308000	304000	302000
R&D Expenses	1734.00	1573.00	1479.00	1512.00	1442.00
Goodwill/Cost in Excess of Assets Purchased	0.00	0.00	0.00	0.00	0.00
Extra Items & Gain/ Loss in Sale of Assets	0.00	0.00	0.00	0.00	0.00

Displayed Currency: Netherland Guilder (1.00:1)
All values are displayed in millions (except employees).

FINANCIAL RATIOS AND GROWTH RATES

PROFITABILITY	1997	1996	1995	1994	1993	5YR AVG
Operating Profit Margin %	8.01	8.57	8.02	8.49	6.95	8.01
Tax Rate %	27.12	36.36	33.68	31.99	29.86	31.80
Net Margin %	11.56	4.80	4.67	5.25	4.65	6.19
Return on Assets %	21.45	10.07	8.84	10.37	9.64	12.07
Return on Equity— Total %	72.40	30.60	26.09	32.66	29.04	38.16
Cash Flow % Sales	7.53	8.45	8.31	8.00	8.59	8.18
Sales per Employee (in 000s)	330	287	259	272	257	281

ASSET UTILIZATION	1997	1996	1995	1994	1993	5YR AVG
Total Asset Turnover	1.49	1.62	1.65	1.67	1.62	1.61
Capital Exp % Gross Fixed Assets	8.54	7.67	8.45	10.92	10.87	9.29
Acc Depreciation % Gross Fixed Assets	43.65	41.07	40.29	39.12	37.77	40.38
Assets per Employee (in 000s)	221	177	156	162	159	175

LIQUIDITY	1997	1996	1995	1994	1993	5YR AVG
Current Ratio	1.91	1.37	1.36	1.35	1.25	1.45
Quick Ratio	1.39	0.78	0.74	0.78	0.71	0.88

Unilever

LEVERAGE	1997	1996	1995	1994	1993	5YR AVG
Total Debt % Common Equity	36.39	66.40	61.28	59.91	54.85	55.77
Long Term Debt % Common Equity	23.56	42.19	39.78	39.45	31.95	35.39
Common Equity % Total Assets	38.64	27.91	28.48	28.84	27.55	30.29
Long Term Debt % Total Capital	18.28	28.00	26.84	26.87	22.00	24.40
Operating Cash/ Fixed Charges	7.03	7.48	6.76	6.62	6.56	6.89

GROWTH %	1997	1996	1995	1994	1993	5YR AVG
Net Sales	7.75	10.15	-3.50	6.39	1.38	4.32
Operating Income	0.64	17.83	-8.88	29.92	-20.74	2.16
Total Assets	17.17	12.14	-2.27	2.60	8.57	7.42
Earnings per Share*	159.73	13.12	-14.56	20.31	-9.73	22.21
Dividends per Share*	27.79	12.76	0.00	5.27	1.73	9.07
Book Value per Share	62.05	9.80	-3.87	7.46	7.92	14.68

Displayed Currency: Netherland Guilder (1.00:1)
*Source: Worldscope. Value may differ from I/B/E/S.
Note: 5-Year Average calculations exclude NAs.

PER SHARE AND RELATED DATA

SOURCE: WORLDSCOPE	1997	1996	1995	1994	1993
Earnings per Share	9.74	3.75	3.32	3.88	3.23
Dividends per Share	2.23	1.75	1.55	1.55	1.47
Book Value per Share	21.82	13.46	12.26	12.76	11.87
Total Investment Return	NA	NA	13.85	-6.91	21.78
Market Price (Year-end)	125.00	76.40	56.38	50.88	56.32
Market Capitalization (in millions)	140183.99	85595.50	63092.42	56720.95	62803.98
Price/Earnings Ratio	12.83	20.37	17.01	13.11	17.46
Price/Book Value	5.73	5.67	4.60	3.99	4.74
Dividend Yield	1.78	2.28	2.75	3.04	2.61
Dividend Payout per Share	22.90	46.53	46.68	39.88	45.58

Common Shares
  Outstanding
  (Year-end) in
  Millions
	1121.47	1120.36	1119.16	1114.91	1115.28

Stock Split/Dividend Ratio	NA	0.25	0.25	0.25	0.25
Type of Share	Certficate Van Aand				

Displayed Currency: Netherland Guilder (1.00:1)
Note: Data is sourced from Worldscope and may differ from I/B/E/S historical data.

48. VEBA A.G.

Just because VEBA A.G. is Germany's third-largest diversified industrial company doesn't mean it's standing pat. This efficient giant continues to make wide-ranging restructuring and acquisition moves. It's also well equipped to compete on prices in a deregulated and increasingly international electricity market. Other VEBA businesses include chemicals, transport, housing development, construction materials, and telecommunications. Using centralized strategic management but decentralized management of individual group companies with independent decision-making, VEBA has a strong commitment to double-digit earnings growth. It expects to accomplish this through enhanced productivity, comprehensive realignment of nearly all divisions, and the international expansion of its core businesses.

The Free State of Prussia established Vereinigte Elektizitats-und Bergswerks-Aktiengesellschaft, or VEBA, as a financial holding company in 1929 to handle the financing of the state's incorporated holdings. The Federal Republic of Germany conceded the majority of VEBA's capital stock to private investors in 1964, and full privatization took place when the government's remaining 25 percent stake was floated on German and international capital markets in 1987. Today VEBA has 450,000 shareholders worldwide, with institutional investors holding 77 percent of those shares. Foreign investors own 44 percent of its stock, including 11 percent owned by U.S. investors.

VEBA operates Preussenelektra, Germany's second-largest utility, which supplies one-fifth of the country's electricity. Coal and nuclear power are the primary energy sources of this profitable division. The company decided to "unbundle" its genera-

338

tion, transmission, and distribution functions to make its operating procedures and cost-effectiveness more discernible to customers. It should do well under liberalized German energy laws because it's already passing cost-savings from its many streamlining efforts on to its customers, who currently pay the lowest prices for electricity in that country. To further solidify its position, VEBA acquired a 12.5 percent stake in the Hamburg utility HEW A.G. and increased its interest in the Berlin utility Bewag A.G. from 10 percent to 23 percent. It owns parts of electric utilities in Scandanavia and the Baltic region, and future non-German transactions are planned. Expansion is necessary because of expected lower profit margins in Germany from heated competition among electricity providers to snare large- and medium-sized industrial customers. Additional cost-cutting in VEBA's electricity unit would be good news for earnings prospects and none of the firm's electricity competitors is expected to be a real threat to its profit margins. The company's other energy business is VEBA OEL, which is involved in petroleum exploration, production, and refining, and owns Germany's largest gas station chain.

Since VEBA has been both consolidating and acquiring, results of individual divisions are considered more important and quantifiable than the somewhat blurred overall corporate returns. You almost need an owner's manual to trace all of this company's transactions. Consider chemicals, from which the company has been deriving strong earnings both at home and outside its borders and which the company says it is dedicated to for the future. VEBA's Huls subsidiary, which makes chemicals such as polymers, methacrylate, and products for the electronics industry, acquired Degussa A.G. to form a separately traded company called Degussa-Huls A.G. in 1998. The prior year the company had divested Huls' polystyrene unit. The company's real estate business has benefited from a considerable increase in housing unit sales and rising rental income. It broadened the regional diversification of its efforts by purchasing a 50 percent share in Deutschbau, the German government's former property agency. VEBA restructured its Trading/Transportation/Services

Division in 1997, with Raab Karcher and VEBA Immoblien merged to form a real-estate services group. That reorganization included a public listing for up to 49 percent of its Stinnes A.G. unit to afford the company the opportunity to finance growth through the stock market. VEBA became the world's number-three distributor of electronic systems and components in 1997 by taking over California-based Wyle Electronics. Raab Karcher has shown dramatic sales gains and earnings growth even without even taking Wyle acquisition into account.

"As a result of groupwide restructuring, all our divisions have solid footing," Chairman and CEO Ulrich Hartmann said in the company's most recent annual report. "They have made a pledge to continue VEBA's quest to internationalize the group—an endeavor we have stepped up since we announced it in 1996—and are making strong headway. With our focus and growth strategy (which involves concentrating on core businesses and elevating them into leading market positions) we are establishing an improved platform for creating future sustainable value for you, our shareholders."

Despite strength in most of VEBA's divisions, telecommunications and silicon wafer manufacturing have been areas of concern. In telecom, where losses have been growing as a network is constructed, VEBA and RWE formed the firm o.tel.o in 1997, with VEBA holding a 40 percent stake. Then o.tel.o bought Thyssen A.G.'s 30 percent stake in the E-Plus mobile telephone network. BellSouth Corporation, expanding its presence in Europe, has said it plans to acquire a stake in o.tel.o. Chairman Hartmann projected having several hundred thousand customers for o.tel.o by year-end 1998.

Meanwhile, VEBA's MEMC unit in the United Kingdom, the world's largest producer of silicon wafers outside of Japan, saw losses widen in early 1998 as market conditions continued in a funk. This was in part a result of the yen's drop against the dollar, which greatly benefited Japanese competitors. However, the bulk of the burden of cost containment and restructuring measures was calculated into the first quarter of 1997 and losses were expected to decline for subsequent quarters. The company believes that with its cost management program in place, MEMC is on its way to greater productivity and reduced capital expenditures. The company's promotional efforts take the importance of the computer world into account. VEBA formed a strategic alliance with StarBase Corporation in 1998 to distribute software-maker StarBase's Star Team 3.0, a suite of team development and management tools, to all of its customers who purchase Compaq Computer Corporation and Digital Equipment Corporation's Windows NT servers.

Looking forward, VEBA management expects electricity to remain the biggest earnings contributor, continuing to set records. Oil returns have been strong, but market conditions in that area worldwide are no sure thing. The newly reorganized Distribution/Logistics and Real Estate Management should have improved earnings, while telecommunications will record high start-up costs. No capital increase is planned for the foreseeable future.

Oh, and expect the acquisitions, restructuring, and cost-cutting to continue as VEBA proves that being a giant doesn't mean you have to simply lumber along.

---

48. VEBA A.G.

Germany   Ticker symbol VEB

One American Depositary Receipt represents one ordinary share

ADR price $57 1/4 (9/16/98)   Dividend yield 1.98%

(Financial data from I/B/E/S International is in German mark)*

BUSINESS DESCRIPTION

TRADING/TRANSPORTATION/SERVICES ACCOUNTED FOR 39% OF 1997 REVENUES, OIL 28%, ELECTRICITY 18%, CHEMICALS 14%, AND TELECOMMUNICATIONS 1%

ADDRESS AND CONTACTS

Address	Bennigsenplatz 1
	D-40474 Duesseldorf, Germany
Telephone	49-211-45791
Fax	49-211-4579501

BASIC FINANCIAL INFORMATION

Capital Structure[†]

Long Term Debt:	3906.00
Total Debt:	5927.00
Common Sh. Equity:	22155.00

SALES BREAKDOWN

Product Segments[†]

Trading/Transportation	31979.00
Oil	22928.00
Electricity	16085.00
Chemicals	11474.00
Telecommunications	253.00

Geographic Segments[†]

Germany	59079.00
Other European	11454.00
North America	8715.00
Other Countries	3471.00

Displayed Currency: German Mark (1.00:1)

*I/B/E/S and I/B/E/S Express are registered trademarks of I/B/E/S International Inc. Copyright 1993–1996 I/B/E/S International Inc. All rights reserved.

[†]Values are displayed in millions.

FINANCIAL STATEMENT DATA

INCOME STATEMENT	1997	1996	1995	1994	1993
Net Sales or					
Revenues	76067.00	68095.00	66323.00	64992.60	61293.60
EBITDA	10124.00	9228.00	8598.00	7542.70	6543.00
Depreciation					
Depletion & Amort	4756.00	4495.00	4497.00	4455.00	4516.90
Operating Income	825.00	1102.00	332.00	-1046.10	-1499.90
Interest Expense	298.00	298.00	265.00	550.20	502.10
Pretax Income	4973.00	4435.00	3836.00	2537.50	1524.00
Net Income	2810.00	2458.00	1915.00	1378.00	825.00

BALANCE SHEET	1997	1996	1995	1994	1993
Assets					
Cash & Equivalents	1276.00	4969.00	4162.00	4195.30	3673.60
Receivables—Net	10021.00	10438.20	8803.00	8812.10	8195.60
Inventories	6559.00	5378.00	5191.00	4917.10	5117.80
Total Current Assets	20959.00	21007.00	20490.00	19962.90	19233.00
Property Plant & Eq.—					
Net	30286.00	28828.00	27487.00	24944.00	23402.30
Total Assets	80595.00	71917.00	67751.00	59854.90	55540.80

VEBA A.G.

Liabilities & Shareholders' Equity

	1997	1996	1995	1994	1993
Total Current Liabilities	14863.00	10902.00	9795.00	10077.80	9387.00
Long Term Debt	3906.00	3129.00	3017.00	3168.00	3224.00
Preferred Stock	0.00	0.00	0.00	0.00	0.00
Common Equity	22155.00	19490.00	17491.00	15576.60	15087.10
Total Liabilities & Sh. Equity	80595.00	71917.00	67751.00	59854.90	55540.80

CASH FLOW	1997	1996	1995	1994	1993
Funds from Operations	8602.00	8191.00	8122.00	6858.90	6438.00
Total Sources	17872.00	9558.00	11049.00	8996.90	6952.46
Cash Dividends Paid— Total	938.00	830.00	846.00	853.20	555.46
Total Uses	17872.00	9558.00	11049.00	8996.90	6952.46
Incr/Decr in Working Capital	-4009.00	-590.00	809.90	39.10	1862.80
Free Cash Flow	3987.00	991.00	-1109.00	216.20	1431.00

INTERNATIONAL BUSINESS	1997	1996	1995	1994	1993
Foreign Assets	15095.00	10007.00	7080.00	NA	NA
Foreign Sales	23640.00	13893.00	12744.00	20145.40	18743.80
Foreign Income	824.00	554.00	818.00	NA	NA

SUPPLEMENTARY DATA	1997	1996	1995	1994	1993
Employees	129960	122110	125158	126875	128348
R&D Expenses	336.00	300.00	312.00	315.00	400.00
Goodwill/Cost in Excess of Assets Purchased	2754.00	1946.00	1783.00	1675.90	1425.10
Extra Items & Gain/ Loss in Sale of Assets	0.00	0.00	0.00	0.00	0.00

Displayed Currency: German Mark (1.00:1)
All values are displayed in millions (except employees).

FINANCIAL RATIOS AND GROWTH RATES

PROFITABILITY	1997	1996	1995	1994	1993	5YR AVG
Operating Profit Margin %	1.08	1.62	0.50	-1.61	-2.45	-0.17
Tax Rate %	39.29	40.61	45.07	39.74	33.51	39.65
Net Margin %	3.69	3.61	2.89	2.12	1.35	2.73
Return on Assets %	4.27	3.92	3.49	3.13	2.21	3.41
Return on Equity— Total %	14.42	14.05	12.29	9.13	5.79	11.14
Cash Flow % Sales	11.31	12.03	12.25	10.55	10.50	11.33
Sales per Employee (in 000s)	585	558	530	512	478	533

ASSET UTILIZATION	1997	1996	1995	1994	1993	5YR AVG
Total Asset Turnover	0.94	0.95	0.98	1.09	1.10	1.01
Capital Exp % Gross						
Fixed Assets	7.43	10.64	13.19	10.20	7.56	9.80
Acc Depreciation %						
Gross Fixed Assets	63.36	62.77	62.65	65.27	65.41	63.89
Assets per Employee						
(in 000s)	620	589	541	472	433	531

LIQUIDITY	1997	1996	1995	1994	1993	5YR AVG
Current Ratio	1.41	1.93	2.09	1.98	2.05	1.89
Quick Ratio	0.76	1.41	1.32	1.29	1.26	1.21

LEVERAGE	1997	1996	1995	1994	1993	5YR AVG
Total Debt %						
Common Equity	26.75	18.74	19.90	24.17	33.56	24.62
Long Term Debt %						
Common Equity	17.63	16.05	17.25	20.34	21.37	18.53
Common Equity %						
Total Assets	27.49	27.10	25.82	26.02	27.16	26.72
Long Term Debt %						
Total Capital	13.36	11.96	12.08	15.33	16.18	13.78
Operating Cash/						
Fixed Charges	21.78	27.49	30.65	12.47	12.82	21.04

GROWTH %	1997	1996	1995	1994	1993	5YR AVG
Net Sales	11.71	2.67	2.05	6.03	-0.05	4.40
Operating Income	-25.14	231.93	-+	N+	N-	-+
Total Assets	12.07	6.15	13.19	7.77	6.28	9.05
Earnings per Share*	13.54	26.89	38.35	67.03	-46.16	12.38
Dividends per Share*	10.53	11.76	13.33	15.38	8.33	11.84
Book Value per Share	12.90	10.16	11.79	3.24	0.88	7.68

Displayed Currency: German Mark (1.00:1)
*Source: Worldscope. Value may differ from I/B/E/S.
Note: 5-Year Average calculations exclude NAs.

PER SHARE AND RELATED DATA

SOURCE: WORLDSCOPE	1997	1996	1995	1994	1993
Earnings per Share	5.7	5.0	3.9	2.8	1.7
Dividends per Share	2.1	1.9	1.7	1.5	1.3
Book Value per Share	44.6	39.5	35.8	32.1	31.0
Total Investment					
Return	NA	NA	16.85	6.32	47.99

VEBA A.G.

Market Price (Year-end)	122.5	89.0	61.4	54.0	52.2
Market Capitalization (in millions)	60907.39	43948.20	29973.91	26243.99	25369.20
Price/Earnings Ratio	21.68	17.88	15.65	19.04	30.75
Price/Book Value	2.75	2.25	1.71	1.68	1.68
Dividend Yield	1.71	2.13	2.77	2.78	2.49
Dividend Payout per Share	37.16	38.17	43.34	52.90	76.58
Common Shares Outstanding (Year-end) in Millions	497.20	493.80	488.17	486.00	486.00
Stock Split/Dividend Ratio	NA	NA	NA	0.10	0.10
Type of Share	Stammaktie				

Displayed Currency: German Mark (1.00:1)
Note: Data is sourced from Worldscope and may differ from I/B/E/S historical data.

49. YPF S.A.

YPF S.A., Argentina's largest company and one of the world's few truly integrated oil companies, deserves more respect. Its oil and gas business encompasses petroleum exploration, development, refining, marketing, transportation, and petrochemical production. Besides interests in about 1,020 wells that contain proven reserves of about 1.4 billion barrels of oil, YFP also has about 9.3 trillion cubic feet of natural gas. YFP owns and operates three refineries in Argentina and operates about 2,800 kilometers of natural gas pipelines. The company operates a retail network of more than 2,400 gas stations in Argentina, Chile, and Peru. Its Maxus Energy subsidiary in the United States has oil and gas properties in Bolivia, Ecuador, Indonesia, and Venezuela. YPF is also a smaller player in petrochemicals, which is expected to be a growth area because it faces no governmental constraints.

The good news from this impressive and increasingly efficient modern company is that its earnings growth prospects over the next several years appear to be excellent even if crude oil prices don't cooperate. Management is firmly committed to improving return on capital from the current 10 percent, which is rather low due to the investments it has made in its refineries to improve product quality, to a more substantial 15 percent by the year 2002. In the meantime, it's likely to churn out a 14 percent gain annually as it improves productivity. Compensation of the firm's senior management increasingly is being tied to performance goals to help make this happen, and the company quickly reduced its capital budget for 1998 by more than 15 percent to acknowledge a sudden weakness in oil prices. Meanwhile, YPF's oil and natural gas production should help the bottom line by growing at a healthy average clip of nearly 6 percent a year over the next five years.

Yet, despite all of those pluses, YPF's share price has been lagging behind other major oil stocks. Of course, lower prices of crude oil, natural gas, and natural gas liquids have taken a bite out of its earnings, and investors have been fretting about unstable emerging markets. But a number of analysts consider all of these circumstances to be short-term considerations in a stock that's a bargain well worth owning for the long haul. No matter what happens, there are now more YPF shareholders around the world for this formerly money-losing company that was privatized in 1993. The government announced in February 1998 it would sell its remaining 20.3 percent YPF stake in the second half of the year, with up to 50 percent offered locally and the rest overseas.

This is clearly not a company that's standing still. YPF is upgrading its natural gas export business, primarily through Chile, and has entered into marketing operations with other neighboring countries as well. It is constantly growing through alliances. In May 1998, YPF, Canada's Agrium Incorporated, and Perez Companc S.A. agreed to build a $470 million nitrogen fertilizer plant in Argentina.

Larger neighbor Brazil offers plenty of potential for Argentina's YPF because that country is opening up its hydrocarbons and power sectors to competition. In yet another alliance, YPF, Brazil's Petroleo Brasileiro S.A., and Dow Chemical Company formalized their $500 million Mega natural-gas venture in 1997, with YPF and Petrobras putting $750 million over five years into a downstream joint venture. An example of the potential in Brazil is the fact that only 3 percent of electricity generated there currently comes from natural gas-fired plants, compared to 47 percent in Argentina.

"Brazil offers a window of opportunity," explained Chief Executive Officer Roberto Monti, who was given the additional title of chairman of the board on April 28, 1998, replacing departing Chairman Miguel Madanes. "Pretty soon plenty of energy will be available at the right prices, so we have to be very aggressive." Monti already has gained a reputation for making things happen quickly. In 1995 he accepted the challenge of running Maxus Energy in Dallas, Texas, a beleaguered company acquired by YPF after it had reported losses for five straight years. He took drastic measures to change that situation and improve the operation, and, by the end of 1996, Maxus had already broken even and was beginning to generate profits.

YPF's exploration and production in Argentina should continue to excel and to be its most important earnings driver in the future. The company has kept costs low while increasing its oil and gas production. In addition, secondary oil recovery now accounts for more than one-third of production, double the percentage of just three years ago. Meanwhile, expansion of natural gas production for exports to neighboring countries will be instrumental in growth. For example, higher natural gas production will be possible due to rising demand in Argentina, and through the start-up of a urea fertilizer plant and an LPG project which together will require more than 200 million cubic feet a day of gas by the year 2001. YPF also has two oil production projects in Venezuela scheduled to start production in 1999.

The company has significantly improved the quality of products manufactured in its refineries, especially gasoline, and in the process has made them much better suited for exporting. Capital spending in refining is expected to remain low for several years. YPF's retail gas stations have been regaining some lost market share of recent years by emphasizing a better relationship with independent dealers and cutting back on an initial goal of significantly increasing the number of company-owned stores. The company will also expand its marketing in Chile and Peru, where it holds only small single-digit market shares. Once again, Brazil offers enormous potential for growth.

"Our goal is to be one of the fastest-growing companies in the international oil and gas industry, while always optimizing the company's resources, avoiding unnecessary risk, and maintaining a sound financial position," Monti said in his letter in the company's most recent annual report. "We will build on our competitive strengths, which include our geographic position, strong relationships in Latin America, ability to deal with national oil companies, and expertise in rationalization and cost-cutting."

49. YPF S.A.

Argentina   Ticker symbol YPF

One American Depositary Receipt represents one Class "D" share

ADR price $25 3/8 (9/16/98)   Dividend yield 3.46%

(Financial data from I/B/E/S International is in Argentine peso)*

BUSINESS DESCRIPTION

AN INTEGRATED OIL AND GAS COMPANY THAT EXPLORES FOR AND PRO-DUCES OIL AND NATURAL GAS. ALSO REFINES OIL AND MARKETS PETRO-LEUM PRODUCTS

ADDRESS AND CONTACTS

Address	Avda. Pte. R. Saenz Pena, 777
	1364 Buenos Aires, Argentina
Telephone	54-1-3292000

BASIC FINANCIAL INFORMATION

Report Dates	Last Annual: Dec 97	Reported On: Feb 19, 1998
Capital Structure[†]	Long Term Debt:	2145.00
	Total Debt:	3638.00
	Common Sh. Equity:	6940.00

SALES BREAKDOWN

Product Segments[†]	Crude Oil Refining	4616.00
	Domestic Exploration	3536.00
	International Exploration	724.00
	Segment Adjustment	-2732.00
Geographic Segments[†]	Argentina	5233.00
	Other South America	281.00
	United States	231.00
	Indonesia & Other	399.00

Displayed Currency: Argentine Peso (1.00:1)
*I/B/E/S and I/B/E/S Express are registered trademarks of I/B/E/S International Inc. Copyright 1993–1996 I/B/E/S International Inc. All rights reserved.
[†]Values are displayed in millions.

FINANCIAL STATEMENT DATA

INCOME STATEMENT	1997	1996	1995	1994	1993
Net Sales or Revenues	6144.00	5937.00	4970.00	4201.00	3958.00
EBITDA	2751.00	2610.00	2104.00	1361.00	1386.00
Depreciation Depletion & Amort	1097.00	1067.00	953.00	701.00	539.00
Operating Income	1624.00	1526.00	939.00	641.00	639.00
Interest Expense	318.00	318.00	255.00	101.00	114.00
Pretax Income	1380.00	1225.00	896.00	559.00	733.00
Net Income	877.00	817.00	793.00	538.00	706.00

BALANCE SHEET	1997	1996	1995	1994	1993
Assets					
Cash & Equivalents	178.00	130.00	135.00	81.00	89.00
Receivables—Net	1101.00	1159.00	1043.00	763.00	811.00
Inventories	288.00	242.00	282.00	274.00	365.00
Total Current Assets	1598.00	1565.00	1501.00	1131.00	1330.00
Property Plant & Eq.— Net	10370.00	9866.00	9331.00	5920.00	5415.00
Total Assets	12761.00	12084.00	11572.00	7725.00	7353.00
Liabilities & Shareholders' Equity					
Total Current Liabilities	2970.00	2371.00	2327.00	1503.00	1237.00
Long Term Debt	2145.00	2566.00	2617.00	695.00	469.00
Preferred Stock	0.00	0.00	63.00	0.00	0.00
Common Equity	6940.00	6374.00	5839.00	5086.00	4966.00
Total Liabilities & Sh. Equity	12761.00	12084.00	11572.00	7725.00	7353.00

CASH FLOW	1997	1996	1995	1994	1993
Funds from Operations	2066.00	2057.00	1907.00	1418.00	1067.00
Total Sources	4997.00	4732.00	5644.00	3053.00	1830.00
Cash Dividends Paid—Total	319.00	293.00	291.00	587.00	167.00
Total Uses	4997.00	4732.00	5644.00	3053.00	1830.00
Incr/Decr in Working Capital	-566.00	20.00	-454.00	-465.00	90.00
Free Cash Flow	1158.00	793.00	-223.00	-6.00	431.00

INTERNATIONAL BUSINESS	1997	1996	1995	1994	1993
Foreign Assets	3061.00	2650.00	2553.00	0.00	0.00
Foreign Sales	911.00	864.00	545.00	0.00	0.00
Foreign Income	216.00	225.00	-48.00	0.00	0.00

350

YPF S.A.

SUPPLEMENTARY DATA	1997	1996	1995	1994	1993
Employees	10000	9750	9256	5839	7514
R&D Expenses	0.00	0.00	0.00	0.00	0.00
Goodwill/Cost in Excess of Assets Purchased	0.00	0.00	0.00	0.00	0.00
Extra Items & Gain/ Loss in Sale of Assets	0.00	0.00	0.00	0.00	0.00

Displayed Currency: Argentine Peso (1.00:1)
All values are displayed in millions (except employees).

FINANCIAL RATIOS AND GROWTH RATES

PROFITABILITY	1997	1996	1995	1994	1993	5YR AVG
Operating Profit Margin %	26.43	25.70	18.89	15.26	16.14	20.49
Tax Rate %	34.71	30.12	7.14	2.15	3.82	15.59
Net Margin %	14.42	14.22	16.54	12.81	17.84	15.16
Return on Assets %	8.83	9.11	12.82	8.22	10.52	9.90
Return on Equity— Total %	13.76	13.99	15.59	10.83	15.54	13.94
Cash Flow % Sales	33.63	34.65	38.37	33.75	26.96	33.47
Sales per Employee (in 000s)	614	609	537	719	527	601

ASSET UTILIZATION	1997	1996	1995	1994	1993	5YR AVG
Total Asset Turnover	0.48	0.49	0.43	0.54	0.54	0.50
Capital Exp % Gross Fixed Assets	7.28	8.81	12.21	9.45	7.20	8.99
Acc Depreciation % Gross Fixed Assets	52.64	52.18	51.02	59.09	59.18	54.82
Assets per Employee (in 000s)	1276	1239	1250	1323	976	1213

LIQUIDITY	1997	1996	1995	1994	1993	5YR AVG
Current Ratio	0.54	0.66	0.65	0.75	1.08	0.73
Quick Ratio	0.43	0.54	0.51	0.56	0.73	0.55

LEVERAGE	1997	1996	1995	1994	1993	5YR AVG
Total Debt % Common Equity	52.42	52.47	63.93	24.75	15.24	41.96
Long Term Debt % Common Equity	30.91	40.26	44.82	13.66	9.44	27.82
Common Equity % Total Assets	54.38	52.75	50.46	65.84	67.54	58.19

LEVERAGE	1997	1996	1995	1994	1993	5YR AVG
Long Term Debt %						
Total Capital	23.22	28.23	29.45	11.92	8.58	20.28
Operating Cash/						
Fixed Charges	7.18	5.77	6.66	14.04	9.36	8.60

GROWTH %	1997	1996	1995	1994	1993	5YR AVG
Net Sales	3.49	19.46	18.31	6.14	1.33	9.48
Operating Income	6.42	62.51	46.49	0.31	44.24	29.67
Total Assets	5.60	4.42	49.80	5.06	-0.94	11.45
Earnings per Share*	7.36	2.67	48.03	-24.00	173.97	27.71
Dividends per Share*	NA	10.00	0.00	0.00	100.00	NA
Book Value per Share	8.88	9.17	14.80	2.42	9.31	8.84

Displayed Currency: Argentine Peso (1.00:1)
*Source: Worldscope. Value may differ from I/B/E/S.
Note: 5-Year Average calculations exclude NAs.

PER SHARE AND RELATED DATA

SOURCE: WORLDSCOPE	1997	1996	1995	1994	1993
Earnings per Share	2.480	2.310	2.250	1.520	2.000
Dividends per Share	NA	0.880	0.800	0.800	0.800
Book Value per Share	19.660	18.057	16.541	14.408	14.068
Total Investment					
Return	NA	NA	6.19	-11.02	NA
Market Price					
(Year-end)	33.700	25.250	21.500	21.000	24.500
Market Capitalization					
(in millions)	11896.10	8913.25	7589.50	7413.00	8648.50
Price/Earnings Ratio	13.59	10.93	9.56	13.82	12.25
Price/Book Value	1.71	1.40	1.30	1.46	1.74
Dividend Yield	NA	3.49	3.72	3.81	3.27
Dividend Payout per					
Share	NA	38.10	35.56	52.63	40.00
Common Shares					
Outstanding					
(Year-end) in					
Millions	353.00	353.00	353.00	353.00	353.00
Stock Split/Dividend					
Ratio	NA	NA	NA	NA	NA
Type of Share	D Accion				

Displayed Currency: Argentine Peso (1.00:1)
Note: Data is sourced from Worldscope and may differ from I/B/E/S historical data.

50. Zurich Financial Services Group

The Swiss know all about the need for a company operating in a small country to make deals and expand beyond its borders. Aggressive Zurich Insurance Company, which celebrated its 125th anniversary in 1998, had expanded into most of the world's key markets within its first thirty years of existence. It provides insurance and financial services in about fifty countries, with its domestic business in Switzerland only accounting for about one-fourth of its premiums.

The company's biggest deal of all took place when Zurich Insurance merged with the financial operations of the United Kingdom's B.A.T. Industries to form a new company, Zurich Financial Services Group, in 1998. The result is one of the ten largest insurance and asset management groups in the world. This newly merged group has two holding companies, Zurich Allied A.G. quoted on the Swiss stock exchange and Allied Zurich Plc. in London. The old American Depositary Receipt program was ended, although the launch of a new ADR program for Zurich Allied A.G. will be considered in 1999. The merger transaction was scheduled to close in the second half of 1998, following the release of second-quarter earnings and audited results prepared under International Accounting Standards for the first time in the company's history. It's estimated the merger will result in an annual cost savings of at least $400 million at the operating income level by the end of the third full calendar year of operations. The new firm headquartered in Zurich has a workforce of 66,000 employees and strong franchises in the key markets of the United States, United Kingdom, Switzerland, and the rest of continental Europe. The U.S. business, which accounted for about one-third of the company's total premiums in recent years, rose to about 44 percent during 1998.

Zurich Insurance shareholders received shares in Zurich Allied A.G., which in turn owns 57 percent of Zurich Financial Services. Existing share holdings in B.A.T. Industries were replaced by shares in two new companies, Allied Zurich Plc., which owns 43 percent of Zurich Financial Services, and British American Tobacco Plc. Joint control of the merged company will be ensured by the requirement for a super-majority, needing 58 percent of votes, on any matter put to shareholders. "This definitive agreement represents an important step in the formation of a new global force in financial protection and investment management businesses," said Rolf Huppi, former chairman and chief executive officer of Zurich Insurance and chairman and CEO of Zurich Financial Services Group. "I am convinced that the combined operations will form an excellent platform for strategic growth in key markets and for continuing earnings enhancements."

In 1872, Gottfried Keller, state chancellor and poet, affixed his signature to the corporate charter that set up the insurance association that was to become the Zurich Insurance Company. Zurich Insurance's products today include nonlife and life insurance, reinsurance, and investment management for customers in the personal, commercial, and corporate market segments. It has made other large deals in the past to increase its global influence in the fast-growing financial services field. For example, it acquired an 80 percent stake in Kemper Corporation in 1996 and purchased the remaining 20 percent in 1998. Zurich's Scudder Kemper Investments international money management unit, in a deal that was completed in early 1998, acquired the investment advisor for the Kemper Funds. This subsidiary offering retail mutual funds, retirement plans, and institutional asset management is 69.5 percent owned by Zurich Financial, with senior Scudder Kemper Investment employees owning the rest. In 1997, Zurich Insurance announced a wide-ranging agreement with Trygg-Hansa, a Swedish insurer, that expanded Zurich Insurance's presence in both the United States and

Scandinavia. In 1995, Zurich Insurance began a joint venture with insurance products with Italy's Banco di Napoli.

This geographically diverse company whose earnings estimates have been on the rise seeks profitable niches in global markets. It offers tailored financial protection and investment management to customers in the personal, commercial, and corporate market segments, guided by an experienced management team drawn from many countries. Zurich Financial has established a new strategy with a corporate structure centered around strategic business units, of which there are 260 worldwide. In individual markets, the traditionally separated branches of life and nonlife insurance are gradually being combined into integrated service organizations. European operations are currently being made more efficient by reducing branches and back offices while more emphasis is being put on underwriting specialties. The U.S. property and casualty insurance operations have posted a strong return, with life insurance premiums and profits growing at a similar rate. Larger underwriters of automobile insurance are becoming more aggressive in pricing to gain market share, making premium growth more difficult. The company's nonlife premiums have been flat due to the company's ongoing conservatism and extremely varied underwriting results throughout its areas of operation.

Zurich Financial management believes its most important corporate challenges currently include: (1) the shift of the world economic order with future relative importance of emerging markets in Asia, Latin America, and Central and Eastern Europe; (2) deregulation and the arrival of new entrants into the market; and (3) technological change which requires agility if a company is to continue being a pioneering organization. In addition, far-flung Zurich Financial has had to deal with considerable foreign exchange volatility. Preparations for the introduction of the Euro, combined with volatile European currencies, influenced European exchange-rate movements and also contributed to the considerable weakening of Asian currencies. This led the Swiss National Bank to continue its policy of a relative weakening of the Swiss franc, an approach that was proving quite successful in early 1998.

355

Just as giant Swiss banks have dealt with investigations into past dealings during the Nazi era, Zurich Insurance announced in early 1998 that it was forming an "international commission of eminent persons" to review disputed life insurance claims arising from the Holocaust period. John Whitehead, deputy U.S. secretary of state under President Ronald Reagan, and Rabbi Arthur Schneier, senior rabbi of New York's Park East Synagogue, are among the commission's four members. The commission will operate independently of Zurich Insurance. A toll-free number was set up to make it easier for potential claimants to make inquiries. Accounting firm Arthur Andersen was retained as advisor, and "to corroborate any findings as required by the commission." Zurich Insurance was one of four European insurance firms that reached an agreement with California Insurance Commissioner Chuck Quackenbush and New York State Insurance Commissioner Neil Lebin to form an international commission that will ensure insurance claims are paid.

50. ZURICH FINANCIAL SERVICES GROUP

Switzerland   Ticker symbol ZUAN (Swiss stock exchange)

Stock price 781 Swiss francs (9/16/98)   Dividend yield 1.5%

Note: Following merger, shares to be quoted as Zurich Allied A.G. on Swiss stock exchange and Allied Zurich Plc. on London stock exchange. American Depositary Receipt program ended in 1998, but Zurich Allied A.G. will consider the launch of another ADR sometime in 1999.

(Financial data from I/B/E/S International is in Swiss francs)*

BUSINESS DESCRIPTION

AN INTERNATIONAL INSURANCE COMPANY THAT PROVIDES LIFE AND HEALTH, FIRE AND ACCIDENT, AND OTHER NONLIFE INSURANCE COVERAGE

ADDRESS AND CONTACTS

Address	Mythenquai 2
	Ch-8002 Zurich, Switzerland
Telephone	41-1-2052121
Fax	41-1-2053555

Zurich Financial Services Group

BASIC FINANCIAL INFORMATION

Capital Structure†	Long Term Debt:	NA
	Total Debt:	NA
	Common Sh. Equity:	NA

SALES BREAKDOWN

Product Segments†	NA
Geographic Segments†	NA

Displayed Currency: Swiss Franc (1.00:1)
*I/B/E/S and I/B/E/S Express are registered trademarks of I/B/E/S International Inc. Copyright
1993–1996 I/B/E/S International Inc. All rights reserved.
†Values are displayed in millions.

FINANCIAL STATEMENT DATA

INCOME STATEMENT	1997	1996	1995	1994	1993
Net Sales or Revenues	NA	37969.40	31683.80	27519.80	27710.10
EBITDA	NA	1962.90	1622.90	2390.50	2288.80
Depreciation Depletion					
& Amort	NA	NA	NA	NA	NA
Operating Income	NA	2335.40	3144.20	8596.20	7280.10
Interest Expense	482.00	482.00	336.20	290.00	327.50
Pretax Income	NA	1480.90	1286.70	2100.50	1961.30
Net Income	1780.00	1138.20	874.10	695.40	613.20

BALANCE SHEET	1997	1996	1995	1994	1993
Assets					
Cash & Equivalents	NA	NA	NA	NA	NA
Receivables—Net	NA	NA	NA	NA	NA
Inventories	NA	NA	NA	NA	NA
Total Current Assets	NA	NA	NA	NA	NA
Property Plant & Eq.—					
Net	NA	423.30	297.80	0.00	0.00
Total Assets	NA	130800.40	95768.06	91469.25	89337.54
Liabilities & Shareholders' Equity					
Total Current Liabilities	NA	NA	NA	NA	NA
Long Term Debt	NA	3921.70	2725.00	1652.00	1503.70
Preferred Stock	NA	0.00	0.00	0.00	0.00
Common Equity	NA	13551.70	10621.16	9601.35	10176.85
Total Liabilities					
& Sh. Equity	NA	130800.40	95768.06	91469.25	89337.54

357

CASH FLOW	1997	1996	1995	1994	1993
Funds from Operations	NA	29983.40	3466.50	5081.50	6384.90
Total Sources	NA	29384.00	4195.20	NA	NA
Cash Dividends Paid—					
Total	NA	273.00	218.40	181.99	159.06
Total Uses	NA	29384.00	4195.20	NA	NA
Incr/Decr in Working					
Capital	NA	NA	NA	NA	NA
Free Cash Flow	NA	1837.40	1622.90	NA	NA

INTERNATIONAL BUSINESS	1997	1996	1995	1994	1993
Foreign Assets	NA	NA	NA	NA	NA
Foreign Sales	NA	NA	NA	NA	NA
Foreign Income	NA	NA	NA	NA	NA

SUPPLEMENTARY DATA	1997	1996	1995	1994	1993
Employees	NA	40981	36522	37354	38280
R&D Expenses	NA	NA	NA	NA	NA
Goodwill/Cost in					
Excess of Assets					
Purchased	NA	1523.50	0.00	0.00	0.00
Extra Items & Gain/					
Loss in Sale of Assets	NA	0.00	0.00	0.00	0.00

Displayed Currency: Swiss Franc (1.00:1)
All values are displayed in millions (except employees).

FINANCIAL RATIOS AND GROWTH RATES

PROFITABILITY	1997	1996	1995	1994	1993	5YR AVG
Return on Assets %	1.36	1.52	1.20	0.99	1.12	1.24
Return on Equity—						
Total %	13.13	10.72	9.10	6.83	7.34	9.42
Tax Rate %	NA	21.59	29.86	17.80	17.53	21.69
Net Premiums						
Written % Equity	NA	299.95	275.33	247.96	298.42	280.42
Combined Ratio	NA	104.88	104.35	83.19	90.35	95.69
Investment Income %						
Inv Assets	NA	7.91	6.67	6.39	7.95	7.23

LEVERAGE	1997	1996	1995	1994	1993	5YR AVG
Total Capital %						
Total Assets	NA	13.72	14.22	12.69	13.70	13.58
Common Equity %						
Total Assets	NA	10.36	11.09	10.50	11.39	10.83

Zurich Financial Services Group

LIQUIDITY	1997	1996	1995	1994	1993	5YR AVG
Benefit & Loss Res % Tot Cap	NA	302.90	263.01	273.58	244.62	271.03

ASSET UTILIZATION	1997	1996	1995	1994	1993	5YR AVG
Assets per Employee (in 000s)	NA	3192	2622	2449	2334	2649

OTHER	1997	1996	1995	1994	1993	5YR AVG
Invested Assets % Total Liab	NA	96.84	99.78	96.11	96.44	97.29
Invested Assets % Total Assets	NA	86.46	88.44	85.65	84.85	86.35
Eq Secs & Real Estate % Inv Assets	NA	23.94	26.83	27.95	29.07	26.95

GROWTH %	1997	1996	1995	1994	1993	5YR AVG
Total Assets	NA	36.58	4.70	2.39	20.92	NA
Total Insurance Reserves	NA	36.69	6.32	5.46	18.54	NA
Net Sales or Revenues	NA	19.84	15.13	-0.69	15.16	NA
Operating Income	NA	-25.72	-63.42	18.08	-2.76	NA
Earnings per Share*	56.18	26.56	26.32	13.43	24.07	28.58
Dividends per Share*	25.00	20.00	25.00	20.00	14.29	20.79
Book Value per Share	NA	19.77	14.34	-5.72	21.66	NA

Displayed Currency: Swiss Franc (1.00:1)
*Source: Worldscope. Value may differ from I/B/E/S.
Note: 5-Year Average calculations exclude NAs.

PER SHARE AND RELATED DATA

SOURCE: WORLDSCOPE	1997	1996	1995	1994	1993
Earnings per Share	38.0	24.3	19.2	15.2	13.4
Dividends per Share	9.0	7.2	6.0	4.8	4.0
Book Value per Share	NA	288.9	241.2	211.0	223.8
Total Investment Return	NA	NA	4.40	-15.35	50.25
Market Price (Year-end)	696.0	372.0	345.0	250.0	301.0
Market Capitalization (in millions)	32642.97	17447.10	15188.86	11376.22	13687.87
Price/Earnings Ratio	18.34	15.31	17.07	16.45	22.46
Price/Book Value	NA	1.29	1.43	1.18	1.34

SOURCE: WORLDSCOPE	1997	1996	1995	1994	1993
Dividend Yield	1.29	1.94	1.74	1.92	1.33
Dividend Payout per Share	23.71	29.63	31.25	31.58	29.85
Common Shares Outstanding (Year-end) in Millions	NA	46.90	44.03	45.50	45.47
Stock Split/Dividend Ratio	NA	NA	NA	0.20	0.20
Type of Share	*Namenaktie*				

Displayed Currency: Swiss Franc (1.00:1)
Note: Data is sourced from Worldscope and may differ from I/B/E/S historical data.